New Concepts in Latino American Cultures
A Series Edited by Licia Fiol-Matta & José Quiroga

Ciphers of History: Latin American Readings for a Cultural Age
by Enrico Mario Santí

Cosmopolitanisms and Latin America: Against the Destiny of Place
by Jacqueline Loss

Remembering Maternal Bodies: Melancholy in Latina and Latin American Women's Writing
by Benigno Trigo

The Ethics of Latin American Literary Criticism: Reading Otherwise
edited by Erin Graff Zivin

Modernity and the Nation in Mexican Representations of Masculinity: From Sensuality to Bloodshed
by Héctor Domínguez-Ruvalcaba

White Negritude: Race, Writing, and Brazilian Cultural Identity
by Alexandra Isfahani-Hammond

Essays in Cuban Intellectual History
by Rafael Rojas

Mestiz@ Scripts, Digital Migrations, and the Territories of Writing
by Damián Baca

Confronting History and Modernity in Mexican Narrative
by Elisabeth Guerrero

Cuban Women Writers: Imagining a Matria
by Madeline Cámara Betancourt

Other Worlds: New Argentine Film
by Gonzalo Aguilar

Cuba in the Special Period: Culture and Ideology in the 1990s
edited by Ariana Hernandez-Reguant

Carnal Inscriptions: Spanish American Narratives of Corporeal Difference and Disability
by Susan Antebi

Telling Ruins in Latin America
edited by Michael J. Lazzara and Vicky Unruh

Hispanic Caribbean Literature of Migration: Narratives of Displacement
edited by Vanessa Pérez Rosario

New Argentine Film: Other Worlds (upd
by Gonzalo Aguilar

NEW DIRECTIONS IN LATINO AMERICAN CULTURES
Also Edited by Licia Fiol-Matta & José Quiroga

New Argentine Film

Other Worlds

Gonzalo Aguilar

Translated by Sarah Ann Wells

NEW ARGENTINE FILM
Copyright © Gonzalo Aguilar, 2008.

First published in hardcover in 2008 by
PALGRAVE MACMILLAN®
in the United States—a division of St. Martin's Press LLC,
175 Fifth Avenue, New York, NY 10010.

Where this book is distributed in the UK, Europe and the rest of the world,
this is by Palgrave Macmillan, a division of Macmillan Publishers Limited,
registered in England, company number 785998, of Houndmills,
Basingstoke, Hampshire RG21 6XS.

Palgrave Macmillan is the global academic imprint of the above companies
and has companies and representatives throughout the world.

Palgrave® and Macmillan® are registered trademarks in the United States,
the United Kingdom, Europe and other countries.

ISBN: 978–0–230–10901–8

Library of Congress Cataloging-in-Publication Data is available from the
Library of Congress.

A catalogue record of the book is available from the British Library.

Design by Newgen Imaging Systems (P) Ltd., Chennai, India.

First PALGRAVE MACMILLAN paperback edition: March 2011

10 9 8 7 6 5 4 3 2 1

Printed in the United States of America.

Transferred to Digital Printing in 2011

To Jorge Ruffinelli, cinephile and friend

To my father, Tuchi, who took me to see
that Buster Keaton picture

Contents

Acknowledgments

In 1999, I put together a study group on film, literature, and theory in which Jimena Rodríguez, Pablo Garavaglia, Lucía Tennina, Julieta Lerman, Joana D'Alessio, Bárbara Rivkin, Julieta Bliffeld, and Germán Conde participated. Together we discussed various ideas that culminated in this book. Jimena Rodríguez, in addition to providing materials and ideas, wrote a paper on Lucrecia Martel's film that helped me rethink my central hypothesis. Pablo Garavaglia spent many afternoons at the Museo del Cine in Buenos Aires consulting materials and journals.

In 2004, Nicolás Casullo generously invited me to teach a seminar in the Master's Program in Communication and Culture in the Social Science department of the Universidad de Buenos Aires. This class was fundamental for me in organizing many of the hypotheses and proposals of this book. I would like to thank the students who shared this seminar with me.

In early 2005, Elvira Arnoux had the kindness to invite me to share the conclusions of my investigation at the Master's Program in Discourse Analysis that she directs at the Universidad de Buenos Aires. There, students discussed my viewpoints and contributed new perspectives.

The following people have lent me a hand with materials, bibliography, or suggestions: Denise Estremero, Lucas Margarit, Ana Amado, Juan Balerdi, Alejo Moguillansky, Gabriel Lichtmann, Gregorio Goyo Anchou, Diego Lerman, Juan Villegas, Rodrigo Laera, Santiago García, Ana Amado, Martín Kohan, Yaki Setton, Cachi from the video store La fábrica de los sueños, Mariano from Estilo, Mariano from Black 2, the guys at La Mirage, Andrés Insaurralde from the library at the Museo del Cine, and Emilio Bernini. Mariano Siskind translated texts and sent them to me from far away. Paulina Seivach, whose statistics and studies I have used here, responded politely to my emails.

Comments on parts of this book enabled me to correct and edit initial drafts. I would to thank Diego Trerotola, Patricio Fontana, Claudia Torre, Santiago Giralt, Domin Choi, Gustavo Castagna, and Hernán Musalupi, who also tracked down material that was near-impossible to find and helped guide me in cinema's industrial complex.

It is difficult to quantify the role that Domin Choi played in the editing of this book. He pushed me to give it shape and collaborated actively throughout the production of the final manuscript.

I want to thank Claudio España for having thought of me for several of his projects, and also Moira Soto, Gustavo Castagna, and Ana Amado, with whom I shared the experience of selecting films for the Mar del Plata International Film Festival in 2001 and 2002.

At the Universidad del Cine (FUC), directed by Manuel Antín, I taught for seven years. I was lucky to meet marvelous students there, many of whom were protagonists in the phenomenon studied here. In that institution I not only learned a lot but also made friends: some of them, boldly, invited me to participate in their movies. I hope not to have let them down as a teacher with this book.

Ana Spisso has given me invaluable help, without which this book would never have been finished.

Vera Waksman remembered the names of movie theaters that we frequented as adolescents.

I would also like to thank José Quiroga, who has made this English edition possible, and Sarah Ann Wells, who, with efficiency and intelligence, took care of the translation.

Finally, Alejandra Laera was more than a reader: she contributed ideas, discussed hypotheses, and accompanied me throughout all the phases of this book. Along with Goyo and Chano, she has offered me a world in which life is happier and more intense.

Introduction

What happens when worlds fade, grow cold, or simply disappear? How can we recognize the other worlds that are beginning to make their presence known, no less intensely, but certainly with less precise contours? These questions, without defined forms and without my knowing precisely the kinds of experiences they referred to, were constantly with me throughout the 1990s. It became increasingly clear that we were experiencing a series of transformations for which a sufficient or suitable conceptual arsenal did not yet exist. In addition to the profound turn our lives took under the neoliberal Peronist government of those years (under which the hegemony currently enjoyed by the same party was established), we experienced a series of global political, economic, and technological transformations that affected the world of labor, the public sphere, and private and intimate life. These changes were not abstract: they managed to shake the mainstays of custom and daily life. The emergence of unprecedented jobs, new urban trajectories, a near-permanent link to computer networks, the intensification of consumption as a form of individual or group identity, the omnipresence of audiovisual media, mutations in the manifestation of sexuality, the incorporation of economic exclusion as something familiar and irrevocable in the social imagination, and the alteration of traditional political practices—these are some of the verifiable changes that we have witnessed in recent years.

My sense that with the new Argentine cinema one could venture some reflections on these transformations was the origin of this book. In my initial musings, neither excessively theoretical nor bluntly practical, the category of *world* began to redefine itself: world as a real or imaginary place that provides its members with codes and affects, certain material and conceptual tools, and a given time and space. Here, what I designate "world" can consist of a certain group or community, a hobby, or, as it was essentially throughout modernity, a job.[1] In Pablo Trapero's *Mundo grúa* (1999, distributed in the United States as *Crane World*), the world of work connects to the world of the story, and together they evoke what no longer is, while in Lucrecia Martel's *La ciénaga* (2001, distributed in the United States as *The Swamp*), the world that breaks down is that of the family. In Martín Rejtman's *Los guantes mágicos* (2004, distributed in the United Kingdom as *The Magic Gloves*), transitory worlds, sustained by a job or a hobby, clash and find outrageous connections: the gym, pornography, the taxi call station, antidepressants, the occupation of dog-walking, the import business. Each of these practices offers a world in which different characters attempt to make a place for themselves. "Services for the middle class," as one of the characters in Rejtman's *Silvia Prieto* (1999) says; or, as I propose here, new forms of working. If something unites these movies, it is the fact that these worlds can barely survive successive contingencies. For example, in Lisandro Alonso's *Los muertos* (2004, "The Dead"), rituals—those acts full of meaning that connect the material and the symbolic—are emptied out, and nature itself is presented as a ruin. Although these films offer up a taciturn or disenchanted diagnosis, they simultaneously allow us a glimpse of vitality and promise. With an openness that other art forms lack in this period, film has transformed itself in recent years into the place in which the traces of the present take shape. It is for that reason that we can turn to movies to respond to the question of why, despite the fact that worlds are in the process of disappearing, something perseveres.

This trace of the present, however, is never exhibited in a pure and transparent manner. One of the tasks of cinema criticism is to construct its own object through movies, with the goal of becoming aware of the relationship between cinema and society. To elaborate this relationship, I paid close attention, in the analysis of the films, to the mise-en-scène, by which I mean the combination of what happens *with* the shot and what happens *in* the shot, or, in stricter terms, the complex combination of the sequences of the shot and its components. And, although it may be impossible to separate these two aspects entirely, it is also the case that they are simultaneously irreducible to one another and capable of independent development to better understand the scope of the mise-en-scène. This means that criticism should circulate in the interstice between the shots and what the image registers, but also that it should be able to explore with relative autonomy the nature of the sequences, on one hand,

and the components, on the other. If we remained only in a reflection on the shots themselves, under the alleged modernist pressure of the evolution of form, the components that connect movies with other practices that are not specifically cinematographic would be lost in the supposed autonomy of the shot. In effect, few kinds of art criticism are as resistant as film criticism to a contextual and sociological reading. If we limited ourselves to a content-based description, however, we would fall into a thematic criticism that would eliminate the significant and specific character of cinematic procedures. We should try, then, to reduce neither the form to the procedures nor the contextual to the components. We should construct a critical articulation that fosters the cultural, social, and cinematographic dimensions of film as a whole.

I am, of course, aware of the risks of a criticism in which a thematic analysis has such a dominant role. From this perspective, it is easy for the particularity of each work to be suppressed in the service of a unity that exists in the method's reductiveness rather than in the objects themselves. Or, worse, the movies are invoked as documents or allegories that are quickly worked through to arrive at the current state of society. It is a risk that I preferred to take, given that in compensation, and in confronting a body of criticism that tends to think in terms of authors, a more sociological gaze helps to construct larger corpuses (not always exclusively cinematographic) by departing from an analysis restricted to authors or movies and thinking the status of the image and of narration by images in society.

From the beginning, my idea was to think not *against* the movies or *about* them but *with* them. I distance myself from both hermeneutic positions and value judgments. Above all, I am interested in approaching the transformations of recent years, assisted by the cunning tricks of the cinematographic form.[2] In dialogue and in debate with other critical positions, I have tried to develop in this book a reading of the new Argentine cinema that is also an interpretation of the changes that took place during the 1990s. By this I am not referring to whether the new cinema put forth a critique of neoliberalism, nor even whether it elaborated a group of images that would allow us to explain neoliberalism's mechanisms. I mean, rather, that we can use cinema—its movies, institutions, festivals, and links to power and money—to investigate the decade's transformations. Attempting to combine thought about cinema with that which exceeds it, I wondered what these films did with the era in which they happened to live.

The book is divided into three chapters: "On the Existence of the New Argentine Cinema," "Film, the Narration of a World," and "A World without Narration (Political Investigation)." In the first part, I analyze the cultural and cinematographic transformations that contributed to the phenomenon of a new cinema in Argentina. In "Film, the Narration of a World," I propose topics (the organization of space and groupings, the return of the real, the omnipresence of merchandise, the treatment of sound, and the use of genres) with the goal of revisiting certain poetics (of Rejtman, Martel, Alonso) or certain works—Caetano and Stagnaro's *Pizza, birra, faso* (distributed in the United States as *Pizza, Beer, and Cigarettes*), Pablo Trapero's *El bonaerense* (distributed in the United Kingdom under the same title), Diego Lerman's *Tan de repente* (distributed in the United States and the United Kingdom as *Suddenly*), and Juan Villegas' *Sábado* ("Saturday"). The third part, "A World without Narration (Political Investigation)," has as its central themes the new forms that "the people" and politics adopted during the 1990s and the way in which movies reacted to the treatment that Argentine cinema had previously given to these issues. In this part I interpret a number of movies produced in recent years, although I place special emphasis on Trapero's *Mundo grúa*, Adrián Caetano's *Bolivia* (distributed in the United States under the same title), and Albertina Carri's *Los rubios* (distributed in the United States as *The Blonds*). In a section titled "Testimony to a Dissolution," I treat issues linked to political minorities, above all to gays, through Anahí Berneri's *Un año sin amor* (distributed in the United States and the United Kingdom as *A Year Without Love*).

The book has three appendices that cover the transformations in the past decade in the exhibition of movies, the modifications that the new Argentine cinema introduced to casting, and all of the releases between 1997 (the year in which *Pizza, birra, faso* premiered at the Mar del Plata Film Festival) and mid-2005 (the year in which I completed this book).[3]

Other Worlds: New Argentine Film is an interpretation that spans many of the films produced in Argentina between 1997 and mid-2005, above all those *operas primas*, or works of young directors who contributed to the phenomenon of the new cinema. In these eight-and-a half years, however, production was so abundant that I have been forced to leave out several valuable movies that were outside the objective I had set myself (that is, to investigate the traces of the present). Some fiction films are not included (such as Marco Bechis' *Garage*

Olimpo, 1999), but the exclusions are most evident in my coverage of the documentary genre, which has acquired such relevance in the film production of recent years.[4] I did not approach this project with the idea of exhausting the subject, nor did I want to write a history of recent Argentine film. Rather, I approached the movies as objects in which we could find keys and codes to understand the present.

1

On the Existence
of the New Argentine Cinema

Each time the new Argentine cinema is mentioned, filmmakers, critics, or the public feel the need to place before the phrase a "so-called" or similar qualifier to mark a certain distance and skepticism with respect to the phenomenon. One of the major successes of a new generation of Argentine filmmakers was to establish the idea that a break and a renovation occurred during the 1990s—that is, that a new Argentine cinema exists, which does not entail accepting that this phenomenon arose deliberately or as part of a shared aesthetic program.[1] The term ultimately became unquestionable given the continuity in the production of movies (many directors of the new cinema managed to make two or more films, even amid devastating economic crises) and given these movies' success outside of Argentina.[2]

If the phenomenon is considered in strictly aesthetic terms, the label might seem problematic. From the aesthetic point of view, it becomes obvious that Lucrecia Martel, Pablo Trapero, Martín Rejtman, and Adrián Caetano belong to universes so different that only someone completely clueless would see them as similar. Yet this perspective ignores the fact that in art, and even more in the specific medium of film, aesthetic criteria are not the only valid ones. In cinema, aesthetic aspects are not necessarily more important than issues surrounding production or culture. Cinema is not made up of only images; organizations and foundations, producers and workers, film schools and festivals, critics and spectators all form a part of it. Production, for example, is present in each stage of a movie (original idea, scriptwriting, filming, postproduction, distribution). Among the virtues of the new generation of filmmakers is an understanding that without a transformation in the film industry, there is no possibility of sustaining a personal project.[3] Thus, although it is true that there are profound differences within the poetics of the new cinema, from other perspectives it is absolutely justifiable to point out that a new creative regime was constituted through the movies of recent years and that this regime could be denominated, without hesitation, "the new Argentine cinema."

Just as the new generation of filmmakers could establish the idea of a new cinema (a currency with a national and international circulation), there is a relative consensus over the events that mark the beginning of this cycle. Despite the "precursors" Martín Rejtman and, to a lesser extent, Alejandro Agresti and Esteban Sapir, as well as the *Historias breves I* of 1995, in which several of the most recognized filmmakers participated,[4] the new cinema was baptized by the Special Jury Prize given to Adrián Caetano and Bruce Stagnaro's *Pizza, birra, faso* at the Mar del Plata International Film Festival of 1997. It was consecrated in 1999 with the award of the prizes for best director and best actor to Pablo Trapero's *Mundo grúa* at the Buenos Aires International Festival of Independent Film (BAFICI). From this point on, the production of films was so abundant that in *Un diccionario de films argentinos (1996–2002)* Raúl Manrupe and Alejandra Portela (2004) listed more than 400 films made during the period. And while it would seem difficult to establish a homogeneous and ordered map, given such a large quantity of movies, I propose in what follows three broad headings that allow us to see the characteristics of this new creative situation: production, artistic production, and the aesthetic proposal.

The One Thousand and One Ways to Make a Film

New Correlations between Production and Aesthetics

During the 1990s, making a movie was an adventure—something that, in Simmel's (1919) terms, moves us outside of the context of everyday life. It was also an adventure in the primordial sense of a search for or the invention of an experience: one goes out with a camera to film, without achievement of the objective being the least bit guaranteed. In earlier Argentine cinema, funding had generally conditioned the film's execution. Directors thought up films that required a certain amount of money and, often with heroic gestures, embarked upon the execution of their project. "Mortgaging the house" to make a movie is a cliché in Argentine cinema, but one based on real stories.

In contrast, the new Argentine cinema had an entirely different relationship with production. Many movies were filmed with the bare minimum of investment, on the weekend, and as a get-together among friends. This is the case with Adrián Caetano's *Bolivia*, which was executed with leftover rolls of film from another production, and of Martín Rejtman's *Silvia Prieto*, which took almost five years to complete before its release in 1999. Pablo Trapero's *Mundo grúa* also took several years and was finished because the filmmaker had his own studio.[5] In these cases, creative imagination was neither subordinated to production nor severed from it: the production was as segmented as the cinematographic execution. Funding was sought for the script, the filming, entry into the laboratory, distribution: none of these phases was guaranteed ahead of time.[6] From the aesthetic point of view, the precarious conditions that surround cinema can be considered stimulating. As Martín Rejtman stated, "[I]t's difficult to talk about risks when there's so little cash to make film and movies are made with so little money. That is, when movies are made by necessity, something new always appears" (quoted in Fontana 2002, 28). Unanticipated difficulties ensured that production was as elastic as possible and that directors often assumed the role of executive producers. Pablo Trapero, for example, signs his movies as "director, screenwriter, and executive producer." If we set aside the potential criticism of this lack of separation of functions (as necessary conditions for industrial efficacy), the new cinema would not have happened if various filmmakers had not also become the executive producers of their own movies.

This situation of segmented production was altered entirely, especially for those who had already completed their *operas primas*, after the 2001 economic crisis in Argentina. With the *ley de cine*[7] ("Cinema Law") in full effect, and with an awareness that the industry needed a solid system of salaries for its employees, producers began to work with scripts as the most reliable calling card to obtain complete financing for a film. (The standard of quality that the new Argentine cinema has achieved is also crucial when presenting a project to international organizations.) In this way, Martel, Rejtman, and Caetano, among others, approached their subsequent productions with a system of funding already in place that allowed them to execute their films with fewer difficulties. Even today, however, a considerable number of *operas primas* continue to be produced in a variety of ways (as independent productions, with state finance, as co-productions with internationals funds or foundations, and so on).[8]

Invention of Unconventional Forms
of Production and Distribution

The production of a movie does not follow an established formula, nor is it necessarily restricted to institutional paths. The vicissitudes experienced during the production of *Mundo grúa, Bolivia, Silvia Prieto*, Lisandro Alonso's *La libertad* (2001, distributed in the United Kingdom as *Freedom*), and several other films made production as much of an adventure as the plot of the film. Directors know that, sooner or later, they are going to have to drop by the Instituto Nacional de Cine y Arte Audiovisuales (INCAA), in particular for distribution and for the conversion to film of movies shot on video. Yet, during a film's production, innumerable options arise that are available to producers (presentation to foundations, at festivals, to NGOs) and others that the movie must create throughout the process of its completion.

Several filmmakers devised alternative networks with the goal of avoiding the INCAA or of creating an alternative culture. Mariano Llinás, Gustavo Postiglione, Raúl Perrone, Ernesto Baca, the movies of Saladillo, the Yago Blas league and countless other examples speak to the strategies of many filmmakers to create an independent cinema (that is, one outside of the sphere of the INCAA) or to form an alternative network of production and reception.[9]

For films that aspire to become part of the commercial market the conditions are no more favorable. The predominance of chain movie theaters and their interest in showing only releases assured of success has meant that many directors have not been able to release their films. Even films that achieved success in film festivals outside of Argentina, such as Celina Murga's *Ana y los otros* (2003, distributed internationally as *Ana and the Others*) and Ana Poliak's *Parapalos* (2004), had to wait years (or are still waiting) to reach the market. Against this background, many directors—taken with the resounding success of mainstream Argentine movies such as Juan José Campanella's *El hijo de la novia* (2001, distributed in the United States as *Son of the Bride*) and *Luna de Avellaneda* (2004, distributed internationally as *Moon of Avellaneda*), both produced by Pol-ka, and with the more discrete success of Martín Rejtman's *Los guantes mágicos* and Lucrecia Martel's *La niña santa* (2004, distributed in the United States as *The Holy Girl*)—began to demand a change in exhibition regulations. Consistent and coordinated pressure led to new regulations known as the *cuota de pantalla* ("screen quota").[10] It is clear, however, that this new regulation did not alter the fate of a sizable tranche of Argentine films, both good and bad: being shown in the limited venue of the theaters of the INCAA. This would require smaller production companies having access to a network of independent movie theaters in attractive spaces where movies would not have to compete with large productions.

The Emergence of a New Generation of Producers

The new generation of producers have profiles that distinguish them from previous generations. Many of them were trained in film schools and know how to maneuver in the international scene (they speak English and know the different foreign sources of funding) and how to connect themselves to projects in different ways. Because they mostly deal with *operas primas,* their only bargaining tool is the screenplay. In this case, the executive producer—often a friend who lives in the same meager conditions as the director—takes on the tasks of translating the script, budgeting, and ensuring that the screenplay is presentable. A new generation of producers emerged under this type of hands-on training. After participating in one or two films, they were able to start their own production companies and have a more active role in the elaboration of films, no longer confined to the search for resources. A full recognition of the key role of these producers in the formation of the new cinema is still pending.

Of the previous generation of producers, only Lita Stantic developed a role in which production could take an aesthetic stance in financing independent projects. This has not prevented Stantic's production company from achieving one of the greatest successes of Argentina cinema of all time (María Luisa Bemberg's *Camila* [1984, distributed in the United States under the same title]) and a very good reception for products of the new cinema (principally, *La ciénaga* and Caetano's *El oso rojo* [2002, distributed internationally as *Red Bear*]). The challenge for new producers is to maintain this profile of renovation and to achieve continuity in the execution of films. Among the new producers, Daniel Burman and Diego Dubcovsky (BD Cine), Hugo Castro Fau and Pablo Trapero (Matanza), Hernán Musaluppi (Rizoma Films), Nathalie Cabirón (Tres Planos Cine), and El "Chino" Fernández (Villavicio Producciones) stand out.

Funding from International Institutions

In the early 1990s, Alejandro Agresti returned from the Netherlands to continue his career in Argentina; he gave interviews, scoured film schools, and criticized the way films were being made in the country. He brought with him a group of innovative movies that provided novel information to young people wanting to become filmmakers. These movies were never released commercially (*Boda secreta* [1989, "Secret Wedding"], *El acto en cuestión* [1994, "The Act in Question"], *Luba* [1990]) but were shown in special film festivals. They had been made with funding from foreign foundations, and, although Agresti experienced difficulties in getting them released in Argentina, they enjoyed prestige and relative success in cinephile networks abroad.[11] Agresti had also been instrumental in the support that Martín Rejtman received during the late 1980s from the Hubert Bals Fund for the execution of *Rapado* (1992, "Shaved Head"), which, despite taking five years to get released, became a cult movie for young people from its first screenings in the Sala Leopoldo Lugones.[12] The admiration that Rejtman's movie inspired was related both to the story it told and to how it had been made. These movies established a production style that would become generalized in later *operas primas*.

If the 1980s were marked by artistic co-production, during the 1990s the support of foreign foundations predominated. Whereas artistic co-production often conditioned some aspects of the making of a film, the support of these foreign foundations entailed only a financial relationship. Among the foundations that had a decisive role in the formation of a new cinema, we should mention the Hubert Bals Fund (created in 1988 and linked to Dutch governmental organizations and to the International Film Festival Rotterdam, the world's most important festival of independent film), the Fond Sud Cinéma (created in 1984 by the Ministry of Foreign Relations of the French government and targeted toward the productions of "developing countries"), Sundance (the foundation of the festival of the same name), and Ibermedia (a fund created in 1997 with contributions from the Programa Ibermedia). These foundations give financial assistance rather than fund a film in its entirety, but obtaining this kind of support is crucial in gaining access to other economic resources.[13] Almost all the movies of the new Argentine cinema received sponsorship from one of these sources, and this was crucial for a new generation of producers (in learning how to present a project and make it attractive and intelligible) and for those directors who entered into the global film scene and had international contacts. (With a few exceptions, earlier *operas primas* had been made in their entirety within Argentina.)

Relationship to the INCAA

Among the most important differences between the new Argentine cinema and the generation of the 1960s (with which it is frequently compared) is that the latter failed in its efforts to break institutional barriers and achieve continuity in production. Under the laws in force at that time, the classification that the Instituto Nacional de Cine gave to a movie once it was made was crucial to recover expenses. Only a rating of "A" ensured that the film would be shown and guaranteed access to the institute's credit financing. A "B" rating ("showing not obligatory") condemned the film to economic failure, excluded it from the benefits of the *ley del cine*, and decreed its certain death. In 1960, two key films of the era (Lautaro Murúa's *Shunko* and his *Alias Gardelito* [distributed internationally as *Alias Big Shot*]) received a "B" grading, despite their quality. This policy meant that the directors of that generation (David Kohon, Rodolfo Kuhn, Manuel Antín, Enrique Dawi, José Martínez Suárez) were unable to establish either a network or a strong voice of their own within the institute. Those filmmakers most closely linked to the movie industry had filled up the INCAA's available spaces, and they were not going to let the younger generation receive official support.[14]

The situation in the 1990s was radically different. In the first place, those directors who had already made several films turned to the INCAA, but they also had other financial sources in co-production or in private capital (Aristarain, Subiela, Bemberg). In addition, another type of producer had emerged. One such producer was Lita Stantic, who, while well aware of the ins and outs of the industry, was also willing to promote *operas primas* and to back new kinds of production. (For example, in the cases of Caetano's *Bolivia* and Diego Lerman's *Tan de repente*, she interceded when filming was significantly advanced or had already finished.) Finally, international circumstances were sufficiently favorable in reinforcing or giving continuity to new movies. Foundations (mainly Fond Sud and the Hubert Bals Fund) and festivals (Sundance, Rotterdam, and the BAFICI) encouraged experimentation and risk and also subsidized projects that previously would have had to search for other sources of funding. (The Mar del Plata and BAFICI festivals also helped in the completion of movies that competed in them.)[15]

In contrast to what happened in the 1960s, the INCAA, in light of the impact of these movies on the festival circuit and their prestige among critics, found itself obliged to cede more terrain to the new generation, who, for their part, searched for a way to capture new spaces and to influence various moments of the decision-making process.

Changes in Artistic Production

Changes in the Training of Artistic-Technical Staff

Film-school training and improved access to sophisticated technology allowed the artistic-technical staff who participated in the new films to make a huge leap with respect to their predecessors. It is not that previously there was no skill in the different areas of the process (the movies of Luis Puenzo, Adolfo Aristarain, or Eliseo Subiela prove this) but that the new staff had a different training and followed a different way of working.

Advances in technical equipment meant technological progress similar in scale to the progress made in the 1970s, when lighter equipment made possible cinema verité, the more intimate documentary (Jean Rouch), political film (*La hora de los hornos* [1969, released in the US as *The Hour of the Furnaces*]), and new ways of representing the urban (*París vu par...* [distributed as *Six in Paris*]). In the 1990s, computers became fully established in various areas of filmmaking and allowed movies that had been filmed in celluloid to be edited digitally. Furthermore, aspects of the film such as sound, color, or final cut could be reworked in different ways.

Skill in the Composition of Shots

It has been pointed out that a correct image is the least that can be expected from a movie, given the technological advances in cinematographic apparatus. In reality, the public's perception of a change in the quality of the image comes not from technological inno-vation but from skill in the composition of shots. In some cases, this dexterity becomes apparent through the decision to film locations stripped of any kind of aura: Rejtman, Villegas, and León have turned the most ordinary bars in Buenos Aires into suggestive places.[16] In *El bonaerense*, Trapero created some of the best sex scenes in Argentine cinema through the fluidity and rigor of his framing. Caetano and Stagnaro constructed, with few elements, a shocking action scene toward the end of *Pizza, birra, faso*. (This is without even mentioning the undeniable virtuosity of Lucrecia Martel or Lisandro Alonso.)

The fact that in the new Argentine cinema we find a strategic use of carelessness provides another indication that we are not dealing here with mere technical innovation. In earlier Argentine film, a shot that was out of focus or sound that was badly processed implied some-thing had gone wrong. The new directors, in contrast, knew how to take advantage of those shots that, according to the criteria of quality, did not turn out well. This is the case with the light reflected in the camera in the images of the warehouse in *Mundo grúa*, with the chaotic hand-held camera work in Ulises Rosell's *Bonanza,* or with the confusing sound in different scenes of *Pizza, birra, faso.* Strategic carelessness becomes one of the aesthetic attributes of these films.

The Policy behind the Choice of Actors

Casting for the new cinema is much more than the incorporation of new faces into the already established cast of professional actors. A rejection of the usual acting styles coexists with the search for different kinds of gestures, corporality, and diction. During castings, only rarely do filmmakers turn to consecrated actors, who, despite clear knowledge of their trade, are often too tied to a kind of realism or *costumbrismo.*[17] Ezequiel Acuña, the director of *Nadar solo* (2003, "Swimming Alone"), has stated that "with those actors, it cost me a lot to get them not to act" (Acuña, Lerman, and Villegas 2004, 162). Even in the case of older characters, where filmmakers not surprisingly usually turn to recognized actors, there is a shift toward those actors less marked by established prototypes and, therefore, more open to the director's molding (for example, Mirta Busnelli, Julio Chávez, Enrique Liporace, Martín Adejmian, Adriana Aizenberg). The most pronounced change can be found in the casting of younger actors. According to Alan Pauls, "[W]e no longer recognize the faces in the new movies. There are no proper names behind the actors. They exist while the movie lasts and they cease to exist when it has finished" (cited in Beceyro et al. 2000). The new cinema transformed the traditional methods of recruiting actors and instituted a reflection on the status of faces, names, and bodies. (For further discussion of casting, see Appendix 2).

Aesthetic Paths

Even before we make any positive decision about their films, the first advantage of these new directors is that they refuse to reproduce the procedures and schemas of the Argentine cinema that preceded them. At the very least, these directors understand what it is that they should not do. Critics have insisted on this point: vices have been banished, mistakes avoided, and bad habits done away with. The lack of an affirmative program (and the consolidation of a negative stance) has allowed each director to follow his or her own path and has also meant that criticism has failed in its attempts to delineate a shared aesthetic panorama for the new Argentine cinema. The problem lies in considering the unity of the corpus in terms of a generational program, shared aesthetic project, or series of stylistic features that the directors would then more or less consciously subscribe to. As no such program exists, in analyzing one film we quickly discover that it shares few aesthetic characteristics with others. However, a relatively unified corpus emerges if these aesthetic problems are considered as epochal features that can be read, with different configurations, in the diverse films of the period.

Breaking with Argentine Film of the 1980s

Two major refusals are written in invisible ink in the scripts and stories of the new movies: of the political imperative (what to do) and of the identitarian imperative (what we are like)—that is, of pedagogy and of self-accusation. In denying these imperatives, scriptwriters and filmmakers construct their stories without the necessity of developing parallel plots involving identity or the political, as the most representative directors—Alejandro Doria, María Luisa Bemberg, Eliseo Subiela, Fernando "Pino" Solanas, and Luis Puenzo—had done in different ways during the previous decade (a legacy that continued with Marcelo Piñeyro, Carlos Sorín, and Eduardo Mignogna, among others).[18] Of course, a political or identitarian reading could be made for any of the films of the new cinema, but the interpretive responsibility remains in the hands of the spectator. Instead of a message to decode, these movies offer us a world: a language, an atmosphere, some characters...a *brushstroke*—a brushstroke that does not respond to questions formulated insistently beforehand but sketches out its own questioning.

One of the definitive characteristics of the new cinema is its avoidance of allegorical stories. These films distance themselves from those that preceded them (for allegory had been the privileged mode by which Argentine cinema referred to context) and from the imperative to politicize to which, according to several critics of distinct orientation, all texts from the Third World are subject. Both Fredric Jameson and Gilles Deleuze maintain that the personal and political are inseparable in the stories told in Third World cinema.[19] Thus, any event, however intimate or trivial, would allow for a reading in a political or social key. The films of the new cinema, in contrast, insist upon the literal and tend to frustrate the possibility of an allegorical reading: the hotel in *La niña santa* is not Argentina; it is, quite simply, a hotel. This does not mean that there is no relationship between public and private, but simply that in our society these relationships are much more mediated; they do not offer themselves up to facile equivalences, nor can they be reduced to the idea that everything must be politicized.

For this reason, the minor stories to which these movies are inclined should not be read as an alternative way to invoke major themes. On the contrary, rather than indicate a theme, the stories work with indeterminacy and open up the play of interpretation. What is the theme of *La libertad, Silvia Prieto, La niña santa*? This thematic ambiguity is reinforced because—and this constitutes the other great negation of the new cinema—these films present neither morals nor characters who denounce injustice and in this way reveal the moral, psychological, or political mechanisms of the plot.

It was Martín Rejtman, with his *Rapado,* who realized that he could construct his own aesthetic program, avoiding the vices of earlier cinema:

> *On the formal level, did you try to distinguish yourself from the bulk of earlier Argentine cinema?*
>
> I tried to show things that Argentina cinema wasn't showing. If everything was explained too much, I chose to be less discursive; if there was a lot of talking, I chose to talk less; if it was clear that there was no narrative system, that every scene was filmed as it came, I tried to be rigorous and to tell the story in a specific way. But it wasn't on purpose that I said: "I'm going to hide the information from the spectator and let him rack his brain thinking about it," because everything that happens [in my films] is very simple. Maybe it requires a little more participation from the spectator in the sense that not everything is stated in the dialogue and he/she has to let each scene develop and end in order for a new one to begin, so that the story can be pieced together. (Quoted in Udenio and Guerschuny 1996)

Cinema as an Investigative Tool

How to begin to film a movie? Many movies begin as though they were documentaries: something that attracts attention is caught on camera. This something can be the nucleus of a story that is later developed into a documentary or into fiction. The lightness of the equipment and the ability to convert from digital video to film means that the note or sketch is already part of the film, just as fiction writers might jot down what occurs to them in a notebook. The traces of this process can be made explicit in a film, as in the case of Ulises Rosell's *Bonanza* or Jorge Gaggero's *Vida en Falcon* (2005, "Life in a Falcon"), or they can be inferred from the film's structure, as in Trapero's *Mundo grúa* or Albertina Carri's *Los rubios.* The "Work in Progress" section of the BAFICI organized by Hernán Guerschuny and Pablo Udenio (from the journal *Haciendo cine,* "Making Cinema") is based on the idea of showing *drafts* to the film world. This characterization applies especially to documentaries, because documentaries are, almost in their totality and owing to the malleability of digital video, works in progress. Before their assembly, documentary materials have a greater impact than would a draft of a narrative film of fiction.[20]

But the idea of investigating with the camera is not alien to films whose screenplays are already completed before filming. The director Juan Villegas, who is also a thoughtful film critic whom no one would accuse of naïveté, said of his film *Sábado,* "The idea of what I wanted to suggest responded to something more intuitive; I hadn't thought it out beforehand. The process was to discover it gradually" (quoted in Acuña, Lerman, and Villegas 2004, 158). Lisandro Alonso, with respect to his projects since *La libertad,* has affirmed, "I want to keep investigating, to try to figure out what I did" (quoted in Quintín 2001). An original idea: screenplay and filming are not successive steps but are mutually conditioned throughout the making of a movie, in a process that can take up to two or three years. In this trajectory, cinema itself is a tool of inquiry and a search that extends until the film reaches theaters.

The Absence of Exteriority

One difference between the new Argentine cinema and movies from the 1980s stems from the composition of screenplays. In the 1980s, responding to the era of the return to democracy, one or more characters embodied the viewpoint with which the spectator was supposed to identify (the morally correct position, the gaze that most adequately interprets what happens), but the majority of the movies of the new Argentine cinema rob the spectator of this possibility.

In Luis Puenzo's *La historia oficial* (1985, distributed internationally as *The Official Story*), the character of Professor Benítez (Patricio Contreras) is central for the *anagnórisis* (recognition) that is produced in Alicia (Norma Aleandro). But Benítez does not fulfill only this role; he is also a progressive teacher, he knows how to get along with students, he does not trick them, and he is a model to follow. This approach can still be found in much later films, such as Adolfo Aristarain's *Lugares communes* (2002). Here, the protagonist, Fernando (Federico Luppi), reacts indignantly to the moral disintegration of society, and it is difficult not to find ourselves in agreement with what he says and with his positions. (In addition, and as in the case of Contreras' character, he is a high school teacher; in both films, the spectator is made to occupy the position of an adolescent.) Federico Luppi has often played this role of the upright man: in Fernando Ayala's *El arreglo* (1983, "The Deal") and in two other Aristarain movies, *Tiempo de revancha* (1981, distributed in the United States as *A Time for Revenge*) and *Un lugar en el mundo* (1991, distributed in the United States as *A Place in the World*). Finally, if Alejandro Agresti was not able to become one of the pioneers of the new generation (despite the fact that his movies, polemical positions, and conception of production caused a genuine commotion in film schools at the time), it was because in his screenplays long speeches tend to create a pedagogy characterized not by its images but by what his characters say. In *El amor es una mujer gorda* (1987, "Love Is a Fat Woman"), for example, the character played by Elio Marchi constantly reflects aloud and gives us lessons on what is happening to us.

All of this is generally referred to as "preaching to the spectator" (*bajar la línea,* or, literally, "to lower the line"). The phrase is apt, as it refers not only to the pedagogical action (at times implying an underestimation of the spectator) but also to the fact that the line (*línea*) of the film extends toward a space that, while working itself out within the script, is actually outside of it. The ethical character does not speak from within the story but has the privilege of being able to judge it from without.

The absence of exteriority, in contrast, is crucial in the screenplays of the new cinema and in some cases manages to make spectators uncomfortable. In Trapero's *El bonaerense* there is no character through whom a judgment can be passed on the actions of the police; in the works of Rejtman and in Villegas' *Sábado,* the characters remain on the same plane and no one appears to judge them or to explain them. (Everything, we could say, takes place on the surface.) The same thing happens with documentaries such as Enrique Bellande's *Ciudad de María* (2002, "City of María"), which refuses to judge its characters from an outside perspective and leaves everything up to the spectator. In fact, there is not a single testimony in the movie from anyone who does not share the believers' faith. (The only intruder, if it can be called that, is the camera-eye, which produces genuine repulsion: "Get out of here! Get out of here!" shout the believers in unison.) In *El bonaerense*, this exteriority assumes an explicit and humorous character: the cop Cáneva maintains that extraterrestrials observe everything that happens on Earth and that "they're outraged about our behavior." On planet Earth (or within the story), however, no one can assume that gaze that judges all and that, through an identification with the spectator, soothes his or her conscience.[21]

By not preaching to the spectator, the films multiply their interpretive possibilities. Although it is difficult to believe that films such as Aristarain's *Tiempo de revancha* or Puenzo's *La historia oficial* offer up multiple interpretive scenarios, how else can we understand the final scene of Rejtman's *Silvia Prieto*? Is it the display of the banality of everyday life or the promise of a possible identification? What is the key scene in a story that is never emphatic and has no upheavals or twists and turns?

Film criticism has perceived this clearly. As Leonardo D'Espósito, a particularly acidic critic who writes for the film journal *El amante cine*, says of Carlos Sorín's *El perro* (2004, released in the United States and the United Kingdom as *Bombón: El Perro*), "Professionally filmed, this 'minor story' stretched to its limits utilizes the landscape and music cloyingly, *pointing out the emotions* that the spectator should experience in each sequence" (2005, 25, my emphasis).

And this is one of the points in which the new cinema has distanced itself most radically from earlier film: in its relationship to the spectator. Open endings; the absence of emphasis and of allegories; more ambiguous characters; the rejection of thesis films; a rather erratic trajectory in the story; zombie characters immersed in what happens to them; the omission of national, contextualizing information; the rejection of the identitarian and political imperatives—all those decisions that, to a greater or lesser extent, can be detected in these films account for the opacity of their stories. Instead of handing over everything to us already digested, these films open up the play of interpretation.

In broad terms, this can also be observed in the titles of these movies: rather than indicate readings, they preserve ambiguity and remain enigmatic. Rather than being descriptions or riddles that will be resolved in the course of the film, titles such as Luis Ortega's *Caja negra* (2002, distributed internationally as *Black Box*), *La libertad* ("Liberty"), *Los muertos* ("The Dead"), and even *La niña santa* ("The Holy Girl") constitute another disturbing element that invites exegesis from the spectator. Other titles are more descriptive but also more neutral, like a signaling that also reveals nothing: *Silvia Prieto*, *Los guantes mágicos* ("The Magic Gloves"), *Sábado* ("Saturday"), *Nadar solo* ("Swimming Alone"), *Un oso rojo* ("The Red Bear"). Compare these with the most emphatic titles of the previous generation, all of which wink at the spectator: *A Place in the World*, *The Dark Side of the Heart*, *Nobody's Wife*, *The Official Story*, *Gardel's Exile*, *Time for Revenge*, *Last Images of a Shipwreck*, among others.

How can we read these two complementary attitudes of investigation and a rejection of preaching to the spectator? It seems risky to give a single answer, but there are at least three elements to keep in mind. In the first place, the mechanism that forces all of our acts to be considered under the lens of the political has stopped functioning. Political responses, in the usual sense of the term, are no longer satisfactory, for the very problems that arise no longer respond to traditional norms. The political imperative does not emerge in such a transparent way. Moreover, successive crises (essentially, the failure to restore institutional and economic democracy) meant that new directors preferred to suspend many inherited certainties. Second, the identitarian imperative, anchored in a stereotyped *costumbrismo* and transformed into a televisual style in which the abuse of the close-up dominated, has also been exhausted as a narrative model. Constructing a screenplay around the question "What are we?" stopped being interesting from the moment the community and history that had given this question significance began a process of decomposition or began to be more defined by contemporary global processes than by national ones. Third, the relationship that earlier directors had with public space was much clearer and more concrete. María Luisa Bemberg made *Señora de nadie* (1982, released in the United States as *Nobody's Wife*) and her other movies from a feminist position; Solanas became the voice of political exiles; Aristarain showed how narrative cinema could uncover the operation of political repression; Puenzo and his screenwriter, Aída Bortnik, showed in *La historia oficial* the necessity to denounce the recent past. These directors identified themselves with, and found a function in, the return to democracy.[22] None of this happened with the young directors who emerged in the late 1990s: those roles were less available, and the social fabric was not so structured that filmmakers could continue to function as a vanguard. In light of the disintegration of the public sphere (whether due to globalization, mass media, or governmental policies), the new filmmakers were not assigned a role in advance.

Instead, they used the language of cinema to investigate their own positioning, their own amorphous desires.

The Dispersion of Narration

Edgardo Cozarinsky has observed, with respect to Diego Lerman's *Tan de repente,* that "there was a starting point, yes; but then the film, with an admirable freedom and economy, went in search of its narration, its story, and began to invent it almost before my very eyes" (2003, 181). Lerman's movie achieves its impact because it carries to its limits a poetics of the accident. A parachute that falls in the middle of the road, in the path of the truck in which the protagonists are traveling, is a good emblem for a film that begins with the wandering around of the adolescent girls Lenin, Mao, and Marcia and ends with the abrupt death of Clara, Lenin's aunt who lives in Rosario. An accident in a narration constitutes a limit because motivated events generally dominate. Even the unexpected (a coincidental encounter) can acquire a certain logic in the goals of a narration.[23]

Paradoxically, in the new cinema the accident is law: unpredictable by definition, it is scattered throughout these stories and their structures. The first term in the series arises by chance. *El descanso* opens with a car embedded in a billboard on the road, *Sábado* can be divided up according to its two automobile accidents in different corners of the city, and *La ciénaga* begins with an accidental fall and ends with a death from the same. In Mariano de Rosa's "Vida y obra," an episode of *Mala época* (1998, "Bad Era"), the protagonist remains mute after a beam accidentally hits him on the head. Finally, Trapero constructs the narrative tension of *Mundo grúa* in a very original way, on the basis of an accident that is constantly promised but never occurs. It is as though the impact that the narrations are trying to process came from the most absolute outside, and for this reason the accident cannot be represented and always remains *off-screen* (in *La ciénaga,* in *Tan de repente,* in *Sábado,* in *El descanso,* in *Silvia Prieto*).[24]

Many movies present an erratic narrative structure, as Fabián Bielinsky, the author of the best screenplay constructed in recent years according to conventional rules, has pointed out in numerous interviews. From the perspective of the author of *Nueve reinas* (2000, distributed in the United States and the United Kingdom as *Nine Queens*), it is clear that the new Argentine cinema is amorphous in its narrative construction. Even the screenplay of *La ciénaga,* very rigorous in its composition, shifts its focus among characters. The story begins by revolving around the relationships formed by Mecha

(Graciela Borges) and her daughter, Momi (Sofía Bertolotto); it moves to focus on Tali (Mercedes Morán), and later José (Juan Cruz Bordeu), to concentrate finally on Luciano (Sebastián Montagna), Tali's son, who dies after falling off a ladder. In contrast to modern film (even in its most transgressive variants), which presented a story and then developed it, contemporary cinema tends to launch, from the beginning, innumerable potential stories, from among which it ends up choosing one or two. This explains a certain nomadism in the plots of these films, along with the sensation that they might drift, at any moment, toward any one of their characters.

Characters outside of the Social

Several years have passed since the birth of a new type of character who, although not absent from earlier films, had never before been so omnipresent: I refer to characters outside of the social world. These figures were equally distant from the oppressed rebels of political cinema who acted to transform the society they had received and from *costumbrista* cinema in which each person was a sign of his place in the social hierarchy. All of a sudden, a series of amnesiac characters began to appear, true zombies who came from nowhere and were headed for the same, obsessed with an indecipherable map. Serge Daney writes,

> In the sixties, the marginalized character was a good theme for a screenplay. A victim of society, a reanimator of utopias, or a revealer of contradictions, the marginal character had something of the anti-hero, sympathetically positive. In order to consider society obliquely, it was enough to follow him; his fall, like that of a falling star, would illuminate it. And now we have Mona [the protagonist of Agnès Varda's *Vagabond* (1985)] who seldom speaks, who makes no claims, takes little, gives nothing, accuses no one, and dies in a no man's land. (2004, 258)

Mona is a character "outside of the social," and the characters of many of the films from the 1990s are marginal in the sense defined by Daney. This marginality carries no sense of change or heroism— "Be marginal, be a hero" went the 1960s-style slogan of the Brazilian artist Hélio Oiticica—but simply the condition of exclusion and absolute disposability.

In Diego Lerman's *Tan de repente,* two girls, Mao and Lenin, wander around without doing anything before they enter into the story. Their names, in addition, signal everything that separates them from modernity: a Mao and a Lenin who don't want to start a revolution; lesbians who don't represent lesbians ("We aren't lesbians," Lenin says several times); they are young people, but they don't turn to this category to justify their attitudes; they are "punks," but this word no longer means anything. We do not know where they live or where they come from, whether they have money or a home. In *Pizza, birra, faso,* the protagonists are young lumpen who are looking not to change but to survive in a hostile world. In *Bolivia,* the illegal immigrant, a former coca farmer, drifts from bar to bar at night, with the single goal of making himself invisible. In *La libertad,* the protagonist, distancing himself from all social contact, demands nothing from anyone and silently proceeds with his task of cutting trees. Emilio Bernini has observed that cinema of the 1990s deals with "closed worlds," in contrast to the desire "to give a global image of society" of the productions of the generation of the 1960s (2003, 90). And Alan Pauls has praised the fact that "the new Argentine cinema is much more interested in showing worlds than in showing characters, heroes" (quoted in Beceyro 1997, 4). These are worlds that are not choreographed in advance, in which the social as containment, oppression, or frame vanishes.[25]

The Return of the Real, Broadcast by Television

In the new Argentine cinema, few films fail to feature a television broadcast. With greater or lesser preponderance, *Silvia Prieto, Bolivia, La ciénaga, Mundo grúa, Tan de repente, Ciudad de María, La niña santa,* Federico León's *Todo juntos,* and Alejo Taube's *Una de dos* (2004, distributed internationally as *One or the Other*), among others, either hand over momentarily the totality of the screen to the television or register the situation of watching it. Even in a film in which the television does not appear, *Sábado,* there is a character (Gastón Pauls) who is presented as a star of the small screen.

It is clear that television occupies increasing space in our lives and that its presence is felt not only in the intimacy of the home but also in public space. The broadcasting of images, news, political events, stories, advertisements, and entertainment has meant that in recent years reality itself has been transformed through the existence and propagation of television, which has modified our understanding of space, time, and belief. In a sense, the real is produced by television, and the return of the real that has been spoken of so frequently recently goes beyond aesthetics, indicating how the mass media have upset our perceptions of the world. In the words of Umberto Eco, television has shifted "from *a vehicle of facts,* considered as neutral, to *an apparatus for the production of facts;* that is, from a mirror of reality it is becoming the producer of reality" (1990, 210, my emphasis).

Cinema, like television, is a machine that produces audiovisual images, but its mode of circulation and degree of influence are on a much smaller scale. By including a scene of television, these movies stage a confrontation between two ways of producing the real, ways that at times enter into tension with one another, exclude one another, or are antagonistic. The realism so frequently ascribed to cinema is nothing more than this: not representing the real but seeing different ways of producing it; not the extent to which reality is measured but the competition in the production of the real. And this happens in movies as different from one another as *Bolivia, La ciénaga,* Federico León's *Todo juntos* (2002, distributed internationally as *Everything Together*), and *Silvia Prieto.*

In *Bolivia,* television manages to occupy the whole shot, expelling cinema, in sporting events (Argentina versus Bolivia in soccer; the boxing match between Mike Tyson and Evander Holyfield) and in the violent movies that the customers consume in the bar as they kill time. It has been frequently observed that national confrontations, in a globalized world, are displaced onto sports, and onto soccer in particular. As the images show an Argentine goal and the sportscaster Fernando Niembro can be heard to say, "The Bolivians are becoming frustrated and disorderly," the music of the band Los Kjarkas upholds a typical discourse of Latin American brotherhood: "[W]hatever bird that emerges from dreams/beyond all reality/soaring, you cross the Andes/carrying a message of fraternity."[26] Toward the end of the movie, the television violence becomes more real than the music, and the character of el Oso ("the Bear") ends up repeating the discriminatory words he heard in the mass media. The contamination between bar and screen is permanent, and the characters, as in the many shots that show them captivated by the apparatus that hangs there, live in a space in which the difference between television image and real space becomes indiscernible.[27]

In *La ciénaga,* television images also accompany the characters constantly, but here it is not contamination but a permanent separation that makes the story move forward. In some shots, the digital image of the news report of the Virgin displaces entirely the filmic images, but this does nothing more than mark an incompatibility, for the procedures of the mise-en-scène try to distance themselves from the conventional forms of media representation. Here, while film leads to suspicion and unease, television is the producer of belief and of a new religion.

It is no accident that one of the films that is most unyielding in its relationship to the language of television incorporates television with the goal of questioning it. In *Todo juntos* the television in the bar is not set up to receive transmissions through the airwaves or cable; it reproduces a written text that speaks to the intimate and incommunicable conflict of its protagonists: "We were practically raised together. She had a key to my house. I had a key to her house. Her mother was my mother's best friend.... We passed six months touching each other, fully clothed. I was able to get an erection, but the very idea of penetration would make me weak." In a film that could be characterized as realist, the televisual production of the real is impossible, because in the time of television the tough core of pain that the movie stages never appears. To approach this conflict, it is necessary to construct, with cinema, a dead time: extremely slow, raw, tense, and viscous, using the apparatus of television but erasing the frenzy of the instantaneous and constantly entertaining time that it tends to broadcast.

One of the best shots of television can be found in *Silvia Prieto*. Marcelo and Brite are in a pizzeria watching the "Lonely Hearts" program, in which marriages are formed (maximum intimacy, maximum public exposure). With surprise, Marcelo recognizes on the screen a former high school classmate, Mario, who declares on the show, "I was having a crisis because my youth was fading." The movie cuts to a shot of the dining room of Silvia's house. She cannot be seen, and later on the television set broadcasts the same program and focuses in on Marta, Mario's future girlfriend. From the sound, we understand that Silvia is in the kitchen. The fixed shot lasts for a bit, and then there is a zoom-in on Marta on the television screen.[28] The image undergoes a genuine distortion; her face becomes larger, despite that fact that the camera has not moved. The indiscretion of television and its procedures is opposed to the distance and slowness of cinema's gaze. But there is something else: no one is watching the television. Silvia is going about her tasks, while the television goes about its own. If she leaves it on, it is because the television is no longer something to be watched. Its temporality, its spatiality, its way of approaching the real (turning the intimate into a public discussion) are already inscribed into our perception, and it matters little whether we turn it on or off. In our daily lives, recent years have also involved a process of learning how to live with the reality that television has produced.[29]

The Realist Manifestation

The realism attributed to the new Argentine cinema needs to be considered along the intersection of two lines: on one hand, in tension with the realism that television produces, discussed above; on the other hand, in its link to cinematographic realism, distinct from other artistic realisms.

For almost all critics—and above all for those who were trained in literary theory—realism is a code. In the negative image attributed to realism, critics of language and literature have contributed the most important conceptual arsenal. Jaime Rest defines realism as "a worldly conception, sociologically and increasingly materialist, characteristic of the nineteenth century, that has formed part of the bourgeois worldview and that tries to reproduce artistically the world 'such as it is seen,' concomitant to the advance in empiricism and modern scientific thought" (1979, 129). In the twentieth century, and above all throughout the 1960s, realism was considered the victorious expression of representation and of an ideological conception in which the sign is ignored in favor of an idea of transparency and an uncritical acceptance of the real (with the real understood as something given and not as a construction). Thus, realism must be unmasked for ideological and scientific reasons because, in the words of Tzvetan Todorov, "one can speak of the *vraisemblance* of a work in so far as *it attempts to make us believe that it conforms to reality and not to its own laws*" (quoted in Culler 1975, 198–9). The contesting of this style reached such an intensity that Paul de Man inverted the terms and no longer defined realism as an ideology but ideology itself as realism: "What we call ideology is precisely the confusion of linguistic with natural reality" (1990, 23). At any rate, this criticism of realism was essentially directed at linguistic and discursive expression. Barthes' phrase "[I]t is the category of 'the real' (and not its contingent contents) which is then signified; in other words, the very absence of the signified, to the advantage of the referent alone, becomes the very signifier of realism" (1986, 148) shows how the contesting of realism was intrinsically related to marking the collapse of the linguistic sign.

The genealogy of realism in film is entirely different. The term begins to circulate at the moment cinematographic codes enter into crisis, as in the case of postwar Italian cinema. Used to name a style opposed to the theatrical and codified nature of earlier cinema, the term "neo-realism" was immediately accepted by filmmakers and critics, despite the fact that it had been abandoned or discredited in other areas owing to the actions of the avant-garde. The "realism" of these films did not stem from narrative or dramatic sources but from the mise-en-scène and from a narration whose codes and causal links were weakened. With the choice of nonprofessional actors and quotidian stories to natural sets, and far from sequence shots and the direct register, Luchino Visconti, Roberto Rossellini, and Vittorio De Sica discovered the documentary potential of film.

Filmic realism would not have acquired its historical importance were it not for the critical elaborations of André Bazin, who considered this movement a turning point in the history of film and established its theoretical justification. To understand Bazin's undertaking fully, we must keep in mind that his writings defend realism but also the notion, key to his position, of the mise-en-scène. (It is known, for example, that he was a staunch defender of the sequence shot as the emblem of modern cinema, as opposed to montage.) We must also consider his conception of the cinematographic image. For Bazin, this is not an iconic representation but an indexical impression, like a fingerprint or, according to a simile with vast consequences in his thought, like the face of Christ in a holy shroud. From this viewpoint, what makes a film realist is its accentuation of the documentary nature of the image (although the story it tells may be fictional). With Bazin's contributions, filmic realism gained credibility, linking it to the most avant-garde, experimental, and modern film.

The name was not contested by later criticism, and the directors of the New Wave, trained at the journal *Cahiers du cinema,* which was founded by Bazin himself, carried out in the field of creation the consequences of his thought: their stripped-down mise-en-scènes, their inclination for the direct register and cinema verité, for the sequence shot and the hand-held camera, for new faces and the familiarity of stories and their places. (Paris is as much a protagonist in the New Wave as Jean-Luc Godard or Anna Karina.) In fact, Eric Rohmer affirmed that "of all the arts, film is the most realist" (2000, 66).

The use of the term "realism" in cinema, after it had been expelled to a greater or lesser extent from other artistic practices, continues to this day. Deleuze himself maintains that neo-realism afforded a description of the real (above all in causal relationships) much greater than we had grown accustomed to in earlier cinema. His objection to Bazin's work was not in the use of the concept but in the fact that Deleuze considered that neo-realism must be removed from the "level of the real" and located in the "level of the 'mental'" (Deleuze 1986b, 11–12).[30] Without considering the word "realism" anathema—Deleuze is far from the alarmist tone of the defenders of *écriture,* Derrida, Barthes, Sollers, or Kristeva—for him the great innovation of neo-realism consists in the fact that it cut the nexus between perception and action, allowing the mental to intercede. The Deleuzian phrase "It records rather than reacts" (1986b, 3) could well be the motto for the various returns to realism that have occurred throughout the history of film.

From this history of the use of the term, it is clear that Argentine film from the 1980s can be criticized not for its realism but for its *costumbrismo,* that is, its attachment to codes of representation that are proper to realist literature or to a certain type of theater inclined toward grotesque realism. Despite the fact that the stories might have been verisimilar in terms of the representation of daily life, the mise-en-scène and acting ended up being theatrical constructions imprinted upon the cinematographic image. This legacy that the new generation encountered produced the following paradox: how is it that in reproducing such natural dialogues, and in representing such common characters, earlier films ended up so phony, so non-verisimilar? The answer lies in the fact that, although this cinema believed itself to be representing the real, what it in fact represented was its codes. The distancing from the earlier *costumbrismo* did not lie so much in a rejection of the codes of representation as in new directors' awareness of the dissimilarities between narration and mise-en-scène—because if the new generation opted for realism, it did so principally in terms of the latter.

This mise-en-scène that evokes the real does not do so on the basis of transparency or the idea that reality must be shown as it is. Reality is not black and white, but the black-and-white images of *Bolivia, Los rubios,* and *Mundo grúa* produce a documentary effect, of a direct and quotidian register. In the words of Claudia Acuña, there is an "explicit intention in *Mundo grúa* to operate as a hidden camera that robs ([Director] Pablo [Trapero] says *to swipe*) pieces of reality" (1999). But this "theft" would not be entirely effective were it not for the editing and combining of materials that accentuates these indexes of the real. Hence, beyond the return to the genre of documentary, there is also a documentary presence in various fictive films of this generation. In reality, as Eric Rohmer saw very well, any film (with the exception of animation) has a documentary basis, whether in the register of bodies, space, or objects[31]—hence the suggestive definition of Serge Daney that "film is that strange art that is made with real bodies and real events" (2004, 288). Argentine cinema tended to accentuate these aspects—in the locations, in the costumes, in the actors, and in the procedures—rather than stifle them or expel them from the mise-en-scène.

In fact, those critics who have wanted to oppose the realist register to the mise-en-scène have had to revert to a negative nomenclature to define a style: the "non-realists," as though the cinema of those directors (Rejtman, Villegas, Acuña, or Lerman) was a reaction to or went against the realism of others (Caetano, Stagnaro, Trapero).[32] Yet these directors do not recognize their work in this confrontation, nor are they willing to attribute the term "realism" to other directors. "To me *Silvia Prieto* is a realist movie and its code is absolutely normal and quotidian," Rejtman states (quoted in Fontana 2002). And Villegas has stated, "[I]n one period I spoke of objectivism, rather than realism, because realism for me is that: not subjectivizing, not emphasizing…which is not my idea but Rossellini's" (quoted in Acuña, Lerman, and Villegas 2004, 167). In any case, the term "realism" turned into an ideologeme of debate, and different aesthetics are defined by directors' interpretations of it.

What these positions reveal (in addition to the fact that filmmakers are not afraid of a term that is still taboo for a certain group of critics) is that many of these antagonisms that structure the modernist debate have run dry in a society in which the artificial production of images is something habitual and generalized. The antithesis of transparency and naturalness or artifice and self-reflection has given way to a different series of conflicts. It is no longer so necessary to show who can unmask the artificial approaches to the real that present themselves as true or natural as it is to see who can offer up better perceptions or faculties to produce the real.

An observation Rejtman made in an interview has the virtue of condensing the two basic lines that we have presented here on realism: the role of television in our perception of the real and the capacity of cinema to come close to our experience of the real. The director of *Los guantes mágicos* says:

In this sense, there are movies, like Ariel Rotter's *Sólo por hoy* [2001, "Just for Today"], which look like television programs. In these cases, improvising means letting actors loose in front of the camera, and letting them do what they want. This kind of *costumbrismo* or supposed realism of a good deal of TV is a bit harmful. In a way, *it becomes something realer than reality.* That's why when you hear someone speak in a different way it may not sound real, whereas for me what it clear is that in everyday life people speak much more like they do in *Silvia Prieto* than in a television comedy like *Son amores.* (Quoted in Fontana 2002, my emphasis)

The Signs of the Present

Of all the artistic practices of the 1990s, it was film that presented the greatest opening up to the present, regardless of whether one explains it in terms of technological, industrial, cultural, political, or aesthetic factors. Yet to access the flux of the present, the new filmmakers had to dismantle and reject what had been done previously and to redirect the cinematic machine. They had to transform the relations between production and aesthetics, to segment the elaboration of films to finance them, to invent unconventional modes of production and screening, to turn to international funding sources, to obtain the recognition of the INCAA and critics, to recruit and train new artistic-technical personnel, to establish a novel approach to casting, to avoid preaching to the spectator by rejecting the political and identitarian demand, to construct open narrations that could include the accidental, to depict characters outside of the social, to compete with other media in the production of the real, and to process the impact of changes in a world that was no longer the same.

I would not like to end this chapter by giving the impression that the panorama sketched here is more stubbornly optimistic than an objective description of what has happened in recent years. Major problems continue to exist in Argentine cinema, in addition to the fact that in Argentina, and in contrast to other countries, a considerable number of movies are produced that do not comply with even the minimal conditions of narrative and aesthetic coherence in cinematographic terms. Many of these monstrosities, moreover, receive the financial and political support of the INCAA. Anyone who has taken the time to watch all the national movies knows what I am referring to. Today, however, any spectator or critic can choose among eight or ten films made in recent years and take an interest in the trajectory of at least two or three of their directors. This is no small feat for a cinematography as meager as Argentina's, which only with great difficulty can list more than ten great titles throughout its history.

2

Film, the Narration of a World

Nomadism and Sedentarism

From its beginnings, cinema has connected groups, publics, communities, multitudes, worlds. In recent years, when the very idea of society appears to be undergoing an unprecedented mutation, to a great extent due to the importance of the media, it is no coincidence that cinema has begun to explore once again, implicitly or explicitly, the possibility of inventing or consolidating associations. The absence or withdrawal of large popular groups as subjects of history led cinema to rest its gaze on a smaller group, albeit one no less revered: the family. It seems evident that not only conjugal matrimonial ties but also familial ideas as entrenched as the heterosexual union, the stability of the group linked by ties of blood, the authority of ancestors, and the sense of belonging are in crisis.

It used to be imagined that parents not only brought children into the world but also offered a world to them, that is, a legacy, an experience, and, eventually, a job and a place to settle. Now, there is a kind of orphanhood to the characters of the new Argentine cinema. Parents do not appear anywhere, and, when they do, it is only to despotically anchor others in a disintegrated order. Despite the fact that there is no family or the family is not visible, it remains inscribed as a reference point. This is why relationships begin to break up: the family is still an operating institution and has not been replaced by another. When characters insist on maintaining this (patriarchal) order, we find ourselves facing a process of disintegration and a paralysis and lethargy that well deserve the name *sedentarism*. In contrast, when the family is absent and the characters have neither a place of belonging nor a home to return to, we find ourselves facing a case of *nomadism*.

Nomadism and sedentarism are complementary signs of new times, but they show different states. Nomadism is the absence of a home, the lack of powerful (restrictive and normative) ties of belonging, and a permanent and unpredictable mobility; sedentarism shows the breakdown of homes and of families, the inefficacy of traditional and modern associative ties, and the paralysis of those who insist on perpetuating that order. Clearly, these are figures of fiction that radicalize and investigate aesthetically and narratively those social components that are increasingly disseminated.

Mobility is important in determining whether a narration is nomadic or sedentary, but it is not sufficient. Pablo Trapero's *Familia rodante* (2004, released in the United States and the United Kingdom as *Rolling Family*) takes place almost entirely within a mobile home that leaves San Justo and arrives at Misiones, on the Paraguayan and Brazilian borders. Yet, if this is a sedentary narration, it is because the family, in the process of breaking down, still gives meaning to the characters' actions. There is a family and there is a home, although they are mobile.

For its part, Jorge Gaggero's *Vida en Falcon* takes place in a single location and documents the days of two men who live inside of two cars parked on the street. The fact that the film's protagonist has adopted this lifestyle after the death of his wife, that he is so emphatically located outside of the social, and that within this car it would be impossible to constitute a family makes this film a key example of nomadism.[1] Thus, what is decisive in this classification is the family as a world of reference and the existence or lack thereof of a stable place (something like a home) to which returns are always possible.

According to its orientation, the narration will emphasize either the detritus of capitalism or the breakdown of sedentary institutions. Film that treats detritus can be recognized by the predominance of erratic itineraries and movements toward the world of waste, drifting, and delinquency (all that capitalism attempts to locate, illusorily, in the margins). In contrast, in film that treats sedentarism, claustrophobia and disintegration win out: families with confused ties, institutions and heroes of the past that function like broken-down automatons, and characters who sink into parasitism.[2] Among Argentine movies made in recent years, Caetano and Stagnaro's *Pizza, birra, faso* synthesizes the coordinates of nomadic film, and Lucrecia Martel's *La ciénaga* has become the most forceful example of the cinema of disintegration. We could, of course, speak of the infinite differences between the two films according to their procedures and mise-en-scènes, but what interests me here, rather than a formal analysis, is the type of preoccupations that they reveal. For they contain a search that cannot be confronted using the instruments of the evolutionary history of modernist film, with its insistence on procedure, the coherent work, and the notion of authorship.

I understand that this classification might generate a certain resistance from the moment it begins to base itself exclusively in cinematographic criteria. However, my goal is to transversally and experimentally make my way through their stories to see how they think culturally and socially with categories that have their own specificity in cinema, such as space, shots, narrations, framing: in a word, the mise-en-scène. I do not consider this a fixed or definitive classification. In fact, I think that *Rapado* has more in common with *La ciénaga*, given its formal rigor, than with *Pizza, birra, faso*, although it shares with the latter film its nomadism. These are *tendencies*, or, if you will, critical constructions to describe disintegrating worlds and the movements of bodies.

Dispersion and Fixity (between *La ciénaga* and *Pizza, birra, faso*)

The claim that in the nomadic tendency we find a shift toward the detritus of capitalism might seem strange in a medium such as film, marked as it is by great economic investment. This is why it is important first to define what type of displacements we encounter and what symbolic and material dimensions are at stake. This nomadic belonging is paradoxical, and it refers as much to groups relegated to the margins as to an elite that travels without paying attention to borders. A good example of this is the success achieved by Caetano and Stagnaro's *Pizza, birra, faso*, Trapero's *Mundo grúa*, Lisandro Alonso's *La libertad*, and Caetano's *Bolivia* in the global culture of film festivals. It is as if the virtues of regionalization and the flight from global capitalism were discovered at these transnational events.

For this reason, the interest in the detritus of capitalism should be understood not as an intransigent or antisystemic position but as a use and often an idealization of the marginal. This is not, however, the only form that nomadism takes: there is also the movement of middle-class people who have no fixed place in life, who have had to abandon their homes or who, through their own decision, live a life of constant movement. That is, I regard nomadism not as a romantic evasion that looks toward precapitalism or as a line of flight, as proposed by Deleuze, but as a contemporary state of permanent movements, passages, and situations of not belonging, along with the dissolution of any instance of permanence.

Without a doubt, we could speak of migration or diaspora, yet the virtue of the term *nomadism* is that it exceeds the national or communitarian. In particular, it deals with a movement through spaces, none of which manages to turn into a point of return (a role that, traditionally, corresponded to the family home, the religious building, or the national soil). In this sense, although they are completely different, Rejtman's *Rapado,* Trapero's *Mundo grúa,* and *Pizza, birra, faso* can all be included in this tendency: they explore what happens when we remain without a home.

In movies that depict characters who are outside of the social, the first thing that surprises us is the link between the global culture of cinema and the idealization of the popular,[3] which has a long history. This alliance between powerful economic investments and attachment to the lumpen, between the nomadism of an enlightened elite and the nomadism of the illiterate, is paradoxically characterized by its rejection of the standardized consumption that global capitalism imposes, at the same time that it enters into one of its variants (the global interaction of film festivals, foundations, and other institutions). In light of this consumption that defines new subjects and wants to include them in the social body, nomadic films capture the existence of characters in the moment in which the force of consumption is exhausted or detained (for example, el Rulo's music, which had been a success, in *Mundo grúa;* the almost absolute dispensability of the protagonist of *La libertad;* the accumulation of scrap metal of the characters in Ulises Rosell's *Bonanza;* the beat-up car that once was valuable merchandise in *Vida en Falcon*). They are excluded and, as such, marked by the dimension of the abject and by their membership in a precarious space: garbage dumps, ramshackle and miserable houses, scrapyards, abandoned sites.

Global spaces (Marc Augé's "non-places") are scarce, and sites that show the peripheral character of this culture abound. According to Augé, "As antrophological places create the organically social, so non-places create solitary contractuality" (1995, 94). Whereas antropological places refer to region and tradition, non-places (airports, shopping malls, highways) are saturated with a hypermodernity. Nomadic characters move through neither of these spaces but through what we could call *spaces of precariousness,* or spaces that they themselves make precarious through their trajectories. There might be social pacts, as Augé writes, but these are always under suspicion; they might seem organic, but this organicity always proves illusory. In *Pizza, birra, faso,* these spaces are taxis but also the unemployment line, an association that lasts only a day, in which any attempt to construct ties turns out to be impossible. (In fact, the characters join the line only with the goal of stealing from others.) Even a monument as important as the Obelisk of Buenos Aires (and monuments aspire to that organicity) is traversed by the characters in its interior and transformed into a dangerous and vulnerable space.

Taxis are an emblem of those transitory contracts that are on the verge of fracturing. In *Pizza, birra, faso,* the thugs el Cordobés and Pablo get into a taxi, rob the passengers, and pretend to attack the taxi driver, who is actually their accomplice. Finally, they fight with the driver and hit him (this time for real), and the pact among the delinquents is broken. Despite the precariousness of these spaces, the fact that they tie together particularity and globalization, and that modernization is in conflict, means that we can speak of *hyperplaces,* rather than places or non-places. As in a hypertext, each field remains recognizable even though it assumes different meanings according to the context.

The hyperplace par excellence is the taxi, and it is no coincidence that one of the first films about globalization (of cinema and of society) takes place entirely in taxis in different cities of the world: Jim Jarmusch's *Night on Earth* (1991), with scenes in Los Angeles, New York, Paris, Rome, and Helsinki. The taxis are similar in nearly all of these cities, but what happens within them has to do with the contingencies and particular situations of each large city: there is neither the organically social nor solitary contractuality. In recent Latin American film, the taxi has become a reduced model of violent sociability, as in Barbet Schroeder's *La virgin de los Sicarios* (Colombia, 2000, distributed internationally as *Our Lady of the Assassins*); *Taxi* (Chile); *Pizza, birra, faso; Todo juntos;* and Gabriela David's *Taxi, un encuentro* (Argentina, 2001, distributed internationally as *Taxi, an Encounter*). What in Jarmusch is dialogue and relatively peaceful encounters, in Latin American films is explosion, crime, violent expulsion. Thus, these forms of transitory sociability create sociabilities that are no longer characterized by their global materiality but by degrees of disintegration in each locality.

Characters trying to implement tactics of pure survival in a nomadism that threatens traditional forms of modern society (classification in the world of work, the drawing up of borders, the implementation of forms of identification and control) move through these spaces. In the words of Zygmunt Bauman, nomadism is the new villain facing what he calls "solid modernity": in contemporary life, he avers, "we are witnessing the revenge of nomadism over the principle of territoriality and settlement" (2000, 13). Within the nomadic tendency, Caetano and Stagnaro have gone furthest in their identification with marginal people, even appropriating their culture. In contrast, in *Bonanza* the world music of Manu Chao is something of a counterpoint to the lives that are narrated. It is as if through an apparently apolitical gaze (because the phenomenon of neoliberalism is omitted) there is an effort to search for moments of resistance to the power of consumption and to construct, with these fragments, parallel universes: a world that becomes a crane, a scrapyard like that of *Bonanza,* the place of retreat into a strange idiolect as in *Pizza, birra, faso.* With the remains of a ruthless era, the collage of a world that ephemerally shelters its characters is constructed.

In its refusal to adopt political positions or whole narratives, this paradoxical nomadism does not manage to constitute an alternative social account in the classic sense of the term. (Associations, when they do not deal with the absolute solitude of the character in *La libertad,* are transitory and unstable.) There is not the least attempt at radical distance from that same capitalism whose detritus it is based on, nor is there a claim for *critical* distance through an elaboration of forms backed up by a grand narrative. What is produced is rather a contamination by this same capitalism, an immersion in it, and a search for an intensity and for interesting situations at its margins, in its extremes or in its remnants (hence the obsession with the lumpen and with urban ruins). These movies are not in search of a finished work; they do not even try to reach *another* form—an unassimilable form, as in Tarkovski or Godard. Instead, they blend with existing forms to investigate the possibilities of these trajectories. Suffice it to compare *Bonanza* with any of Rosell's other movies (co-authored with Andrés Tambornino and Rodrigo Moreno), such as *El descanso,* or Stagnaro's stint on television with *Okupas* (2000).

Strategically, these filmmakers reject or disdain the modernist myths of self-consciousness or authorial style: form does not stride out ahead discovering things; it is reorganized and defined in the course of its realization. It is as though, by approximating television in this respect, there were a tendency to work directly on the editing table with raw materials, letting these orient the film. Form rests more in the investigation into what is found while filming than in the priority of the alternative account that the modernist mise-en-scène offers. Rather than privileging a thought based on the shot, these directors act as investigators of the outside. *Bonanza,* for example, is the result of near-ethnographic expeditions into the outskirts of the city of La Plata, and *La libertad* grew from an anthropological, economic, and spiritual interest in a woodcutter in the state of La Pampa.

In contrast to the nomadic movement toward remains and margins, the sedentary tendency presents a spiral movement toward interiors. The key is the insufficiency of the family order, and one of the disturbing characteristics of *La ciénaga* resides precisely in the lack of definition of parental links in the film's first scene. During these initial moments, the spectator functions, like the characters, as a zombie who slips between life and death without reference points to interpret his or her own situation.

As in the nomadic tendency, consumption marks the characters, but rather than being rejected it imposes its ruthless and omnipotent machine, permanently anchoring the characters in situations of disintegration. (One of the protagonists of *La ciénaga* does not stop shopping, even from the bed, and a promised shopping trip is never fulfilled.) The society organized around patriarchal authority, with all that this implies, disintegrates in these films, testifying to the shift from a masculine imagination (which dominated human life for centuries) to a feminine imagination in film. These movies might be made by women who thematize this not wanting to return home (*no querer volver a casa*, in the words of one of Albertina Carri's titles), or by men, such as Luis Ortega, Santiago Loza, or Federico León, who made films that put forth bitter critiques of patriarchy.

In Luis Ortega's *Caja negra,* Dorotea (Dolores Fonzi) begins to discover that just as her surrogate mother (her grandmother Eugenia Bassi) ties her to the simulacrum of a family, the reencounter with her father (Eduardo Couget), who gets out of jail, reveals that this family is isolating her from life. Trapped in a family marked by aging and apathy, Dorotea wastes her youth and can only execute a game of seduction with a random neighbor, with whom she is united above all by a relationship of camaraderie and favors.[4] In Santiago Loza's *Extraño* (2003), Axel (Julio Chávez) moves around constantly, yet the image of the train track that traces a line across the screen shows the illusory nature of his movement and the disintegration of his familial affections. Meanwhile, Erica (Valeria Bertuccelli) shuts herself up in her house, expecting a child, remembering her friend, and never mentioning, not even in her conversations with Axel, the child's father, who never appears. In Federico León's *Todo juntos,* the return of the protagonists to their own homes is impossible, and the phantasm of the family lies in wait for them in the impersonal places that they traverse.

As Ana Amado points out (2002), the nomadic tendency can also be observed from the perspective of the family order, although from this perspective what predominates is less an account of disintegration than the absence of families, especially of mothers—in *Pizza, birra, faso; Bonanza; La libertad; Mundo grúa*—whereas in *La ciénaga,* mothers abound and multiply. In *Bonanza* not only is there no mother, but all of the familial lifestyle is organized around typically masculine occupations, to the point that the protagonist's daughter (la Vero) is a woman with masculine behaviors and mannerisms. Flight or disintegration offer alternative answers to the same situation, but they entail diametrically opposed movements that might coexist within the same movie.

The Precarious Orders of Chance

On the edges of these two tendencies, in each of these movies and beyond all that separates them, the same threat lurks: ruins, the unthinkable, what is beyond our control. Thus, we find an investigation into the fortuitous, the accidental, and the random, which links the experience of film—of the act of filming—with a reflection on those ruins (be they spatial, as in the cinema of nomadism, or temporal, as in sedentary cinema). These are narrations in which the accident causes the story to move, as in Tambornino, Rosell, and Moreno's *El descanso,* Juan Villegas' *Sábado, Mundo grúa,* and *La ciénaga,* among others.

El descanso opens with a car embedded in a billboard on the side of the road; *Sábado* can be divided up according to its two automobile accidents in different corners of the city; and *La ciénaga* begins and ends with accidents: the first is a fall, the second a death. Finally, *Mundo grúa,* in a very original way, constructs the tension of the story through a work-related accident that is constantly promised but never happens. There is realism, but above all there is an excess of the indexical effects of a real that appears not as a previously organized order but as an amorphous mass from which the unexpected can spring. These indexes shape an excess of the fortuitous real that overwhelms bodies and makes them explode from within and from without. Cuts, wounds, anomalies: a charge of intensity that the human body cannot endure.[5] From the wounded bodies of *La ciénaga* to the anomalous body of Eduardo Couget in *Caja negra,* from the violent bleeding to death of one of the characters in *Pizza, birra, faso* to the obesity that excludes el Rulo from the world of work in *Mundo grúa.* We could, of course, consider the possibility of a coincidence, but when has Argentine cinema seen such a proliferation of ruins and bodies out of step? Could it be that the changes wrought in the 1990s have been so profound, abrupt, and unexpected that the accident has become one of the possible figures through which to contemplate and narrate the present again? Or is it that film distances itself from the consolation offered up by narratives in which the characters are essential to the course of events and tends instead toward a weak symbolization of the accident?

Ruins constitute the complementary face of the accident: if the latter is the remnant of modern time that persists, ruins are what remains of its space. In the new Argentine cinema, ruins or ramshackle and precarious houses, in the literal sense, are to be found in a great number of movies. From *El descanso,* where a vacation complex is constructed in an abandoned hotel; to Mariano Llinás' *Balnearios,* which tells the story of a flooded town; through *Pizza, birra, faso, Caja negra, Bonanza, La libertad, Los muertos,* and so many others.[6]

At the beginning of *Otra vuelta* ("Another Turn") by Santiago Palavecino, perhaps the director of the new generation who sustains the most modernist poetics—in his shots the presence of Antonioni can be felt; in his score there is an evident evocation of Godard—there is a long shot in which the protagonist, in a white overcoat, appears to move with difficulty through a space in ruins. This space is one of the service stations that had been a launching point for the modernization of the region. It constitutes an emblem of the town to which the protagonist returns, where the privatized factories of the YPF oil company are now huge mute structures.[7] The ruins are shot at an angle; rather than elements of an allegory, they constitute the realm in which a story of loss and missed encounters is developed. These are not the ruins of a prestigious antiquity or of the now far-removed nineteenth century; they are—like the service stations—ruins of modernity. How can we construct an experience if modernity has swept away traditions but can no longer sustain itself as permanent renovation and provider of meaning? How can we create experiences from variability, precariousness, and accidents?

Through ruins and the accident, these stories open themselves up to the present and to the recognition that there is no longer a prior narration that would indicate which paths to follow. Ruins and the accidents are there before the story begins, and this renders all subsequent connections weak. With this precariousness, each movie begins to elaborate a possible way out, a glimpse of experience, always in danger. Palavecino turns to a modernist form and transforms these ruins into citations of Antonioni's *The Red Desert;* Lisandro Alonso pursues an asceticism that brings him to a state of nature as prior to modernity as it is to tradition. Martel tries to reflect on an evanescent category like the accident using another category that is no less evanescent (that of desire); Trapero defers the accident because, by locating it in the future, he shows that narration without modern work is impossible. Finally, Rejtman appears to have gone even further, inserting the randomness of the series into chronometrically constructed narrations where everything is determined beforehand. Observed from the ruins of modernity, some movies of the new Argentine cinema set out to achieve the impossible: to construct order by incorporating chance.

Chance, Bodies, Tragedy

In the denouement of *La ciénaga,* one of the children, Luciano, falls off of a ladder and instantly dies. This scene is one of the few in the movie that resort to a somewhat artificial rhetoric, if we compare it with the fresh and unique shots of the rest of the movie. Perhaps this mannerism, with its film school tricks, that takes hold of the movie constitutes an effort to recover composure after the narrative has been shattered, thereby resolving abruptly, in a single stroke, the diversity of the stories that had been at stake. In the beginning, everything in *La ciénaga* seems to revolve around the relationships between Mecha (Graciela Borges) and Tali (Mercedes Morán) and between Momi (Sofía Bertolotto), one of Mecha's daughters, and the maid Isabel (Andrea López). Later, the story focuses on José (Juan Cruz Bordeu), Momi's brother, to culminate finally in Luciano (Sebastián Montagna), Momi's son, who dies by falling off the ladder. The narration *chooses* one of the most "innocent" characters of the story and incarnates the wickedness of chance in his seven-year-old body.

Undoubtedly, Luciano's death is anticipated in many ways (he has an accident at the same time as Mecha's that is elided, he tries not to breathe, he is told "You're dead" in a game, he gets locked in a car), but none of these explains or justifies a death that makes all interpretation seem foolish or arbitrary in light of the absurd vacuum generated. In reality, neither innocence nor punishment matter, insofar as chance—in contrast to what happens in classic narration—is not motivated but enters into the story to shatter it, with all of its despair, power, and lack of justification. The rhetoric (the shots of the empty rooms that come after Luciano's fall) rises up to reorder something that has been presented as too threatening, that not only devastates the characters but also puts the very form of the movie at risk: as if the analytic gaze that the film sustains is trying to hold itself upright despite knowing that it has been dealt a harsh blow. There is a zone of the narration that is outside of all control; there is a dark and undefined force that throws the characters permanently into wells. For this reason, bodies cannot stand up straight or rise up, and the two most important ascents that are produced (the boy climbing up the ladder and the Virgin revealing herself in a stain in a water tank) must yield in the face of this tectonic force that causes them to be dragged down, to fall, to lie down, or, simply, to be unable to get up.

One of the difficulties critics faced with this film was that they were unable to attribute any affiliation to it. Some chose to repeat the words of the filmmaker; others turned to what was closer at hand: the films of Leopoldo Torre Nilsson.[8] Although there is a similarity in the tight, claustrophobic situations that reproduce social conflicts (in addition, of course, to the presence of Graciela Borges), a fundamental difference lies in the fact that desire and the fall in the films of Torre Nilsson are consequences of a psychological crisis in the characters and of a dramatic crescendo in the story. In contrast, in *La ciénaga,* desire never manages to be sufficiently powerful to yank the characters out of their extreme apathy, and the fall happens not because of the violence of transgression but because of disintegration or degradation. Suffice it to compare, in light of their astonishing thematic overlap, the scene of the boy's death on the ladder in *El secuestrador* (1958, "The Kidnapper") with the equivalent scene in Martel's movie: whereas the former constitutes the explosion of class antagonism, the latter is the work of chance. Luciano does not want to see *something else,* as in the case of Nilsson's adolescents, but is moved by his curiosity about a dog's barking. The characters of *La ciénaga* have no consolation because their drama is beyond desire. (For this reason, the figure of the boy and his whim closes the story.)

Of course, beyond its affinities with the work of Torre Nilsson, *La ciénaga* can clearly be classified in terms of a style: naturalism, as

Deleuze describes it in his *Cinema*. In naturalism, the *originary world* (recognizable by its amorphous character—in this case, the swamp) reemerges in all of the characters with its bubbling up of elemental drives. This originary world, in Deleuze's words, is "the set which unites everything, not in an organisation, but making all the parts converge in an immense rubbish-dump or swamp, and all the impulses in a great death-impulse" (1986a, 124). He adds, "There's an identical parasitic impulse everywhere" (130).[9] The singularity of naturalism is that it makes this drive cut through all spaces: in Martel's movie, the amorphousness of the swamp seeps into the civilized circles of the pool and Mecha's bed, creating an aquatic realm, constantly rendered opaque, through which the characters attempt to move. This opacity also affects glass, mirrors, clouds, the water tank and its stain, the river, the shower, and the very air, converting it into a greasy and viscous layer. In an oppressive climate, the characters move like zombies, without ever being able to interpret their own situations (a tension between the analytical obsession of the camera and the para-sitism of the characters), and what always remains truncated is their desire in a world stripped of consolation and sexual satisfaction.

Already in the first scene it is indifference and nothing else that unites the characters on the terrace: they are aimlessly adrift, dragged around by their chairs. They are never able to recognize the space in which they live as a world subject to interpretation and to change. They are, so to speak, floating. Like the believers who move en masse in front of the television cameras and the water tank, their great difficulty consists in the fact that they cannot separate their desire from what they say and from the opacity that surrounds them. Momi sees the maid as a sister–girlfriend; Tali, the fatalist, thinks that things can't be any other way; Mecha believes that the world ends in her television and telephone and at the edge of her bed. In Momi, the first character who literally sinks into the pool/swamp, desire must flow toward her own family in a series of impossible relationships, like that of José with his sister Verónica (Leonora Balcarce), or is concentrated in the figure of the maid, transgressing all social rules. Luciano, the only character who tries to see what he can only hear, falls with a crash to his death. That would appear to be the law of the swamp: whoever desires to leave it sinks more deeply into it, squelching around in the most pathetic way. (And some, like the father, interpreted by Martín Adjemián, lack the strength even for that.)

However, there are some shifts that establish a moment of abandonment, even if they do not mark a way out of the zombie state.

This movement is nearly imperceptible, and for that reason critics maintained that the movie had a circular structure or form (as it begins and ends in the pool). This is not the case: the story takes place in a spiral, and toward the end a small leap or movement occurs that can in no way be interpreted as a return to the first scene. Whereas at the beginning of the film the characters behave like zombies, toward the end one of Mecha's daughters, Verónica, is able to separate the world of desire from the visual world: "I didn't see anything," she says of her pilgrimage to see the Virgin in the water tank. In the scenes of collective psychosis previously shown on television, the characters saw what they wanted to see. This statement by one of the daughters is, in contrast, the strongest trace of what remains of the death of Luciano: a certain rationality appears in the words of someone who can question the existence of God or faith after the inexplicable death of the boy. This is a small negative illumination that announces that certain beliefs will need to be reconstructed, starting from scratch, from the remnants of what remains.

Ways Out

Scenes of dancing or parties allow the new directors to show not only a state of bodies, tastes, and uses of free time but also the conflicts among various social sectors and classes. Such key scenes have marked, as scenes of religious confession did in the 1980s (*Camila, La historia oficial,* Oscar Barney Finn's *Contar hasta diez* [1985, "Count to Ten"]), a great number of Argentine films of the 1990s, from Marcelo Piñeyro's *Cenizas del paraíso* (1997) to *La ciénaga* and *Pizza, birra, faso;* from Lucho Bender's *Felicidades* (2000, released in the United States as *Felicidades* and internationally as *Merry Christmas*) to Daniel Burman's *Esperando al mesías* (2000, released internationally as *Waiting for the Messiah*) and Rejtman's *Los guantes mágicos.*

In *Pizza, birra, faso,* the party scene is only the promise of an entertainment that is never fulfilled. The protagonists try to enter a club but are unable to so. In the final scene, they choose to rob the ticket booth. In this sequence, the camera remains distanced and cold, as though lying in wait, with designs on entering a world prohibited to it. Violence separates the groups and reveals a spirit of solidarity among the robbers that speaks to a possible community of values, synthesized in the film's title. In its role as witness, the camera eye attends this party with classical shots, those of an action film, but it takes the side of the robbers and identifies with them. Caetano and Stagnaro take pleasure in showing this subculture, following it, highlighting its features, and celebrating its vitality at the margins of the law. The only thing that can end these stories from the outside is the law, represented by the police, a nomadic cell of sedentary power. (This final irruption occurs not only in *Pizza, birra, faso* but also in *Bolivia*.)

In *La ciénaga* the party scene is threatened by the confrontation between the Kolla Indians and the provincial bourgeoisie. And the reason for the fight is Isabel, the maid who works in Mecha's home. With a nervous, restless, and disoriented camera that mingles with the carnival's frenzy, Martel follows the participants into the final confrontation, in which José, who had wanted to impose the dominion of the home on the maid in a public space, is wounded by el Perro ("the Dog," played by Fabio Villafañe). The scene's shots are the opposite of those in *Pizza, birra, faso,* and with paradoxical effects: whereas Caetano and Stagnaro opt to use distance to identify with the protagonists, Martel's camera, immersed in the situation, does not let up its analytic gaze on the *machismo* and patriarchy of the small town. This position allows Martel to maintain a certain negativity, a certain critical gaze, full of suspicion, and in tension with the nervous filming, almost trancelike, which mixes with the social groups that clash over the maid. The party is not, as it is habitually read, the space of subversion but a reaffirmation of the greatest social regressions: women as the object of desire and aggression, the paternalistic *machista* gaze as the reason for encounter and quarreling, violence as a way to resolve conflicts, automatist dancing as a supposedly genuine expression.

In Martel's movie, the oppressed are simultaneously objects of desire and of repulsion. According to the mythology forged by the masters, the poor eat cheap fish from the river, are incapable of answering the telephone, have sex with dogs, and are ignorant of civilized ways—in short, everything, sublimated, that is reproduced within Mecha's family. The landowners uphold the myth that their servants rob them, but it is Momi who ends up keeping something of the maid's. The alliance (or love) between these two groups, which their attendance at the same party seemed to promise, and which was the sign of Argentine culture in the 1990s, is as impossible as it is fictitious. Martel distances herself with conviction, as she had already done in her short film *Rey muerto* (1995, "Dead King"), from condescending or complicit representations of the popular. However, something of the affection for the popular characters that Caetano and Stagnaro have been criticized for can be found in Martel's film: it is as though these characters could offer up to us the secret of a way out of parasitism.

Other than Verónica's almost imperceptible movement, the only other shift is found in Isabel, who avoids repetition: the maid is the only person who abandons the fateful circle of the swamp, transforming it into a spiral. In a world marked by infertility and impotence, Isabel is the only one who becomes pregnant. Her partner, who goes to the threshold of Mecha's house to look for her, is el Perro, an emblematic character who condenses all that is threatening and sinister lying in wait for the members of the family (the African dog-rat in Verónica's story, the dog that is the incidental cause of Luciano's death, the mangy dogs that move throughout the film). The world of the dominated is inaccessible and perhaps for that very reason promises a possible resistance: Isabel's fate is, in reality, beyond the story.

If the spiral of *La ciénaga* drags all of the characters into a sedentary disintegration (with the exception of Isabel), the nomadic mobility of *Pizza, birra, faso* traps all of its characters and pushes them toward a flight that ends tragically. El Cordobés is stopped by the police, Pablo dies, the others disappear. The only one who is able to cross the border is Sandra (Pamela Jordán), who, in the final scene, boards the boat that will take her to Uruguay. As the voice from a squad car radio is heard, the camera records the city from the ferry as if it wanted to attach itself to the promise of this escape to another country, of Sandra with the stolen money in her bag and a baby in her stomach. "Women," says Oliver Mongin in *Violencia y cine contemporáneo* ("Violence and Contemporary Film"), "when they do not succumb to the fascination of violence, when they do not wish to occupy violently the place of violent men, are almost always the instrument of a regeneration. And with good reason: women respond to destructive violence with the violence of birth, of procreation" (1997, 50). The family of the future, in a movie that extols the virtues of a lumpen nomadism, promises a moment of arrest, of foundation, or, at least, of happiness in a family without a father.[10] It remains unclear, however, how hopeful we can be with respect to this new order that Sandra will create.

Whether in nomadism or in fixity, in the nomadic fleeing or in the sedentary sinking, the same world is vanishing, and not even narrations appear to offer much consolation. Remaining, as a last refuge, is hope, for, as Walter Benjamin said, "It is only for the sake of those without hope that hope is given to us" (1986, 88).

Intensities of Faces and Bodies
(*Rapado* and *Todo juntos*)

Martín Rejtman's *Rapado* and Federico León's *Todo juntos* present a stylized vision of nomadism and sedentarism. This is not because they are extreme versions of one tendency or the other but because they trace in a single stroke the stylized lines of (respectively) drifting and stagnation. Rejtman's characters (such as Gabriel in *Silvia Prieto* and Alejandro in *Los guantes mágicos*) often have no home and are in perpetual motion. Never stopping, they travel by car, plane, train, motorcycle, or skateboard. As in the films of Wim Wenders, these forms of transport merge with the film, which is itself transformed into the means of transport for a gaze regulated by the dialectic between a global order of simultaneity and the search for the local. It is true that in *Rapado* we find families who sit around the dinner table, but it is equally true that these ceremonies are the testimony of something that is ending; the film's adolescents think only about planning their escape. Where to? Anywhere. As Beatriz Sarlo notes, "[T]here is much talk of nomadism and the characters in *Silvia Prieto* have something of the nomad: these young people live where they can. One goes to Los Angeles, Silvia to the beach town of Mar del Plata; there is something nomadic in all of this. The Armani jacket is a kind of nomadic horse that passes from one town to another" (quoted in Birgin and Trímboli 2003, 144). Mar del Plata, in one way or another, has functioned as a soft version of Mexico in U.S. movies, the place to which those fleeing the law escape. The characters of the new Argentine cinema who go to Mar del Plata are not fleeing the law but searching, perhaps, for a breath of fresh air or a change of scenery. *Silvia Prieto,* Diego Kaplan's *¿Sabés nadar?* (2002, "Do You Know How to Swim?"), and Ezequiel Acuña's *Nadar solo* all feature scenes in beach towns.[11] As the characters always travel to these spaces during the winter, the beach becomes something useless, where only the remnants of summer vacation are to be found, as in Alejo Moguillansky and Fermín Villanueva's *La prisionera* (2005, "The Prisoner"). This city is not a place to stay but one station more in the characters' trajectory: nomadism is the sign of the instability of affective ties with the world.

Nomadism constructs a cinema of space and of movement in which places are never sufficiently endowed with meaning and history. In sedentarism, in contrast, places are overloaded, and they trap and enclose bodies. More than trajectories or routes, what matters in films of sedentarism are physical reactions and gestures. This is why they tend more toward close shots and close-ups: the corporeal gesture constitutes the trajectory. No movie corresponds more fully to this category than *Todo juntos*. The film tells the story of the break-up of a couple who are connected to a large, absent, but nevertheless oppressive family that operates through telephone conversations. Rubén the father, Marta the mother, Nicolás the cousin, Gasloli the childhood friend: all keep watch, invisible, on the other end of the line. The camera hounds the only two characters who appear on screen, their faces a map that orients us in a shadowy world, already disintegrating—hence the importance of the prologue, in which the male protagonist (Federico León) is seen on video slaughtering a pig. Throughout the story he will appear like a zombie, someone who has lost his own gestures and cannot be bothered to find them, but in the first scene his face is seen undergoing all kinds of contortions: intrigue, ecstasy, fear, admiration, recklessness. This is the energy of a body that can do *something* without its Siamese twin, his girlfriend (Jimena Anganuzzi), with whom he had done everything and from whom he is separating. It is as if in the solitude of the open space, his body could expand and explode, whereas in the rest of the film it is contracted and static. The sedentarism of the characters, once more, is the disintegration of an order, of a world.

The Long and Tortuous Path of a Couple's Separation

The story of *Todo juntos* takes place almost entirely in bars, Internet cafés, and taxis. With the exception of the first scene, in which the video camera captures the protagonist slaughtering a pig, the rest of the film registers the comings and goings of a couple who have shared their entire life together ("they were raised together") and who now face a break-up. The situation has something of the autobiographical documentary (León was in the process of separating from his partner, none other than Jimena Anganuzzi) and of a mise-en-scène of the relationship between director and actress: "In a movie," León has declared, "the relationship between director and actress is always one of power. In fiction, he also has control over her. As much as it may be the epilogue, the man directs what is going to happen" (M.B. 1983). The film can be read as a triple exorcism: of the fictitious couple, of the real couple, and of what a director and an actress can do when everything has finished. It is an exorcism that excludes the prolegomenon of the rupture (the time for arguments has expired and the relationship is over) and limits itself to showing the ways in which a couple end a relationship that has already run its course.[12]

Despite the fact that these are the only two characters who appear onscreen (in a city that appears emptied out and deserted), several secondary "characters" are summoned through the various telephone calls that the two partners make, obsessively. Their voices are never heard, but their silent or invoked presence in the couple's dialogues is an ominous shadow projected over the entire story. Through the telephone wires, the bodies of the characters are tied to an exterior that is defined as a threatening offscreen space (*hors-champ*). The calls to parents, to friends, to the friends of cousins show the growth of the characters in two families that did everything together. The problem, then, is *exteriority*. For this reason, rather than finally break up in their own apartment, the characters act out the break-up in public places: nothing remains that is theirs alone. "These are private situations in public spaces; they are unable to take their problems home," León has affirmed (M.B. 2003). Or, better yet, they are "semipublic" places, like the telephone booth that the female protagonist uses in the first conversation, or Internet cafés, in which they can maintain the most intimate of relationships while being exposed to the gaze of others. Even the most private aspects of a person (the personal and confessional notes in a planner) are read by the male protagonist into the telephone, and the strange text that tells of the sexual initiation of the couple is "transmitted" by the television in a café.

Although his training was in theater, León works with a cinematic language that differs radically from the dramatic scene. In terms of procedures, *Todo juntos* explores offscreen space and the close-up. In contrast, continuity with the theater can be found above all in the dialogues and in the search for a rhythm comprising colloquial phrases that are nevertheless structured as in a poem: "Are you going to do something tonight?"; or, when he reads her agenda: "Algeria all day long. Swimming: make up. Dance. Episodes: a little dance with old cash, like practicing for when we have many bills like these, but new. We're going to be able to do a lot. Always keep in mind that time passes quickly; we can let it pass." If there is something that makes León's theater resemble a spell it is, precisely, the rhythm of his dialogues, which reach a lyricism through the raw material of everyday conversations. These are dialogues, then, that come from theater but acquire the potentiality of cinema through the peculiar use that León makes of offscreen space and the close-up.[13]

The common places in which the action of *Todo juntos* takes place—cafés, Internet cafés, taxis, corridors—are places of transit that are not transformed by those who occupy them. The transitoriness is accentuated by the soundtrack's lounge music, which belongs to the spaces and not to the characters; neutral, it is not summoned up by anyone. The shots (in general, medium shots) remain fixed; that is, the mise-en-scène petrifies the environments and makes them stranger through the *raccords* that modify them. Thus, one of the cafés in which the couple meets is registered by various shots that are linked to one another only with difficulty, disturbing the continuity of the space constructed by the mise-en-scène and giving the impression that such spaces are not traversable, are divorced from one another, lack an exit, and imprison or asphyxiate the characters. The offscreen space, then, continues to add elements to comprehend the space in a difficult and fragmented way. (Of the first café we see almost nothing except a few chairs and what appears to be a first floor; of the taxi we see only the backseat; of the Internet café, the illuminated telephone booth of the protagonist.) The space must be constructed through the characters and through the spatial fragments that their bodies offer up to us.

This difficulty is exacerbated by the fact that these bodies are frequently shown immobile and tied to chairs. The camera never assumes a distanced point of view (there are no long shots) and, to narrate conflicts, opts for close-ups. The depressed and tearful faces of the couple contain the signs that allow us to follow closely their states of mind. According to Deleuze, three functions are generally ascribed to the face: "it is *individuating* (it distinguishes or characterises each person); it is *socialising* (it manifest a social role); it is *relational* or *comunicating* (it ensures not only communication between two people, but also, in a single person, the internal agreement between his character and his role)" (1986a, 99, my emphasis).

The cinema of Bergman or Bresson, in particular, through the close-up, disrupts these three functions. Something similar happens in León's movie: there is no individualizing gesture, because the two heads emerge from the same body, now dead. His face is stamped on hers, and vice versa. The socializing function of the face fades entirely as well. "Come here, I don't want them to see my face like this," he tells her, as though he himself does not form part of the social gaze that points her out or condemns her. In the movie, others are erased or emptied out: the city streets do not contain the gazes of strangers, the voices on the phone never take shape in a face, and the seducer is only a murmur. No one looks at them; or, if we follow the director's intention to tell the story of a break-up "as though it had been filmed by them," it is the couple who erase the others and their gaze. Finally, the relational face is abolished, because the only two faces that we see have nothing left to communicate to one another; or, better, there is no communication with the other in *Todo juntos* because the "other" is already constituted by the couple's history. They have said everything to each other and shared everything; what they are unable to share is the break-up, the abandonment, the separation (to relate *a* face with *another*).

She has only reproaches for her ex, and he has only threats; in each of these acts, the other is already there and can do nothing, because everything he or she does is determined and judged beforehand. Her reproaches are based on the supposition of what she already knows, as there is nothing about him that she does not already know: "You don't even want to talk," she tells him. If there is no communication in the reproach, it is because the other cannot wish for anything that is not already determined beforehand: *I know you very well, I know that you don't want to talk, even though you might pretend that you want to talk; in reality you do it to satisfy me, but I'm not satisfied because I know that you're pretending, even though you might deny that you're faking,* etc. In his case, in contrast, the threat prevails: "If I go out to buy cigarettes, maybe I won't come back." Yet he does come back, for what ties him to her is the threat itself, rather than its realization; in this way, the relationship—as in Kafka's parable "Before the Law"—is prolonged indefinitely. He doesn't want so much to leave her (even though the relationship is over) as to show her that he is leaving her. She offers only reproaches, and everything that he does will inevitably spawn new ones. The reproach and the threat prolong indefinitely their separation.

In reality both the reproach and the threat are the effect of a deeper reality: there is no *other* to look at. Separation has as its goal the creation of an other, but how is this possible when the other is the same? The paradox of this entire situation is made clear in one of his statements: "The fact that I think you're foolish doesn't mean that you're foolish." Nothing, however, is more spurious that this reasoning: as both are in reality only one, the fact that he considers her foolish *makes* her foolish. The two faces are the sides of the same thought and the same spirit runs through them. Jimena Anganuzzi's character says it explicitly: "I need you to think...being alone and thinking is really difficult and I make an effort." In the reproach and the threat the characters exchange a single and obsessive communication: look at how you've left me, *I no longer have a face.* As Deleuze says with regard to Ingmar Bergman: "Bergman has pushed the nihilism of the face the furthest, that is its relationship in fear to the void or the absence, the fear of the face confronted with its nothingness" (1986a, 100). Paradoxically, the reproach and the threat end up being directed at that which unites them, prolonging the relationship indefinitely rather than leading to the longed-for separation. For, to separate, they would need a *third,* someone to recognize the individuality of that face, to communicate with it, allowing it to circulate once again in the social world, returning the gaze of someone, anyone at all.

This desired third is also a threatening offscreen space, but in a different way than the family. The family converts these two people into one ("We were practically raised together. She had a key to my house. I had a key to her house. Her mother was my mother's best friend"), and its reality is the continuity of the relationship ("My mom and your mom are going to keep seeing each other," she tells him). The third that they need is someone who could divide them, moving through three to arrive at two. Throughout the story, this third appears as a promise: in the mise-en-scène in the café, the sign in the window reading "Desserts" (*postres*) is transformed by framing into "three" (*tres*). When he reads to her from her planner over the telephone: "They should be three: my exclusivity, your variety. Already three was spoken of, without me. I never became friends with Romina because of the intimacy between the two of them, beyond what happened or what might happen." But each equally needs to be with the other to reach three and separate. What these two characters need to end their relationship once and for all is a third from the most absolute outside and not, of course, from the family. In the end, they seem to find him in a taxi driver.[14]

The taxi driver without a face (who appears exclusively in the offscreen space) *gives* her a face, and then gives him one. When her boyfriend gets out of the car, threatening never to return, the taxi driver (an expert in the art of love) assures her that he will come back and, in the meantime, offers her a candy bar. They begin to talk about family issues and, when the boyfriend returns, the taxi driver asks her, in a smooth and velvety voice, to take off her black sunglasses: "Take them off. Why not? I want to see your whole face. Ahhh, *now I can see your whole face.* Why don't you come up front here with me, come here a little while. Will you let her come up here?" This is followed by two prolonged fixed shots: the first is of the boyfriend, downcast, with a small fragment of the front seat that moves and the panting of the taxi driver and his ex-girlfriend as they make love. The

second—after the change in positions—is her face, while the movements of the car and the panting of the taxi driver and her ex-boyfriend
can be felt. The separation seems to have finally occurred: her face is
seen for the first time by another and it inspires neither pity nor com-
passion but desire. The gaze of the other splits these bodies; she can
move into the front seat and contort with pleasure. We do not see
these faces shot through with pleasure, because they no longer have
to do with the relationship between the couple but with its ending.
We must now imagine how, through the gestures of new love, they
are transformed into *others*. The pleasure of each of them is inaccessible and the "all together" of the title breaks up. Or is it that instead
of taking advantage of this third to say goodbye to one another, they
manage to include him in a new unit in which the two of them become
masochistic spectators of new exchanges?

Despite what has been frequently repeated (even by the director),
this scene is far from constituting a rape. The taxi driver does not
invade the couple's space, forcing them to do something against their
will (it is they who pass to the front seat), nor are there traces of violence
or physical aggression (the taxi driver behaves like a gentleman and is
even concerned about the physical safety of his passengers). The sex
does not manage to be pornographic, although it is certainly obscene.
It is literally "offscreen" ("outside of the scene"). The final liberation
is paradoxical: they continue to be "all together," but in this case
there is something they are not going to be able to share (pleasure).
They have found that third, and as a consequence the relationship is
about to end. The film's ending, however, is full of ambiguity. It is
morning, and the two protagonists are seated at a table outside, in
what appears to be a gated community in the countryside. He gets
out of the shower; she talks on the telephone (the link with the others
is reestablished) and sits next to her partner, telling him: "They're
going to come and get us." This sudden first-person-plural pronoun
restores the "all together" that has repeatedly threatened to disintegrate throughout the film. The end of the movie, yes, but is it the end
of the relationship?[15]

Shifts in Experience

Within the nomadic tendency, there are varying and at times
opposing options. Trapero's *Mundo grúa,* for example, endows the
protagonist's neighborhood with affect, transforming it into a *place*.
(The nomadism consists in the fact that he must leave it to find work).

In contrast, in Rejtman, places appear emptied out, whether they are *non-places* (airports) or those sites frequented by the characters (the video arcade in *Rapado,* the Chinese restaurants in *Silvia Prieto,* all of the temporary residences of the characters in *Los guantes mágicos*). Already in his first film Rejtman had sketched out the lines of his world with incredible vividness. Perhaps only Lucrecia Martel and Lisandro Alonso have been as categorical in their aesthetic ambitions. Yet to an even greater extent than in the films of these other directors, Rejtman's three feature-length works establish a code so distinctive that the spectator begins to feel at ease only several minutes into the film. And one of the features of this world is that the characters are permanently moving around. What is more, their obsessions tend to have to do with making their bodies into faster, more mechanical, and more impassive machines of movement. The long traveling shots that open *Rapado,* following the motorcycle of Lucio (Ezequiel Cavia), are transformed into a traveling shot from the motorcycle itself, as though body, machine, and camera have become a single entity. This is why the nomadism of Rejtman's films goes beyond his characters. It is things themselves that constantly circulate, move, generate a story and a meaning: counterfeit bills, a watch, sneakers, a vacuum cleaner, video game chips, as well as airplanes, motorcycles, and the skateboarders who cross the street at the film's end. Rejtman's cinema is a map on which people and things ceaselessly trace itineraries.

In contrast to his two later films, in which circulation precedes the characters, *Rapado* is, so to speak, the most romantic film of his filmography—not because there are references to romantic literature (there is nothing further removed from Rejtman that romanticism), nor because it tells a love story, although the two protagonists end up forging a relationship with others: Damián with a girl he meets in the street (Cecilia Biagini) and Lucio with Gustavo (Gonzalo Córdoba), the guitarist of the band Estrella roja ("Red Star").[16] By "romanticism" I mean that *Rapado* is the only one of Rejtman's movies that narrates a moment in which a character *voluntarily* abandons the sedentary to enter into a nomadic mobility. Like the stories that form part of Rejtman's book of the same title, *Rapado* is centered on adolescent characters who have not yet entered university or the workforce (their time is neither scheduled nor commercialized) and who have just finished, or abandoned, high school. They are at an undefined moment, filled with fears and promises. As the song by Estrella roja goes: "It was a bad year/I can't remember a worse one/I was in the street/without a job and without love/no one said anything good, anything bad/anything about me."

In this need to abandon the world of the family, the motorcycle becomes a talisman that allows for escape and the intensity of velocity. The story begins when Lucio is robbed of his motorcycle, money, and sneakers, and continues with a search for a motorcycle to replace the stolen one. With his friend Damián (Damián Dreizik), Lucio fantasizes about building a motorcycle, and after several failed attempts, he manages to steal a scooter that he hides in his house and on which he escapes the city. When it breaks down, he has to abandon it and return. The story ends with Damián meeting a girl in the street and with Lucio going to sleep—and sharing a bed—at the house of Gustavo, the guitarist whose band he had by chance heard on a cassette found in the stolen scooter. In the final scene, Lucio leaves the guitarist's house and heads toward the bus stop. Gustavo's brother passes by with a group of skateboarders, and Lucio greets him as he realizes that once again he has forgotten his watch in his friend's house.

The characters in *Rapado* are almost twenty years old, in *Silvia Prieto* they are a little under thirty, and in *Los guantes mágicos* they are, as one of them states, "closer to forty." Each movie functions as a description of worlds at a certain age. In *Silvia Prieto* the nomadic mobility is found in taxis, in *Los guantes mágicos* it is in the cars for hire, and in *Rapado* it is on the motorcycle, a sign of adventure, adolescence, and isolation.[17] The characters have no parents in either *Silvia Prieto* or *Los guantes mágicos,* and their families are coming apart or have only recently formed. In *Rapado,* in contrast, we witness various familial scenes, lunches or breakfasts in which the characters have nothing to say. "Did you know that in the Northern Hemisphere the drains flow in the opposite direction?" Lucio's mother says at the lunch that follows her arrival from Canada. She receives no response. During dinner, Lucio's family reacts with mechanical movements and exchanges insubstantial words. Toward the end of the film, over breakfast Gustavo undermines the authority of his mother when she offers coffee to Lucio. Families are not quite "dysfunctional," but their capacity to give meaning to the world of these adolescents is exhausted.[18]

The vacillation of the characters in *Rapado* lies in the fact that they do not want to forge a new order but only aspire to the intensity of escape. Lucio's final melancholy emerges from the fact that he is unable to restore the velocity of which he was a protagonist in the first sequence. Perhaps he restores it with the simple act of cutting his hair, which offers him the sensation of individuality or liberty or, unconsciously, with the second forgetting of his watch at the end of a story. (In Rejtman, each event is part of a series.) Might this forgetting be an oblique way of experiencing the weight of the chance but intense encounter that he has just had with the guitarist? We do not know for sure whether it was romantic or simply the beginning of a beautiful friendship: as in *Silvia Prieto* and in *Los guantes mágicos,* sexual contact appears to be elided. And here, unlike the scratched-up back of Gabriel in *Silvia Prieto,* there are no marks that something has definitely happened. However, the doubling and play with situations that make the story move leads us to suppose that Lucio found a new intensity that substitutes, in a different world, his urban trajectories with his motorcycle. At any rate, this encounter is furtive, isolated, and transitory. Lucio remains adrift and perhaps will meet Gustavo again only to ask him to return his watch.

With the gaze of an entomologist, Rejtman shows, in *Rapado,* the functioning of a cold world, one in which everything is transitory and in movement. Yet he also shows how, in those transitory situations and in those movements of flight, one can find, even if only for an instant, the gleam of an experience.

The Return of the Documentary

Art is covered by a sick veil.

—Sabzian, in Abbas Kiarostami's *Close Up* (1990)

In 1953, the young people who would go on to form the Nouevelle Vague attended a screening of Roberto Rossellini's *Viaggio in Italia* and would discover that it was possible to make films with very little. "Just a car, a couple, and a camera," commented a very young Goddard (1989). The great Rossellini had taught them something once again, in deepening, as Bazin understood with great lucidity, the neorealist tendency of his first films. Neorealism is not merely a question of themes (the dregs of society in the streets) but a series of procedures (the sequence shot, the elliptical and erratic narration, the stripped-down mise-en-scène, the use of natural sets, the depth of field, and a furious drive to take hold of the real). Both Rossellini's reception in France and the defense spearheaded by Bazin and his protégés are fundamental to our understanding of what realism means for cinema, and, above all, to clearing up the confusions that stem from the translation of the coordinates of literary realism into cinematographic language.

Italian neorealism emerged from the ruins of postwar Europe, and this origin marked it indefinitely. This was not a realism that based itself in conventions and a relatively established social imaginary (as was the case in literature and the visual arts) but one that emerged when all beliefs had entered into crisis, when all certainties had been devastated, like the major cities of Europe. The sensation of fluidity, transparency, neutrality and the naturalized connection between events had been the cause of literary realism's splendor as well as the reason for which its detractors set out to demolish it, demonstrating its artifice, its surplus value of codification, its class ideology—first the bourgeois, then, with social realism, the proletariat—that did not distinguish between the real and its representations. In contrast, cinematic neorealism opposed a series of movies that were too similar to theater or distanced themselves from everyday life; it also showed the disconnected and erratic character of the event, its resistance to being inscribed in preconceived schemes. It was a *register* of surfaces (streets, gestures, bodies, displacements) at a moment when the ruins of postwar Europe would not permit any conventional or consolatory realism.

To achieve this effect, the Italian neorealists (the early Visconti, De Sica, Rossellini) grounded themselves in the technological power of cinema, which provides us with images that capture, all of a sudden, the infinite details of the real. (Compare, for example, a shot of an automobile or a human expression with a literary or pictorial description of the same.) For filmic images are not iconic or symbolic but indexical. In Peirce's terms (1885), they are signs that "respond to a direct physical connection," that are point-by-point equivalent to nature.[19] That is, they are traces that physical reality leaves on the plate or film and that, beyond film's formal aspects (framing, the selection of the object, temporal fading together, etc.), maintain a remnant that can be summarized in the formula "It was like this."

The virtue of the defense of realism mounted during the 1950s by, among others, Bazin and Sigfried Kracauer (whom only a clueless person could accuse of naïveté) was that it shifted the debate over the cinematographic image from the iconic order to the indexical. Kracauer did so when he spoke of film's affinity with physical reality, and Bazin, when he upheld the primacy of perception over the signified and the dynamic and innovative character of what he called the neorealist *image-fait.*[20] "A fragment of reality anterior to sense" (2000, 282): this is how Bazin defined the *image-fait,* thus opposing the old iconophobic French tradition that would reemerge in the late 1960s, in *Cahiers du cinema,* the journal that he had founded. With a conception of culture as a system of signs, the iconophobes argued that there was a necessary link between the predominance of the bourgeoisie and realist representation. ("We are devoted," Philippe Sollers wrote, "to deconstructing the mechanisms of bourgeois literature in a critical way, elaborating the formal organisms that are not recoverable through the bourgeois ideology of classical representation.") Many years later, this belief was revealed as false, from the moment the proliferation of simulacra and computer-generated images displaced what Sollers called "classic representation," without producing upheavals in the modes of domination. Once the cycle of the modernist criticism of representation was closed, cinema's drive for the real, its capacity to register surfaces and to document what exists, returns.

But this *image-fait* did not come alone. The neorealists used it as a testimonial core, fostered by its symbiotic relationship with fiction, in a dialectic that returns from time to time in film (the French New Wave, British free cinema, Brazilian New Cinema, and even the upsurge of documentary). In recent years this dialectic between the *image-fait* and fiction has appeared with such force that one of the most successful films, Roberto Benigni's *Life Is Beautiful,* had to include neorealist leitmotifs—the bicycle and horse from Vittorio De Sica's first two films, the boy who is an impotent and overwhelmed witness—with the goal of attenuating and neutralizing them. The boy does not die because of what he says, as in Rossellini's *Germany Year Zero* (1948); instead, he confuses the concentration camp with a fairy tale.

In comparison, this return is shown in all its splendor in Abbas Kiarostami's *Close Up,* which gave another turn of the screw in the relationships between documentary and fiction by presenting the testimony not of a deed but of a desire. It does not matter that Sabzian lies; much more decisive is that he finds in the reality of images a path via which desire encounters its truth. In the face of the elements and ruins, each new realist film promises the convergence between trace (the remnant of the real that remains on the surface) and desire (those configurations that are formed with each index collected) to give shape to a belief.

The Poetics of Indeterminacy: Renouncement and Liberty in a Lisandro Alonso Movie

To me he's a sage. Someone who isn't interested in society, who creates his own world. People talk about Whitman, Rousseau, Nietzsche, and other names I've never heard of.

—Lisandro Alonso, speaking of Misael, the protagonist
of his film *La libertad*

The necessity of registering and using the indexical character of the filmic image has returned with vigor in many recent Argentine films. *Mundo grúa, Bonanza,* and *Bolivia,* to name only three, are based as much on scenarios that are already set up, so to speak, as in the mutual fostering among fiction, documentary, and improvisation. One film, however, goes further than any other in this drive to record, to the extent that the idea of narration in its classical sense vanishes: Lisandro Alonso's *La libertad.* "I don't want to tell a story," Alonso has stated. "I'm only interested in observing."

The story that unfolds in the film is very simple: in the first scene, a young man seated by a bonfire devours an armadillo. It is night; lightning can be seen in the distance. This man is Misael Saavedra, a woodcutter who lives in the countryside, in the province of La Pampa, far from the city and his family. Throughout an hour and fifteen minutes, the only thing that Alonso does is follow the life of this woodcutter: Misael cutting firewood, Misael defecating, Misael washing his hands, Misael carting his wood to sell, Misael buying things at a store. *La libertad* ends with the same scene that it begins with: Misael eating the armadillo with the lightning behind him. Misael Saavedra is a real person, and the movie simply shows us some of the scenes of his life as a woodcutter.

There are no anecdotes or dialogues in the movie, except when Misael sells wood, talks on the telephone, or buys sodas and cigarettes. Otherwise, he is alone and has no contact with other people. Given its lyrical power and the scarcity of information it provides, *La libertad* is far from a documentary. It is a question not of showing how a woodcutter lives in the Argentine countryside but of uncovering the mystery of so much wisdom. The succinct script recalls Cesare Zavattini's idea that for an hour and a half, one should film a worker who leaves her house, goes shopping, peers into shop windows, and returns home. Yet whereas Zavattini wanted to investigate social ties, Alonso's *La libertad* is the story of someone who has decided to isolate himself from the world. The woodcutter has chosen an ascetic life, withdrawn and solitary, with no religious, political, or utilitarian justification. Misael is the nomad who flees the city to find his home in nature and his livelihood in trees.

The anomaly of a movie that observes something as apparently simple as a day in the life of a worker is underscored by its title. As with certain artistic works of the twentieth century (seminally, Marcel Duchamp's ready-mades), the title radicalizes the indeterminacy of the object. Duchamp chose a urinal and gave it the title *Fountain*. With the same logic but in an entirely different universe, Alonso registers the activity of an isolated woodcutter and titles the result *La libertad*. This poetics of indeterminacy had a powerful effect on spectators and explains why Whitman, Rousseau, and Nietzsche have been invoked in relation to the film. But what does the praise of Misael have to do with Whitman's multitudes, Rousseau's general will, or the German philosopher's obsession with the will to power? I prefer the definition given by the filmmaker himself: "It's a mirror, but empty." This indeterminacy allows each of us to project, on that trace, his or her own idea of liberty and to respond to Alonso's provocation.

But liberty is not only part of the character; we cannot fail to recognize it also in a new director, under the age of thirty, who takes it upon himself to execute, without concessions, a work that is singular, unsociable, luminous. Both liberties meet without changing places or entering into contact with one another. Saavedra exploits the virtues of his renouncement, and Alonso those of the man with the camera, which consist, as Kracauer says of Proust, in being a witness, an observer, an outsider (1989, 36). We could add: a harvester of traces. The director observes the woodcutter, bears witness to his activities, tries not to meddle in his world. Each takes advantage of his knowledge of his trade: if nature offers up to the woodcutter a perpetually renewable raw material, the art of cinema offers up to Alonso the distance of the sequence shot and the indeterminacy of meanings, extracted from the perception of surfaces.

Fleeing from Pity

We can recognize the gaze that takes an interest in Misael's fate in other Argentine films of recent years: it is the attraction toward those characters who are outside of consumption, who could be deemed "popular characters,"[21] if the representation of such characters were not already marked by stereotypes and the most elemental attributions. With the exception of the films of Leonardo Favio, popular figures in earlier Argentine cinema tended to be anachronisms from the past. Poverty and *costumbrismo*,[22] or poverty and overacting, were common modes of representation until new forms of registering the real relocated this type of character to the very center of contemporaneity. El Rulo in *Mundo grúa*, the maid in *La ciénaga*, the immigrant in *Bolivia*, the trash picker in *Bonanza*, the kids in *Pizza, birra, faso*: all of these bodies form a gallery of dispossession and precariousness. Undoubtedly, Misael belongs to this lineage, but his gesture is so emphatic, his separation from society so irreversible, that he appears to be guided by a secret or plan that will never be revealed to us.

With the exception of Martín Rejtman in *Silvia Prieto* or Juan Villegas in *Sábado* (which treat the seemingly less interesting characters of the middle class), these lumpen or needy characters, in the past associated with populism, proliferate in the new Argentine cinema. Yet we cannot speak of a continuity with earlier representations of the popular, because the *sympathetic link* that saved those characters from utter misery has been irrevocably severed. These characters don't ask for our pity; they are indifferent to it: they form their own world and do not need any outside redemption. *La libertad* goes even further, because it takes an interest not in the problem of the conventionality of representation (that *costumbrista* style that, in the Argentine tradition, is the real substitute for theatrical or literary realism in film) but in the fact that complete ascesis is required to capture surfaces or indexes. Alonso is not concerned, like Rejtman, with deconstructing *costumbrismo*, nor with attacking it, like Caetano, with violence; he simply ignores it, through his indifference or lack of interest. As witness, observer, or outsider, he goes in search of an innocent gaze, of a pure experience, of an uncontaminated surface, and he finds it in nature and in the woodcutter Misael. Alonso is not concerned with the conventional narrations to which cinema has accustomed us; he is as extremist in his aesthetic as Misael is in his life.

The idea that experience belongs to those popular characters draws *La libertad* closer to movies such as *Pizza, birra, faso, Bonanza*, or *Mundo grúa*, but the fact it considers that full sovereignty can be fulfilled only in escape and in solitude places its protagonist in a very unusual place: Misael renounces the idea of being a popular character to be transformed into someone who, in the most adverse conditions, adopts an individualist way out. He has a secret, but this does not depend on his belonging to a group, collectivity, or people. Misael eludes, renounces, and is able—almost—to do without others. He discovers, in his refuge, the wisdom of necessity.

Two Territories

The indeterminacy of liberty demands at all times the making of decisions. This is why the freedom of each epoch is based on its capacity to refuse something that is imposed on it. And this "something" that structures subjects and their perceptions in contemporary life is consumption. We could consider the movies of the new Argentine cinema according to their strategies for dealing with consumption: the proliferation in series of trinkets in *Silvia Prieto,* the nostalgia for a productive world in *Mundo grúa,* the robbery and pillaging of *Pizza, birra, faso.* In *La libertad,* exteriority itself is conceived as a world of consumption where one must negotiate under ignoble conditions and where only the art of bargaining is worth anything. Thus, Misael has to go out to sell cheaply the wood he has cut so carefully. He begins by offering fifteen trunks at two pesos each and ends up selling them for one peso and eighty cents each—a total of twenty-seven pesos (approximately nine dollars), ten of which he spends almost immediately at the store. Another detail: his buyer calls the trunks "posts," stressing their utilitarian character.

This scene of the sale that the film stages is fictional and constitutes one of the modifications that the director introduces into the woodcutter's story. "The only difference," Leandro says, "is that in his daily life he doesn't sell the wood but instead works for a salary" (quoted in Quintín 2001). In the image that the film offers up to us, Misael regulates his work and his moments of rest in his territory, but to survive he most go out to sell the wood and battle with consumers in an outside that emerges as a space of plunder. With this substantial directorial change, Misael is divided in two: inside of his territory, he offers himself up freely to nature; outside of it, he needs to transform the results of his freedom into commodities. The woodcutter who has transformed his necessity into liberty must resign himself, to maintain his individualist utopia, to the mercantilization of his surroundings, subject to permanent physical and monetary mediations. Alonso imposes this limit on the life that serves as the basis for his project: either a free nature or the commodity's threat.

This is why Misael Saavedra and Lisandro Alonso's praise of nature has no hint of romanticism: it is a calculated way out of the sinister and threatening realism of the commodity. Whereas the commodity in *La libertad* is something sublime, incommensurable, that which still has no concept, nature is a refuge and a dwelling, a secure and inhabitable place. It is the withdrawing into a circular time that offers not so much positivity as the possibility of avoiding a world in which everything is quantifiable. Within this small piece of sovereignty, Misael finds the moment that eludes contingency and exchange, when trees are wood and trunk, and not posts.

Ascetics of the World, Unite

> Not renouncement but detachment.
>
> —Giacinto Scelsi, *Nuova Consonanza—le parole gelate,*
> Rome, November 1985

The question that filmic realism poses is subsequent to that of literary realism and, to a certain extent, presupposes it: How can the world be reenchanted? Literary realism was able to emerge as a style because the world had become disenchanted. Religious, magical, or superstitious interpretations were no longer able to explain connections among events: a quantifiable universe in which each object found its cause. In contrast, filmic realism owes its existence to the fact that it emerged from the ruins of the war. In that moment when nothing seemed to be able to sustain itself, cinema took advantage of its traces to draw lines, sketch affections, and establish trajectories: to shore up a *belief*.

Anchored in the real (the fragment of Misael's biography), Alonso's movie adds that *plus* that makes it a treatise on a possible and desirable life. ("To me, he's a sage," Alonso has declared of his protagonist.) The film lacks pedagogy: the indeterminacy lies, to a great extent, in the fact that we never know the precise reasons for the director's approaching Misael. Only the film's title indicates that it is about liberty. But what kind of liberty? Do we find ourselves facing a negative liberty, as in the absence of constrictions or obstacles? Or does the movie offer us a positive liberty, in which the self-determination of the subject coincides with something broader? A positive liberty assumes a greater social organization that would offer opportunities for this will to be manifested (Bobbio 1993). However, *wisdom,* for the director as well as for the protagonist, is more a subsistence economy than a production of knowledge and rules for life. Rather than establish a collective agreement on ends and means, it consists in fleeing from all contact, to such an extent that the very encounter between filmmaker and protagonist is marked by discretion and the absence of interferences.[23]

Misael's liberty is, in reality, a negative one, of withdrawing, of solitude. His greatest wisdom consists in having transformed necessity into liberty, even if to do so he must renounce human society. This is a renouncement that can, of course, never be entirely fulfilled: Misael has to haggle to sell his wood; he must call his family so that they do not worry; he needs to go to the store to get a soda. He does all of this to return to his territory, where no one enters and in which he can do what he needs without anyone watching. I think I understand the difficult terrain that Alonso ventures into: that of the celebration of asceticism and retreat, of separation and renunciation, of individualism and whims. He shows an attraction for those marginal characters who can set aside worldly worries and who see social relations as a restriction or impediment. This attitude has more of a philosophical or religious genealogy than a political one, and it marks the type of interests that orient the director's gaze. In a pessimistic reading—and the indeterminacy of the film also accepts this interpretation—liberty is withdrawn from the realm to which it genuinely belongs: that of human society. (For how long can Misael's self-imposed exile last, and how can a community of purely negative liberties be formed?) In a more comprehensive reading, Misael's is a small utopia in which happiness requires neither the taking of power nor the agreement or dissent of others: a nomadic wisdom of a man who escapes, of which we are offered a delicate model. It does not matter that this is not the liberty we would want or that as a concept it might be narrow and restricted. For seventy-five minutes, Alonso succeeds in making it beautiful, real, desirable, and livable.

Commodities and Experience

In contrast to other art forms of the period, including literature, cinema in Argentina in recent years has had such a powerful obsession with the flow of the present that a cultural critic would be able to use its films to inventory the transformations of the 1990s. The extension of globalization; the transformation of labor; alterations in elite, mass-media, and popular culture; the predominance of consumption; and the crisis of the popular (or its end) can be regarded, with their refractions and displacements, as signs of a present that emerges in filmic images. In fact, we can detect one of the most decisive transformations of those years, the invasion of commodities into all forms of daily life, in various movies of the new Argentine cinema.

As though nothing is safe from the reign of its form, the commodity seems to leave its trace in every still.[24] The titles themselves already manifest this fact: thus, *Pizza, birra, faso* defines its characters, through slang, by what they consume; *Los guantes mágicos* bestows a magical nature, typical of the commodity form, on the products that its characters hope will be their salvation (a shipment of gloves that arrives from Hong Kong, the new capital of cinema).[25] Enrique Bellande's *Ciudad de María* begins as a sketch on religious belief and ends up as an economic treatise. It explores how the industry that takes place around the Virgin generates a new order in a city that had been fueled by the steel trade. Daniel Burman's *El abrazo partido* chooses as the space for its narration one of pure commerce, a shopping center in the commercial district of the Once neighborhood, and a type of framing that leaves its characters hounded by cheap commodities that reach the very edges of the screen. Gaggero's *Vida en Falcon* begins with an old commercial for the Ford Falcon and ends with the same, to recount the life of someone who lives on practically nothing.

Consumption and the exchange of commodities also define the characters with whom, according to their criteria, we can make something like a periodic table of elements. One of the films apparently furthest removed from this problem, Martel's *La ciénaga,* presents us with one of its protagonists (the mother, played by Graciela Borges) prostrate in a bed and bewitched by one of the most widespread forms of publicity in recent years, commercials for objects sold via television. By means of an ellipsis, Martel suppresses the act of purchasing, but the terrain of the bedroom ultimately shifts to flaunt a small refrigerator, the result of this style of consumption. By introducing selling and purchasing into the bedroom, previously reserved for marital relations (particularly listless in this movie), Martel gets to the heart of one of the transformations of the nature of the commodity in daily life: its eruption into intimate spheres.[26] The sinister and unlocalizable ubiquity of the commodity, the global character inscribed in products, the satisfaction and immobilization of desire, and, finally, the capture of the consumer's body (all features that the commodity had previously possessed but that reached their culmination in recent years) are the marks read in the body of Graciela Borges' character. Prostrate in her bed, she lacks the possibility of an experience. And this could be one of the key themes of cinematographic narration in recent years: the commodity as one of the most powerful threats to the existence of experience. Few works have been as radical in staging this threat as the films of Alonso (*Los muertos,* as well as *La libertad*) and of Martín Rejtman (*Silvia Prieto* and *Los guantes mágicos*). Whereas in the former this threat assumes the form of an exteriority, in the latter the commodity is the environment in which one lives, which must be traversed to reach an experience.

Cinema of Remains:
Lisandro Alonso's *Los muertos*

In the wake of Walter Benjamin, Giorgio Agamben begins his book *Infancy and History: Essays on the Destruction of Experience* with the ostentatious affirmation that "Indeed, [man's] incapacity to have and communicate experiences is perhaps one of the few self-certainties to which he can lay claim" (1993, 13). However, when Agamben avers a few sentences later that "experience has its necessary correlation not in knowledge but in authority—that is to say, the power of words and narration" (14), he makes clear the restricted character of his definition of *experience*. The Italian philosopher refers to the link that binds tradition, memory, and collectivity, which, since the ancient Greeks, has defined the term.[27] This is what Benjamin termed *Erfahrung* (in opposition to *Erlebnis*), which had been called into question during modernity and, more specifically, through the Great War.[28]

This same conception is what leads Nicola Abbagnano, in her *Diccionario de filosofía* (1961, "Dictionary of Philosophy"), to consider that "exceptional experience" or "mystical experience" is a contradiction in terms, or mere rhetoric.[29] Yet, in modernity, the *unheard-of* (*inaudito*) is constituted as the very mark of experience, manifested in our daily speech in expressions such as "I had an incredible experience" or "I want to experience new things." For just as there is an experience that is nourished by what it receives from tradition, there is another kind, typically modern, that is linked to contemporaneity, openness, and experimentation. The avant-gardes took this form to its limits when they suspended the first notion of experience. In this sense, it is no coincidence that in those same years Benjamin would proclaim, in his essay "Experience and Poverty," the end of one type of experience and the emergence of another (1989, 167–73). And although it is certain that experience as transmission and legacy of the older generations seems to be irreparably eclipsed at the beginning of the twentieth century, it is no less certain that, after nearly one hundred years, the liberation of traditions that manifested itself as the promise of a new kind of experience (that of modernists like Albert Einstein, Paul Klee, or Adolf Loos, according to the examples given in "Experience and Poverty") had also been overshadowed.

More recently, the new has manifested itself as an obstinate repetition of an empty ritual. Facing this double decline, the fundamental task consists not in defending one type of experience over the other but in combining the two, or in examining what happens *between* them. Neither *tabula rasa* nor false return to traditions that have already withered: both modalities continue to persist as muffled echoes, waiting for the operations that would show their value and radiant core. Lisandro Alonso's two movies, *Los muertos* and *La libertad*, testify to how this clash of two kinds of experience takes shape.

A Journey with No End

As in certain traditional travel narratives, *Los muertos* "tells" the story of the journey of a man, Argentino Vargas, who gets out of jail once his time has been served and goes up river to be reunited with his daughter. The jail is in Corrientes, near the city of Goya, from where the protagonist sets off by canoe along the Paraná River. The typical vicissitudes of the fictional travel narrative present themselves along the way: the overcoming of an obstacle, the recognition of a long-lost friend or acquaintance, an affair with a woman, and, finally, his reunion with his family. All of these events take place, however, as muffled echoes of an experience that never emerges. The over-coming of an obstacle (the delivery of a letter to his daughter from a fellow prisoner) is no significant hindrance. The erotic explosion is, in reality, an apathetic encounter with a prostitute. The conver-sation with the friend is an effort to reestablish forgetting. Finally, the reencounter takes place not with his daughter but with her son (Vargas' grandson), with whom he laconically exchanges a few cold words.[30] The expiation of guilt or the process of radical transforma-tion of the hero's voyage never occurs, and the narrative progression of the journey contrasts brutally with Vargas' impassivity.

Los muertos, Alonso's second film, follows at least two of the lines that *La libertad* had traced. The motto that drives *La libertad* ("I don't want to tell a story, I'm interested only in observing") can also be applied to the later movie. Both films register the encounter of two solitudes, that of the protagonist and that of the filmmaker—or, better stated, the encounter between two types of experience of solitude that are in opposition: the traditional and the modern, that of the knowledge of survival and that of the knowledge of cinema, that of the people from the countryside and that of the man with the camera ("witness, observer, outsider") who comes from the city.

The other line that the two films share is the representation of the outside world (what lies beyond the ranch or the jail) as a space of plunder where mercantilization stands in the way of relationships between people. In *La libertad,* Misael's only encounters with other people are with the man who buys wood from him and with the store employee who sells him drinks. In *Los muertos,* once out of jail, the protagonist enters into a series of economic exchanges that define his stay in the town: he goes to buy food ("three and two, five," the shopkeeper affirms) and a shirt for his daughter, and he sleeps with a prostitute. The small amount of money given to him when he gets out of jail for his work as a carpenter is his only link to the characters he will encounter during his journey: "How much do I owe you?" to the taxi driver; "You sell a lot of wood? How much do they pay you?" to the brother of María, the woman to whom he must deliver the letter. The scene of the encounter with the prostitute is, from the point of view of its images, entirely pornographic, but it is ultimately de-eroticized by the way in which it is filmed. "Love for the prostitute," Benjamin affirms in his *The Arcades Project,* "is the apotheosis of empathy with the commodity" (1999, 511). In this scene, however, the empathy (with the merchandise, not with the prostitute) is so profound that the amorous act does not reach apotheosis. (Alonso cuts before the orgasm occurs.) The scene is shown with the automatism and abstraction of the commodity.[31]

If the threat of the commodity had an impact only on the characters, it would not be so terrifying. This threat, however, affects the form in its entirety. In the film's interior, in its narration, the absence of experience as transmissibility and legacy—Vargas tells no one about what has happened to him and only manages to say, in one of the film's most confessional moments, that he does not want to remember anything—is substituted by the transmission of quantities. In its exterior, in the relationship that the film establishes with the spectator, the form must negotiate the threat of prefabricated stories, of a commercial cinema that, evading all experience, does nothing more than repeat over and over what has already been told. Facing the prefabricated narration into which cinema itself has been transformed, the crystalline register of exteriority in *Los muertos* works with indeterminacy and avoids causal explanations and links. Just as the protagonist gets away from the town, suffocated by an environment in which the only contact with other men and women is through economic transactions, the filmmaker goes out intentionally in his search for a different kind of cinema, far from the cinema-as-institution.[32]

The knowledge of cinema that Alonso contrasts with the cinema-spectacle or with the cinema-commodity is made evident in the protagonist (the other) as a radically different knowledge: that of survival in the jungle or the woods, a survival that can *almost* do without the market. The woodcutter in *La libertad* eats an armadillo; the former prisoner in *Los muertos* consumes a honeycomb, a drink that is given to him, and a goat that he finds on the riverbank.[33] The experience of which Agamben speaks, linked to the authority of tradition and in danger of extinction, remains inscribed on the body as *skill.* Despite many years spent in jail, the protagonist of *Los muertos* still knows how to move around in the jungle: he can row a boat, orient himself, recognize different types of trees. This is an em*bodied* (*incorporada*) experience, in the most genuine sense of the term. The director is even obsessed with recording manual and corporeal skills: working with wood, collecting fruit, destroying a honeycomb, killing a goat.

This skill inscribed on the body must confront two hostile objects in different moments of the film. The first is when Vargas decides to buy something for his daughter and must head toward the commodity. The salesperson hands him three shirts and tells him three different prices. The protagonist finds himself facing two problems: first, he has little money and, second, he has to imagine the measurements of his daughter's body. ("I have no idea what she must be like," he confesses.) He chooses, as we might have imagined, the cheapest shirt.[34] In this way, his relationship with his daughter becomes something abstract, determined by the commodity. The fact that at the movie's end she does not appear renders this clear.

The second hostile object appears toward the end of the film and concludes the protagonist's journey on the river, in a part of the film in which the world of commodities would appear to have been left behind. During the journey, Vargas had forged a spontaneous relationship with nature, in accordance with his necessities, for his skill allows him to take from the world what he needs to survive, but it does not allow him to perceive or experience that which is foreign to him. At the end of the film, he arrives at his daughter's ranch and finds one of his grandson's toys, a little doll with an Argentine soccer jersey, which he takes in his hands and later throws to the floor. Vargas' contemplation of the object is highlighted by the shot, but what for the spectator could be cultural (a little football player, a commodity, a child's toy), for Vargas is a *nonimage* because it lacks the instrumental character that he seeks in all that surrounds him. Clearly, this thing will not help him to survive, and this is why he throws it to the floor. The opacity of the object reveals the precarious character of Vargas' perception, which distinguishes only what is useful for him: if the protagonist is dead (as in the film's title), it is because he was not able to overcome the human condition. His perception is governed by his necessity to survive, and, outside of useful objects, Vargas cannot see a single thing. His subjective experience can never be made objective.[35] Miniaturized, the body of the little soccer player is transformed into an allegory in which the body becomes inert, a dead piece, a hollowed-out body.[36] For corporeal skill allows for survival but creates neither community nor meaning.

In no moment is this better illustrated than when his incorporated experience is shown in all its splendor, when he kills a goat. Vargas slits its throat with a machete, as he had done with his brothers. In the words of the director, "I wanted to show that the protagonist had maintained his ability to kill intact. And when the moment arrived to begin filming, Argentino did it in such a quick and natural way that he surprised us all."[37] The goat, which the protagonist killed out of necessity, does not manage to become a scapegoat. A repetition without a ritual, an immolation without expiation, this killing can be neither a sacrifice nor a promise; it is a fragment that cannot be integrated into any meaning (any life) beyond corporeal skill. Hence, these characters are *the dead*. Literally, the film's title seems to refer to the two bodies (presumably those of the protagonist's brothers) that are shown lying at the film's beginning, but the title's resonance permeates the entire story, impregnating its characters, actions, atmosphere. Alonso defines it as such: "They are resigned, rummaging through remains, without thinking about what's to come" (quoted in Pérez 2004). The experience as legacy is transformed into "remains." Moreover, the characters lack the possibility of opening themselves up to experience as a future. (The journey does not manage to shape itself into either a story or an adventure.)

With this experience—and Alonso goes in search of it where it appears to be waiting for us, far from the cities and artificial life[38]—only the minimum can be achieved: survival, which is a form of death in life. Skill is a withdrawal into an instrumental vision of the world. Even the protagonist's relationship with his daughter is converted into something abstract, determined by the commodity. The reason for his trip ends up being an absent body. And the relationship with his grandson in the end comes down to nothing, as though it were little more than an encounter between two people who cannot perceive one another, and nothing more than the opacity of children who already belong to another world.[39] As in *La libertad,* with this experience one cannot create a community. Yet whereas in the earlier film this experience suggested withdrawal (and hence could be called *liberty* and could be spoken of in terms of "wisdom"), in *Los muertos* it is only the exhibition of a mutilation that finds its most variegated representation in Argentino Vargas' character.[40]

Dialogue among the Dead

Los muertos never ceases to mark a difference between observer and observed. As though to underscore this difference throughout, the film ends with the music of Flormaleva, performed by one of the band's members, Catriel Vildosola, who is one of the most important soundtrack artists of the new Argentine cinema. This electronic music is as far from the world of the protagonist as a movie camera. Yet, if experience is in decline and what is decisive is what is produced *between* two possible types of experience, how does this *between* acquire a nearly corporeal presence, pervading the spectator? From the knowledge of cinema and of art, Alonso makes use of two basic procedures: the sequence shot and the indeterminacy of meaning.

In *La libertad* as well as in *Los muertos,* the sequence shot at medium distance, attempting to trap the characters in its enveloping frame, is characterized by meticulous and delayed observation. The point of view upheld throughout almost the entire narration, corroborated by the shot in *Los muertos* in which the camera moves away on a truck, is that of the filmmaker, a position of testimony and registering that explains the documentary effect that certain parts of the film radiate (medium distance, always exterior, but concerned with recording everything), reinforced because the protagonist has the same name as the actor who plays him.[41] In contrast, in the jail scenes the shots multiply, generating a paradoxical sensation of diversity. In the town and on the river, the cuts are scarcer and the diversity of perspectives reduced. The documentary effect diminishes now that the camera, in contrast to ethnographic or nature documentaries, does not move forward with the protagonist but waits for him: the character enters into a nature that has already been explored.[42] This is a world deprived of magic and sacredness, but also of future and novelty. In this way, the sequence shot tends to guide us not toward the landscape or toward what is going to occur but toward what the characters do, allowing us to observe them without interruptions or abrupt cuts. The sequence shot opens itself up to time, but not to the full time of narrativity or of redemption. In the words of Kracauer, "[He is] thrown out into *the cold infinity of empty space and empty time*" (quoted in Frisby 1986, 120, my emphasis).

The indeterminacy extends throughout Alonso's films but is anchored in a gesture that has to do with the specifically cinematographic (or artistic) nature of this experience. A great deal of the effectiveness of *La libertad* lies in its title (chosen by the filmmaker), which fostered the indeterminacy of the meaning of the woodcutter's story. The function of the title in Alonso's first film is fulfilled in his second by the sequence shot, a sort of prologue or prelude. It is a decentered, fluid, somewhat inebriated image that spins around itself and manages to record the totality of space, obverse and inverse. In its trajectory it manages to show, obliquely, an arm with a machete (later we will understand that it is Argentino Vargas') and two cadavers with their throats slit (which we will later assume, without any greater clarity, are his brothers). The sequence shot ends with a fade-out in green and can be incorporated into the rest of the story as a dream of the protagonist.[43] Yet this possibility should not erase the singularity of this scene if one pays attention to its grammar, so different from the rest of *Los muertos*. In the "Prologue," in contrast to the rest of the film, the point of view is absolutely evanescent, vertiginous, without an anchor. This establishes the prologue as an underlying core through which the film's entire poetics is defined. It is, in every sense, an incommensurable and incorporeal shot that opens up to the indeterminacy of meaning.[44]

Although sequence shots belong to the patrimony of modern cinema's procedures, indeterminacy is situated slightly beyond. Like the little soccer player that Vargas holds in his hands, it is the fragment ("remains") that cannot circulate without collapsing the modes of abstract exchange that the commodity proposes and the modes of demarcated exchange that survival imposes. In the face of a quantifiable world, what is undetermined does not manage to constitute redemption or liberation, but it does open the way for a recognition of the precarious and powerful character of both experiences. In this sense, *Los muertos* goes further than *La libertad,* because whereas in the first movie the illusion of reciprocity was possible (liberty, in solitude, of the woodcutter and filmmaker), in the later film there is a threshold that cannot be crossed: the others are dead, and waiting for their return makes no sense. The film's intelligence, in any case, consists in taking the fragments of the ruins of the dead and making them circulate, leaving them undetermined and with their own luminosity.

Silvia Prieto, or Love at Thirty

The relationship between commodities and experience is also central in Martín Rejtman's films. Here, however, we do not find opposition or escape, as in the work of Lisandro Alonso, but something very different: the commodity is the threatening realm in which experience must make its way. As in Alonso's films, here we are also in a world of quantities: "I served forty-eight regular coffees, twenty espressos, and fifteen coffees with milk," says Silvia Prieto. Yet whereas in *La libertad* and *Los muertos* this quantification forms an exteriority (something from which both characters and film attempt to flee), in Rejtman it is the space within which the characters move.[45] If something characterizes *Silvia Prieto,* it is the very close framings of urban signs, usually posters of businesses or advertisements that frame the lives of the characters and within which they must move. A shot of a pharmacy window displaying different products (Yastá, Fanta, Rexina, Seven-Up) acquires a new meaning when Silvia Prieto (Rosario Bléfari) and Brite (Valeria Bertuccelli) appear with shirts advertising a powdered soap and giving away samples. They themselves become shop windows, commodities: in fact, the powdered soap is called Brite, like Sylvia's friend—or is it the other way around?[46] Once again, the global character is inscribed in commodities and captures the bodies of the characters, like a one-size-fits-all glove. Commodities possess magical properties from the moment they permit the metamorphosis of objects and of bodies.[47] The characters of *Silvia Prieto* move within this world of signs (brand names, logos, names, posters), and it is within this world that they must choose a way of life.

Affective ties, in addition, tend to begin with an economic transaction. In *Rapado,* Damián meets a girl who asks him whether he has some money; immediately after, Damián gives her a kiss instead of the money. In *Los guantes mágicos,* Valeria says that her relationship with Alejandro "began with an economic arrangement." It is not, then, that money and affect are opposed; rather, we must detect the chemistry by which one thing transforms into another. Characters free themselves not by fleeing from the commodity but by following, incorporating, and resignifying its transformations, and by anticipating them.

The Decision to Change One's Life

Silvia Prieto's story begins with her categorical affirmation that "nothing was going to be like it was before" and ends with another, no less emphatic: "at that point nothing mattered to me anymore." In the manner of structuralist critics who recommend reading the beginning and end of stories to interrogate the nature of the narration, we can juxtapose these two sentences to reveal the transformation of the protagonist, in a sequence that begins with a strong decision (to change her life), continues with a sudden dispossession (she discovers that others have the same name as she does), and ends with utter detachment.

What approximates Rejtman to his mentors Eric Rohmer and Roberto Bresson is choice. "Rapado," the short story that is the source of Rejtman's first film, begins thus: "Lucio makes a sudden decision: he walks into the barbershop—it is six-thirty in the evening, almost summer time—and decides to shave his head." And, shortly after: "[H]e decides, again almost suddenly, that he will steal a motorcycle" (Rejtman 1992, 87). The two decisions speak not to an absolute will incarnated in a subject but to small strategies, somewhat necessary, somewhat hasty, that someone takes to move forward. Nothing really changes for Lucio after he shaves his head, and his theft of the motorcycle is to restore what has been previously stolen from him. "No one chooses anything," says Fabián, one of the characters in "Algunas cosas importantes para mi generación" ("Some Things That Are Important for My Generation"), also in the book *Rapado*. Yet choices for the characters in Rejtman's literature are never sufficiently meaningful or transcendent (and here his poetics diverges from that of Rohmer or Bresson). Like Lucio's choice in "Rapado," they are sudden, capricious, unexpected, even for those who make them. In addition, they are never heroic or superhuman (or tragic): Silvia Prieto decides to work in a café, and Alejandro, in *Los guantes mágicos,* chooses for his taxi a Renault 12, hardly the most attractive car, or a car-screen (*auto-pantalla*), as Alan Pauls deems it (2004). This is how the voice-over of *Silvia Prieto*'s protagonist begins: "The day I turned twenty-six *I decided* that my life was going to change.... At noon I got a job in a café. I was completely determined. Nothing was going to be like it was" (Rejtman 1999, author's emphasis).

The choices are made not in a vacuum but in a world that is already commodified, where no object comes to us uncontaminated. Before beginning a system, choices are inserted into a preexisting one (except, as we saw, in the case of *Rapado*). This applies not only to the characters but also to the mise-en-scène: the components of the shot are objects or places that have already been circulating, from Chinese restaurants to common places, from knickknacks to clothing. Affect does not displace the commodity, just as choice does not annul the series: simply, the former give the latter a transitory tone, affirming a singularity that the serial world tries to deny. Affect and choice do not alter the economy of things but resignify it.

Choice and series constitute this double system that is defined according to the subjects and objects implicated: Silvia Prieto and her life, Silvia Prieto who decides that her life is going to change, the life that changes Silvia Prieto. The objects are those things that can circulate, including work, the body, clothing, names, and even life itself.[48] This double system initiates on the part of the subjects a decision to take or to do something to appropriate, exchange, or give away something (shaving one's head, stealing a motorcycle, giving someone a sweater); on the part of the objects, it initiates *seriality* (motorcycles, any motorcycle; life, any life). The series, based on reproduction, bestows a certain neutrality—which comes from exchange—on objects like the little doll that Gabriel (Gabriel Fernández Capello) buys in Los Angeles. A souvenir, a fake handicraft bought in a knickknack store, it is exactly the same as so many neutral objects that lie waiting for new tourists to choose them. In Rejtman's works, no objects are outside of the series.[49] Appropriation, exchange, or giving away lends new meanings to these neutral objects, taking them out of the series to insert them into a different one. Gabriel gives the little doll to Brite (donation), but Brite says it looks like Silvia Prieto, and she gives it to her; Silvia throws it into the street; Santiago picks it up, takes it to his room, takes it out of circulation (appropriation), and puts it on his shelf of found objects. The series, like a screen, possesses a neutrality that only cracks when the subjects' choices project meaning. Something similar happens with the series of names, like that of Silvia Prieto. Is there, however, anything simultaneously more neutral and less neutral than a name: that which has no meaning but is at the same time extremely meaningful?

As they are narrated, the two systems refer to one another. The way in which subjects circulate begins to be reproduced in a series: "He hears steps approaching, running," we read in "Rapado." "He sees the owner of the motorcycle. They are the same age. Both have shaved heads. He stands up in front of Lucio. They both try to get their breathing back to normal" (Rejtman 1992, 89). Silvia Prieto, who makes the decision, discovers that she also forms part of a series, that of the other Silvia Prietos. By means of a decision, the seriality is detained through the force of appropriation and subsequently acquires individuality: "A prudent amount of time passes and the motorcycle, Lucio thinks, is unrecognizable. With its new paint it has changed completely; in the woods it would be completely unnoticed. What's more, he had put an Ángelo Paolo sticker on the gas tank. Then he decides to take the bike out" (90–1).[50] From this point on, the motorcycle is recognizable as belonging to Lucio.

In a reduced field such as the series, and with a limited temporal reach, no appropriation is definitive. On one hand, we have the decisions that others have made beforehand, as in the proper name. For how is it possible to appropriate a proper name? On the other hand, we have the chance that governs the series and shows the contingency of any choice. Why are Gabriel and Silvia together if not because of Brite and Marcelo's relationship? How can we explain the coincidental encounter with Armani or the trajectory of the little doll? The decision, then, is not pure and uncontaminated but refers to what precedes it.

It is not difficult to realize that we are facing a narrative regime: Rejtman takes or constructs an act and subjects it to the two systems, the series and the decision. With this double system, Rejtman is also able to discard a certain idea of narration based on exceptionality and adventure. Hence, there is no hierarchy among characters, and none stands out more than the others. Experience and value, Rejtman's movies seem to say, are found in the series, in random choices, in chance, and not in the exceptionality of the adventure. (In his narrative, the spare and concise style highlights the neutral, rather than unusual, character of the events.) Thus, the two processes set a narrating machine into motion.

It would be an error to consider this double system only from the point of view of its capacity to produce stories or encourage narrative procedures. Our interest in this regime lies in the fact that through it, Rejtman speaks of a great many things—above all, of contemporaneity. Like Rohmer, Rejtman is an archeologist of layers of time: who will be capable of comprehending the profound reach of Ángelo Paolo? How many people will remember the advertisements with bellbottoms and the content young people from the famous ascendant lower-middle class, now defunct? Why were Chinese restaurants so popular at a certain time? Why does the coat of Silvia's mother suggest class, distinction? Who are those who identify with the New Order song that Alejandro dances to in *Los guantes mágicos* or with the León Gieco song that Cecilia discovers on television? Each contemporaneity has its "typical places"—the phrase is from *Los guantes mágicos*—and Rejtman's movies tend to work with the features of each world (its typicalness), according to the biological cycle of each his characters. In *Rapado,* for example, the family is the realm in which decisions find meaning, whereas in *Silvia Prieto* families no longer exist (except for the two characters who are twenty years old: Santiago, the boy who keeps the little doll, and the bassist of the group El otro solo ["The other alone"], the son of the second Silvia Prieto). Ezequiel Acuña, the director of *Nadar solo,* has spoken of this situated and generational character of Rejtman's movies:

> Coming back to Rejtman's *Rapado,* in my case it had to do with important experiences in a certain point in my life, around adolescence, besides the fact that this is also, to a certain extent, the theme of the movie. That's why *Silvia Prieto* and *Los guantes mágicos* don't interest me as much; they don't have that *silence* and something personal that I find in *Rapado.* (Acuña, Lerman, and Villegas 2004, 155)

Every generation finds itself at some point searching for the means to access an experience.

Silvia Prieto is a movie of characters who hit thirty and know that something is going to change, just as *Rapado* is the story of kids who are almost twenty, and *Los guantes mágicos* deals with characters who are closer to forty. The characters are out of sync, because they are always a little less than they thought they would be: in Rejtman, the former high school classmate who reminds us that things did not turn out the way we imagined never fails to make an appearance. These are the coincidental encounters in which characters connect again with a world in which the possibilities of choice *appear* to be unlimited.[51] This is why they are always a little less. "The only strange thing," Silvia remarks, "is that I have less of everything, but the proportions are what they should be. Less of a pulse, lower blood pressure, less red cells, less white cells, less of everything" (Rejtman 1999, 96). In the process of describing what she lacks, what she no longer has or what was taken from her, Silvia moves from decision to dispossession, which she finally is able to transform into detachment. This ascetic channel saves the protagonist in a world in which she no longer seems to have a place.

The Rhythm of Comedy (the Neutrality of the Series)

According to film critics, Rejtman's movies show two strong influences: the screwball comedy and the films of Robert Bresson. However, little has been spoken of Max Ophuls, the director whose work probably most closely resembles Rejtman's. The circulation of objects in Rejtman's stories recalls that of the earrings in *Madame de...* (1953) and of the interlinked couples of *La ronde* (1950).[52] Given that the mise-en-scène in Rejtman's films is so stylized and elaborate, it makes sense that critics have tended toward finding many more deliberate affiliations in his work than in that of other directors of the new Argentine cinema. Yet the sparseness and neutrality of Rejtman's point of view is far from the sources of his inspiration, and it is this difference that allows us to ponder the peculiarity of his films.[53]

Silvia Prieto has neither climax nor upheavals, and although things (many things) keep happening, the film has a regular rhythm and a mise-en-scène without emphasis. It is somewhat odd that this uniform rhythm subtends a comedy, a genre conventionally governed by the crescendo of plotlines and the punch line. Rhythm is what is most original in Rejtman: it is neither the rash succession of situations of the screwball comedy nor Bresson's intense blowing nor Ophuls' decadent melancholia. Like these, Rejtman maintains an unflappable, observant distance, and, like these, he circulates objects to give sense and form to the narration. Whereas the others place emphasis to provide keys to reading their films, however, Rejtman's films repeatedly reestablish neutrality.

This neutrality is based on the fact that Rejtman's system of shots and tone tends to suspend any value judgment. In the work of Ophuls, in contrast, the object that circulates is the testimony of a desire and the evocation of a past, like the earrings of *Madame de...*, which have an affective, economic, and commemorative value. They are not knickknacks. In Bresson's stories as well we find objects that, put into circulation, construct a story, like the donkey that goes through different owners in *Au hasard Balthazar* (1966, *Balthazar*) or the bill in *L'Argent* (1983, *Money*), which is based on Tolstoy's novella "The Forged Coupon." Yet in the randomness of circulation there is a *belief* that organizes all of Bresson's poetics and that could be synthesized in the words of one of the characters in *L'Argent*: "If I were God, I would pardon everyone." The *pardon* offers potential religious, political, social, or cinematographic readings.[54] The prominence that the object imprints on the screen is far from Rejtman's utopia of "a world where everything is worth the same" (Pauls, 2004).

This contrast makes itself most evident in the confrontation between *Silvia Prieto* and the screwball comedy. In *Pursuits of Happiness: The Hollywood Comedy of Remarriage* (1981), Stanley Cavell designates his corpus "comedies of remarriage," as all begin with a fight and end with a second marriage of the same couple.[55] Cavell writes that "this *freedom* is announced in these film comedies in the concept of divorce" and is complementary to the love that is fulfilled when the couple decides to marry again (1981, 110). There are also three weddings in *Silvia Prieto*. One is the marriage of Silvia and Marcelo, which occurred many years ago and which they remember along with Brite in the home movie they watch on Silvia's television. The second is between Mario Garbuglia and Marta, the result of their participation in the matchmaking television program, which takes place at a big party that the station pays for and that Marcelo and Brite take advantage of to get married themselves—the third marriage. When Silvia receives the former prison inmate who substitutes for Gabriel, she shows him the video of the marriage and tells him that it is Garbuglia's.[56] How is it possible to inspire laughter with today's passions, so different from those of the screwball comedy? How can we speak of freedom or love when a wedding is already in itself an economic transaction, as the television couple, Mario and Marta, whose wedding is televised and organized around publicity, show? What is it that makes Silvia deceive someone she does not know and show him a false video, as she affirms in a voice-over, "[A]t this point nothing mattered to me"? With this gesture and with the purpose of not "deceiving" the former prisoner, Sylvia plays with the series of weddings and of wedding videos: typical scenes that work as well for some people as for others. Whereas in the screwball comedy the characters, in the process of apprenticeship, affirm an irreparable love, Silvia here enacts detachment: she lets the series function, and she declares herself unnecessary. Whereas the circulation of objects establishes evocation in Ophuls' films, pardon in Bresson's, and an affirmation of love *and* freedom in the comedy of remarriage, in *Silvia Prieto* it opens up into the emptiness of detachment. Yet how did this path that began with such an ambitious decision ("to change one's life") culminate in the recognition of dispossession and in the revelation of detachment?

The Gift: From Dispossession to Detachment

A theme that I'm always talking about: economics. My movies don't talk about anything else.

—Martín Rejtman (quoted in Pauls, 2004)

An extensive fade-out precedes Silvia Prieto's encounter with her double (Mirta Busnelli) in a café. The two women are not alike; they share no friends or acquaintances; nothing that they have done links them. They are doubles in only one aspect: they have the same name. The name, in principle, is a sign that gives no indication or precise description: "Silvia Prieto" could be young or old, tall or short, good or bad. Yet this autonomy of the signifier does not account for Silvia Prieto's experience of dispossession, because what happens to her is much worse. All of us (or nearly all of us) have a name that designates us in a contingent way.[57] Names *designate someone* in a determined world. What happens to Silvia Prieto is that she discovers—beginning with a comment made by Armani, the man she meets in Mar del Plata—that this name no longer designates only her. The name that removes us from the series returns to sink the protagonist once again into the series. This dispossession, whether real or symbolic, destroys the world based on decision that Silvia had constructed for herself up until then. "I decided that my life was going to change," she affirms at the beginning of the movie. Something (a *name,* not a person) decided that my life would change, we seem to hear in the fade-out. In the face of the appropriation and dispossession that regulate the economy of the first part of the movie, the gift[58] emerges: that detachment with which Silvia gains experience, based not on what she decides to do but on what she makes circulate, what she gives, or what she watches disinterestedly.

A pure present produces disequilibrium in the world. Taking a commodity out of circulation, moving it into the zone of affect, expecting nothing in return: these are the features of one of the oldest and most antieconomic activities, to present the other with something. Of course, even with the present—that gift with something violent about it, with which we set ourselves up in another person's life—the marks of symbolic capital of the commodity can still be there, manifesting social status, power, economic riches, or a generosity that creates obligations. In an essay from his book *Pascalian Meditations,* Pierre Bourdieu questions the gratitude and disinterest that have been attributed to the present and shows how the act of giving something supposes an interval of time that anticipates a reward or a transformed return (the gesture made with an eye toward obtaining something material or symbolic in return, not always admitted) (1999, 257ff).

Here we will limit the debate, which in the field of sociology has infinite derivations, to the fact that in the world that Rejtman constructs, the disinterested or pure gift is possible. And this is despite the fact that in his films there is no naïveté with respect to the act of giving. Alejandro's birthday party in *Los guantes mágicos* shows the present to be a variant of economic exchange: Piraña and Susana give him the dog Luthor; the dog walker gives him dog walkings; Cecilia gives him the dog walker's taxi rides to pick up Luthor.[59] Valeria constitutes the exception to this generalized exchange: she gives him an argyle sweater. As Alejandro wears only plain clothing, this gift provokes a disequilibrium in his habits that is reestablished in the following scene: Alejandro wears only striped clothing for the rest of the movie. Valeria does what no one else does; she is able to add an object to that world and to set herself up in his body, in an expenditure without recompense. To state it simply: an act of love and generosity. The same occurs with Alejandro and his love for cars, and for Renault 12s in particular. When he manages to get into one, he "borrows" it and takes it to a car wash. He leaves the car where he found it; now it is impeccable.

The series of presents in *Silvia Prieto* is no less abundant: a tupperware container with twelve hundred dollars that Silvia's ex-husband gives her, the answering machine that her dealer gives her, the little doll that Gabriel brings to Brite from Los Angeles, the shampoo that Silvia Prieto gives to Silvia Prieto,[60] and, finally, the lamp made from a bottle that Silvia gives Gabriel. Of all these presents, the most disinterested are the dollars from her ex-husband and the answering machine from Devi. Silvia and Brite, in fact, work by giving away things: they give out free samples of soap powder to passers-by.

A gift (Silvia's ex-husband gives her twelve hundred dollars without asking for anything in return[61]) constitutes the first disequilibrium in the story, and the return to a final equilibrium is achieved through the detachment that Silvia carries out. In contrast to the present that adds an object to the world and that is the product of a decision, detachment allows an already existing object to follow its path without the intervention of a personal, affective, passionate, or evaluative register. The apathy at which Silvia arrives, her withdrawal to observe from a distance the circulation of objects without establishing values, is not a passive attitude but produces a particular type of experience. Silvia detaches herself from her little bird, her coat, marijuana, the money that her ex-husband gives her, the little doll that Brite gives her, her name (she goes by Luisa Ciccone), her documents of identification, and, in the last scene, her wedding: "[A]t that point nothing mattered to me anymore." The phrase is typical, circulating like a cliché, but it manages to establish an experience. This suspension of values is analogous to the practice of the director himself, who has managed to suspend evaluations of the things that circulate and are exchanged on screen to such an extent that interpretations of his films are obliged to highlight one element over another to establish meaning.[62] This is what Barthes deemed, in one of his last seminars, published posthumously, *the neuter*. In the face of this "obligation to choose," which, for Barthes, is the "pure expression of the anti-Neutral," (2005, 183), Silvia ends up adopting a similar gaze to that of the movie itself. What matters is to observe at a distance the mechanisms of exchange rather than, through decisions and affirmations, interfere in them.

Silvia's ultimate apathy contrasts with that of Brite, especially at the story's end. Brite becomes pregnant; Silvia pretends to be (but she throws out the pregnancy test that Brite gives her in the bathroom). Brite remains with Marcel; Silvia remains without a partner. Finally, Silvia wanders around the city with an ace of spaces, the card given to her in a disco in exchange for her identity documents; with this same object Brite beats her at a game of cards. It would appear that Silvia Prieto is left with nothing. Yet, on closer inspection, a particular vibration perturbs this character who remains without a face, a past, a future. Now she can observe at a distance and look at things with a certain detachment: a sort of ascesis and withdrawal that is not so different from the gaze sustained by the movie itself. In a world in which everything has a price and is there to be exchanged for something else, Silvia Prieto adds what was not there before. Someone has decided to step away from the world to observe, without fear or hope, how it works.

Sound, Track Separate

Perhaps you insist on seeing film as "images and sounds." And if it were the other way around? If it were sound and images? Sounds that let us imagine what is seen and to see what is imagined? And if film was also the ear that perks up—like that other ear, the dog's—when the eye is lost? Walking in the open country, for example.

—Serge Daney (2004, 130)

Among the many aspects that distinguish the movies of the new Argentine cinema from their predecessors, one of the most crucial is the treatment of the soundtrack. Even in the most celebrated films of the 1980s (Adolfo Aristarain's *Últimos días de la víctima* [1982, "Last Days of the Victim"], *La historia oficial,* or *Camila*), the soundtrack was treated according to whether it dealt with the score, dialogues, or ambient sound. The sound was subordinated to the task of completing the narration and achieving the best technical and expressive finish for the film. In many of the movies of the 1990s, in contrast, sound acquires more autonomy and is not necessarily destined to follow behind the images. Through sound, the stories acquire new meanings and directors try to search for a stylistic mark. Of course, none of this constitutes a novelty as such (Hitchcock asked Bernard Hermann to treat the sound of the flocks of birds in *The Birds* as though they were part of the score; Ennio Moricone, influenced by one of John Cage's disciples, made music with footsteps, drops of water, and wind in the initial sequence of Sergio Leone's *Once Upon a Time in the West* (1968); Hugo Santiago, in *Invasión* [1969, "Invasion"], used the musical laboratories of the Di Tella Institute[63] to treat sound as *musique concrete*). But I am not following an avant-garde logic whereby things are legitimated according to their degree of novelty; I am detecting transformations that have the capacity to foster different aspects of film. I am not claiming that Lucrecia Martel's *La niña santa* or Rejtman's *Los guantes mágicos* is revitalizing the treatment of sound, but something different (more modest but not for that reason less significant): all of these films treat sound as a significant material that has a relative autonomy with respect to the image or that provides it with new dimensions.[64]

Sound in the movies of the new Argentine cinema is not stratified into music, dialogue, or ambient sound but generates a true network of sounds in which the indiscernible is in tension with differentiation. For example, dialogues are treated as soundtracks, and many times their sound texture is equally or more important than the meaning of the words. In *Los muertos,* the protagonist speaks on the river bank, interspersing his words with terms from the indigenous language Guaraní, most likely incomprehensible to the spectator, but with the goal of accessing the tonality of the voices of the characters and their otherness.[65] In *La niña santa,* the murmurs and hushed dialogues create a significant dimension of sound that has nothing to do with the meaning of the words. The effectiveness of Rejtman's dialogues lies less in what the characters say than in the repetitive, lazy, and automatic character of their phrases. "Another part of my 'method,'" the actress Rosario Bléfari writes half-jokingly and half-seriously in her text "Rodaje" ("Filming"), "is what we could call the touchstone or the principal axis of the theory: the almost obsessive insistence in listening for the adequate tone in all spoken words. There is nothing that infuriates Rejtman more than an off-tune cadence" (in Rejtman 1999, 115). The obsessive repetitions of Juan Villegas' *Sábado* and the lazy voices of the characters in Ezequiel Acuña's *Nadar solo* create sound that provides these movies with their recognizable and original style. Finally, two films as different as *Pizza, birra, faso* and *La ciénaga* coincide in the fact that both use dialogues as soundtracks. The dialogues are not only what the characters say to each other but also a tonality, a noise or a musicality that runs through the stories transversally. Converging only in this point, the two films diverge once again. The soundtrack in the dialogues of Caetano and Stagnaro's movie is the tense and furious insult of a group of marginalized youth that is outside of the bourgeois myth of language, that is, of the word as a coin of useful exchange. (In Caetano and Stagnaro's movie, words serve not to say something but to get attention.) In contrast, *La ciénaga* investigates all the folds of the provincial bourgeoisie's voice and its feverish nuances of control and submission; the other side of this voice is the almost silent body of the maid, drawing the desire of Momi, Mecha, and José, without ever entering into dialogue with them.

Although any one of these films could be used to reflect on the dimension of sound in the new Argentine cinema, few filmmakers have made such intensive use of sound as a significant material as Martel in *La niña santa* and Rejtman in *Los guantes mágicos*. Strangely (it can only be a coincidence), the protagonists of both films, which were released almost simultaneously, have problems with their hearing.[66] A noise without origin sets up within them, unsettling them and preventing them from sleeping. The soundtrack is thematized; no longer only the technical-expressive function, it also sets the story itself into motion.

La niña santa and the Closure of Performance

He is longing who flees from his mother.

—Lezama Lima, "Llamado del deseoso"

La niña santa begins where *La ciénaga* ends.[67] "I didn't see anything," Verónica says to Momi after making the pilgrimage to the water tank in which the figure of the Virgin had supposedly appeared. The conflict between desire and belief in the earlier film was just barely sketched out, for belief was always outside (on television, in the faithful who would converge around the water tank). In contrast, in *La niña santa* belief is central for the two adolescent girls, torn between mystical rapture and religious doctrine, between the desire to interpret their inability to fit into a world and the rules that the catechism offers on how to deal with desire. These two girls are cousins, Amalia (María Alché) and Josefina (Julieta Zylberberg). Amalia lives with her mother Helena (Mercedes Morán) and her uncle Adolfo (Alejandro Urdapilleta) in a hotel; their lives are changed when a medical conference is organized there. In addition to attending catechism classes (and wondering about her mission within the divine plan and the world), Amalia has a strange experience. During a musical demonstration of a thereminvox,[68] one of the conference participants, Dr. Jano (Carlos Belloso), comes up behind her and places his body close enough to touch hers. Jano, who has developed a game of mutual seduction with Helena, does not know that Amalia is her daughter, and he will find out only at the film's end. Although the movie has several other characters who provide nuance in a complex story, this triad of protagonists (Amalia, Jano, Helena) constitutes the basis for a reading of the film.

The character played by Carlos Belloso has a name so obviously symbolic that it is difficult not to notice it. In fact, it had already appeared in Martel's earlier film. In *La ciénaga,* two little girls, in front of a fan that deforms their voices, sing the following children's rhyme: "Doctor Jano, surgeon/today we have to operate/in the emergency room/a girl your age/She is twenty-one/You are one year older/Doctor Jano, surgeon/Don't go falling in love."[69] In Roman mythology, Janus is the god of doors, limits, and thresholds. He has two faces, one that looks toward peace and the other toward war. In *La niña santa,* the mythic significance of this name opens itself up to various readings: Jano's double face refers to the relationship he forges with Helena and her daughter, unaware of the link that binds them, or it relates to his double life, as family man and as the pervert who harasses young women in the street, or to the fact that Jano is the ambivalence of the threshold of Amalia's initiation into adulthood. The actor who plays him defines the character with these words: "To me, the script has a ton of myths. The first thing that I thought of is Little Red Riding Hood and the big bad wolf. Jano is the innocence of wickedness, and the girl is the wickedness of innocence" (quoted in Lerer 2003). The actor is correct as to the dominant characteristic of the characters in *La niña santa:* their ambivalence.

Ambivalence cuts through all the characters, even those who are secondary, whom Martel treats with a subtle hand. The catechism teacher (Mia Maestro) tries to teach her students to be chaste and to recognize the divine call, but she is passionately in love with a man who initiates her into the world of sex. (The guilt makes her cry in the movie's opening scene, as she sings, "I surrendered everything.") The teacher wants to eliminate ambiguity and cannot stand the gruesome tales, not included in the class plan, that her students bring to her. Miriam (Miriam Díaz) is obliged to work as a cook for her mother Mirta (Marta Lubos) but is a kinesiologist and one of the film's most sensual characters. In a more televisual register (and in this sense Mónica Villa is an excellent choice for the part), Josefina's mother speaks constantly of "good manners" but exclaims "filthy, cheeky Indian (*china*)" when she discovers that the maid has brushed her teeth in the kitchen sink. Something similar happens with the protagonists. Jano, a professional and a family man, goes out into the street to harass an adolescent girl. Later, toward the end of the film, he threatens Amalia that he will tell her mother and goes up to Helena's room, but he ends up saying nothing and instead kisses her passionately. Josefina, not wanting "premarital relations" (she repeats the phrase she learned in catechism, as does Amalia when she tells Josefina, "How resplendent your hair is"), has anal intercourse with her cousin and, when her mother finds out, offers her the story of Amalia's ambiguous relationship with Jano, which she had promised to keep a secret. It is not so much that she betrays her cousin as that she saves herself. She understands, unlike her friend Julieta, that one must learn to live with this duality. ("I have the gift of learning," she affirms.) Finally, Helena uses the hotel as a seduction scene for Jano and ends up performing herself in the dramatization that ends the medical conference. Of all the characters, she is the most dependent on the outside gaze, hence her duplicity.[70] The ambivalence that these characters establish with their acts relates to the necessity of upholding the order of social representation, that is, of what must be seen by others and what must remain hidden. Despite the fact that this is a fiction starring almost exclusively women, the masculine gaze (and thus the importance of Jano) is fundamental in assigning the characters' roles, principally those of mother and daughter.

The only characters who do not present this ambiguity are Dr. Vesalio and Amalia. Dr. Vesalio circles the hotel like a satyr pursuing nymphs. In addition to embodying a typical masculine obsession, his attitude leads him to be expelled from the conference. In his pursuits, in the velocity and anxiety that have transformed the world into something stripped of all density, this man misses the link between mystery and desire. Amalia, as Belloso says, embodies "innocence" or sanctity: in her integrity and in her candor, this young woman enters into the tragic logic of desire once she has thrown herself into the social world. She masturbates, pursues the man who harassed her, and kisses her cousin on the mouth with the same purity with which she maintains that the fall of a man is a miracle, sings a religious song, and upholds that she now has a mission in the divine plan. Amalia believes in what she sees and hears, and she is the only one who looks behind her to see more, to see everything, in order to comprehend the divine call.[71]

This ambivalence dominates the traditional relationships that the feminine figure has been subject to throughout history, in the polarity mother–lover and woman–mother.[72] In *La niña santa,* the woman–mother is Josefina's mother, whereas the woman–lover is Helena, who is observed admiringly by men at the pool and, according to her brother and to Jano, should be an actress ("You should give up everything and devote yourself to acting").[73] The house of Josefina's mother, as she insists throughout the film, is the opposite of the hotel, a space of passage in which no family is possible. Amalia, the holy girl, fractures the logic of each, because in the divine plan that she imagines, her disturbing figure refers to neither of the two models, or, better stated, contests what is central about them: to be seen and to be represented. In this vision of woman, men impose their logic with an exterior and disciplinary gaze that becomes social and totalizing (divine) (Cavarero 1998, 303).[74] This is why Amalia escapes the gaze and penetrates the labyrinths of hearing, touch, and divine will. Amalia does not submit, like her mother, to the gaze of a man, to the order of representation, to the game of the patient who falls in love with the doctor ("Dr. Jano, surgeon/Don't go falling in love"), but touches and listens to the call.

The apprenticeship of the characters, as in the case of the precocious Josefina, is to understand that they live in a world of appearances, in a world in which one must play a role (Daney 2004, 192). Thus the movie ends in a scenario, just as the performance is about to begin. The performance, as is stated more than once, is the *closing* of the conference. However, the movie ends before this closure happens, on the threshold where Jano's performance as doctor, and Helena's as patient, is about to begin. Martel shows that desire, in this society, cannot be represented and that each time it is staged, vision imposes its orders, its hierarchies, imprinted by masculine visual control. This is why Amalia is the only character for whom desire can be expressed without being subordinated—not only because she escapes from visual ordering but also because in her world, in her divine plan, there is no sin.

La niña santa: *An Acousmatic of Belief*

In the triangle that dominates *La niña santa*, the competition between mother and daughter establishes a counterpoint that turns around the desired figure of Jano, a character that Belloso plays with little sensuality or seductiveness. This counterpoint constructs two entirely different zones with respect to sound: the sound that pesters Helena is opposed to the call, also difficult to interpret, that hounds her daughter. The mother suffers from Ménière syndrome, a mysterious illness whose causes are still unknown and whose effects are devastating: a deafening and bothersome noise that can lead to madness. The persistence of these noises transforms Helena into a *case* and into an ideal candidate for the conference's final performance.[75] In contrast, Amalia is captive not to any noise but to the call, a supernatural and inaudible voice that alerts her to her role in the divine plan. Something like divine omnipotence that makes her seek out Jano (making the random encounter appear providential) is repeated, in modified fashion, in the encounter between Helena and Jano or between patient and doctor, because Jano specializes in Ménière syndrome. (The random encounter is providential.) Mother and daughter are opposed in the compositions that they choose as emblems: the sensual song that Helena dances to in front of the mirror and the poem of the *romancero* (Spanish folk ballad of medieval origins) that she dances to and recites contrast with the carols and litanies to the Virgin Mary that Amalia sings and recites.[76] Beyond the differences in the sound profiles of the characters, Helena's noises speak to a deficiency compensated for by visual exuberance. Her image is trapped in the mirror, and this is where we see her when Jano discovers her or when she dances in her room. With her coquettish obsession with how she is perceived, Helena finds pleasure in the visual field dominated by the masculine gaze.[77] In contrast, Amalia penetrates into the aural labyrinth, using sounds, touch, and even the sense of smell to trap Jano, the man whom she wants to save. She leaves the visual order to move in a different realm, one made up of sounds, smells, and surfaces.

In the Catholic tradition, the conflict between the visual and the aural has always played a central role. "He who has ears to hear, let him hear," Jesus said at the end of his parables, and almost all of the mystery of the religion hinges on the words that the Angel says to the Virgin in the Enunciation, to such an extent that there were theologians who affirmed that the Virgin had become pregnant through her ear.[78] In Romans 10, we read, "Consequently, faith comes from hearing the message, and the message is heard through the word of Christ." Visual imagery has also had a persuasive function in the religion, above all in Catholic propaganda, but it seems to depend on a different aspect of belief than that of sounds.[79] Whereas sound relates to presence, the interior, and withdrawal, the image imposes distance, exteriority, and the differentiation of elements. Visuality imposes a relationship of power and domination different from that of sound. "The doctor has a very good eye," Vesalio says, referring to Jano's choice of Helena for the final performance.

In the face of this world of visual clarity, aural confusion emerges, and causal relationships are upset. The origin of a sound can appear belatedly, or it can hide itself in the folds of space. A term from cinematographic theory helps us to make our way through this aural labyrinth: acousmatic designates a sound with no recognizable visual source (one which is heard without seeing the cause of the sound).[80] Yet the term also evokes, in the words of Robert Stam, "highly personal intra-familial associations. The voice of the mother for the child still within the womb is strangely acousmatic. Within the history of religion, the term evokes the voice of the Divine entity which mere mortals were *forbidden* to see" (2001, 217). Michel Chion affirms that acousmatic sound is "magic or perturbing" and that it "symbolizes the incorporeal double of the body" (1999, 173). In *La niña santa* the relationship between cause and effect is inverted; only after hearing a sound do we see the source that produces it. The explosion that Amalia and Josefina hear at the side of the road comes from young men who are hunting, as the image shows; the noise of a body falling in Josefina's house is, as the image shows, from a naked man who falls from the second floor; the mysterious noises that are heard in the thermal baths of the hotel are, as the image shows, ones that Amalia makes to capture Jano's attention. This revealing of the source, however, does not diminish the mystery of the world of sounds, which has its own logic. In these dark places, Amalia finds her fortress of escape from the order of visual control.

Characters become disturbed when the cause of the sound is hidden. This is what happens to Jano when Amalia strikes one of the railings of the pool. The first scene in which this causal disturbing becomes clear (visual) is the thereminvox scene. While the severe musician plays the instrument in a shop window, the spectators, Amalia among them, stare, fascinated, at this mysterious sound without an origin. Up until this moment the story has moved along in counterpoint between the hotel and Helena's seduction of the recently arrived Jano, on one hand, and Amalia and Josefina's catechism classes, on the other. The thereminvox scene disturbs this counterpoint because in it there is an encounter (a touch) between Jano and Amalia. The instrument also narrates again, with music, the conflict between belief (the music of Bach) and the seduction of the flesh (Bizet's *Carmen*) that runs through the protagonist. She enters into this "call" that mixes together two different plans: to make Jano know love (to turn the other cheek) will be her salvation. For Amalia, desire does not establish a system of prohibitions and hierarchies; it is an energy that runs through everything without guilt or conventions: from the long kiss that she gives Josefina to her pursuit of Jano. Amalia does not give herself over to the gaze of the other: she follows a sound.

Between the Call and the Performance

In the face of the masculine and visual logic of domination, feminist theory has imagined various possible alternatives, whether from within the visual field itself or in the potential of other senses, principally touch and hearing.[81]

The medical conference's "performance as an end" is a phrase mentioned several times throughout the story. The movie ends, precisely, with a suspended performance, as though there is something that could not be seen or represented in the logic of the film; the performance "closes" the story of Jano and Helena along with that of the conference.[82] After frustrating the possibility of seeing Helena and Jano in the performance in a deferred realization of desire, the movie inserts a different ending, that of Josefina and Amalia swimming in the pool, while Amalia asks, "Hello, hello, can you hear?"

The performance between Jano and Helena, in which he plays the doctor and she the patient, fulfills in a sublimated way the amorous relationship between them, always anticipated but never consumated. It seems that the desire of both will finally be performed/represented,[83] even if only in the traditional mode of the man who knows and the woman who is a patient and allows herself to be "observed." The conquest has been anticipated in the discussion of the colors of Helena's dress (once again the visual as a way of seducing) and with the kiss, the product of a misunderstanding, interrupted because of the performance. There, the woman–lover becomes actress and patient at the same time and transforms from a woman who seduces into a woman who is subordinate to the gaze and knowledge of the other, a man. Helena loans her ear so that Jano can examine it and ends up adapting herself to the role to which the masculine gaze subjects her.

In contrast to the woman–mother and woman–lover opposition, Amalia, the holy girl, puts forth the disequilibrium of *absolute surrender*. The stories read in the catechism seminar stage a third model that questions and undoes the others. The catechism teacher, it is true, cannot deal with the stories of the woman who dies in the accident and of the profane woman who gives up everything to care for the misfortunate. Yet, beyond their morbidness, these stories fit into a logic of sacrifice that does not question doctrine. The ghost of the dead mother saves her son's life and the profane woman abandons everything to devote herself to charity. What can we do, however, with the story that Amalia and Josefina read, in which a woman "dressed in Divine Charity" affirms that "it is better to suffer more in our world for the salvation of one soul than to to be in the glory of Our Lord?"[84] And even more—although the teacher does not know this part—since this disequilibrium leads Amalia to become impregnated with the body of the man whom she wants to save (she sniffs his shaving cream with relish, then puts it on her shirt) and to pursue him? Amalia finds her *mission*, but this mission situates her beyond the rules of the religion that acted as her starting point. The girl–adolescent chooses the world, "our world," with all of its passion and all of its senses. She is a desiring subject rather than a desired object produced by the gaze of others.

Amalia triumphs: she is a girl and she is holy; she is beyond performance or representation in a world in which these frustrate all possibility for desire.

Los guantes mágicos: Noises on the Surface

The acousmatic provides the image in Lucrecia Martel's films with a prominence and a depth accentuated by the superimposition and fragmentation of bodies, creating a striated realm for the offscreen space (of its sounds or of the unseen). In contrast, sounds in Rejtman's films are almost always within the image: the immense loudspeakers, the engine of the Renault 12, or the gym-goer who pants and puffs, almost always in the frame, almost always visible.[85] Rejtman's is a smoothed-out space. His motto is "cinema is surface, never depth" (1999, 130). Sounds are not somewhere else (behind, to the side, underneath); they are signs inscribed in the image. In the positions of characters and of objects Martel and Rejtman differ as well: whereas in the work of Martel a body is always behind another body, Rejtman locates bodies along the same line, as though, instead of being distributed in space, they are drawn on the same screen.[86] The enemy of the mise-en-scène in Rejtman is the perspective that creates the depth of field, because this tends to create an abominable system of hierarchies. In an interview with Alan Pauls (2004), Rejtman said that in his movies there exists "a kind of utopia: a world where everything has the same value." This neutrality and sparseness, already evident in *Silvia Prieto,* is spread so extensively throughout *Los guantes mágicos* that in this film we can speak neither of dramatic progression nor narrative climax. This extends to a mise-en-scène that never privileges a character with a close-up or uses a shot/reverse shot for dialogues and that does not establish a hierarchy among the characters through their location in space.[87] The scene of snow in Buenos Aires, for example, which could have inspired a certain delay, underscoring the event as miraculous, is limited to a brief and lovely scene of the protagonist getting out of a car: a neutral register for an extraordinary event. It is even difficult to determine what *Los guantes mágicos* speaks of, what its theme is and what its definitions are. The leitmotifs of Rejtman's narratives and films undoubtedly appear, but everything is presented on the same surface, without relief or emphasis.

Because of the number of events that occur and the at times outrageous and unpredictable shifts or tangents, it is as difficult to summarize the plot of *Los guantes mágicos* as that of *Silvia Prieto.* The story begins on a rainy day in the taxi (a Renault 12) of Alejandro (Gabriel "Vicentico" Fernández Capelli). In the backseat the passenger Sergio "Piranha" Romano (Fabián Arenillas) recognizes him. According to Sergio, the taxi driver had been a classmate of his brother Luis (Diego Olivera), now living in Canada. He invites Alejandro and his girlfriend Cecilia (Cecilia Biagini) to have dinner at his house, but the couple fight, and Alejandro decides to go alone. Susana, Piranha's wife, is a travel agent and also a busybody. To mend the relationship, she calls up Cecilia and recommends a trip to a spa in Brazil. When Cecilia returns from her trip, Alejandro goes to the airport to pick her up and meets Valeria (Valeria Bertuccelli), a stewardess with whom he begins a relationship. Because of his fight with Cecilia, Alejandro ends up living in Luis' apartment, which he gets through Piranha. Cecilia meets Daniel (Leonardo Azamor), a dog walker, and begins a relationship that hinges on the tranquilizers that they consume. Then Luis comes from Canada to film a pornographic movie, moves back into his apartment, where Alejandro is living, and sets up a gym and an impromptu studio where he films various scenes with the Russian actors who have traveled with him to Argentina. From conversations that he has with his brother, Piranha comes up with an incredible business idea: to import magic gloves from Hong Kong, taking advantage of a cold front moving in on Buenos Aires. The first shipment is a success, and Alejandro sells his car to invest in gloves and continue importing. The second shipment, however, takes longer than expected to arrive, and when it reaches the port of Buenos Aires, the heat frustrates all possibility of selling the merchandise. The characters end up thus: Susana travels to Brazil and does not return; Luis returns to Canada to pursue his career as a pornographic actor; Cecilia develops a relationship with Hugh (Pietr Krysav), one of the Russian-Canadian porn actors; Piranha keeps making money; Alejandro, who continues his relationship with Valeria, goes from being a taxi driver to being a bus driver. Oh, and I forgot: before Alejandro and Cecilia separated, they fought over the fact that Cecilia did not want to go out dancing ("I don't want to be surrounded by eighteen-year-olds"). The last scene shows Alejandro in a club dancing to New Order's "Vanishing Point."[88]

Sheltered from a World

At the end of *Rapado*, Lucio is waiting for the bus that will take him home. The brother of his new friend passes by with a group of adolescents who are skateboarding. Lucio watches the group with interest and then touches the little doll he has been carrying, only to discover that once again he has left his watch at a friend's house. The seduction of the skaters coming toward him, harmoniously and at full speed, is better understood through the lens of the short story "Quince cigarillos" from Rejtman's *Velcro y yo*: "In a sort of trance, the six skater girls turn in circles around a stereo, as though it were an object of adoration in a primitive cult. I recognize in these circles the construction of a *perfect and closed world* from which I am excluded. All of this sweat for an abstraction, I think. I don't know if I'll ever be able to enter into that world" (1996, 89). The *world* is the capacity to organize with the series an idea of community, an intensity of temporality, a pleasure in meaning. All in all, it is a shelter, in the fullest sense of the word: a refuge that gives equilibrium to perpetual movement.

The idea of the magic gloves leads the characters to an obsession with making money, and Alejandro to hilarious and ruthless exchanges. (He ends up losing it all and becoming a bus driver.) As in *Silvia Prieto,* the motif of the plot (the confusion of the names, the glove business) appears once the worlds within which the characters circulate have already been introduced. (A fade-out marks, in both films, this shift.) The series are already in operation; we need only ask what the characters do with them. Both protagonists have their world; beginning with this fade-out, they enter into the series of names or of magic gloves, with which they can barely construct another equilibrium.

Before the magic gloves business appears, the characters' lives move through three series: the series of health, work with the body, and transportation. The *series of transportation of passengers* (as Valeria ironically deems it) opens the film and is part of what the second Silvia Prieto (Mirta Busnelli) defines as "services for the middle class"—from the highest rung of international flights that Valeria, the charter stewardess, never reaches to the lower rungs of long-distance bus rides and dog walking, a genuine service for the middle class. Alejandro feels a special affection for the Renault 12, and not just his own.[89] With a few alterations (a mirrored ball, colored lights, and dance music), the car can be transformed into a miniature disco, which is what Alejandro likes most. In this series, there is continuity among play, pleasure, and the workplace: not only does Alejandro enjoy his car, but Valeria says that she is a stewardess because airplanes remind her of the dollhouses she played with as a girl.

The *series of health* is found crouched within the bodies of all the characters and is introduced with a certain consistency at the age of forty. Alejandro is thirty-six, and as his doctor tells him, "You are closer to forty than to thirty." It is a strange time of life because illnesses do not tend to have an organic origin, as happens in old age, or a purely emotional one, as in youth. They are a mixture of both, and this depresses the characters even more: "Is depression organic or emotional? Do the two states combine to become more intense, or do they cancel each other out?" asks Daniel, the dog walker. Cecilia and Susana also enter into this world of depressed people and turn to the series of antidepressants and sedatives: a true catalog (and Rejtman's cinema finds narration in catalogs): Valium, Xanaz,

Melatol, Alplax, haloperidol, and many others.[90] "Is yours organic or emotional? Your depression, I mean," Cecilia asks Daniel. And he replies: "Mine is one hundred percent emotional, let's not screw around. If it's somehow organic, I'll kill myself." (That is, Daniel affirms that he is *still* young.) The series of health refers also to the comic series of doctors: Alejandro goes first to an ear doctor and ends up with a prescription for glasses from an optometrist who presents his motto as soon as he enters: "First I prescribe, then I examine."

The *series of work with the body* arrives with Luis and appears with relative persistence in Rejtman's literature. "Barras" ("Bars," in *Velcro y yo*), one of his most successful stories, tells the story of a girl who works bagging groceries in a supermarket and, after being fired, discovers the advantages of having a gym in her own apartment. She moves from barcodes to the bars of gym equipment. Rejtman's interest in gym culture lies in the fact that it constitutes its own world, with its own food, drinks, vitamin supplements, and routines (see Beatriz Sarlo in Birgin and Trímboli 2003, 131). Just as depressed people find comfort and a topic of conversation with others who suffer from the illness, gym-goers construct among themselves a world of belonging. Fragile, perhaps, but not for this reason insignificant. The end of "Bars" reads: "The four [gym-goers] seem to have reached an *equilibrium* in their lives where routine transforms easily into pleasure and pleasure into routine" (Rejtman 1996, 65, my emphasis).

Equilibrium is an ideal in Rejtman's movies. There is something more, however, for this fascination with gym-goers or porn actors is related to work, with the production of money and with a verifiable progression: work on the body has the peculiarity that it is clearly perceived. Muscular "toning" (each world has its own slang) allows what work can no longer achieve in society—progressive and sustained progress with visible results—to be achieved within the body itself. In *Liquid Modernity,* Zygmunt Bauman lucidly observes that "postmodern society engages its members primarily in their capacity as consumers rather than producers" (2000, 76).

What is key about this change is that "[l]ife organized around consumption...*must do without norms*" (82, my emphasis), because it can never be satisfied. This means that "being in shape" (as Piranha's brother says to Alejandro) is an ideal that can never be entirely fulfilled, even though it can be measured at first glance. In a world that is permanently changing and that denies us recognition, carrying the traces of work in the body itself is not insignificant: we need only consider Luis and Alejandro's bodies and the advice on going to the gym that Valeria gives the latter. In the pornographic actors this use of the body for work reaches its apex, for what matters is less an action (working out) than being well-endowed by nature. The risk here is shown in one of the last images of the film, when the characters see the cover of the pornographic video and cannot recognize Piranha's brother because he is wearing a mask. He could be anyone: he gains a body but loses a face.

At any rate, for someone as disoriented as Alejandro, living with Luis becomes a nightmare, for his down time, full of dreams and incomprehensible noises, clashes with the corporeal sounds and regulated and full time of the pornographic gym (in the same room where he sleeps). Luis exits the story just as he enters: he returns to Canada and continues the same job, and the experience of the magic gloves remains only as a bad memory. In contrast, Alejandro suffers a series of losses, beginning with that which defines him, the Renault 12. His movement from taxi driver to bus driver is not auspicious, especially since he is nearing forty. However, he does gain something: a girlfriend and the possibility of continuing to go to the club to dance to New Order's "Vanishing Point," a song that finds hope in the notion that "life is short but love is strong."

Of all the films of the new Argentine cinema, Rejtman's most fully attacks the idea of the signified, searching for its own flight line (its "vanishing point") in sounds, perception, materials. As with the name Silvia Prieto, which means nothing, what sets the story into motion here is the signifier. In *Los guantes mágicos,* the flight line is the music that Alejandro dances to.[91] With this song, the taxi driver manages to transform noise into music. In the face of aging, time, and the inclemency of life, Alejandro cannot return to twenty, but he can, as he dances, feel an intensity that releases him from the demands of the present.

Speech Acts

There is a world that contains these others, and it is Rejtman's. The neutral, the leveled mise-en-scène, the hilarious series, and the discrete and ascetic composition are among the features that make his films immediately recognizable. The most identifiable element of his films, however, is in the field of sound and in his treatment of voices. With the material of common expressions, the filmmaker works obsessively on the search for a *tone,* artificial and neutral, that runs throughout the film.

For this reason, rather than being an expression of content, the dialogues are sound or, to use the actress Rosario Bléfari's expression, previously quoted, a "cadence." At the same time that we say *something,* we say the saying itself. Or, to use an expression of Paul Valèry, quoted by Paolo Virno in an epigraph to *Quando il verbo se fa carne* (2003): "Before it even *signifies* anything, all emission of language *indicates* that *someone is speaking.*" And we express a meaning not only in the content of what we say but also in the tone, the cadence, or the volume. Rejtman's voices move from the guttural to the fully articulated (the voice-over), just as the sounds move from deafening noises to a pleasant melody. In *Silvia Prieto,* the limit is reached (or heard) with the performance of the rock band El otro yo and the bassist María Fernanda Aldana shouting and screeching herself hoarse. The event forms a world based on something that is beyond the sign or articulated speech.[92] Something similar happens with Alejandro in *Los guantes mágicos* when he breaks up with Cecilia because, according to her, they are too old to go dancing at a club and gets together with Valeria, with whom he goes out dancing several times. As they dance, their dialogues are muffled by the music, but this does not prevent their relationship from growing stronger. Rather than what is said (or screamed), what matters is that they want to talk and make themselves visible to one another.

We could therefore sketch out a decibel meter of the new Argentina cinema, based not on what characters say but on what they mumble, whisper, shout, or babble. It would be a map of tones, showing the meaning of tones and not of words. In this map, *Pizza, birra, faso* would register the highest decibels; the insults hurled by the characters would mean nothing more than the impossibility of communicating with each other. (To give just one example: "What are you doing, you son of a bitch?!? Are you crazy, son of a bitch, fuck your mother! Asshole, son of a bitch, I'm going to kill you!!") In *Pizza, birra, faso,* the real is the insult. According to Silviano Santiago, the insult in subaltern classes has to do with the absence of a perceptible enemy (2004). Through the insult, they show their discomfort with the world; hate does not manage to articulate a story or a meaning. In contrast, Lisandro Alonso's two films form maps of silence in which the voices, when they appear, do so with the sole goal of growing quiet once again. These voices border on the incomprehensible and the inaudible: one must speak minimally and in a low voice because society is impossible. Tambornino, Moreno, and Rosell's *El descanso* extracts a good part of its humor from the voice of José Palomino Cortez, whose Peruvian intonations refer to professorial rhetoric and the diction of radio announcers. On our map, the film would be a country superimposed with the mass media. The humor stems from our witnessing how, in contemporary life, we are spoken to by the media. One of the most central and striking regions would be occupied by Lucrecia Martel. With a multidimensional project, Martel has not only worked on the voices of her principal characters and their different intonations but also left behind, out of the frame, a series of whispers and incomprehensible voices that remain unintelligible. It is as though in these voices something of the desire as opacity that defines her films is encoded. There are expressions, dialogues, statements, but these never reach their destination. Finally, on this map, there would be an island: Rejtman Island.

On this island, the dialogues are revealing for the processes of defamiliarization and familiarity that they provoke. They seem artificial, sound monotonous, do not register ups and downs. If we listen to them with greater attention, however, are they not closer to the daily speech of the middle-class than any other movie? Image and sound are defamiliarizing machines that do not go in search of the unexplored (as in Alonso and Martel) but work with the material of typical places or, per Silvia Schwarzböck, "an audiovisual guide of common places" (1999).[93] In one scene in *Los guantes mágicos*, "typical places" are referenced, taking on the form of an audiovisual guide: long traveling shots of the streets and touristy monuments of Buenos Aires are shown to the Russian actors. The sequence shows a procedure characteristic of Rejtman: to see the familiar through foreign eyes—discovering what is attractive about the Monument of the Spanish or the Obelisk or, as in *Silvia Prieto*, a Chinese restaurant or average barbeque place. Something similar happens with voices in his movies. In the beginning a tone seems strange to us, but after a while it seems that if we listen to ourselves speak, we are actually much closer to Rejtman's world than to any other.

In this way, Rejtman's movies begin with the principle of the series and banish with a single stroke affections that are anchored in audiovisual language, above all in television, such as confession, emphasis, unburdening, emotion, vehemence, pathos. Or, in the language of the cinematographic mise-en-scène: the close-ups, the hierarchization of bodies, the acceleration of editing, the dramatic crescendo, and the depth of field. The first figure that corresponds to Rejtman's cinema is the *withdrawal of distance*. His films always observe at a moderate distance, locating characters on the same plane, locating typical phrases in such a way that it is as though we are hearing them for the first time. For this reason, the second figure is the *find*. With neither emphasis nor underlining, the find is not displayed but must be discovered by the spectator. The path of *acsesis* that Silvia Prieto and Alejandro follow is also that of the spectator and of Rejtman's work: withdrawing to learn to look, listen, confront the exceptionality of the typical. In a world overpopulated with images and messages, this detachment is not a bad way to draw near to colorful surfaces and the nuances of sounds.

The Use of Genre: Trips and Detours

The new Argentine cinema is not, in broad outline, a cinema that turns to genre. Many of its films, however, have used genre partially and in a very specific way. Turning to the frame of expectations that each genre establishes beforehand, to its codes and its rules, many films have found a launching point that ends in often unclassifiable results. *Silvia Prieto, Tan de repente, El bonaerense, Un oso rojo,* or *Sábado,* for example, without belonging strictly to a given genre, allow us to see certain generic forms against the light, whether as citation, basic scheme, or narrative ideal. This is immediately obvious, for example, in the extremely common genre of the crime or detective narrative. In the 1980s, this genre allowed filmmakers to reflect on the violence of the recent dictatorship years. Movies such as Adolfo Aristarain's *Últimos días de la víctima* (1982), Juan Carlos Desanzo's *En retirada* (1984, "In Retirement"), Sergio Renán's *Sentimental* (1980, released in the United States and the United Kingdom as *Sentimental*), José Martínez Suárez's *Noches sin lunas ni soles* (1984, released in the United States as *Nights without Moons and Suns*), and Aníbal di Salvo's *Seguridad personal* (1985, "Personal Security") dealt, more or less explicitly, with the recent years of violence, often in a political vein, as in the first two screenplays written by José Pablo Feinmann. In all of these cases, however, filmmakers turned to the conventions of the genre, and this did not inspire a corrosive reading, against the grain.[94] The crime as enigma, the central figure of the police detective or private investigator, the schema of the persecution as the structure of the plot, even the presence of the femme fatale, are elements that trace a line of continuity among the classic proposals of the genre and its variants in the 1980s.

In contrast, in the new Argentine cinema, there is an implicit but obvious refusal to turn to this genre. Perhaps the movie that most closely approximates the conventional paradigm of crime or detective fiction is *Un oso rojo,* although its combination of crime and Western ends up producing a rather original hybrid from the point of view of genre.[95] The other film that could be included in this genre is *El bonaerense,* but its point of view and the use it makes of the rules are so particular that, to define its forms, it is first necessary to make a series of detours.

Surprisingly, one of the most common genres in the new Argentine cinema is the comedy. Or perhaps that surprise stems from the fact that, since the 1950s, Argentine film has shown itself to be somewhat reluctant to revisit a genre with one of the more interesting traditions. (The 1940s saw the execution of solid comedies by directors such as Manuel Romero, Leopoldo Torres Ríos, Carlos Schlieper, and Carlos Hugo Christensen and by talented actors such as Pepe Arias, Osvaldo Miranda, Juan Carlos Thorry, and Niní Marshall.) Rejtman's films; Villegas' *Sábado;* Alejandro Fadel, Martín Mauregui, Santiago Mitre, and Juan Schnitman's *El amor (primera parte)* (2005, "Love [Part 1]"); Diego Lerman's *Tan de repente;* Juan Taratuto's *No sos vos, soy yo* (2004, "It's Not You, It's Me"); Gabriel Lichtmann's *Judíos en el espacio*; Pablo Trapero's *La familia rodante;* and Sergio Bizzio's *Animalada* (2001, "Animal") are some of the movies that could be deemed comedies or that play with the genre. What is most original about several of these movies is that they try to combine the timing of the comedic genre with the dead or empty time of the new cinema. The bet is a risky one, and although some of these movies die trying, all appear to uphold the idea that the only real laughter is that which arises from this encounter. Laughter is provoked on one hand by the genre and on the other by the discovery of the real.

Comedy: Speed and Chance (*Tan de repente* and *Sábado*)

Tragedy is the necessity of having your own experience and learning from it; comedy is the possibility of having it in good time.

—Stanley Cavell (1981, 238)

Comedy is tragedy plus time.

—Woody Allen, *Crimes and Misdemeanors*

Without warning, just like that, *Tan de repente* (all of a sudden). As its title suggests, Diego Lerman's *opera prima* is the result of a clash of various speeds. The first part of the film demonstrates this with a rigorous system of shots and an almost mathematical precision. On one hand, we have the slow time, of medium and fixed shots, and pans that show Marcia (Tatiana Saphir) going to work. An employee in a lingerie shop, Marcia is somewhat unattractive, struggles with her weight, and in her loneliness cannot stop calling an ex-boyfriend to whom she cannot work up the nerve to speak. On the other hand, there is the convulsive and accelerated time of Mao (Carla Crespo) and Lenin (Verónica Hassan), two bold young women, dressed in black and with short hair, who steal a motorcycle and play on pin-ball machines and are followed by a nervous hand-held camera, in a series of travellings and rapid editing. The back and forth between these scenes marks an opposition between Marcia and Mao/Lenin, the fat girl and the thin ones, yoga and frenzy, work and idleness, boredom and adventure, the reality principle and the pleasure principle.

But all of a sudden, in the street, Mao sees Marcia and falls in love. From this point on, the two speeds start to collide and to contaminate each other. Mao and Lenin pursue Marcia and finally manage to meet her face to face. "Do you want to screw?" Mao says to Marcia impetuously. What are Mao's intentions with this declaration without further ado? Does she want to enter into the slowness of her brand-new object of desire, or is she trying to accelerate the other's life? All of the humor in this first dialogue stems from this play of speeds:

> "Is there something wrong with you?" Marcia says indignantly.
> "I fell in love," Mao states...."*Give me some time*....Don't you like sex?"
> "Without love it doesn't interest me."
> "Don't talk about love because that's got nothing to do with it."

The comedy emerges from the clash of speeds, which is also a clash of genres: Marcia's *costumbrismo* (and the dead time of work) and the road-movie nomadism of Mao and Lenin (and the full time of adventure). With force and with threats, Mao and Lenin manage to drag Marcia into their time, taking her away on a road movie: stealing a taxi, entering the highway, traveling to a beach, encountering the sea. With Marcia's voluntary entrance into the sea (as a kind of test), the first part of *Tan de repente* ends: the duo becomes a trio, and the different speeds merge into one.[96]

The second part takes to the extreme the story's unexpected events. The young women hitchhike to the coastal town of San Clemente del Tuyú. They are picked up by a veterinarian (Susana Pampín) who tells them about the orca whales in the aquarium and invites them to visit it. However, and also unexpectedly, the protagonists decide to go to Rosario because, according to Lenin, "one of my great-aunts who I'm not sure is still alive lives there." After a ride in a truck and crashing into a parachuter on the highway (which gives rise to a song in an invented language that will return at the film's end),[97] Mao, Lenin, and Marcia reach Rosario, where they search for and find Aunt Blanca (Beatriz Thibaudin). "The road movie," Cozarinsky writes, "is being transformed into a *costumbrista* comedy" (2003, 181).

The arrival at Blanca's house, where two other guests, Delia (María Merlino) and Felipe (Marcos Ferrante), also live, maintains the alternating rhythm, but its logic changes entirely. Whereas in the first part two speeds of the present confronted one another, in the second the rhythms of the present clash with those of the past. The combinations become more complex: two trios encounter each other, but the alternation is maintained in the relationships of Mao and Marcia on one hand and Lenin and Blanca on the other. With the arrival of Delia and Felipe, the encounters multiply, and the story ends with three unexpected pairs: Lenin and Marcia together on a bus en route to Buenos Aires, with the parachuter's music in the background (the pleasurable incorporation of chance into their lives); Mao and Felipe in the aquarium seeing the feats of the orca whale (incorporation of the adventure); and Blanca, who dies, with Delia, who takes charge of Blanca's house and her chickens (incorporation of domestic happiness). It is Blanca who, with a full vitality and her sudden death, ends up adjusting the energy of the other characters.

When they arrive at Blanca's house, the protagonists' velocity stops and layers of time begin to accumulate. Marcia turns up in a flower-power dress, and Delia's manners seem to be from another era. We could say that, in the humor of stereotypes, the movie moves from punk frenzy to hippie good vibes. But whereas Marcia and Mao try to continue the story from the first part (finally, in Rosario, they make love), the weight of the past splits Lenin in two. Mao and Marcia discover, with great delight, that Lenin's real name is Verónica. In this way, a new layer of time is incorporated into a film that up until now has been pure present. (Even if it was an open present, like that of the road movie.) On one of the walls of Blanca's house, there is a panel with old photographs, and Verónica draws near more than once to observe them. Wisely, the camera emphasizes nothing, but it is not difficult to notice the intensities that run through Verónica–Lenin's body and that will culminate in sobbing and a failed phone call to her mother after Blanca's unexpected death. Tragedy advances rapidly, because the "all of a sudden" also includes, or includes above all, death. The fall of the parachute triggers the comic absurd, and Blanca's fall, during a boating excursion, the tragic absurd. The tragic and the comic are two potentialities of the only thing that interests us in *Tan de repente:* life as an adventure.

After stopping in Blanca's house, the movie in its final dispersion recuperates its tone of absurd comedy, in the style of the Finnish filmmaker Aki Kaurismäki. Ultimately, the genre allows Lerman to investigate our ways of perceiving time, interpreting it through chance, fate, the unexpected, the inevitable. In the song that Blanca sings, in a performance that recovers something of her youth and destroys her age, we hear: "We struggle against fate/if time has separated us/because God wanted it that way."[98] Whereas the first part of the movie consists of the triumph of speed and adventure, the second is constituted by the discovery of experience and the magic of everyday habits. Through Blanca, we see that Mao, Lenin, and Marcia can incorporate other speeds and other temporalities to later return to their lives.

People Who Come and Who Go

Juan Villegas' *Sábado* is another of the new Argentine cinema's comedies. Its tone recalls Eric Rohmer, as does its inclination for the theme of probabilities and chance, so dear to the French director. In his first film, Villegas constructs a story that follows the crossing of paths of three couples and that takes place during an entire day between two car accidents. The three couples are Camila (Camila Toker) and Leopoldo (Leonardo Murúa), Gastón (Gastón Pauls) and Andrea (Eva Sola), and Natalia (Mariana Anghlieri) and Martín (Daniel Hendler). The first crash, between Martín and Gastón, occurs at the film's beginning, and the second, between Martín and Leopoldo, toward the end. Although the couples do not know each other, different coincidences cause them to run into each other, and hilarious dialogues ensue. Camila, who is a journalist, interviews Gastón and ends up sleeping with him. Andrea and Martín meet at the police station, where they went to report a car crash, but the relationship ultimately does not work and they break up abruptly. Leopoldo and Natalia run into each other at the entrance to a beauty parlor and decide to meet up at midnight, but she skips out on the date because she runs into Gastón and goes to have a drink with him. They do not begin the anticipated relationship, however, because Gastón takes advantage of Natalia's trip to the bathroom to leave the bar in a taxi. Camila returns home with Andrea (they had met in a café) and runs into Leopoldo at the entrance; she says good night to him without letting him in. The last scene repeats the first, but the following morning: Natalia is at home with Martín, and they are preparing tea and pastries. After they exchange a few sad and unfortunate words, Natalia understands that everything is ending, and a tear falls from her eye. Martín asks whether she is crying and she denies it. Although it is a comedy of misunderstandings, *Sábado* is also a movie shot through with melancholy.[99]

In addition to the coincidental encounters, the dialogues, which never cease to spring from the most banal themes or the most awkward misunderstandings, give the film its particular texture. Its degree of artificiality and defamiliarizing effect has led some critics to group *Sábado* with Rejtman's work. However, the same effect is in reality a product of two logics that are quite different from— perhaps even opposed to—one another. In contrast to what happens in *Silvia Prieto* or *Los guantes mágicos,* in *Sábado* the subject is always implicated in what he or she has. What makes conversations happen is the desire to be loved and the fear that one is not. In *Silvia Prieto* the characters put typical phrases into circulation; in *Sábado* they try, tirelessly, to embed themselves within them. Leopoldo and Camila in a car:

Leopoldo: Do you want me to be quiet?
(Silence)
L: Why don't you say it?
Camila: Say what?
L: That you want me to be quiet.
C: I didn't say anything.
L: Do you want me to be quiet?
C: Yes, be quiet.
L: Okay, if you want me to be quiet, I'll be quiet.
(Silence)
C: Okay, if you want to talk, talk, but don't be annoying.

In the movie, the processes of *crystallization* of love of which Stendhal speaks ("I call 'crystallization' that action of the mind that discovers new perfections in its beloved at every turn of events" [1966, 221]) confront what we could call *processes of decrystallization*. Although the conflict that runs through every couple is never made transparent, we can infer that Camila and Leopoldo, and Natalia and Martín, are facing definitive break-ups. In the first case, it is because she is no longer in love with, or even attracted to, Leopoldo. (Their last encounter is particularly pathetic, when he appears with a stuffed animal as a gift, which she accepts condescendingly.) In the case of the second couple, the break-up is implicit because they no longer understand one another, and everything that they say leads to a misunderstanding. The relationship ends not because it is facing a huge crisis but because spontaneous and frank dialogue can no longer take place.

In this process of decrystallization, the features of the loved object are no longer the source of new idealizations but the repeated discovery that the other is someone ordinary (even if we once loved them). Natalia, who has just met Leopoldo, finds his messy hair attractive (that is, it has the capacity to undergo crystallization); Camila, his girlfriend, finds it "disgusting." As love is already gone, each question is received as the answer to another question, and each act of communication culminates in a misunderstanding. As Barthes says, "[T]here is always a terrorism of the question; a power is implied in every question. The question denies the right not to know or the right to indeterminacy of desire" (2005, 107).

When there is crystallization, in contrast, there are no questions, or questions form only part of a game of seduction in which neither suspicion nor irritation has a place. This function of crystallization is fulfilled by the well-known actor Gastón Pauls, who plays himself. In contrast to what occurs in the rest of the film, the dialogue between Gastón and the women forms not a part of the paranoid counterpoint but a game in which any question can spawn any response, because desire is already present from the beginning. Camila the journalist asks Gastón:

Camila: If you had to choose between being who you are and being someone completely unknown, what would you choose?

Gastón: What's the first thing you do when you get up in the morning?

C: How old were you when you kissed a girl for the first time?

G: How old were you when you tied your shoelaces for the first time?
C: Favorite season of the year.
G: Thursday.
C: Favorite insult.
G: Water heater.

The three women desire Gastón Pauls not for who he is ("I am me," Pauls says at one point) but because he is the famous Gastón Pauls. Given his place in the media, he is already crystallized; the question of whether they desire him makes no sense, as Camila makes plain when he asks her, after they have made love, "Did you sleep with me because you like me or because I'm Gastón Pauls?" Camilia responds that it is a stupid question and not worth answering. Andrea, his first girlfriend, has already told him that if he weren't Gastón Pauls they never would have met. And with Natalia the fact that she wants to sleep with him because he is famous is so evident that the actor leaves the movie by taxi, never again appearing. For the others the conflict is in the fact that their relationships are ending; for Gastón Pauls it consists in the fact that he is so crystallized in the eyes of others that any relationship is impossible. Every process of crystallization works against a process of decrystallization. This is why in Pauls there is no *process* and why he is the only person who does not change throughout the story. For there is no possible *beginning* for poor Gastón: the others do not know (*conocer*) him, but they recognize (*re-conocer*) him, only approaching him to ask for an autograph or to sleep with him.[100] "It's difficult being famous," he says again and again, and confesses, "Sometimes I'd like to be unknown for awhile." Thus, while the conflict of the other characters is that desire has already died out (entering into the process of decrystallization), Pauls' conflict is that desire is already present beforehand (the process of crystallization happens outside of him). With an anti-televisual mise-en-scène (in the sequence shots, in the acting, in the framing, in the ellipsis), *Sábado* is the only movie of the new Argentine cinema to invoke all the stars of the small screen, showing us how the media installs itself within the chemistry of our desire. Nothing gives us such a full and sublime pleasure as the restitution of a famous person.

Sábado is a movie about the desire for the other and how, when this desire becomes opaque, lovers fall into drama. Complementarily, observing these missed connections and misunderstandings makes us laugh. In an article with the hyperbolic title "The Last Representative of the New Wave," Rafael Filippelli correctly notes, "It is as though

the comedy were the director's and the drama the characters'"
(2001, 8). *Sábado*'s laughter emerges from the typical procedures
of comedy: "the periodic repetition of a word or of a scene,
the symmetric inversión of roles, the geometric development of
misunderstandings" (Bergson 2002, 35), and from an intense use
of chance and coincidence. The car crashes are repeated symmetri-
cally; the characters run into one another as though they were the
only inhabitants of the city; phrases are repeated in an inverted or
modified fashion. (Gastón tells Natalia that she has "the face for
short hair"; in an earlier scene, Leopoldo has told her that she has
"the face for long hair").

Natalia explains the theory of chance in the film and holds that
probabilities do not exist. What already happened is the only thing
that was probable, and what did not happen would be improbable.
In this conception, chance is the insufficiency of probabilities in fore-
sight. Natalia carries this conception to its most absurd consequences
and treats the future as if it were a given: each of the six sides has
the same probability of coming up, but, as she avers in her obstinacy,
only the one that came up was the one with *all* of the possibilities
of coming up. If all these comic misunderstandings slip permanently
toward drama it is because coincidence is paradoxically linked to the
fact that the characters do not want to see the truth of their desire. To
what extent does Martín, the typical comic character of the distracted
man who gets into car crashes, use his absentmindedness in order not
to see that Natalia is no longer in love with him?[101] The more or less
coincidental encounters with Gastón Pauls—aren't they evidence of
the fact that he is an object of desire par excellence, on this side of
desire? And the random encounter between Camilia and Andrea—
doesn't it happen because of Camila's need to tell someone that she
slept with Pauls (the pleasure of having done it lies in talking about
it) and because of Andrea's need to recognize that she is one of many
conquests of the man who seduces without having to devote himself
to seducing?

The end of the story is beyond all dialogue and all comedy. Rather
than a happy ending or anagnorisis (or recognition), we see Natalia
unable to avoid tears, pretending not to cry when faced with Martín's
questions. The kiss, anticipated in the first scene, never happens, and
the reencounter that the screwball comedy promises (the wedding
or remarriage) fails. For only an instant, and very faintly, the movie
lets us see the autumnal melancholy that is its inspiration: the death
of love.

The Return of Comedy

One feature allows us to explain the return of comedy in Rejtman, Villegas, or Lerman, despite the fact that it cannot be extended to all comedies of the period and although there are great differences among the movies. This feature is the dialectic between order and chance. What is it that made this clash so attractive to these directors? Why, in a certain moment, did the comedy's discretionarily ordered coincidences become the theme of so many films?

One reason is that the rejection of the identitarian demand opened up a greater field of thematic possibilities and freed directors from profundity and density. The question "Who are we?" was displaced by "How do we desire?"—with all of the humorous and melancholic consequences that this question triggers. Another explanation is that the order of preference of cinematographic tastes in 1990s Argentina was modified: the films of Eric Rohmer and François Truffaut, the screwball comedy and Howard Hawks displaced the cinephile pantheon of Ingmar Bergman and the psychological drama. There were, in addition, new discoveries: the films of the Kaurismäki brothers, Jim Jarmusch, and Takeshi Kitano were the revelation of a global slapstick that works with dead or empty time and more contemporary materials. Yet perhaps the most significant fact is that through chance and the unexpected these stories investigate the functioning of a world beyond what its subjects might like—because desire is rarely what a person wants, and comedies show us precisely that. Through misunderstandings, accidents, and the absurd, we discover, through laughter, that we are closer to the automaton than to the omnipotent living being we think we are. Comedy is a very apt mode to speak of the setbacks of desire; it is the genre that shows why it is so complex to obtain something that we desire and why not getting it can be, from the outside, so funny. *Silvia Prieto, Tan de repente,* and others show what gets in the way of our desires and, through laughter, speak (although they might appear to be speaking of something else) of how difficult it is to move around in a world that is increasingly strange.

Pablo Trapero's *El bonaerense*: The Genre of Corporatism

Let's begin with genre. At least three genres meet in a particular way in Pablo Trapero's movie *El bonaerense*: the crime film, the police procedural drama, and the *Bildungsroman,* or novel of individual development or formation. The first is a variety of crime fiction and the second is one of the least prestigious examples of detective films (both were very important in the films of the 1940s); the third has a more dispersed presence in the history of film, but not for this a less important one.[102] The *Bildungsroman* genre establishes continuity and a dramatic crescendo in the narration, whereas the other two, which Trapero reads against the grain, provide the point of view. *El bonaerense*[103] tells the story of Eduardo "Zapa" Mendoza (Jorge Román), who, for having inadvertently participated in a crime, must abandon his hometown and join the Buenos Aires police force to avoid jail. Zapa becomes a cop and, once he has become a corporal, encounters an old friend who has tricked him in the past and whom he decides to betray. But Zapa himself is then betrayed by his superior, Captain Gallo (Darío Levy), who injures Zapa's leg with the goal of simulating an armed encounter. Now lame and with his new promotion, Zapa returns to his hometown.

Fox established the police procedural genre in 1945 as a semidocumentary style that presented "an explanation of police procedures from the prism and protagonisms of the agents of law" (Coma and Latorre 1981). Mervyn LeRoy's *FBI Story* (1959), with James Stewart and the legendary J. Edgar Hoover in a cameo, is a good example of a genre that never produced great works, in contrast to films that could be called antiprocedural, such as Orson Welles' *Touch of Evil* (1958), and others that took the suppositions of the procedural to its limits, such as Raoul Walsh and Bretaigne Windust's *The Enforcer* (1951). Through archival materials and with propagandistic goals, the procedural drama is an antecedent of television shows that use documentary videos of clashes between delinquents, persecutions, and arrests. *El bonaerense,* despite being far from a procedural (its goal is not to promote the supposed advantages of the Buenos Aires police force), tells the entire story from the point of view of the institution, through several of its members.

Another subgenre within the detective film but one that, in contrast to the police procedural, is based on the point of view of the marginal or outside of the law is the crime film. The best example of this genre is, undoubtedly, Raoul Walsh's *White Heat* (1949), with James Cagey, but there are numerous films in which the delinquent assumes the narrative voice (through the voice-over, and the camera accompanies him in his misfortunes, as in Jacques Tourneur's *Out of the Past* [1947] or, in a more contemporary version, Quentin Tarantino's *Reservoir Dogs*

[1992]). In the United States, the crime film has had a critical role, as it has not only promoted identification with the criminal but also shown society as dark, violent, unpredictable, and morally murky. As Javier Coma and José Maria Latorre point out, "[T]he citizen who decides to break the law and become a criminal expresses in many cases the insufficient ethics of the System" (1981, 104). The similarity between Trapero's film and this genre lies in the fact that adopting the protagonist's point of view excludes what does not belong to him or what he does not perceive. In the substation where Zapa works, two drunk cops shoot at point-blank range two young people, also presumably drunk, who go by on a motorcycle. The conflict is shown from Zapa's point of view (it is a subjective gaze), and in the moment shots are heard we see not the victims, who are not in the frame, but the cops who fire. Throughout the film, those who are outside of the police world are shown as bodies without outlines, without names, who represent trouble or a threat and whose greatest interaction with the police is in violent confrontation or to register a complaint.[104] In the same way as in the crime film, the story limits itself to a gaze that gives a tone to the entire narration.

Yet why invoke the police procedural if *El bonaerense* is far from being an edifying and pedagogical film? Why refer to the crime film if the perspective adopted is not that of the criminal but that of the agent of the law? The presence of crime and of all the characters and elements (police, guns, violent acts) directed at putting a stop to it suggest the multiform and extended detective genre that predominates in a good part of cinematographic production. Trapero's movie hands us all of the elements (armed confrontations, violent situations, shots, bodies, crimes, criminals, defenders of order, etc.), but any reference to a determined typology within the genre is bound to fail. If it is necessary to turn to approximate models that are incompatible with each other, such as the police procedural and the crime film, it is because the reading against the grain of these genres explains the *paradoxical initiation* that determines Zapa's entry into the institution: Zapa becomes part of the police force, the institution that combats crime, because he commits a crime.[105] This paradoxical initiation is repeated several times throughout the novel of Zapa's education: each time a change occurs in his institutional situation, we find crime and reward (never punishment) bound up together. He joins the police force because he commits a crime; he enters into confidence with his superior because he picks a lock; he gets a promotion because he participates clandestinely in a robbery. The borders between the crime film and the police procedural begin to vanish precisely because the stories of the criminal and of the institution that persecutes him blur together. The territories that the law traces are not as clear as the premises of the genre would seem to demand.

It is Zapa's own uncle who initiates him, who takes him out of jail and helps him to enter into the institution. From that point on, Zapa discovers a new world where corporate and affective ties are so powerful that everyone who enters the institution is immediately marked by a *double identity* of police officer and family member.[106] "Uncle Ismael" is, for his part, a higher-up in the Buenos Aires police force. Through his contacts, he puts his affective ties to work in the institution. He sends Zapa to San Justo, where he gets in touch with Pellegrino, another police officer who does a favor for Uncle Ismael by admitting his nephew. To join this world, Zapa is stripped of many of his attributes, which he will recover during the story. His name is no longer Zapa but Enrique Mendoza; his age is no longer thirty-two but twenty-eight (the age he needs to be to sign up); he loses his home, his family, his hometown, and also his trade.[107] The scene of passage is magnificently represented with the moment in which the protagonist's hair is cut: Zapa looks at himself in the mirror and finds Mendoza the trainee. Thus begins the novel of education of the young man who came from the provinces.

On the first rung of his slow and discrete ascent, Mendoza is a trainee and works as a servant. (He cleans the substation.) When he begins the course he transforms, in the words of his instructor, into a "larva" and an "animal." We can observe a clear process of infantilization in the classes (law, physical education, structure of the institution, narcotics, technique and practice of arrest) and in the repeated slogan of the teachers: "What are you laughing at?" The first ascent (not in degree but in the eyes of his superiors) occurs when Mendoza recovers his trade: he picks a lock and wins the sympathy and protection of Captain Gallo, one of the most charismatic leaders in the force. Mendoza becomes a "kid," an affectionate term that Gallo uses with him, and receives from this man a Browning from his own collection: "it's *personal*... when they give you your own, you'll give it back to me." The uncle's lesson (that of the value of personal relationships above institutional ones) acquires a new meaning for Mendoza; his relationship with his superior is based on favors and the exclusion of institutional mediation. Later, Gallo will name him assistant to Cáneva, who deals with collecting bribes or "extras"— the duality is also present in language. The new leap in his mediocre ascent through the ranks is due to his own merits, and in this case it is the institution that gives him access (the "diploma"). "You're a cop now," Mabel (Mimí Ardú) tells him. Then comes the moment when Mendoza can apply everything he has learned. Two scenes of arrest and confrontation with criminals further the paradoxical character of all of the protagonist's advances. In his intervention in a fight between gangs we see Mendoza for the first time in a strictly police activity; terrified, he barely knows how to control the group and only manages to fire shots into the air to frighten the rabble-rousers or to calm himself down. The second scene is superb. It consists of a shoot-out with a group of presumed criminals, in which Mendoza is admonished by a superior because he forgets to draw his weapon. The effectiveness of this scene lies in Trapero's maintenance of the police point of view to the extreme; we are never able to obtain a clear image of those who fire *from the other side*. Exteriority is a black, confusing, and impenetrable hole from which aggression and brutality erupt.[108] This is a key passage in Mendoza's novel of apprenticeship, because it is his *baptism by fire*. The scene lacks heroism. Mendoza has no talent or capacity to carry a weapon and act as a representative of the law, but he survives the shoot-out and can now consider himself part of the force. The following scene shows him trembling in a bar while he speaks with Gallo, who attempts to calm him down.

The last phase of Mendoza's education begins when the Pole (who had betrayed him with the safe) contacts him and offers him a role and part of the profits in an attempted robbery. The invitation allows Mendoza to organize his scene of revenge and to betray the Pole in cahoots with Gallo. The latter character gives him a final lesson and shows him why he should not confide in him with an educational response: "You trust me, don't you?" In the same moment he invokes trust, he kills the Pole and wounds Mendoza in the leg to invent a scenario of resistance on the victim's part. Mendoza's face is stained with the Pole's blood, and this is his *true* baptism by fire (not in the name of the institution, but in what is outside of it). In addition, Mendoza recovers his nickname, as the Pole shouts, "What are you doing, Zapa? Have you gone crazy?" Officer Mendoza wanted to get revenge on his ex-"boss" (as he calls him) but he was not able to see that his actual "boss" could be worse. For this reason, Mendoza becomes lame, but continues his ascent to corporal and later gets a transfer to his hometown, where he is warmly received by the police there.

Pedagogies

Zapa's apprenticeship occurs within his own body: he returns to his hometown diminished, without being able to understand very well what is being said to him, with nothing to say. His ascent in the institutional hierarchy corresponds to a physical and moral degradation. And his lameness converts his failure into a visible image and a daily burden. At any rate, Zapa learns to see the complexity of dependency and how education (in the case of a police officer) is subject to the whims of superiors. (The situation grows much worse when the dependency becomes indissoluble and without any possibility for change.) "Trust" as an act becomes, in this world, the greatest weakness; affections can never erase the hierarchy. Despite the protagonist's illusions, Gallo will never be his accomplice. Zapa discovers, finally, that this world that provides him with affect and shelter is the same one that subjects him to a cold and irreversible betrayal. He also understands the most important lesson: affect and betrayal are part of the same thing, in an institution that defines itself on the basis of personal relationships. Outside of the coldness of rules and norms, the passions of love and betrayal are an effect of the same process.

As Zapa learns, the spectator also experiences an apprenticeship that, in principle, is based on the suppression of an exterior judgment that condemns the characters without appeal. It is no coincidence that the film aroused indignation, especially among certain parts of the left. At the Havana Film Festival, for example, critics and spectators expressed dissatisfaction with a narration that at no point offers the comfort of a condemnation of what takes place. What is truly uncomfortable in *El bonaerense* is that we cannot identify with a single gaze that condemns the action of the characters. There is no character who allows us to judge what is happening; there is no avenging individual (as tends to happen in U.S. film) and no speech that offers the spectator the relief of feeling that he or she is recognized as a subject who judges the events from an external and impartial gaze. To accentuate this fact, Trapero erases all contextual political referents. Although the film can be linked to a famous expression of then-governor Eduardo Duhalde, "the best police in the world," the association is left up to the spectator; there is no reference in the movie that would lead us to connect the narration with political events of the era.[109] The possibility of an exterior gaze is instead parodied in the "aliens" who, according to Cáneva, are observing earthlings (not only police officers) from their planets and who think that humans are doing very, very badly.

The fact that none of the characters provides a model of moral conduct does not mean that all are on the same level. Gallo's bravado and Zapa's awkwardness contrast with the impotence of the captain who comes before Gallo and with Mabel's indignation. In fact, Mabel interrupts her passionate relationship with Mendoza because she condemns his subordination to Gallo and his excessively transgressive practices (and I say "excessive" because Mabel is far from the role of the avenging figure or one with an ethics strictly opposed to that of the institution). All of these confrontations occur within the codes of the world of the police; they do not affect the workings of an institution that seems to have no outside, as it does not accept the regulation of an objective order (the law).

El bonaerense incites us not to make a moral judgment but to observe how a world operates—a world, that of the police, that is capable of providing its members with shelter and something like a family, as the scene on Christmas Eve shows—paradoxically, as well, in a space watched over by the Virgin Mary and her purity, a symbolic protection that is evidently not heeded in the actions of its members. The story also invites us to understand what leads a good person like Zapa to enter into the criminal networks of the police institution. To see, then, how this production of belief operates can be more interesting than abiding by an evaluative or politicized reading of what happens.

Two logics intersect constantly in the story of Zapa's apprenticeship: the affective and the institutional. These, as we know, are incompatible from the moment an institution demands a depersonalization of relationships and is governed by norms that regulate relationships and exclude or suspend the affective. This is why the fact that Zapa joins the police because he commits a crime is so serious, as is the fact that he enters, through his uncle's influence, through a recommendation of an affective nature and not because he has a particular aptitude for the job. Not only is his entry marked by personal connections, but all of his life in the institution is deeply marked by a series of loyalties and favors that place charisma over effectiveness and the corporate moral over social rules. In fact, the most important phase of Zapa's apprenticeship takes place in the shadow of the political boss, Captain Gallo, who weaves a series of alliances based on privileges and acts of power that move past institutional orders. (Thus, against the instructions of the captain, he forces the secretary of the police station to pay Mendoza his salary by taking money out of the "petty cash," uses his influence to find him an apartment with cheap rent, and "personally" loans him a gun.[110]) Yet this communitarian or corporate life that will supposedly offer Zapa an affective refuge is also what provokes the betrayals that leave him disabled.

There are at least three betrayals in *El bonaerense*. The first occurs when the Pole betrays Zapa by sending him to open a safe for some thugs; the second when Zapa gets back at the Pole by revealing his plans to Gallo; the third when Gallo, having set up the shoot-out scene, wounds Mendoza and keeps the money.

In Part 1 of his *Cinéma*, "The Movement-Image," Deleuze analyzes how in U.S. cinema the figure of the traitor predominates in historical films and how betrayal is one of the paths to arrive at the Good (1986a, 215–16). Borges, in his "Theme of the Traitor and the Hero" (*Fictions*), shows another possible function of treason: to render visible the codes and values that link a group together. Paradoxically, treason is one of the most effective means to shore up a belief, and for this reason it is as functional to a cause as heroism. The betrayals in *El bonaerense* are far from heroic; instead, they produce unmentionable personal benefits and, rather than indications of possible integration, are the most obvious signs of disintegration. In the case of the Pole, the betrayal is directed against an employee and a friend (the Pole was like a father, we hear at one point in the film); in the case of Gallo, a subordinate is betrayed, indicating the disintegration of social and institutional ties.

Betrayal is a natural consequence of the way in which institutional life in the Buenos Aires police force is organized. When trust (the hope for a symbolic reward) is placed not in an institution but in people, everything is implicitly subjected to their fickleness and interests. (Here, trust is based on affection and not on shared rules.) And this subjection is even greater if, in the absence of a personal relationship such as that between Zapa and the Pole, there is no other protection than an institution such as the Buenos Aires police. This is the most important lesson that Mendoza learns: in an institution in which rules are never clear and affections are always present, betrayal is the only way to get ahead.

Ultimately, in this world, Zapa or Officer Mendoza can construct very little.[111]

3

A World without Narration
(Political Investigation)

Politics beyond the Political

An odd, tacit division of labor seems to have arisen in film during the 1990s: with few exceptions, the political (in the classical sense of the word) was allocated to documentaries, and fiction films tended to avoid it. Very few movies (*Garage Olimpo, Los rubios, Mala época*) were concerned with mixing both worlds and with asking how fiction can represent political events.[1] Despite their differences, documentaries and fiction films coincide in the fact that the incitement to political action is linked to the past. This has meant that the status of the political in the new Argentine cinema has provoked a certain perplexity. Horacio González affirms:

> *El bonaerense* touches upon all of these themes and takes care to remain within the realm of petty crime organized in police stations, in a phase of *pre-political* initiation. Thus it easily fulfills what eventually has been celebrated in these films: the lack of judgment or, as it is said, "preaching to the audience [*bajar la línea*]."
>
> Of course, this is a more profound problem that cannot be resolved by the voluntary resignation of indictment that underlies (*should* underlie) any artistic or political venture. But it is clear than a style that decides to put in voluntary suspense the immediate judgment of themes that contemporary debate charges with values decided "beforehand" (with respect to political violence, ostensibly), should reinstate with adequate artistic means the power that fiction always has: *that of perceiving the values that make public space possible*. Once the famous objection of "preaching to the audience" has been avoided, one

has to show that art can, in itself, carry all the burden of its own truth. (González 2003, my emphasis)

Two lines of argument intersect in Horacio González's article. On one hand, in his writing on cinema he links the political to public space and popular mobilization, and he sees cinema as a medium that should intervene actively and directly in this sphere. González reads cinema with the filmmaker Solanas (whom he defended in his book on the film *Sur* in the late 1980s) as a starting point. Yet in the text quoted above, his argumentation—which includes an implicit reference to Jacques Rancière's essays—moves from a concept of political *praxis* in the cinema (with Solanas as an ideal) to an activity of clarification or consciousness that continues, in a more contemplative line, the earlier proposal. Each perspective complements the other to propose that when this notion of public space is absent or displaced, we find ourselves in a *prepolitical* realm.

There also were critics who spoke of "depoliticization" in the new Argentine cinema, as though the backdrop of the political were unchanging, and as though there did not exist in these works a need to reformulate the terms themselves. The fact that when the political is addressed in the new Argentine cinema, critical discourse culminates in its negation (as *prepolitical* or *depoliticization*) leads us to wonder whether we might not instead redefine its status—no longer as something displaced (what is unprecedented will always be prepolitical) but as a category that acquires new powers and qualities in a medium whose function changed radically during the 1990s. That is, before launching a condemnation, wouldn't it be worthwhile to ask whether the political in cinema requires a redefinition of our assumptions? Ultimately, we are dealing with an aesthetic debate: not what film does with a political that is exterior to it but how the political offers itself up to us in the form of these movies.

The Metamorphosis of History

The legacy these new filmmakers inherited was not an easy one. History had changed, but the model of political cinema that *La hora de los hornos* offered in its era was still considered valid by some, including Solanas himself. With *Memorias del saqueo* (2003, "Memories of Looting"), Solanas took up his own work from the 1970s. In addition, the Groupo de Cine Liberación (Liberation Film Group, the group co-founded by Solanas during the 1970s) was the only aspect of Argentine film that had a strong impact internationally and that gained credibility in film theory. For these new filmmakers, however, it became clear that the subordination of artistic practices to the struggle for national liberation—the struggle of the Liberation Film Group in the 1970s in their questioning of cinema as an institution—had expired.

Based on the events of December 2001 that brought about the fall of then-president Fernando De la Rúa, *Memorias del saqueo* records popular mobilizations and investigates different instances of corruption in the early government of Carlos Menem, which was responsible for the political and economic debacle. A documentary with a testimonial and political character, *Memorias del saqueo* takes up the proposal of *La hora de los hornos,* inspired by the days in which political mobilization, after a low point during the 1990s, once again occupied center stage. Yet what is odd about this *return* is that the film speaks of the political as though the conditions of its practice had not been transformed during the 1990s. Of course, to rehabilitate this notion of the political (which revolves around the idea of active groupings, permanent mobilization, and a demand for social change), the movie has to leave out some information. The most notable of the silences of the narrator (Solanas himself) is with regards to Menem's reelection in 1996 with more than 50 percent of the vote. If the point is to celebrate the continuity of popular consciousness over the years, the charges of betrayal and lies appear weak (after all, a number of Peronists supported neoliberalism). This is not a malicious omission. *Memorias del saqueo* needs to suppress whatever would call into question political actions as a successor to the epic of the people (a link already present in *La hora de los hornos*).[2]

What Solano suppresses (as much as we may not like it, the sovereign and political decision of the majority of Argentines to approve Menem's reforms in that moment) should be the center of a reflection on whether the people interpolated in *La hora de los hornos* still have the homogeneity and epic charge that *Memorias de saqueo* suggests. One of the characteristics of film from the 1990s is, precisely, to show that not only have times changed, but also that the people, to whom Solanas directs his film, no longer exist.

Superimposed on this legacy of political film we find those 1990s films that, responding to the identitarian demand, also found a political function: to clarify recent events concealed by official history, to denounce injustices, and to offer up national allegories—or, to say it with the title of one of the era's successes, *Darse cuenta* (1984, "To realize," Alejandro Doria). Film accompanied the process of democratization that began in 1983 and devoted itself to consciousness-raising. However, it became increasingly clear that this function diminished the possibility of a cinematographic self-reflection and tended to subordinate stories to a moral already known beforehand. For this reason, in all of these narrations the moment of *recognition* was of central importance, revealing the unbreakable character of the protagonist and the operation of society. It was, in addition, the moment in which the spectator was offered a *message* that had to do with Argentine identity. No shot sums up this entire tendency more effectively than when, in Alejandro Doria's *Esperando la carroza* (1984, "Waiting for the Carriage"), the camera focuses on Mónica Villa's face, laughing enthusiastically with tears in her eyes at the false wake of her grandmother, only to later look squarely at the camera and, rupturing the film's grammar, say to the spectator: "I am laughing at all of us." The grotesque style was considered in this moment a key element in understanding Argentine identity.

The new Argentine cinema chooses other narrative mechanisms. The prototypical character of the unbreakable fighter who was decisive in the plot development of several movies of the 1980s, including Adolfo Aristarain's *Tiempo de revancha* (1981) and Fernando Ayala's *El arreglo* (1983), is nowhere to be found. Nor do we find the mobilization in the streets that, like a prism, captures the light of history and offers an interpretive key for the entire narration, as in Luis Puenzo's *La historia oficial* (1984), Oscar Barney Finn's *Contar hasta diez* (1985), or Alberto Fischerman's *Los días de junio* (1985, "June Days"). Finally, it is not easy to find in the new cinema national allegories or revisionist readings of the past, as María Luisa Bemberg's *Camila* (1984) created for the nineteenth century and Alejandro Agresti's *El amor es una mujer gorda* (1987) and Lita Stantic's *Un muro de silencio* (1992, distributed internationally as *A Wall of Silence*) did for the years of dictatorship. Yet, when we look more closely, we can see that we are not dealing with only a narrative choice. In fact, the cinema of the 1980s seems to have given to the new Argentine cinema a prescription for what *not* to do. To watch *La historia oficial* and *La ciénaga, Los días de junio* and *Silvia Prieto,* or *El amor es una mujer gorda* and *La libertad,* is like traveling to two different planets. And is not insignificant that whereas in the 1980s the political was expressed as transparency (or the need to make things clear), in more recent films it appears as *opacity,* frequently read as apolitical or depoliticized.

If movies are not subordinated to a cause and do not propose to raise consciousness, then, it means that they do not recognize the existence of a political obligation that is prior to the film. The question is whether *in the film itself* we can find a politics and what the contemporary events are that allow us to ponder the political dimension of these films.

What Is to Be Done? Or, the Difficulties of the Call to Political Action

"What is to be done?" is the political question par excellence because it emphasizes *human action,* that is, those decisions, linked to the public, that have a bearing on contingency (Flores D'Arcais 1996, 18–20). In the social imagination of the 1980s, this action was linked to political mobilization and to a people that made itself present to force or provoke decision. During the 1990s, this image quickly vanished: in national terms, civic participation began to be discredited and popular mobilization disregarded; in international terms, the phenomenon of globalization presented new challenges for transformative action.

The implementation of neoliberal prescriptions by Carlos Menem's Peronist government implied profound changes in all realms, but perhaps nowhere so much as in political practice. Subject to the dictates of an economy regulated by iron-clad laws, action could only appear as a whim when confronting that which appeared to be fatal. Through the fetishism of fatality, efforts were made to suppress the plurality of viewpoints and to discredit free action with the goal of imposing a pragmatics of power. This truly political action of the government (presenting itself through figures of inexorability and as beyond the political) had as its most disastrous consequence the degradation of public space, of all the realms in which the elaboration of an action of social change was possible.

Added to these consequences, from which society will surely need years to recover, are those of a globalization that advanced during the 1990s (from the Argentine perspective, with a surprising speed). Coupled with the degradation of any possible alternative in the national sphere were the processes of an unprecedented globalization, one that accelerated too quickly to be understood immediately. According to Zygmunt Bauman in his *In Search of Politics,* "the truly potent powers of today are essentially exterritorial, while the sites of political action remain local—and so the action is unable to reach the quarters where the limits of sovereignty are drawn and the essential premises of political endeavours are—by design or by default—decided. The separation of power from politics is often referred to under the name of 'globalization'" (1999, 190).

These two phenomena made Jacques Rancière's observation that "the disenchanted opinion spreads that there isn't much to deliberate and that decisions make themselves" (2004a, viii) a daily experience during the Menem years. In this context, few realms remained safe from the processes of devastation, dismantling, or *restructuring* (a word frequently invoked during the period). In the case of film, Julio Maharbiz's disastrous administration as head of the INCAA demanded new tactics to obtain what in an underdeveloped country is inevitable: state protection (another term frequently employed during the period, but always in a negative sense). In contrast to what happened in other industrial sectors, fortunately for film all of the institutions of the medium agreed on a law and principles of protection, recognized and consecrated by the reforms of the constitution made by the Asamblea General Constituyente of 1994. Through protests and organized pressure (and in a favorable global context, because almost all countries promoted the protection of audiovisual production), different groups in the industry obtained the enactment of a law that fostered and regulated production. Thus, we should not minimize a victory won by those from the film world through the skilled use of audiovisual media.

Although this was the case in the corporate or professional context of filmmaking, the situation within the films themselves was completely different. Toward the end of the decade, a group of movies in which the political occupied a very different place than in previous productions emerged. I do not believe that this indicates a conformity with the new conditions of power that globalization imposed or with the extreme apathy and lack of belief that, according to some analysts, spread through almost the entire population (particularly young people). First, by not being subsumed by an exterior action, the new cinema abandoned a restricted and unilateral concept of the political. Film aesthetics, these movies seemed to be telling us, cannot access action or political consciousness directly without first reflecting on its own form. But not only this: it is in its form that film, unfailingly and without recognizing an obligation from without, should find its own political justification, one not given beforehand. Thus, Lucrecia Martel affirms the following: "I think that I find meaning in my existence if I commit to maintaining a critical look at my situation as a middle-class Argentine woman. In that place I locate myself within Argentine cinema. I think that Argentine cinema has a *political function* in those terms" (quoted in Quintín 2000, my emphasis).

Because this function is not previously ascribed, every response is a political option in and of itself. Martel's reflection would surely be different from the response of Lisandro Alonso or Pablo Trapero, the director least inclined to accept political readings of his films; regardless, this indeterminacy means that directors' opinions matter less, making them, in the words of Roland Barthes, "one more guest" (1986). The director can be more or less consciousness of form, but by abandoning all pedagogical or denouncing attitudes, he or she ceases to have absolute power over the effects. Rather than film being something that reaches us in the form of a message, the screen is a surface on which both director and spectators inscribe a meaning that may or may not be political.

For all these reasons, and despite appearances to the contrary, Argentine cinema of the 1990s is the most genuinely political—that is, as cinema. It opens up the space of indeterminacy; it considers meaning not as a message transmitted but as that which is constructed with shots and with mise-en-scènes; it makes us see and hear imperceptible or less grandiose forms of domination, as with the family in *La ciénaga*, with labor in *Mundo grúa*, or with immigrants in *Bolivia*. This disposition is what allowed it to trace, like no other art form of the period, the changes experienced during the 1990s. The presence of immigrants, the breakdown of institutions, the change in the status of labor, the role of memory are not subjected to a declaration of principles; instead they are an object of investigation realized with cinematographic form.

A detail from *Bolivia* allows us to contemplate the indeterminacy to which I am referring. There are no explicit references in the movie to the world of the political—no parties, no political or governmental representatives, no references in the dialogue to events of public life— nor is there much information about what takes place outside of the bar. However, when Freddy goes to Rosa's boarding house and they make love, we see, on her bed, a postcard of Eva Perón. There is no detail shot that underlines this fact; there is no dialogue that explains the presence of this photograph. It is merely one object of Rosa's among others. How can we interpret this photograph? How can we understand this almost imperceptible mark of the political, part of the life of one of characters about whom we know almost nothing (except that she is Paraguayan and works in the bar where the movie takes place)?

The story that Caetano narrates displaces the ties of traditional domination in favor of a less represented one (discrimination against foreigners) in which the dominated (those who turn to the figure of Evita) are transformed into those who want to expel this new group (immigrants from neighboring countries). In this passage, the protective figure of Evita moves from one pole to the other. There is something more, however: doesn't this photo on the bed point to the fact that the political has been transformed into a private, intimate matter, a past that we hold with the same devotion as a saint's image, and that this is a passion *that cannot be spoken*? Because if there is something that marks the character of Rosa (other than her relationship with Freddy), it is the humiliation that others inflict on her, which finds its limit in the protective image of Eva Perón, hung in her room in the boarding house.

None of these descriptions, however, seems to respond to the question "What is to be done?"—a demand that the movies of the new Argentine cinema reject or ignore.[3] Or perhaps they respond in an unconventional way—with their investment in a language that examines its own possibilities or with their descriptions of worlds—to what has been done (or is being done) in the field of cinema as an industry. It is this very detour from the norm that establishes the political in 1990s film.

The Political: Nothing More, Nothing Less

In the text cited at the beginning of this chapter, Horacio González speaks of the duty of fiction to "perceive the values that make public space possible" and at the same time expresses a certain doubt about this capacity to perceive, given that these values are "decided beforehand." Yet this capacity to perceive is precisely what *El bonaerense* proves, and for this reason the film refrains from resting on these judgments. Rather than a question of values (about which we could be in agreement), what is important is to see *operations*. Which spectator who goes to the cinema does not agree that the business of politics is corrupt and often covers up, rather than fights, crime? How many spectators disagree that Bolivian immigrants should be treated without discrimination of any kind? Rather than resting on a judgment that has already been passed, as in the case of many films from the 1980s, these movies show us, through cinematographic form, how a world operates: *El bonaerense* and the institution of the police, where affect and corruption are mutually reinforcing; *Bolivia* and the harmful discourse that anticipates and presupposes physical violence; *Mundo grúa* and the transformations of labor; *Los rubios* and the operation of memory. Between indeterminacy and the recording of an operation, the new cinema establishes a different possibility of thinking the political.

Goodbye to "the People"

In Argentina in the 1990s, the traditional category of the *popular* underwent a profound change.[4] In political terms, the party that had traditionally been considered the representative of the popular (the Peronist or *justicialista* party) rose to power and implemented a neoliberal program, such that, although we could say that Menem's government was populist, it was so in a very different sense than earlier governments formed by the same party. In cultural terms, although the popular had previously maintained a tension with or resistance to media appropriation, during the 1990s we could say that the growth of mass media and the culture industry ended up absorbing (and depoliticizing) almost all expressions of popular culture. In Argentina, the efforts of Menem's government to demobilize and evacuate the contents of the idea of *the people* (*el pueblo*)— which began to give way in political discourse to the more neutral *people* (*la gente*)—intersected, whether intentionally or not, with the growth of what Renato Ortiz deems "international-popular culture" (1994), the sign of the times of globalization. Pablo Alabarces, a specialist in the study of popular culture, went so far as to claim that "the nineties were—could be—neopopulist because the people no longer existed" (2004, 23). This concept of "neopopulism," in place of the traditional "populism," does not mark a mere postmodern inflection, the tendency to add "neo"s and "post"s to all terms. It indicates a more profound crisis: that of the category of the people itself. This categorical crisis was so profound that many theorists have spoken of its definitive eclipse, and others have tried to forge alternative concepts, such as Hardt and Negri's "multitude" (in their *Empire*). Populism continued its successful career in the 1990s, while the people began to disintegrate or simply abandoned the stage.

This new crossroads was ignored by many commentators, who continued to read Menem's populism in light of Peronism (which can be useful with respect to the concepts of verticalism, pragmatism, and personalism), minimizing the components of a populism with global characteristics. As José Nun pointed out, "[W]hen we speak of a political regime, it is much more difficult today to label it *populist* without previously analyzing to what extent it refracts in particular ways a transformation in the styles of political representation that affects the majority of neoliberal democracies" (1995, 75). In fact, and despite the differences between them, in questions of style Menem shares features with Perón, but also with George W. Bush. All of this perhaps finds its explanation in the vast growth of mass media (including television, radio, the Internet, surveys, publicity) and in their role in how politics is conducted. "The people" to whom these leaders appeal is often electronic. The masses as a subject, a key figure in political theory, gave way to, in Peter Sloterdijk's words, *the postmodern mass,* which "is a mass lacking any potential, a sum of microanarchies and solitudes which can barely recall the era in which, excited and driven toward itself through its loudspeakers and general secretaries, it should have and wanted to make history, given its condition of a collective pregnant with expressivity" (2002, 18). If the people are missing, then, it is because there are no transversal lines that unite different "microanarchisms." Nor is there a part that can assume the representation of the whole: although it may return in the future, it is certain that in the 1990s "the people," in the sense in which it had been known until then, made itself scarce.

Under these new conditions, defenses of the continuity of the popular in the mass media that, rightly and hopefully, had been formed in the years of the return to democracy (principally in Jesus Martín Barbero's *Communication, Culture, and Hegemony: From the Media to Mediations*) began to seem too optimistic, products of a euphoria that, during the 1990s, declined irrevocably. Democracy and the popular, ultimately, did not encounter each other again, and much less within the space of the mass media. Cinema, which from the days of *The Battleship Potemkin* had been an ideal language for inspiring the people to action, discovered that "the people" had been transformed into something else.

The new Argentine cinema not only rejected, explicitly or implicitly, the legacy of political cinema of the 1970s; it also launched a critique of the consideration of the people as a privileged political subject and of cinema as one of its potential weapons. And if in some films a nostalgia for the popular can still be detected, it is in terms no longer of a promised social transformation but of cultural practices—what I deem the people as cultural repository, although it would be more precise to say that what appears is more correctly defined as *lumpen* than as *the people*. Outside of the world of labor, and moved by necessity, this underclass constitutes not the promise of liberation (as the people could be) but fits of disorganized and rash violence. Not the poor struggling against the rich but miserable people taking advantage of other miserable people, as in *Pizza, birra, faso,* when the protagonists rob a disabled beggar. The other way that the people, or what remains of them, appears, is as *otherness,* something that we cannot have access to, a situation presented in *Los rubios, Los muertos,* and *La ciénaga.* In this mode, the people have become something cold, removed, televisual. The world of the people that gave sustenance to certain political action has disintegrated, and these movies offer up to us something different.

The People As Political

In the films of the 1990s, the people are missing. One scene illustrates this transformation perfectly. In Trapero's *El bonaerense,* the protagonist encounters a *piquetero* protest (see note 3). Zapa, off-duty, wants to cross the street and has to wait until the protest passes by to continue on his way. Although the camera does stop to observe the multitude, it accompanies the protagonist. The spell that the masses might cast never happens, and the protest is unable to intervene in history. It is, as it were, a run-in of little consequence. It is as though *El bonaerense* had come across a fragment of Solanas' *La hora de los hornos* or his *Memorias del saqueo,* yet, in contrast to the other filmmaker, Trapero shows no interest in making the popular protest an actor in his story.

In *Silvia Prieto* the young women who hand out laundry detergent manage to mobilize to protest the death of a colleague. Yet whereas in political film the multitude fills and exceeds the screen, in Rejtman's film the march is marked by a gap. Whereas in the earlier films the shots outline faces twisted in shouting (as in the famous poster for *La hora de los hornos*), the scene in *Silvia Prieto* registers apathetic or inexpressive faces. In addition to the mildly comic effect of the salesgirls' clothing, there is a certain indifference or inertness in the characters (they are all seated and appear tired), which contrasts with the agitated, restless bodies that characterize earlier political film. Marcelo and Brite arrive by taxi, work their way through the protest, and ultimately abandon it because they have a reservation at a Mexican restaurant. The protest demands safety ("improved safety on the job, no to impunity" the posters read) and the mise-en-scène underlines the local, specific, and contingent character of the protest. The group of salesgirls struggling for something fair does not correspond to the traditional category of the people, nor is it interested in doing so: the concerns of Silvia Prieto and her friends are of a different order.

In this respect, however, no film goes further than Albertina Carri's *Los rubios*. In her eagerness to demonstrate that her parents' struggle was mistaken, Carri presents a series of interviews with "the people" (from a poor neighborhood to which her parents moved to continue armed resistance during the last dictatorship) clearly juxtaposed with interviews with intellectuals (who are generally shown through video and television).[5] The former radicals' "everything set up politically" (*todo armadito políticamente*), in the words of the filmmaker, is opposed to the neighbors' discourse, which is unreflective (but not without logic), naïve (but not without wickedness), full of gaps and lapses. Carri breaks with one of the tacit principles of documentaries of these years, which generally limit themselves to the testimony of participants. This is an "I lived it" that finds in the story of the neighbor who turned her parents over to the military regime a disturbing gaze. With this testimony, Carri removes from "the people" the idea of consciousness and deliberation that the voice of the radical grants them. In fact, a fragment of her father's book that the protagonist reads deals precisely with this transformation of the multitude into the people by way of consciousness:

> The population is the masses, the school of fish, the gregarious group, indifferent to the social, submissive to all power, idle in the face of evil, resigned in its pain. Yet, even in this habitual state of dispersion, in the spirit of the *multitude* there is a profound underlying sentiment of its originary unity; the affront and injustice accumulate anger, elevating the tone in their affective life, and one day, in the face of a sentimental clash that acts as a powder keg, passion explodes ardently, the crowd becomes *the people*, the flock becomes a collective being: egotism, private interest, personal worries disappear, individual wills fuse and submerge into the general will; and the new, electric, vibrant personality directs itself to its goal, like an arrow to its target, and the torrent destroys when something is in its way.[6]

This transformation, however, never occurs. Carri attacks one of the strongest pillars of the popular in cinema and in Argentine history: the belief that resistance and an inalienable consciousness lie within the people.

In these three cases we can thus see how newer films make reference to the people in order to show their absence. In neither *El bonaerense* nor *Silvia Prieto* nor *Los rubios,* despite their clear differences, does this absence generate nostalgia. These three movies present new possible groupings that no longer need the fusing power of the people. The institution in Trapero's film, chance and the commodity in Rejtman's case, and the family in Carri's work function as affirmative spaces. There is no nostalgia for what is lost but an effort to overcome postmodern solitude.[7]

The Masses As Cultural Repository

If "the people" is not a political subject to which filmmakers can appeal, they can nevertheless turn to it as a cultural promise. With a long populist tradition that harks back at least to the nineteenth century, popular characters have appeared as purer, more authentic, more full of life. A closer look, however, shows that we cannot speak in these movies of "the people" as a cultural repository, for the characters who appear neither represent a group of people nor allegorize it but circulate outside of this category. In any case, the interest in such life forms and their cultural practices stems from the fact that they are marginalized, nomadic, unpredictable. The category of *lumpen* that for Marx characterized those who were at the edge of economic classes is perhaps the most precise. In *Pizza, birra, faso,* in a scene that refers to Buñuel's *Los olvidados* (1950, *The Forgotten Ones*) and also to an Argentine filmmaker of the 1960s, Leonardo Favio, the protagonists attack a beggar in a wheelchair and rob him of all his money. Whereas in the work of Buñuel or Favio the critique was directed at the tendency in social film to soften the image of popular or marginal groups, in *Pizza, birra, faso* its meaning lies elsewhere: these characters do not know how to orient themselves in a world in which the enemy has disappeared or is otherwise inaccessible.

The separation between *represented world* and *modes of representation* allows us to analyze the type of populism that Stagnaro and Caetano stage in their work. On one hand, the represented characters are assigned to the dimension of the abject or discarded. On the other hand, the means of representation are contaminated by images of consumption in the mass media. As Silvia Schwarzböck says with respect to this cinema, "[T]he middle class tends to represent marginal lives with the lens of the crime section of newspapers and television news. That is, they imagine a universe that is more intense, but where one cannot live a calm life, because death and danger are the order of the day" (2000, 50). This affirmation, however, warrants expansion: this projection is not limited to the "middle class," because this same *lumpen* (as the scene in which the kids in *Pizza, birra, faso* watch *Dog Day Afternoon* on television) also conceives of itself as coming from that space. We find ourselves facing a populism of the mass media that cannot always see that this same *lumpen* is an *inverted reproduction*—but ultimately a reproduction—of that dominant power. This is the structuring paradox of the nomadic tendency, which threatens its capacity for resistance. The actor-character of *Pizza, birra, faso* becomes a garbage collector on a cop show.[8] Undoubtedly, Caetano and Stagnaro reject some of the more conventional characteristics of populism, such as its dramatic styles or a kind of symbolic reward, which is the conclusion that populism always reaches. "In populism, the other, who seems to have nothing, has everything or almost everything," Grignon and Passeron point out (1992). As late as 1995, two films were made in which Luis Brandoni plays this neighborhood character, a little shameless, but nevertheless lovable, as the tango professor of José Santiso's *De mi barrio con amor* (1995, "From My Neighborhood with Love") and the street vendor in Santiago Carlos Oves' *El verso* (1995, "The Verse"). A typical way of representing these characters in film is to show them, in a rather romantic way, as very affectionate people, condemned to disappear under new conditions.

Even in the most populist movie of the period, Ulises Rosell's *Bonanza (En vías de extinción)*, "the people"—as the title itself states—is condemned to be part of the past. Bonanza Muchinsci and his children La Vero and Norberto are the protagonists of this documentary film in which there is neither a voice-over nor characters who gaze directly into the camera. The protagonist is somewhat odd. In his youth, he was part of one of the most spectacular bank robberies in Argentine history; now, at around the age of seventy, Bonanza sells scrap metal, hunts for animals to sell, and forages in small-town junkyards, turning him into a true political boss (*cacique*).[9]

Ulises Rosell began to record Bonanza's life while filming a short, "Dónde y cómo Oliveira perdió a Achala" ("Where and How Oliveira Lost Achala," *Historias breves*), in his warehouse on the outskirts of La Plata city. The poster advertising the movie depicts Bonanza as a king, complete with a crown and a gigantic viper wrapped around his neck. And, in truth, Bonanza is a plebeian king, surviving on odd jobs and political clientilism.[10] One of his speeches shows the character's morals: "We've got to beat the drums....Come on, there's a gang that's messing around: I'll call my people and....Let's go." This "let's go," as one might imagine, does not bode well. In contrast to other movies in the new cinema, politics does appear explicitly profiled in the posters that Bonanza's boys put up, but to the camera-eye the identity of the candidate is irrelevant (his face can be made out only obliquely), as are his ideas. What matters is how Bonanza and his people know how to take advantage of a corrupt political system. To paint a fuller picture of the situation, we should state that Bonanza speaks poorly of drugs ("the great problem facing young people") and that the neighborhood has a worse enemy than he, a criminal who respects nothing, without tradition or affective ties with the people. Bonanza, let us say with a word from the history of film, is a *godfather*.

The vision that the movie has of the character is absolutely celebratory, and it is not difficult to see in its viewpoints a continuity with the type of populism that, although previously linked to political viability, now takes pleasure in finding itself "an endangered species." The world of the Bonanzas seems full of adventure, wisdom, experience, rather than a precarious situation or a damaged life. Intense scenes occur one right after the other, as with the celebration of each of the skills that the characters present, from hunting vipers, to taking apart a car with an ax, or playing with swings made from tires in ponds and in the mud, behind the sheds where the families live. Rosell wants to remain outside of the story and, just as the characters never look into the camera, we never hear the voice of the director or of interviewers asking questions. Instead, the director's desire is to blend with his characters. This can be seen in the bricolage montage that evokes the skills of the plebian king: with the same talent as Bonanza Muchinsci (render unto Caesar what is Caesar's), Rosell constructs a captivating story with remnants, chance or careless shots, scenes captured off the cuff, the recycling of heterogeneous materials.

At some point, however, the irrevocable distance between the young director (a student at the Universidad del Cine) and the trash picker must make itself present. And this happens, more than anywhere, in the score, which only by chance reproduces the music that the characters listen to, turning instead to the sounds of world music. Manu Chao and Kevin Johansen show how the valorization of this life stems from a globalized vision that discovers the benefits of the local and of the slightly "savage" life of those who remain outside.[11] The Grignon and Passeron quotation above is fulfilled in Rosell's film; in reality, Bonanza, who appears to have nothing, ends up having it all.[12]

One of the descriptive details of *Bonanza* provides us with another insight into how this type of populism found approval in various media during the 1990s. As in several movies of the period, television appears, but it does not manage to occupy the totality of the screen, as the Bonanzas' life is radically different from one dazzled by television. The only moment at which the camera lingers on the television screen is when we see a show in which Alberto Olmedo plays "Manosanta," one of his most popular characters. Acclaimed by the public and journalists as a comic genius, Alberto Olmedo (1933–1988) received an unexpected acceptance in cultured circles and in the academic world.[13] Oscar Landi, after a successful seminar in the Social Science Department at the Universidad de Buenos Aires, wrote the book *Devórame otra vez (Qué hizo la television con la gente, qué hace la gente con la television)* ("Devour Me Again [What Television Does with People, What People Do with Television]"), which assumes a total and polemic defense of the comic. It is precisely in the figure of Manosanta that Landi finds a bridge between "the repertoire of precariousness and of foraging for work (*rebusque*)" and "the picaresque zone," as a demonstration both of the fact that "when crisis yanks away all the handrails, magic is not the last hope but rather one more way of making a living (*rebusque*)" and of the "avant-gardism of peripheral magic." Landi concludes that Olmedo, "master of improvisation, represented like no one else the grotesque, that which has no meaning, the parody that allows us to keep living in an Argentina with a lengthy crisis" (1992, 29–34).[14]

The clichés that survive in Landi's gaze are not new. They have a long history in Argentine cultural interpretations: the survival tactics of the popular classes, their inventiveness, their wit. In the context of the crisis and the growth of the mass media, this popular inventiveness acquires new forms, and Landi calls our attention to this. But more than Olmedo's or Bonanza's supposed genius, what interests me here is what artists or intellectuals do with it: how, for example, they project a *fascination for cynicism* that appears to be more a displacement of the political impotence of intellectuals during the 1990s than an effect peculiar to Olmedo or Bonanza, or how they assume an *imaginary way out* when, in the case of *Bonanza* and *Vida en Falcon,* what we are in fact witnessing is the misery of a life that can be romanticized only through elisions and editing.

Paradoxically, many features of popular culture appear in a film in which the continuity of populist tradition is no longer possible. Santiago García's *Lesbianas de Buenos Aires* (2004, released in the United States as *Lesbians of Buenos Aires*) is a documentary without men that questions the *machismo* and discrimination to which lesbians are subjected. Excluding *machismo* (one of the essential components of a fossilized Argentine popular culture), popular culture appears as a repository and also in political terms. Soccer, cars, the singer Gilda, and the praise of "the working-class (*populares*) woman in the National Encounters of Lesbians," against feminists who carry around Simone de Beauvoir's book and those who "love teaching," are the components that return in this populism, but populism is impossible not only because there is no *machismo* (one of populism's most persistent features) but also because it puts forth antagonisms of a different order. The small scandal of women playing soccer (Mónica) or assembling cars continues in the couple seeking a child or the young woman (Claudia) who introduces her girlfriend to her parents.

The vital and ideological recuperation of these events in popular culture extends to political struggle. The director, also a noted film critic and expert in the classical period of Argentine film, inserts from the very beginning of the film images of certain emblems of power: the presidential house (*Casa Rosada*), the national cathedral, the Congress.[15] In addition, unlike most films from the period (outside of those that are traditionally political), the film shows street protests for the gay pride march, which are also shown in Goyo Anchou's *Safo, historia de una pasión (una remake)* (2003, "Safo, the Story of a Passion [A Remake]"). Criticized by Mónica, an activist of the previous generation and member of the Comunidad Homosexual Argentina (CHA, Argentine Homosexual Community), who considers them "copies" and "counterproductive" because they do not help the effort of assimilation, the protests are defended by Claudia in a counterpoint that shows the vitality of these minority struggles and their different ways of making themselves visible. The movie, undoubtedly, also proposes this goal. Without huge cinematographic claims, García knows how to set up the scene so that this visibility finds its expression in images. In one of Mónica's testimonies, a passer-by crosses in front of the camera in the neighborhood of Primera Junta, indifferent to the filming. "This is the famous invisibility of lesbians," Mónica remarks.[16]

Within the series that we are setting up, what is surprising about this film is its return to the features of the politically and culturally popular, in an environment in which these acquire a radically different meaning. "The people" thus return, but they are made up of only women; masculine reason is dismissed. "Something's missing," as one of the young woman jokes. However, this lack no longer produces guilt but the discovery of another dimension of affect in which the lifeless common places of Argentine culture acquire an unusual vitality.[17]

In the 1990s, the genuinely popular can return on the sole condition that it denies itself in the same moment in which it takes place.

The People As Otherness

In the evocation of the people as cultural repository there is a certain comforting complicity, imaginary or real. In contrast, in the people as otherness, we find opacity among relationships; the inaccessibility of this far-removed culture; and the suspicion, not always explicit, that populist artifacts show not popular culture but an idealized image that it has of itself. The paradox of this gesture is that it must deny popular culture at the same time as it draws closer to it: it represents it as a gap or emptiness, absence, opacity, but *something* is being represented. How does it make this double movement that, in image and sound, shapes this beyond?

In its elaboration of changes produced in our understanding of the popular, *La ciénaga* is one of the most sophisticated and attentive films. Critics make a mistake when they aver that Solanas' *Memorias del saqueo* presents *another voice* that complements Martel's, because this denies what Martel says about the popular and how she represents it. According to Jacques Rancière, "[T]he people is, first, a way of framing" (1991, 95). And *La ciénaga* frames in two ways: through mass media and through "geometric framing."[18] Martel's ethics represent "the people" behind the frame, in silence. In her films, "the people" is never a subject but an object distanced by the television screen or door and window frames.

In one of the film's most abrupt scenes, the digital television image suddenly takes over the entire screen: it is as though film has been displaced in order that television, with all its brutality of the real, realer than reality itself, can present itself. This grainy and glassy image of the television screen shows the visit of a reporter to the house where the Virgin is said to have appeared. One system of beliefs survives in another, that of religion on televisual. To reject both leads to nihilism, as this belief establishes a powerful real. The relationship between belief and desire is the nucleus of Martel's work and, in this scene, it shows us its other, hidden face: the absolute and noncinematographic image of religious and televisual beliefs. The common place of the alienated people reemerges with all of its power because the only salvation consists in "not seeing anything," as Verónica says at the film's end.[19]

The other way of framing is much more faithful to the idea of the people as otherness; although it establishes an exterior gaze, it does not presuppose an essential idea of the subject (as someone who can be alienated). At key moments, as when Isabel leaves the house, the characters of the people (the *Kollas,* in Mecha's graphic expression) are seen through windows or frames. Momi, who desires Isabel, sees her leave through the window frame. This distance, this mediation that the frame obliges itself to enact with the world, is made violently concrete when Momi accompanies Isabel to meet el Perro ("the Dog"), a character with a significant nickname linking him to a threatening and sinister otherness. It is not superfluous to recall that dogs are the supposed object of desire of the Kolla Indians ("They screw dogs"), and a dog is the protagonist of the story of the "African rat" (a pet dog who becomes a sinister beast); in addition, a dog provokes Luciano's accidental death. Momi accompanies Isabel to a club in a poor neighborhood where el Perro, his friends, and neighbors meet to play pool, dance, and listen to music. When she arrives at the door, Momi stops and is witness to a conversation between Isabel and el Perro. The discrete camera stays with her, and the spectator views this conversation from afar, framed by the doors of the club. We do not hear what they say and, at first, the meaning escapes the spectator entirely. (Later we will learn that she went to tell him she is pregnant and this is the reason that she leaves the house.)

The people are, in this case, inaccessible. On television they are accessible, but at the cost of utter artificiality. In reality, both visions complement the cinematographic language itself: facing an image extraneous to film (that of the television) that imposes a false knowledge (but not for that reason less real), the filmic image can express itself only if it recognizes its own impossibility. Setting up frames, distances, silences: the people are always beyond, and film cannot represent them except as a mute tongue and an unattainable image.

When *La ciénaga* presents popular characters without these mediations, as occurs most notably in the party scene, violent confrontations happen. This is because for Martel the system of domestic labor silences others and terrorizes through insult and through neglect (or with the *derecho de pernada,* the feudal right of the lord to sleep with the wives of his subjects, as in the case of José). In *La niña santa,* Josefina's mother refers disdainfully to "Indians" (*chinas*), and neglect is made clear through that ubiquitous character, one of the hotel's maids, who appears periodically in the rooms with a disinfectant, without being summoned by anyone. It remains odd, at any rate, that in her short for *Historias breves* Martel showed an interest in the world of the popular, using as her soundtrack a Lía Crucet song and telling the parable of the dead (*macho*) king. Complementing what happens in *La ciénaga*, the inaccessibility in this film does not imply an idealization. Popular groups are not exempt from relationships of control and servility, because the masculine oppression of the king and his decadence runs through all of society and through all social classes.[20]

Nostalgia for Work

One of the virtues of Enrique Bellande's *Ciudad de María* is to make clear, from the vantage point of film, recent transformations in the world of labor. A documentary filmed between 1997 and 2001 in San Nicolás, in the province of Santa Fe, it tells of the changes in the city from the moment in which the Virgin appears to Gladys Motta, on September 25, 1983. Little by little, the religious fervor over the Virgin grows until it transforms San Nicolás in the mid-1990s into a true religious city. Traditionally known as the "city of steel" for its Somisa factory, the basis of the town's economy, San Nicolás began to be known as the "city of María (Mary)," ultimately receiving one and a half million pilgrims a year.

An inflection point in the story of the city is the closing of the steel factory in 1991 and the brutal firing of more than seven thousand workers. Bellande, a native of the city, organizes his documentary around two central themes: the pilgrimages to the shrine and the figure of Gladys Motta. The two culminating points of this organization of the material are the mass pilgrimage of 1998 and the interview of the woman who saw the vision. The pilgrimage closes the film, but despite having interviewed several people close to Gladys Motta, the movie never obtains an image of her. "Impossible to film her, isn't it?" the director asks at one point.

Bellande is principally concerned with the economic transformations that the phenomenon produces and with the presence of the mass media, which feeds into the belief in the Virgin. One of the greatest challenges that the film takes on is a blow-by-blow struggle with the television image. Bellande is not an unfair opponent, and he cedes the entire screen to the television, reproducing in three parts the transmission of the pilgrimage of the blind Christian Reboa, who goes off with the requests of the children of the public hospital and with a jacket from the television station that sponsors his cavalry.[21] In addition, the camera records the labor of the reporters and the presence of television stations.

The unfolding of the microphones and cameras of radio and television transforms the city into a spectacle and its habitants and the faithful into protagonists, in the eyes of God and of the cameras. Worship is no longer the relationship between God and the believer but a triangle; a third eye watches and transforms everything into a spectacle. Bellande points to the extended stay of the media in the city with an object that is as present in the documentary as the little statues of the Virgin: the microphone. With all the technology in the world at their disposal, the priests also become mediocre showmen, and the scene in which one of them tries to entertain kindergarteners in a catechism class is particularly pathetic; the priest tirelessly attempts to imitate the television hosts that he has seen. The worship of the Virgin is set up like a spectacle, and the two most fervent beliefs of the 1990s are united, as in *La ciénaga:* television and religion.[22] The flows of superstition that run through one and the other are the raw material with which Bellande constructs *Ciudad de María.*

Yet not everything is television in the movie: after showing Gladys' house, speaking with the priest Pérez and a psychiatrist (a character who should be in the psychiatric ward, but as a patient), showing the inside of the newspaper *El Norte* (also a protagonist in the phenomenon of the Virgin), and, finally, giving space to the television image and to Christian, the blind man, Bellande reveals his weapons. The film moves to a fade-out that clearly indicates that we are entering into a different logic. Then we see the numbers and signs that indicate the beginning of a film (9, 8, 7,...), cuing us into the fact that we are facing the celluloid of filmic material. The scenes that follow, observed from the present, appear to be from a science fiction film: two men wearing safety hoods are smelting (the black and red contrast with one another). This scene is followed by images of a desire for a modernity that, in the present of the movie, is already in ruins. Schoolchildren wearing the white public school uniform are leaving a secular school. (How can we not think here of the schoolchildren of the private, religious school saying that they have two mothers, one on Earth and the other in Heaven?) Young people work at huge drawing tables in an enormous room (how can we avoid thinking about the religious processions?); two doctors perform an operation (how can we not remember the psychiatrist's chattering?); and a mock-up that becomes the city is shown, without a space for the chapel. The sun rises and the voice-over of an advertisement says, "All of this is steel," and ends by affirming, "Steel is life" (how can we not think of the song the faithful sing, "God is everything"?).[23]

Of course, an eye trained in cinematographic practices could view these images of modernity with suspicion. (They are, lest we forget, from an advertisement.) For this reason, rather than referring back to a golden age, the advertising spot is the index of a lost time, a different time when the other (the worker) was still symbolized, even with a hood and visor.[24] In contrast, in contemporary life, workers appear nowhere, as in the case of Gladys' husband, a former employee of the Somisa factor, who is never filmed. Thus, film is linked to the modern city, workers, and steel, whereas television appears linked to the postmodern city, to believers, and to superstitions.

After the Somisa advertisement, the television image reappears. Minister Triacca, a sinister union leader, claims that the closure of the Somisa plant will not have "social consequences." In response to an *escrache* (see note 5) made on Triacca's house, a man holds up the image of the Virgin of San Nicolás and says the Lord's Prayer; "I'm a Catholic just like you," he shouts. This man, who asks to go back to work in an appeal to religion, does not understand the surprises that his conversion has in store for him: from now on his new job will be religion itself. After the images of Minister Triacca we see neither unemployment nor a ghost town but the (unplanned) arrival of a new type of industry: the pilgrimage. The candidate for mayor calculates ten pesos per person, which means that the 400,000 pilgrims celebrating the fifteen-year anniversary of the Virgin's appearance will bring 4,000,000 pesos. *Ciudad de María* shows the passage between modernity and postmodernity, and it does so around belief and images. From the worker to the believer, from the citizen to the consumer.

According to Zygmunt Bauman, in the postmodern world, "[s]tripped of its eschatological trappings and cut off from its metaphysical roots, work has lost the centrality which it was assigned in the galaxy of values dominant in the era of solid modernity and heavy capitalism" (2000, 139). And in Argentina some cities, such as San Nicolás, linked their destiny to this heavy capitalism that found in steel one of its symbols. Yet, in times of precariousness, and once large industry had been dismantled, the city found a raw material almost as lucrative as steel: belief. It has been observed by many authors that in the post-Fordist world, ideas and information generate more wealth than material products (Bauman 2000; Virno 2003).[25] Belief transforms into the raw material of spectacle and wealth; this is why those who before appeared as enemies or unpleasant memories of the past (priests) are suddenly transformed into the best vendors, because they manage discourse and performance like no one else, and because they have at their disposal an impressive arsenal of highly effective images. In the Somisa commercial we see doctors, students, workers, architects, engineers, a baby, a couple in love, but no priest, who, according to that ideology, would be unproductive and reactionary. In the present, however, the city is succeeding. Are we thus witnessing a kind of infinite loop in which capital no longer makes the sacred profane, according to Marx and Engle's famous hypothesis in the *Communist Manifesto*, but instead the sacred and capital have joined forces? One and a half million pilgrims are also one and a half million consumers who make of worship their true labor.

The Powers of the False

The intimate and even rather reserved relationship that Gladys Motta has with the Virgin is transformed, after 1991, into a spectacle. In the eyes of the filmmaker, Gladys' figure is marked by mystery and density. With sound judgment, the movie does not refute her, nor does it try to demonstrate that she is crazy or a charlatan. On the contrary, it shows proof, such as the photograph of arms marked with the Virgin's presence and pages written in a very refined calligraphy for someone who did not finish grade school. Rather than oppose truth and falsity (thereby exposing Gladys Motta as an impostor), Bellande chooses a more interesting and forceful path—to show the elemental and coarse nature of the cult of the Virgin: the pilgrims who sing as though they were at a soccer match, the *gauchos* who shout "Long live the fatherland!" and defend the slogan "fatherland, family, property," the desperate people who seek the water from the sacred cistern. "Yesterday," writes Serge Daney, "it was the truth of lies. Today, the powers of the false. A sign of the times" (2004, 204). Because *Ciudad de María* is a documentary that has the camera move among the characters without judging them, it is the spectator who uses the film to make hypotheses, take on positions, and draw conclusions.

Ciudad de María testifies to all of these transformations, entering into a power struggle with the spectacle. It does so in the only way possible: without adopting a position of exteriority, without judgment, by presenting the spectator with all the evidence. It is worth asking, however, whether Bellande does not end up fascinated by the phenomenon he wants to portray. The *distance* printed on the image without recourse to exteriority is central here. Although the director achieves a fecund juxtaposition between what he witnesses and the filmic advertising clip from the past, this juxtaposition deteriorates at the film's end, when the celebration of the Virgin takes control of the image, with her entrance into the shrine. Is this a recognition that it is impossible to resist the seduction of the spectacle? A declaration of arms in the face of world that has proven itself to be stronger than steel? Or the final staging for a spectator who has learned to *watch* the history of San Nicolás?

Labor As a Possible Narration

Despite what many reviews of the film have suggested, *Mundo grúa*'s effectiveness stems not from its capacity to capture scenes of daily life but from its peculiar narrative structure. With its dispersed, elliptical narration, Trapero's movie testifies to the experience and situations of its protagonist, el Rulo (Luis Margani), for whom *labor* narratively structures time, constructs links, connects him with the past, and sustains a perspective on the future. In the face of this expectation that labor will provide the character with a future (deeply rooted in the social, rather than personal, history of the protagonist), the film's structure is that of the *pure present*, for labor never manages to construct the sustained and integral narration that el Rulo fervently desires.

For this reason, as *Mundo grúa* moves forward elliptically, assembling slices of life, these ellipses never move backward in time: the flashback is strictly prohibited according to the film's logic, and labor cannot impose a stable story. The past is presented not in images but in the words of friends who recall "Paco Camorra," the successful song from the early 1970s by the group Séptimo Regimiento ("Seventh Regiment"), in which el Rulo played base.[26] In the present itself, it is embodied in the figure of his son Claudio (Federico Esquerro), a slacker and a guitarist in a rock band. As Trapero says, "[T]he son functions in the movie like a flashback of el Rulo in present tense. The son is a young Rulo, or el Rulo could be his son as an older man" (quoted in Acuña 1999). Yet in these confrontations with the past (whether in the image of Claudio or in the memories of the song), the film's narrative time reveals what separates it from the past, for if the son functions as a kind of flashback, it is because his life has similarities to the past of his father without being identical to it. There is nothing further from the concert that Claudio's group gives than the stories recalled by el Rulo and Adriana (Adriana Aizenberg), the owner of the neighborhood shop who becomes his girlfriend.[27]

There is a difference, then, that emerges from the confrontation between el Rulo's present and another present that is similar, although not equal, to his past. The basic difference is that whereas el Rulo cannot even begin to consider abandoning the world of labor, his son does not want to enter into it. The sociologist Maristella Svampa synthesizes this idea masterfully in the title of one of her essays: "Identidades astilladas. De la patria metalúrgica al heavy metal" (2000, "Splintered Identities: From the Metallurgical Fatherland to Heavy Metal"). What is produced in between (what the movie does not represent in images) is the movement of history, the modification of the status of labor and, therefore, of the temporality in which we live. In the present of *Mundo grúa,* the act of living creates time, but a *splintered* time, without labor, that is proper to the historical moment in which the movie takes place, the 1990s.

If *Mundo grúa* were a sociological essay we could speak of the precariousness and neglect that workers face. The movie, however, at no moment attempts this kind of reading but something quite different: the experience of time in contemporary life and the problem of how to construct a narration from the remnants of an unstable and temporary job. For el Rulo, work is what makes his world function, what makes it beautiful. The love for machines that possesses him, and all of the male characters, extends to his relationships with people. "You work with a lot of care" is the first flirting compliment he gives when he meets Adriana, as though this makes her more attractive. Later, he tells his son that he is "practicing" and learning on the machines, as though work also represented the possibility for an education and to begin again. His friendships (especially his friendship with Torres, played by Daniel Valenzuela) are linked to work, as we also see in his affection for his mother and for Adriana. (He welds a bar in his mother's house and installs a metal curtain for Adriana's store.) Even his relationship with his son is implicated: "Don't you think about getting a job?" he asks. The entire conflict is unleashed in the final words that he says to Claudio before kicking him out of the house: "This can't go on like this....I work every day....I can't support you anymore."

The phrase "I work every day" structures el Rulo's time. For this reason, his being fired means the collapse of the only possible narration that the protagonist imagines in his life. As he says to the man who gives him a ride to the bus station, in the South: "With the mess we've got now, with work and all that, I practically don't remember all of those things [in reference to the hit song]....*I don't feel like going around talking about it.*" If he had a job, he would talk about it; he would bind the present to the past and head toward a future. Yet this possibility never emerges or unfolds in the movie.

As el Rulo's world is articulated around labor, his son's life is incomprehensible to him. Even el Rulo's youth, with his band, was structured by the need to search for a means of support. How can his son deny the only thing that could organize his world? The difference between the two is made clear in one of el Rulo's many expressions of disapproval toward his son: "Lots of partying and little memory." That is, without work there is no memory; there is no possible narration of time. These are two distinct ways of living temporality: whereas his son feels comfortable in the present as dissipation (with neither links to the past nor projections of the future), el Rulo still tries to give meaning to his existence through work. This desire is so strong—or so necessary—that he must abandon his affective world (his mother, Adriana, his neighborhood) to go south to work with a crane in a quarry. To achieve stability, to continue to live in the world of labor, he slips into the paradox of having to abandon his affective world. As there is no work, there can be no narration: that is why the movie is a succession of presents that can be linked neither with images from the past nor with images from the future. Hence, the movie does not end (in narrative terms) but is suspended in a close-up of the protagonist returning to Buenos Aires after losing his second job. The narration that *Mundo grúa* offers up to us is, like the identity of its characters, splintered.

Crane World, Film World

> "How do you feel up there?" el Rulo asks.
> "Like a bird," says the man in the crane.

The world changed during the 1990s: power became less accessible, less representable. In Trapero's movie, we see a waiting room, represented by a set of stairs that supposedly leads to the bosses, who never appear, even though they make the cranes move. "They're putting up all the money," Torres says to el Rulo as they climb a set of stairs that leads to nowhere. Union meetings are no longer held to take power but because the workers' lunch hasn't arrived or because they need to "defend [their] work sources," as someone says in one of the CTAs[28] in the South, where el Rulo goes to work.[29] In this context, there is something heroic in el Rulo's defense of his job, and the movie identifies with him. The fact that he maintains his desire despite everything makes his emblematic song not the hit "Paco Camorra," part of an already closed past, but Canaro's "Corazón de oro" ("Heart of Gold"), which ends el Rulo's story. This identification between the protagonist and the director's gaze reaches a love for film itself, already represented in the love for machines. The crane world is the film machine whose pieces (shots or gears) must be assembled for something to function.

How do machines function? How can they be fixed? How do we maintain them or make them run correctly? In *Mundo grúa,* machines proliferate: the car engine that was supposed to take el Rulo home stalls; the shop in his house, where work continues as a hobby; the metal curtain of Adriana's store, which el Rulo fixes and which leads to his relationship with her; the different cranes that he must learn to operate; the car that carries the mechanic (Rolly Serrano) to Comodoro Rivadavia; the bass made, piece by piece, by a luthier; the bars that el Rulo welds in his mother's house.[30] In fact, the movie begins with a machine that does not work and that Torres, el Rulo's friend, must repair.

The most important machine is, evidently, the crane of the title, which runs through the movie in various ways. In Claudio's party scenes, for example, it appears miniaturized in a pinball machine that moves around a metal ball instead of construction materials. The fact that the camera itself climbs into the crane and merges with it through its panoramas of Buenos Aires shows how in these shots the director's intent fuses with that of the actor. For what is the crane, besides a symbol of labor, if not a tool of film, for those shots in which the image appears to be floating, acquiring its own flight? Isn't the crane one of the icons of film, of its power and splendor?[31]

If *Mundo grúa* goes further than *Ciudad de María,* it is because it remains more faithful to the idea of film as a space of resistance (as an alternative to labor and to belief). One of the film's loveliest scenes is the one in which el Rulo and Adriana go to the movies after having dinner in a restaurant. Two fixed shots, and only two, sum up their experience at the movies. The first is a long shot of the seats in which we can make out the light emanating from the projector behind the spectators, while we hear the screams of what appears to be an action movie. A cut, and the second shot: el Rulo and Adriana from behind (as he tries to hug her), looking at two large film projectors that can be seen through an enormous window.[32] "Look at how beautiful it is!" the protagonist exclaims, at the same time that he recognizes the Geneva drive mechanism that it shares with other machines.

Just as the narration is analogously organized, then, with the impossibility of finding a job, the protagonist's desire is assumed by the film in all of its consequences. By means of this identification, *Mundo grúa* constructs a story in which the loss of labor and the desire to have it are part of the same machinery.

Thought and Labor

Mala época is one of the few movies of the new cinema in which we find satire and social criticism. The film is composed of four chapters articulated organically, and the presence of satire as a moral criticism of custom makes the film, made in 1998, one of the few that establishes links with the cinema of the 1980s.[33] This referencing is made clear in the construction of secondary characters, constituted by colloquial and *costumbrista* elements and by a certain image, with a lengthy tradition, of Buenos Aires identity. In addition, classic politics occupies a prominent role, through the figures of Vicentini, an unscrupulous political candidate, and Carlos Brochato, a corrupt and bureaucratic union leader.

This remnant of earlier film does not prevent *Mala época* from being an example of the new cinema, not only because of the presence of a group of technicians and actors who will later appear in other productions but also because the satire takes place parallel to the narration of the four stories: Nicolás Saad's "La querencia" ("Homeland"), and the unfortunate adventures of a small-town guy in the city; Mariano de Rosa's "Vida y obra" ("Life and Work"), and the revelation of a worker on a construction site; Salvador Roselli's "Está todo mal" ("Everything's Wrong"), and the love stories of adolescents at a private high school; and Rodrigo Moreno's "Compañeros" ("Classmates"), and the story of a soundman for political events who falls in love with the girlfriend of his boss, a sinister union leader. None of these narrations—quite disconnected and linked not by their novelty but by the desire to construct an allegory—ends up absorbed by satirical lessons. The stories maintain a certain zone of autonomy, less concerned with underscoring that we live in a bad time, particularly the chapters directed by Mariano de Rosa and Salvador Roselli, which concentrate on more elusive conflicts almost always treated badly in Argentine film. Roselli enters into the experience of an adolescent who discovers, simultaneously, love and betrayal; Rosa approaches, with a rigor bordering on abstraction, the relationship between labor and thought, or, to refer to a famous conceptual pair, between manual and intellectual labor.

The story of "Vida y obra" is simple. At a construction site, Omar, a Paraguayan laborer, pursues a young woman who ultimately reveals herself to be the Virgin. The message that the Virgin gives him, in Guaraní, is that the workers should unite and think about who they are. In keeping with this message, Omar convinces his co-workers to stop working because, he argues, "If we work we can't think." Omar then begins to reflect, jotting down his revelations in a small notebook. The foreman, Luque (Martín Adjemián), decides to call the union, and Carlos Brochato (Carlos Roffe) arrives with some thugs to force Omar to return to work. In addition to hurling insults and growing furious when Omar speaks to him in Guaraní, Brochato attacks him physically. Omar defends himself, pursuing the other man through one of the floors of the job site, and, by accident, knocks down a support and causes a cement block to fall on his own head. This renders him permanently disabled as well as mute. A voice-over explains that the only thing he can now do is think, lamenting the fact that the Virgin came to him "too late." The episode ends with a shot of the notebook in which Omar writes in an incomprehensible scribble.[34]

In *Ciudad de María* and in *Mundo grúa,* the nostalgia for work was produced because work structured a world. Whether as belief or as narration, the time of labor offered the frames and principles that allowed for an articulation of human action. Yet in both cases this action was linked not to politics but to daily life. Somisa's past or el Rulo's job lends a fullness to daily experiences, affective relationships, the return home. In contrast, in "Vida y obra" *political action as a lack* is presented in all of its splendor.[35] From the moment of the revelation of the Virgin, which comes to substitute the workers' desires for the women passing by on the sidewalk, the job is suspended because the entire group affirms that it must begin to think: "If we work we can't think." This suspension is not a strike, although its effects are the same in terms of production, to such an extent that the union leaders arrive not to support the workers but to force them to work—that is, not to think. For by thinking the workers discover that they could also be foremen. The revelation of the Virgin is, then, the putting into operation of a faculty that manual labor prevents, that of thought. This faculty leads Omar to art and to writing, an apparently unproductive activity that is possible only if he cancels his activity as a bricklayer. The protagonist returns to manual art of a different kind; the blank page is the possible space of thought, speculation, and a search. One form of labor replaces another and, in between, life, rebellion, the negation of the world of labor that had been his lot. Political action is cancelled (only the union can call a strike, says the leader), and for this reason Omar reaches the limit: it is no longer a question of improving labor but of suspending it and leaping into another reality.

Paradoxically, through the accident, Omar achieves his objective, although his body must be rendered useless. Unable to perform his work as a bricklayer, he also remains without speech, and we can gain access to his experience only through the voice-over that constitutes the trajectory of his pure thought ("The only thing I can do is think"). "The Virgin came too late," he laments, and the revelation of the mutilation in which he was living (working without thinking) is replaced by another (thinking without working). The scribbling is the revelation, the pure act of writing, contemplation and the way out of the world of labor. Yet this entire experience is incommunicable—except for the spectators who also exercise contemplation and thought.

"Vida y obra" closes the circle of labor: to the desertion of narration and of belief, it adds the absence of politics. Whereas in *Ciudad de María* everything was marked by longing (for what was and no longer is), "Vida y obra" treats labor in the present tense, as something less mythic and omnipotent but flawed. Rather than resort to its epic status, Mariano de Rosa displays its drama, because although labor structures people's lives (as in *Mundo grúa* and *Ciudad de María*), it also severs them. Perhaps this fact seems less crucial once the eclipse of labor is imminent, but "Vida y obra" has the virtue of showing that what becomes the cause for worship once it has disappeared can be insufficient while it exists. Religious and transcendent belief, the miracle—so premodern and so postmodern—lies in wait from without (in *Ciudad de María*) or from within its very center (in "Vida y obra"), but in both cases one thing is clear: labor, which had satisfied the lives of subjects, did not mean emancipation.

Words That Wound: Discrimination in *Bolivia*

For a certain vein of film criticism, the stereotype is evil incarnate. It is still uncertain, however, whether we can think without turning to stereotypes or whether stereotypes in fact help us to think, in certain situations. "We all create stereotypes. We cannot live in the world without them," Sander Gilman writes (1985, 16). Although they can be paralyzing and seem opposed to novelty and modernist sophistication, stereotypes can be of great use in investigating certain social relationships. Of all the films of the 1990s, Adrián Caetano's *Bolivia* has been most frequently seen as a stereotyped representation of popular groups. Is this the case, or does the movie offer a more complex and distanced meditation on stereotypes?[36]

Caetano's feature film, based on a short story by Romina Lafranchini, confronts one of the most central stereotypes of our culture: that surrounding Bolivians, or, as they are derogatorily referred to, *bolitas*. Originally, the adjective Bolivian could refer to a national identity, but further examination reveals that physical appearance and social status are the defining factors. ("He doesn't look Bolivian" is a common expression.) These are widespread social stereotypes that tend to play an active role in the imaginary, linguistic, and perceptive configurations of the average Argentine. "Because there is no real line between self and the Other," Gilman writes, "an imaginary line must be drawn" (1985, 18). Thus, stereotypes banish the other behind a line made up of different judgments ("Bolivians are thieves"; "They don't bathe"), which also tends to preserve the integrity of the (also imaginary) group that emits them.

Despite their simplicity, the practical function of stereotypes tends to be quite complex, establishing a series of prejudices that can be quite independent of what happens in real life. If a "young man" goes in search of a job and finds one, he is someone who has decided to assume responsibility for his own future. If the young man is "Bolivian," we find ourselves facing someone who has come to take work away from "Argentines" (an argument that, strangely, does not apply to Uruguayan or French workers). These prejudices form a *structural instance* that has the capacity to incorporate even that which seems to resist it: no matter how much you bathe, you're Bolivian and, for this reason, dirty. Or, to reaffirm the stereotype, "He's Bolivian, but clean" (as in the phrase "He's Jewish, but a good guy"). Through its mechanisms, the structural instance guarantees a great capacity for absorption that, through repetition, confirms certain relationships of power.[37]

Although artistic stereotypes take their form from social stereotypes, they tend to form a sort of *second degree* of the latter, as they can either reinforce or deconstruct them, showing their artificiality. It is enough to turn on the television to find a proliferation of stereotypes and to see also how, in some cases, the stereotype is ironized. Because of its violence and its harshness, the stereotype of the

Bolivian tends not to appear on television (at least, I can recall no representation), which, in a way, allows the stereotype to continue on its way through the social imagination. In other cases, in particular with gays and transvestites, the strong modifications in the social imagination have led to a wider range of stereotypes. In comic programs in particular, stereotypes are a source of laughter and ridicule. Laughter in such cases has no liberating effect; it reaffirms power and established opinions. Social stereotypes are so strong, have such longevity, and are so interwoven with "common sense" that it is not easy to deconstruct them or reveal their operations. A work of art should lead us to perceive stereotyped characters as such and also show us the *structural instance* that produces them. And this is what *Bolivia* does.[38]

Bolivia tells the story of Freddy (Waldo Flores), a Bolivian who goes to work at a bar in the Constitución neighborhood of Buenos Aires as a "helper" (waiter, grill cook, and dishwasher). His boss is the typically paternalistic Enrique (Enrique Liporace); the clients are taxi drivers—el Oso ("The Bear," Oscar Oso Bertea), Marcelo (Marcelo Videla), Mercado (Alberto Mercado)—and other figures, including Héctor (Héctor Anglada), who is gay.[39] Also working at the grill is Rosa (Rosa Sánchez), the other server and, eventually, Freddy's lover. The story's structure is circular, and the sign that opens the movie ("Grill Cook Wanted") also closes it, after Freddy has been killed by el Oso in a fit of rage.

In an ideological—that is to say, superficial—reading of the movie, the two characters who are saved are Rosa, an emblem of the victims of the reactionary *machismo* of a certain social class, and Enrique, the supposedly understanding boss who functions a little like a second father. (A friend who gives advice is less a friend than a quasi-father.) Yet *Bolivia* shows something more: it stages how the structural instance produces the stereotype of the Bolivian.

The Failure to Adjust

Bolivia displays the artificial and constructed character of stereotypes through the discrepancy between discourse and events, in a split that finds its first manifestation in television.[40] The distorted and slightly banal exhibition that the television image produces opens the movie with a soccer match between Bolivia and Argentina. The split between the visual and the aural is already present in this fragment: the goal scored by Argentina contrasts with the music of the popular Bolivian group los Kjarkas. Later, the television shows a scene from the fight between world champion Mike Tyson and Evander Holyfield, the opponent whose ear Tyson bites off. The sublimated violence of sports reproduces and anticipates, in a distorted way, the material violence that will explode in the bar at the story's end. But the stereotype's falseness and link to power is presented, as in a mise-en-abyme, in the bizarre North American movie that takes place in Buenos Aires that is being shown on the bar's television. Marcelo, the taxi driver, perceives this clearly when he comments: "The bad guys are always the *latinos,* the Latin Americans, the blacks, even the Haitains, *absurd!* They're terrible."[41] Yet, Marcelo will later back up el Oso in his fight with Freddy, who is Bolivian; although he can detect perfectly the presence of stereotypes in a movie, he cannot see how they function in his own life.[42]

Through the difference between the characters' discourse and narrated events, a conflict is produced that leads the spectator to consider with distance and suspicion everything the characters state about other people. This is true of even the most understanding characters, such as Enrique (or especially of these characters, as good intentions and paternalism do not obscure the oblique presence of prejudice). "Freddy, be careful because that girl is a real bitch," Enrique says of Rosa. Throughout the movie, we see Rosa only struggling with different offers of sex in exchange for money or job security. What is it that makes her "a real bitch"? Nothing more or less than the asymmetry of power relations.

This discrepancy between what we see and what we hear is most obvious is in the protagonist himself. Let us pause on Freddy's image. Not only is he Bolivian (that is, he was born in Bolivia) but he also looks Bolivian (the stereotype of what a Bolivian should look like). One can be Argentine and look Bolivian, or be Bolivian and not look it. But Freddy is and looks Bolivian. However, in his actions—and even in his name—he fulfills none of the requirements of the Bolivian stereotype: he is not submissive; he is not retiring ("you know that they're all quiet and then they swipe at you"); he is tidy (in one scene he is freshly bathed and, in contrast to the others, always clean-shaven); he is seductive and elegant, and knows how to inspire respect. In fact, Freddy is the story's heartthrob, developing a relationship with Rosa, the woman the others all desire and whom they can access only through money or favors. With Freddy, Rosa establishes a disinterested relationship based on reciprocal exchange among equals (an immigrant who works under the same conditions and with whom tips are shared).

Dodging one stereotype, Freddy manages to avoid another: that of the irreproachable hero. He fights, lies, is reckless, does not know how to move around in the city. Rather than a stereotype, Freddy represents, historically, a prototype of a certain type of Latin American and Eastern European migration proper to the 1990s. "The farm laborer or peasant (*campesino*)," writes Silviano Santiago, "leaps past the Industrial Revolution and falls by foot, swimming, train, boat or airplane, directly into the postmodern metropolis. Many times without the intermediary of the necessary consular permit" (2004, 52). As he tells Rosa, Freddy was a farm laborer in his country of origin; if he does not appear to be, it is because globalization has reduced, when it has not erased, regional features and other marks of belonging. (Freddy narrates his past as a farm laborer as he plays on a pinball machine depicting the Addams Family.) Nevertheless, some critics have argued that Caetano reproduced stereotypes. Might it not be that the "prison-house of the image" is so powerful that we see a Bolivian stereotype where in reality none exists?[43]

From the point of view of the narration, *Bolivia* denies, in the character of Freddy, one of the characteristics that Bolivians are saddled with in Argentina, and yet the stereotype functions as much for the other characters as for critics. At the start of the film, a character who falls asleep in the bar (clearly a good-for-nothing) tells Rosa, "Stop busting my balls, black girl" (*negra*), and insults Freddy as "poor, black, wimpy" (*negro muerto de hambre, cagón*). What does the insult "poor" (*muerto de hambre;* literally, "starving to death") describe when uttered by someone who sleeps in bars because he has nothing of his own and who hurls his insult at someone who is working? Its efficacy lies in the fact that the phrase is false in terms of facts but true with respect to the imagination to which it appeals.[44] For this reason, any story told about discrimination must confront and narrate this fact: why stereotypes, despite everything, form a nucleus of power that only with great difficulty can be destroyed by facts.

Reality As Insufficiency (the Prison-House of the Image)

A stereotype, then, is an image constructed with words and gazes that involves power relations. In this construction, *Bolivia* puts the visual image, as opposed to dialogues, into operation. Whereas the linguistic exchanges between characters establish hierarchies and update power relations, the visual mise-en-scène is based on the equivalence among different viewpoints. Although it is difficult to determine a logic to the mise-en-scène given the abundance of takes, there are three types of shots that combine to construct the space of the bar in which almost the entire story takes place (in addition to the detail shots and the extreme close-ups that, at the film's beginning, introduce us to its atmosphere).

In the first place, high-angle shots tend to show the actions of the workers and clients: they are like notes of the restricted and regular movements that organize daily life in the bar. Seen from above, the characters seem to move like marionettes under our gaze. This type of shot, neutral in its description of movements, is particularly expressive when money is involved. When el Oso pays for his sandwich or Héctor leaves some coins on the bar, the high-angle shot is closer and lasts longer, highlighting the importance of economic transactions in the narration's development. (This is fundamental for the drama of el Oso, from the beginning a man hounded by debts.) These shots correspond to the special economy and economic space of the bar.

The most frequent type of shot in *Bolivia* is the medium shot, which shoots the characters at eye level and establishes a relationship of equivalence or respect among them. The image underscores the human component that words tend to deny. This type of shot is short, is articulated with the logic of the shot–countershot, and varies constantly to give space to all the characters. Its theme is the gaze and the alliance of antagonisms among the characters, and it generates a space charged with meaning in which power relations are constantly present.[45] As these relationships unfold, it is as though the camera, through medium shots, is maintaining an equal status for all of the characters.

Third, there are the long shots of the bar that are almost always taken from the zone occupied by the television, so that the characters talk among themselves as they direct a gaze at one side of the camera. Here the gaze is not shared among the characters but is anchored by a hypnotic point in space. The television images that impel the characters are not neutral: power relations appear here as spectacle, as in the soccer match between Bolivia and Argentina, the fight between Tyson and Holyfield, or that strange U.S. movie that takes place in Buenos Aires.

Despite this abundance of takes, there is a very strong absence from the system of shots in *Bolivia*: there are no point-of-view shots. We accompany the characters' gazes, but at no point do we assume their positions or see through them, as if the camera, obsessed with their gazes, does not want to be identified or confused with them. This mise-en-scène that seeks to transform gazes into an objective and palpable material, presenting them without choosing any one over another, breaks down precisely in the final scene when el Oso shoots Freddy. (The frenzied editing of the fight scene has already anticipated the rupture in the logic of shots sustained until this moment.)

The scene plays out as follows: after fighting with Freddy, el Oso and Marcelo leave the bar and go to Marcelo's taxi, where they call a tow truck. El Oso opens the glove compartment and looks at himself in the rearview mirror. He sees his nose bloodied from the blow that Freddy landed on him. The character discovers himself in a position that inspires not respect but scorn (the origin of resentment), and he decides to cleanse his blood with that of the *other* (the one who is guilty for this physical wound, who is also, in his eyes, painfully symbolic). The camera then locates itself inside the taxi, behind both characters. When el Oso takes out the gun, the camera moves to a shot from the point of view of el Oso: we see the revolver pointing and Freddy in the doorway of the bar, and we hear a shot being fired.

Although there is perhaps a suggestion of the spectator's own guilt here, what is decisive is that the relations of control and exclusion acquire, here, an objective status by means of a point-of-view shot (as if el Oso's subjectivity were not his but something that he shares with reality). The discriminatory gestures that the camera had been registering from without are therefore embodied in el Oso. Moreover, although the act of violence is personal (el Oso takes revenge on Freddy), the structural instance that guarantees it has a long sedimentation in social stereotypes: an Argentine punishes a Bolivian. All the weight of controlled aggression throughout the story falls on Freddy, and the image itself, which had remained impartial, is impelled to confirm the "prisons of image" within which, according to Alice Walker's expressive formula, the stereotype is enclosed (quoted in Shohat and Stam 1994, 198).

The Insult As the Production of Identity (the Prison-House of Language)

In contrast to the visual equilibrium that the mise-en-scène establishes until the conflict explodes, disequilibrium emerges in the language of the characters. Appearing intermittently yet persistently, the insult increasingly makes its way through the polite dialogues that tend to regulate life in a bar. At the level of discourse, the insult is the mode in which the place of the other is constituted in a type of enunciation that draws its strength from its capacity to physically interpolate the interlocutor. Extremely crystallized forms of speech, insults are what Judith Butler deems "words that wound" because, although they are speech acts, they have a violent performative character in addition to producing, in the case of acts of discrimination, a social subjection based on preexisting power relations (1997, 18). An insult like "shitty black" or "dirty Bolivian" never has the same offensive and corporeal effect as "shitty white." In each insult the social structure and position that the subjects occupy is also enunciated.[46]

In *Bolivia,* the most discriminatory offenses come from el Oso, who ends up killing Freddy. To follow the discourse of this character (the definition of resentment) is to see how discrimination and stereotypes function on the basis of suppositions, gaps, and contradictions. At first, the basic distinction that he makes is between "people from my country" and "people not from my country" ("from *outside*"). Of those who come "from outside" he says that "*someone* opened the door for them" and "they rake in money in a day," an affirmation that renders el Oso a subject of universal generosity, a would-be victim of foreign ploys. These "people from outside" are interchangeable, because the one who "screwed him over" is a "Uruguayan son of a bitch," Paraguayans are "shitty blacks," and the "Paraguayan Chilavert" was right when he said that "Bolivians are all fags" (a declaration that comes immediately before the physical aggression that unleashes the conflict). The substitution of Uruguayans for Paraguayans and for Bolivians reveals the mechanisms of his discourse, because in reality Uruguayans do not trigger the racial and national hatred that Paraguayans, Peruvians, and Bolivians generate. El Oso's paranoid delirium operates according to linguistic *substitution* and in a *reactualization* of power relations.[47] Another victim of the economic system, he finds symbolic consolation by locating himself, by means of the insult, on the side of the powerful (taking advantage, in addition, of the contingent fact that he is not "Bolivian," nor does he look it).

The Paraguayan author Augusto Roa Bastos has said that "on a dead-end street, the only way out is that street." And this phrase is valid for the labyrinth of discrimination that el Oso has entered into: without his knowing it, his own rash and unthinking discourse offers up the way out of this entanglement. When he totters around half-drunk and Freddy moves to help him, el Oso rebukes him: "You think I need a *Bolivian* like you, you think I need help from just *anybody?*" (my emphasis). When el Oso's body falls, racist discourse comes to save him, to prop him up. Racist stereotypes, writes Sander Gilman, appear when self-integration is threatened (1985, 18). Ultimately, discourse encounters its limit and the insult becomes physical punishment, always on the offense: el Oso punches Freddy and throws him behind the counter at the bar. The acceleration of the story is then unleashed, marked by a frenetic editing that culminates in Freddy's breaking el Oso's nose and the exit of the taxi drivers. From the taxi, el Oso shoots at Freddy and gets him in the heart. We encounter the suspension not only of speeches, the words that wound, but also of the sound itself. A slow-motion camera, in the style of Sam Peckinpah (undoubtedly one of Caetano's strongest references), and at the end the movie's initial situation is reestablished: Enrique again puts up the "Grill Cook Wanted" sign that opened the film. It is as though *Bolivia* distorted time and the story lasted exactly a day; between one morning and the next, the other is expelled.[48]

Yet, as el Oso himself says, the "shitty Bolivian" is also an "anybody." It is not that el Oso could be Freddy (a typical means of contesting racism, telling the victimizer that he could be the victim, as though racism were a psychological, rather than structural, problem). Rather, there is an object on which discrimination is exercised who is *an anybody*. This is the absurd and empty backdrop against which discrimination is exercised, and not the fact that in reality Jews or blacks or Bolivians cannot be how they are described.

The victims find themselves in the paradox that they are simultaneously an anybody and a determined someone. The "anybody" does not mean that people are equivalent but that they are equal and that, from their identities, they negotiate their difference. El Oso wants to deny Freddy this possibility: the other is an *anybody* (which he means to be derogatory) and he is a *someone* ("someone opens the door for them"). Like any plebeian who is hurt and wants to be considered an equal, el Oso tells the bar owner, "You're going to respect *me*." But when he adds that "you think that I'm that Bolivian [*bolita*] who's over there sweating?" he frustrates any possibility of reciprocity that, in modernity, establishes respect or the possibility of its existence. Understanding the *anybody* as a space of universal substitution in which rights should come before power would have saved el Oso from the humiliation of self-loathing and from the frustration of meaningless violence.

Through images and words, *Bolivia* constructs a barely visible, if not invisible, reality, in the culture of Buenos Aires, of the existence of increasingly energetic and powerful migratory cultures. If

Caetano's movie approximates his characters by means of an affirmation and negation of stereotypes, it is because stereotypes continue to regulate our relationships with these communities and these cultures that often prosper at a few feet from our homes but that we are still unable to see.

Los rubios: Mourning, Frivolity, and Melancholy

Que le lecteur ne se escandalise pas de cette gravité dans le frivole.

— Charles Baudelaire,
"Le peintre de la vie moderne"[49]

In a division of labor never made explicit, in recent Argentine cinema the documentary has been assigned the task of taking charge of the historic past. Although there are exceptions, such as Cristian Bernard and Flavio Nardini's *76 89 03* or Marco Bechis' *Garage Olimpo*, in almost all fiction films of the new cinema references to our political past are nonexistent. In the genre of documentary, in contrast, beginning with the historical and testimonial reflection opened up by Andrés Di Tella's *Montoneros, una historia* (1998, "*Montoneros*, a Story") and David Blaustein's *Cazadores de utopías* (1996, "Hunters of Utopia"), the obsession with the past has grown in recent years to the point where a good chunk of documentary production is dedicated to investigating Argentina's political past.[50]

The most revisited era during the 1990s was not the period of the military dictatorship of the late 1970s and early 1980s but the entire decade of the 1970s, with a special emphasis on armed, militant organizations. It is as though, once the revision of the dictatorship had been completed, an increasing interest in reflecting on and documenting the years immediately prior opened up in all fields of culture. Hugo Vezzetti's book *Pasado y presente: Guerra, dictadura y sociedad en la Argentina* (2003, "Past and Present: War, Dictatorship, and Society in Argentina") in the field of criticism, Martín Caparrós and Eduardo Anguita's monumental work *La voluntad: una historia de la militancia revolucionaria en la Argentina* (1998, "Will: A Story of Revolutionary Militancy in Argentina"), and the movies cited above are a sign of this shift. It is not that debate about the dictatorship has been eliminated. Rather, the idea that state terrorism is qualitatively different from other, more particular forms of violence and that state violence should be condemned and repudiated in all of its forms managed to establish itself in society with relative success. Once this success had been obtained (principally as a result of the action of human rights organizations and law suits against those involved in the military coup), the path was cleared for a debate on the 1970s, which could build on the irrefutable supposition that civil violence in no way justified the repressive, illegal action of the state.

A previously unknown element contributed to this necessity to rethink those years: the fact that many of the children who had been direct victims of state terrorism were now in their twenties and thirties and had begun to use film as a means of expression. María Inés Roqué, Albertina Carri, and Andrés Habegger (all children of known *montonero*[51] militant activists assassinated by the government) found in film a means of processing the work of mourning. Yet how can one mourn when the necessary establishment of justice is defective or partial? How can one recover this childhood past, in which one lived in relative ignorance of what was happening?[52] Finally, how can one liberate energies when the key pieces in this process are missing: the body of the dead person, the condemnation of those who are responsible, and a reliable story of the victim's last days?

María Inés Roqué's *Papá Iván* (2004), Albertina Carri's *Los rubios,* and Andrés Habegger's *(h) historias cotidianas* (2001, "Stories of Everyday Life") are movies, histories, testimonies to get out of mourning.[53] In different ways, these three movies function as "epitaphs," as María Inés Roqué states explicitly in her *Papá Iván:* "I thought that this movie would be a tomb, but it isn't." Only *Los rubios* manages to leave mourning behind. Rather than a film-epitaph, Carri elaborates a film of artifice (*film-del-postizo*), or one of people's public roles.

It is not difficult to say why these young people turned to film to process their pasts. The indexical character of the cinematic image allows for the construction of a testimonial space that is very effective for memory, including photographs, voices, audio recordings, documents, people who knew the victims, records of collective events, and so on: an entire visual and auditory arsenal for mourning work. At the same time, as though this visual space were insufficient to touch that which is ineluctably extinct, these three documentaries return—above all in interludes—to haptic images, that is, to images with a texture that suggests the tactile through prominence, strong contrasts, and different surfaces.[54] These include the leaves of the trees seen from above in *Papá Iván,* the posters with three-dimensional effects in *Los rubios,* and the shots of the river with glimmers of light in *(h) historias cotidianas.* With the exception of this last film, in which there is also a thematic angle (the Río de la Plata is the place where the bodies of the disappeared were thrown), these haptic images work with the dialectic of near and far, of image and nature, of visual deception and tactile verification.[55] It is as though in the face of the distance of visual memory, these stories were conceding a moment of pure sensation and fusion with their object (memory itself). Whereas in *Papá Iván* and *(h) historias cotidianas* the haptic images are beyond language (a nature that will no longer be the same: the river is hiding something; the transient nature of the leaves on the trees now connotes an absence), in *Los rubios* they are made up of language (the titles and posters inserted in black and white have prominence). This is because Carri's movie shows most thoroughly the "failure of visual representation" (Amado 2004, 76) as testimony and document.[56] Thus, owing to its virtualities and despite its limitations, film is a potential space for mourning work.

Of these three films, only Carri's has the words "The end" coincide with a way out of mourning; the other two end up failing in their efforts.[57] From the beginning María Inés Roqué posits her goal as the definitive burial of her father, yet toward the film's end the shadow of this father becomes so powerful that the effort to settle accounts with him is in vain. Roqué begins her mourning work with the idea that her father abandoned her, but the various testimonies recorded in her film insist so much on his heroism that the abandonment moves into the background and her father ultimately settles in as a monument, inspiring respect, distance, and a certain reverential fear. "I always said that I would rather have a living father than a dead hero," Roqué recalls, but she never manages to question whether her father was, in fact, a hero, or the nature of this heroism. Mourning transforms into a celebration, and the filmmaker, always a daughter, ends up on a one-way street.[58]

All of this despite the fact that Roqué has access to one of the most stunning testimonies in political documentaries made in Argentina— that of her own mother. By explaining her differences with her ex-husband (her rejection of violence as a political instrument) and by showing that other civic activities were possible, Roqué's mother contests a weak historicism that seeps through in nearly all other documentaries: one that states that violence was the only possible path and that the natural thing in that era was to opt for armed struggle. ("You had to be there" is constantly repeated in political documentaries.[59]) The mother's testimony, however, seems marred by personal grudges, particularly when it is compared with Miguel Bonasso's, which, appealing to his heroism, installs Roqué once again in the space from which the film itself had wanted to remove him. The present, in the face of past actions, seems diminished; present aspirations seem banal, frivolous, and insignificant in light of the ambitions of militant activists from the past: to change history, to save the nation, to transform society; in short, to make a better world. At no point does Roqué manage to displace the "living hero" to reencounter her "dead father," and this failure fuels the intensity and beauty of *Papá Iván*. It is significant that one of the final testimonies, that of one of Iván's fellow activists, affirms that Iván died as an upright man, stating, "We can't ask anything more of life."

Andrés Habeggar's (*h*) *historias cotidianas,* in contrast to the films by Carri and Roqué, has a more institutional insertion (the group HIJOS) and a dual goal: to recover the intimate experiences of the children of the disappeared who give their testimony and to show the different ways in which the protagonists try to bring closure to their stories when they cannot find it in juridical reparation. The parenthetical (*h*) of the film's title symbolizes the gap or hollow (*hueco*) that disappearance left in the daily life of those who give testimony. The film's chapters are entitled *huellas* ("Traces"), *historia* ("History"), *Hijos* ("Children"), and *hoy* ("Today"). Habegger, the son of a well-known disappeared *montonero* radical and survivor of the Trelew prison in southern Argentina, interviews six witnesses, who present different aspects of the conflict.[60] In contrast to Roqué and Carri, the director never becomes involved, preferring to limit himself to a more traditional organization of testimonies, perhaps because he firmly believes that politics is located outside of the film rather than within it.[61] In contrast, *Papá Iván* and *Los rubios* consider form fundamental because it is within the filmic narration itself that the possibility of memory and an opening up to the present are at stake.

Of these three films, *Los rubios* is the only one that appears to get out of mourning, and it does so because it questions the political project of the father and, by extension, of the armed organizations of the 1970s. Its position is not that these people were cowards—bravery is present above all in the intense testimony of the young photographer whose life was saved thanks to the militant activists Carri and Oesterheld. Rather, it foregrounds other aspects: the deflation of the past, the questioning of parental decisions, why it is worth giving one's life to a cause.

In contrast to other political documentaries, Carri's does not emphasize the narration of the past. She turns to an actress (Analía Couceyro)
to represent herself, also acting in the film as director, and surrounds her
with technical-artistic collaborators (Jésica Suárez, sound editor; assistant directors Santiago Giralt and Marcelo Zanelli; the camerawomen
Catalina Fernández and Carmen Torres). Facing the heroic actions of
the past (they placed themselves at risk, gave their lives for what they
believed in), with palpable remorse over the fact that today nothing is
worth giving one's life for, *Los rubios* shows a vital present, painful
but without guilt, with an activity (making film) no less honorable than
that of her parents, Roberto Carri and Ana María Caruso (making
the revolution). There is a world with which the director identifies
(cinema), just as her parents had found a world in activism. Yet Carri
goes further. Her parents' move to a poor neighborhood is the object
of different objections, among which a critique of the populist attitude
that idealizes the supposed beneficiaries of its actions stands out. In
reality, these beneficiaries perceived her parents as "blonds" (that is,
as somehow foreign or different from them). All of this misfortune is
symbolized by the noise of a typewriter in a neighborhood where no
one else has one, which ends up being heard by some neighbors whose
highest ideal is "peace and quiet." After Carri's parents disappeared,
says one of the informers, a neighbor whose hair is dyed a harsh black,
there was "super peace and quiet." The very struggle of her parents is
ironized: "I remember my father and his rage and his tireless toil until
his death."

Why is it worth it to give one's life for a cause? *Los rubios* responds
with a Witkiewicz poem, reproduced with raised letters in the film,
that provokes the haptic sensation cited above:

> if everything could be like that
> like memories
> i would love all of humanity
> i would die for it, happily

To die with delight for humanity, but on one condition: that past and
present be one and the same. However, the poem's conditional shows
that this fusion is far from taking place. Instead, one must choose in
the present; one cannot live forever anchored in memory. In addition
to its content, it is also fundamental that this quote is a poem, as *Los
rubios* responds with neither pamphleteering nor a discourse of justification or historical explanation. Confronting her parents' choice of

political militancy, Carri responds with a choice of aesthetics as the territory in which it is worth living or giving one's life. In this decision and in her own terrain, she meets up with her parents, who gave her life and who gave their lives. In this imaginary encounter, she arrives with three amulets: aesthetic appearance, the perception of a young girl, and memory from the perspective of a vital present.

Mourning and the Pose

Edward Said's distinction between filiation and affiliation in *The World, the Text, and the Critic* (1983) helps us understand Albertina Carri's effort to respond to the legacy of her parents. Filiation wants to impose a continuous series, without sutures, symbolized in the father–son relationship; affiliation comprises "peculiarly cultural associations between forms, statements, and other aesthetic elaborations on the one hand and, on the other, institutions, agencies, classes, and amorphous social forces" (1983, 174–5). In this passage from filiation to affiliation, from being the daughter of disappeared parents to being a film director, Carri is able to complete the trajectory of mourning.

Parents and daughter reencounter one another in the title, *Los rubios* ("The Blonds"). All three are blond, which in the film's logic means to be both different and rebellious. Whereas the parents are "blond" for their adoption of a cause (that of the people), their daughter is "blond" because she is a filmmaker, interested in poses, props, appliqués, the fake or false. At the moment at which they reencounter one another, they also diverge: all three are blond, yes, but for different reasons. In this separation, Carri begins to construct her *affiliation* for aesthetics, or the cunning tricks of cinematic form.

In contrast to nearly all other political documentaries on the disappeared, *Los rubios* not only speaks of "art history" but also uses more complex aesthetic procedures beyond the mere documentary interview. Contiguity and the confusion between fiction and testimony, constant self-references, expressive repetitions through editing, the contrast of fixed and moving images, and other devices distance Carri's film from the fixed genre of the political documentary, generally made on the basis of interviews, documentary images, and the informative use of the videograph. Instead of portraits of politicians or party posters, political marches or archival images, film and editing equipment surround the actress who plays the director in her studio. Here, she is framed by two posters: one of Jean-Luc Godard (his gaze multiplied innumerable times in a poster for a retrospective of his work) and another of the mythic John Waters' *Cecil B. DeMented* (2000). *Los rubios* distances itself from political documentary and seeks out an affiliation with Godard's avant-garde films and with Waters' parodic aesthetics of trash, his frivolity that foments the sinister. It is no coincidence that the actress Analía Couceyro wears glasses that evoke Godard's when she reads aloud the letter from the INCAA and sits like Melanie Griffith in the publicity for Waters' film as she listens to testimonies. *Cecil B. DeMented* tells the story of a film director and his collaborators who act as a guerrilla cell of independent filmmakers against Hollywood, sporting wigs and other accessories to kidnap a successful actress.[62]

One of the posters inserted throughout *Los rubios* makes reference to this drama of filiation and affiliation: "i don't think that my family knows anything/and what's most likely is that you are your parents' daughter/i also thought i was king solomon's son/rasputin's/mata hari's/and nothing/you see/it turns out i'm my parents' daughter." Mata Hari, the World War I spy who become a film heroine (Marlene Dietrich, Jeanne Moureau); King Solomon, the hero of a children's book; and Rasputin, libertine sorcerer of the Tsarist court.[63] Once again poetry provides a possible flight for the gaze of a little girl who is still searching for explanations (or for the young woman who is looking for explanations for the perception of the girl she used to be). The prose poem excerpted here, Olga Orozco's "Solferino" (1998, 258), tells of an imaginary incursion into the world of childhood, marked by magic and the presence of the strange, signified here, as in Baudelaire's famous text, by gypsies and by the magicians of children's stories. Suspending the contents of filiation, *Los rubios* investigates all of the folds of affiliation, the different, perhaps unspeakable, intensities of a girl who grew up as an orphan, without any explanation.

Carri offers us not a character anchored in the past but a difficult confrontation between a present that she remembers and a past that drifts away. All of this explains why the director refuses to present herself in the process of mourning: it would do nothing to offer to the gaze of others the contrite but soothing scene of the daughter of the disappeared in mourning. The pose of mourning is concealed from us by a sleight of hand, and this frivolity has bothered critics of *Los rubios*. Even in the scene where this trauma of the mourning appears most explicit—when the actress plays Albertina as a young girl, on her birthday, making three wishes that are really a single wish: that her parents return—the distancing is extreme (Kohan 2004a).

In another scene, the crew starts up a discussion when the INCAA refuses to support the film, and Albertina abruptly interrupts her colleagues: "Let's get to work." The work of film displaces the work of mourning. In the past we see her as a daughter without parents; in the present, as a film director. "In place of the family," Ana Amado writes, "she forges a fraternal community, made up of her mini-film crew. Their blond wigs, like a masquerade of filiation, in exchange for blood as the certification of an alliance" (2004, 77). A documentary on the disappeared, *Los rubios* is also a documentary on the process of filming, and on a group of friends united by cinema.

As Carri made the movie, it does not make much sense to claim that she did so only to forget. Carri offers us a frivolous pose, but nothing about this is simple, for the film tells us that watching, listening, and understanding the image constitutes an entire process of apprenticeship. It is not simply about making memories, about placing five or six talking heads to evoke the past from their own experiences and broadcasting three or four judgments about the historical past, interspersing them with archival images. Memory has many more complex mechanisms, and the most perverse may be that of paralyzing us in the past, suppressing the present: a memory of traces that has lost all projection of the future, a permanent mourning that insists on a perpetual burial of the dead. The director herself asks at what point "obstinate memory does not become a mere whim."

To negotiate this crossroads, Carri turns to frivolity. This is a truly risky pose, given the gravity of the conflict, because it has the potential to make the spectator impassive (or lead him or her to *indolencia,* the state of being unmoved or unaffected).[64] And Carri seems to take pleasure in throwing us off track and in locating the processes of suffering beyond our gaze. According to Sigfried Kracauer in his book on Offenbach (1938), two types of frivolity existed during the period he studies. One was linked to cynicism and the idea that social hypocrisy was necessary, given man's wicked nature. The opposing type is found in the frivolousness of Halevy, Offenbach's librettist, who dedicated himself to an irony based in the conviction that paradise was lost (1938, 205–7). With the seminal scene of the countryside, *el campito*[65] (an idyllic place where Carri spent her childhood), the director's frivolity intermingles with an ability to discern and an ironic capacity with respect to what her childhood had and no longer has. "I don't like dead cows, I prefer beautiful architecture," the director says at one point. This statement, on the very surface of frivolity, links the cows of the countryside (fantasy) to the sinister architectonic refractions of the concentration camp where her father was held, to the photographs of the woman who had met her father in the camp, and, finally, to a position that is "at the antipodes of the realism of the slaughterhouse" (Amado 2004, 46). That is, frivolity here had to do not with cynicism but with disenchantment, for Carri loses paradise twice: first when her parents are taken from her and later when she realizes that her parents had been in a much more terrible place, when the idyll of the countryside becomes something else. Her frivolity is not at the antipodes of the sinister but is instead a way of dealing with it as contiguity; it is a way of emptying out the subject (abandoning pathos) to see the workings of the past and of memory. The detour of the aesthetic leads not to an apolitical gaze but to a different path, where form and event condition one another.

The inclusion of the music of the group Virus, which at first might seem to be another act of frivolity, should also be read in this sense. With the lyrics of Roberto Jacoby (one of the protagonists of the avant-garde Torcuato Di Tella Institute of the 1960s and a participant in *Tucuman Arde*[66]), Federico Moura's group opened up an unprecedented space in the years of the return to democracy, showing, against the "protest" music then in vogue, that fun and distraction can also have a political character. (Among other images, I remember the partisan protests with which the group illustrated on a big screen its album *Recrudece* at a 1982 concert.[67]) Virus was the most political group of the 1980s, just as Carri's is the most political of the documentary films on the disappeared—not only because it works on memory but also because it puts forth the possibilities of making a community with the signs of the present.[68] For this reason the frivolity that would appear to be a capricious gesture is, in reality, a critique of the identification and idealization of the past.

The Gaze of Children

Little has been written on the relationship between political theory and childhood. Whether with wisdom or with common sense, treatises—from Aristotle to Bobbio—do not include children, for as subjects they are at the margins of the public sphere.[69] In modernity, the arrival of adulthood was marked by the entrance into public life; the fact that there had been child monarchs and that monarchs had treated their subjects like children was seen as an outrage. In an effort to avoid well-known images from fascism, Nazism, and Stalinism and to construct a benevolent image, the last military dictatorship in

Argentina and its attending journalism used a famous photograph of the dictator General Videla with a little girl.[70] This image attempted to cover up the greatest outrage of the dictatorship years: the kidnapping of children (many of them born in captivity) and their subsequent handing over to substitute families (generally part of the military or linked to the repression). In paranoid fashion, the military dictatorship believed that these children were potential subversives and that it was necessary to extract them from the "evil" influence of their families. Hence, one of the darkest acts of this period of genocide: the attack against those who, by definition, participated neither in politics nor in public life.

Crimes committed against children do not expire,[71] because they are considered crimes against humanity, and they have been fundamental in the proceedings against many of the participants in the military dictatorship pardoned by Carlos Menem's government. In recent years, several books have moved to other zones of political life, revisiting the lives of activists during the 1970s and the relationships among families.[72] In Argentina, the unwitting participation of children in the violent political struggles of the 1970s had conflictive aspects, because the shift from rural guerrilla movements (Ernesto "Che" Guevara's *foquista* theory[73]) to the urban realm meant that the struggle was no longer separate in military terms from the spaces of daily and familial life. In this shift, organizations, particularly the *montoneros,* did not establish a political difference for minors and, in many cases, encouraged their members to continue life within the familial nucleus.[74] In this context, the *foquista* theory, for all of the criticisms that have been directed against it, makes a lot of sense: by abandoning what was his and going into the jungle to struggle, the guerrilla did not put the lives of his family in danger.[75] In fact, all of Guevara's children are alive. In the case of the Argentine guerrilla movements, specifically urban in character, daily life became militarized, and the zone of the private that could have been sheltered from political action and the demands of full-time activism was dissolved.

In addition to making note of the acts of illegal repression that characterized the dictatorship years, *Los rubios* finds one of its core themes in the relationship between childhood, politics, and repression.[76] The director's own testimony, orally reconstructing a moment that she barely remembers (she was only three years old at the time), when "two men" arrived; the representation of the kidnapping with playmobile dolls; the story of her parents' fate that she hears at the age of twelve; the visits to the "countryside," where her childhood took place—these are the most important aspects of an issue that runs through the entire film, with different modulations. When her parents were kidnapped, Carri was three years old; that is, she had learned to speak recently, she had a natural inclination to believe in magic, and she had no understanding of politics. This is why she sets up a reading of the kidnapping with what she has at hand: little dolls, fantasy, and action B-movies. Film, which is now her trade, provided her during her childhood with both company and the shaping of a sensibility.

One of the key points in Martín Kohan's article is his assertion that the child's gaze that Carri constructs "depoliticizes" the kidnapping. In opposition to this gaze, Kohan offers as exemplary the testimony of Carri's nephew, referred to both in *Los rubios* and in the documents compiled in Juan Gelman and Mara La Madrid's book *Ni el flaco perdón de Dios* ("Not Even God's Weak Forgiveness"). These testimonies speak of children who fantasized about killing the dictator Videla. Although I do not believe that the testimony of a five-year-old who "spoke at length on the one thousand and one ways of killing Videla" *politicizes* anything, the proliferation of children in Carri's movie seems more inclined toward questioning a way of doing politics (that of her parents) that transforms children into the material of a political problem.[77] In fact, Carri references her nephew's testimony and points out that her sister, the boy's mother, has prohibited her from including it. Carri complies with this wish, and we could say that she refuses to subject this child, her nephew, to the process that she herself was subjected to, that of not having a private life separate from the demands of public life.[78] In this light, a scene that may initially appear irrelevant acquires its full meaning. Analía Couceyro stays in the neighborhood talking with a group of children about the house in which the Carri family lived. The kids are of various ages; one or two are possibly the same age as Carri when her parents were kidnapped. We cannot speak in this case of a reliable testimony, but we can speak of a strange, invented world that children enter into. Through these testimonies, the movie shows the nature of a perception and the modes of imagining that could have been the director's own when her parents were taken from her.

In turning strategically to children, *Los rubios* not only refuses to depoliticize; it also offers a resounding political critique of 1970s activism: in politicizing all aspects of social life, this activism ended up putting at risk realms that should have remained sheltered. Even the epigraph from her father's book *Isidro Velázquez*, which Couceyro reads in the film, speaks of the disappearance of "egotism" and of "private interest" in place of a "general will," a term from Rousseau that acquires different nuances when considered from the point of view of those who do not form a part of it. By investing their entire life in political activism, they dragged their children, who were in a position neither to choose nor to comprehend this engagement, into the struggle. One of the few testimonies of a fellow activist of Carri's parents describes it thus:

> I feel that they [Albertina's parents] made a great effort to assume a different life, kids and all....They did this by dedicating their entire lives to political activism. So, I have images where the kids were always there, obviously the weapons were there, the kids, *everything mixed together*. At a certain point Ana and Roberto were giving it their all, hoping it would bring some good. I don't know how they lived it in the last stage; I think it was already a circle, a challenge that they couldn't back out of. (My emphasis)

In *Los rubios,* just as children proliferate throughout the narration, the story itself acquires childlike forms, from the use of the playmobiles to represent her parents' kidnapping to the trip to the countryside where Carri spent part of her childhood.[79] These two forms, which bind interiority and fantasy, are self-sufficient. The playmobiles are shown, but never the players; the little dolls acquire life through editing, and the inorganic world of toys becomes organic and appears to move on its own. In the case of the countryside, this self-sufficiency is achieved by means of an extensive circular panning that the director herself explains to the actress playing her. Both spaces are counterposed to the neighborhood where her parents went to live, shown as a hostile, amorphous space, one that the film crew wants to leave as quickly as possible. In contrast to the life-size scale of the neighborhood, we have the game's miniaturization.[80]

The self-sufficiency of these worlds attempts to suture the fantasies of a memory (the director's) that is reopened and riven through by history. As Susan Stewart writes, "[T]he miniature, linked to nostalgic versions of childhood and history, presents a diminutive, and thereby manipulable, version of experience, a version which is domesticated and protected from contamination" (2001, 69). This miniaturization stresses the childlike perception that the movie seeks out; in its self-sufficiency, it retranslates outside events, including political violence, family life, and free time. In fact, the movie opens with a "typical family" (father, mother, son or daughter) of playmobiles entering a house. It ends with the kidnapping of the parents set up as a B-movie, the kind of super-action film that Carri might have seen on Saturday afternoon as a child, as in Robert Wise's *The Day the Earth Stood Still*.[81] The psychedelic soundtrack of the kidnapping scene is taken from this movie, whose music was composed by Vernard Hermann, responsible for the exceptional music of Welles and Hitchcock. Once again, the aesthetics of film offers the means to leave mourning behind.

What the film confronts head on, then, is childhood perception and political action. Through children's actions, *Los rubios* questions certain attitudes of Carri's parents and emphasizes one of the most difficult aspects of the 1970s, the role of children in armed organizations. Yet because the movie offers up to us not only the construction of a past but also the gaze of a survivor, the following question emerges from the conflict: How is it possible to construct an identity without parents in a society that interpolates these victims exclusively as children, which does not allow them another identification?

Albertina Disappears

Gran parte de cuanto creemos, y así es hasta en las últimas conclusiones, con idéntica obcecación y buena fe, nace de un primer engaño en las premisas.

—Marcel Proust, *Albertine disparue*

Carri's peculiar mourning process is not limited to a critique of her parents' action or to an opposition between aesthetics and politics. A third element is necessary to find a way out of mourning and to implicate the other two: the opposition between present and past and the construction of a unique space in light of the gaze of others. "In my case," we hear in the film, "the stigma of a threat remains from those days of terror and violence, in which saying my last name meant danger and rejection. To say my last name in certain circles still meant strange gazes, a mixture of *uncertainty and pity*" (my emphasis). In this respect, frivolity is opposed not so much to melancholia or suffering as to nostalgia and tragedy. Frivolity does not have a permanent character; rather, it is an inclination that is, in certain moments, displaced by suffocation. After the interview with the neighbor who turned her parents in, the director must open the window of the car in which she is traveling because she feels that she cannot breathe. And in other moments we see her remorseful or overexcited (especially in the interviews with her parents' former neighbors).

It is not, then, that *Los rubios* conceals tragedy or pain but that these emotions must be articulated in terms of the other two actions that we see the director performing: directing (that is, given over to her work) and obsessing over how to face the past from the position of the present. Carri refuses to present herself exclusively in the pose of mourning or to offer up a tragic character. It is not so much that she does not believe in a possible reconstruction of the past (the truthfulness of what happened is not something that the film places in doubt) as that she does not believe she should invest her life in the contemplative cult of the past.[82]

In ideological terms, *Los rubios* does something different than other political documentaries because it suggests, when it does not express it directly, that her parents' past was not heroic (although her parents themselves might have been) and that it did not necessarily shape a more profound experience (as proof we have the testimonies of the activists, in which everything is "all set up"). Carri, like her parents, has passions. Yet her passions are not the same as theirs. They dedicated their lives to politics; Albertina devotes hers to film. She also has her struggles (with the INCAA, for example), goals (making movies), likes, and doubts. She does not approach life dazzled by heroic actions that seem to her unrepeatable (in contrast to the melancholia that we can detect, for example, in Blaustein's *Cazadores de utopias*). Instead, she constructs her own space within which she can speak and watch. This is what is most important about her film: to consider the past from a present that has no desire to be suppressed for the sake of worship or mourning without end.

With the goal of completing this process, Carri turns to an actress to represent herself, for what is at stake in this movie is the same thing that defines the stigma of her life: how to construct an "I" when she is already inscribed in the gaze of others. The movie states this explicitly: "How could she construct herself without that figure that gave her the beginning of her very existence," those "strange looks" that in times of "terror or violence" suggest "danger or rejection" and, now, "uncertainty and pity."[83] The "terror and pity" that, according to Aristotle, provoke tragedy, find here an atypical execution: pity tends to be present in these looks, and the author's present and her "frivolity" (in reality, the distractions that we all have a right to have) provoke uncertainty. Pity definitively culminates in a perverse effect, demanding that the other assume the pose of pain. If he or she does not do so, he or she is considered *impassive* (*indolent,* "without pain"). There is no public life for these people beyond what links them to what their parents have done. A fold is then presented, an "uncertainty" that Carri can investigate only by showing (and showing herself) the construction of this watched body of the daughter eternally condemned to mourning. By choosing to have an actress play her, Carri preserves her trade (as director) and embodies this "I" produced by "strange looks." She also returns the gaze of children, her schoolmates, who with "cruel little eyes" would ask her why she lived with her aunt and uncle. Like a modern Antigone, she asks to bury her parents and shows how, for her public performance, kinship is contingent (which removes not even a hint of her pain and her mourning).[84] Against the construction of the gaze of others, she makes her own construction, forging for herself a present and a future.

It would perhaps not be a bad idea to ask why Albertina Carri made this movie. The first response is simple: to make others. Because the mourning work is complete, the demand to speak about her last name, her inheritance, her "stigma," will no longer be a burden for these new movies. Carri made *Los rubios* to continue filming. Another hypothesis is the polemical character of her project in cinematographic terms: the director tacitly critiques other documentaries made on the issue, shows that the differences between documentary and fiction in film are of degree and not of kind, and battles the idea of reconstruction as something organized, chronologically ordered, and without gaps or detours.[85] A third response is therapeutic and is based on the distinction between the work of mourning and the work of film, which condition each other to do something with the material of the past and memory.

A fourth response is eminently political. *Los rubios* shows that the death of Carri's parents is a problem linked to intimacy—hence the splitting of herself into two—but that the death of radicals is a public and social problem. This is why Carri turns to Analía Couceyro for the scene of the three wishes that she makes as a girl (the scene in which she draws closest to intimate pain, and thus the scene that is most comforting to the public) and at several moments also implicates herself with her own body. (She forgets that she could have remained behind the cameras.) She takes a blood test, interviews her parents' former neighbors, visits the concentration camp where her parents were held. Film can process private life but is undoubtedly displayed for a public gaze. Carri ceaselessly evokes this private life yet insists on the social significance of her experience, marked by the brutality of the oppressors and, later, by others who tried to transform her into a perpetual daughter. Rather than displaying the state of her personal feelings, with great intelligence Carri chose to show all the factors that made her childhood paradoxically happy and unfortunate.

The Testimony of a Dissolution: On Anahí Berneri's *A Year without Love*

A vein of sadism and masochism runs through contemporary film, and it has found an immediate reverberation with the public. We could say that sadists and masochists abound, and the success of vampires, tough guys, and gangsters, so plentiful in today's films, proves this.

—Victoria Ocampo, *"Henry V y Laurence Olivier"* (1947)

The representation of gay characters in Argentine film reaches back to the first national sound film, *Los tres berretines* (1933, "The Three Crybabies").[86] The film stars Luis Sandrini, an actor who would become one of the great stars of Argentine film. The plot treats three great passions of Buenos Aires: tango, soccer, and film. At the margins of these lovable and sympathetic *berretines*, linked to the popular and to the city of Buenos Aires, a flamboyant character prowls around. Interpreted by Homero Cárpena, he is not difficult to identify as a homosexual. With his exaggerated mannerisms, his pronunciation of words in French, and his fastidious outfits, he parades around, restless and excited, surrounded by women, with whom he clearly shares only friendship, gossip, and a passion for movie stars (*un berretín femenino*). A character with roots in vaudeville, Pocholo reproduced a stereotype that transformed a threatening subject into the object of laughter. This passion for the mannered gay is no less a part of the culture of Buenos Aires than elsewhere. Indeed, we could consider him, as Borges wrote in a contemporaneous essay entitled "Nuestras imposibilidades" ("Our Impossibilities"), a fourth *berretín:* the art of ridicule (*la cachada*), or, in a less favorable interpretation, "the Buenos Aires ease with hatred."[87]

In his essay, Borges locates this ridicule in the context of an emergent mass culture. "Nuestras imposibilidades" begins by analyzing the audience's reaction to two films, King Vidor's *Hallelujah!* and Josef Von Sternberg's *Underworld.* As if ridicule and homosexuality were irrevocably linked in mass culture, the text ends with references to sodomy and the assertion that "the thugs of Buenos Aires" worship "the active agent, because he mocked his friend," in a gesture that he deems "fecal dialectics" (Borges 1999, 120).

Yet there is something more to this character from *Los tres berretines*. He is also a diehard aficionado of film. The stereotype thus includes characteristics considered part of the same family: to be gay is, ultimately, to be a spectator, an aesthete, a passive subject. The movie recognizes the common roots that forge a link between the homosexual and the aesthete, one that has seen numerous interpretations. From Oscar Wilde and earlier still, the link between homosexuality and aesthetic pleasure spanned the twentieth century, particularly in the stereotyped vision of mass culture. Many years after *Los tres berretines,* but with the same aspirations of ingratiating itself and of representing the popular, nationalist populism, in a presumably more elaborate formulation, broadened its scope to unite intellectualism, homosexuality, and passivity (that is, cowardice). Witness the following assertion by José Hernández Arregui: "Raúl Scalabrini Ortiz is a national writer. Jorge Luis Borges is a colonial writer—more perfect than a musical sphere in Pythagoras' mind.... A night bird of colonized culture, [Borges represents] the landless, *effeminate literary colonialism* that we are referring to" (1969, 26).

An entire series of prejudices are present in Hernández Arregui's observation. For him, imperialism can be transmitted only if there are passive subjects willing to accept and eventually, as in Borges' case, cultivate it. Manuel Mujica Láinez, whom Hernández Arregui refers to numerous times, and whom the anti-imperialist film *La hora de los hornos* transformed into the emblematic character of colonial penetration, is the most likely victim of this gendered/*machista* interpretation of imperialism. In this image, the people are behind the figure of the *macho* (as Perón was called, even well into the 1970s). This *passivity,* which *Los tres berretines* had the virtue of embodying in the figure of the film critic and which Hernández Arregui projects onto cosmopolitan writers, experienced diverse modulations throughout the twentieth century.

Although the effeminate character whose purpose was to ridicule and ward off the supposed threat of homosexuality continues to be very present in the media, especially on television, this formation has undergone many changes in recent years. Other stereotypes have appeared, forming a cast of characters broad enough to include, among others, the serious and thoughtful homosexual who does not seem to be gay and the transvestite who elicits both open sympathy and hidden fantasies. The regime of visibility has shifted (again, especially on television), and this has minimized the transgressive charge of certain sexual acts. It has also meant that the inclusion of homosexuality in some works can be linked to the market or constructed as a concession to the spectator's tastes (and to nonexistent, imaginary transgressions). The homosexual is one more possibility of available identification, and the formerly repulsive character of this figure has diminished considerably in the field of visual representations. In this way, including gay characters in stories is much more complex, as it can be inadvertently converted into a form of audiovisual political correctness.

Anahí Berneri's *Un año sin amor* (2004) relegates all of this to the sidelines with a violent shove, and here lies the film's extremely contemporary vision. Not only does the film manage to recharge the sense of gay sexuality and of desire more generally; it also enters into a zone, that of sadomasochism, in which the imaginary sympathy of the spectator with respect to homosexuality is rendered more complex, and even impossible. With neither stereotypes nor "tolerant" representations that would maintain a fictional acceptance of homosexuality, the movie does not hide behind a supposed transgression to approach a gay character and his world. It is not transgression that matters but the condition of desire and what this puts into play.

An adaption of Pablo Pérez's novel of the same name—an autofiction or novel in the form of an autobiographical diary—*Un año sin amor* tells the story of a writer who becomes HIV infected and suffers the vicissitudes of the disease.[88] The movie begins on April 26, 1996, with a voice-over spoken by Pablo (played by an excellent Juan Minujín) and a shot of the computer screen on which he writes his diary. (The letters on the screen also serve as the opening credits.) Visibly suffering from his illness, Pablo's only relationships are with his Aunt Nefertiti (Mimi Ardú), with whom he shares an apartment; his remote father (Ricardo Merkin), who sends him money monthly; a student to whom he gives private lessons in French (his only job); and his friend Nicolás (Carlos Echevarría).

Having decided to forge sporadic relationships through ads in a magazine and furtive encounters in gay meeting places, Pablo embarks on a search for sex and pleasure that leads him to pornographic movie theaters and to a leather bar where sadomasochistic sessions take place, directed by the police officer Báez (Osmar Núñez). In the sessions at the club, Pablo meets Alejandro (Javier Van de Couter), a tall, bald young man whom he has run into before. With the complicity of another participant at the leather bar, Juan la Hiena (Ricardo Moriello), Pablo enters into a master–slave relationship with Alejandro, beyond Officer Báez's surveillance. However, Báez finds out about the plan and invites Pablo to his house, where he and Alejandro prepare a sadomasochistic torture session, ending the hope of initiating a sexual relationship outside of the master's gaze.

This is the story of Pablo in the world of leather. In parallel fashion, the movie shows his visits to the hospital and the doctor and his efforts to publish a book of poems that finally leads to the publication of the novel/diary *Un año sin amor*. (The movie uses the book that was published by Perfil press in 1998.) When his family finds out about the book, with names only slightly altered, the wrath of Pablo's father falls on him, and he kicks him out of the house. After a few frustrated calls to his friends Nicolás and Juan, Pablo walks into a pornographic movie theater, in search of sex. Rather than ending, the story is suspended, without us knowing what the protagonist's future will be.

Although there are no psychological descriptions in the movie, certain signs allow us to make a hypothesis about Pablo's history. In the past that is not recounted in the film, Pablo lived in Paris, where he had a French boyfriend. Facing the diary written on Pablo's computer, we find the handwritten diary of his ex-boyfriend, in which a few sentences can be read describing a frustrated encounter with Pablo that never comes to fruition. In light of these notes, the spectator wonders whether Pablo left his boyfriend or broke up with him while the other was suffering from an illness. The note dated July 12 appears to indicate this: "I remembered him today in agony, even though I was never a witness to his agony."

Although Pablo was not a witness to his partner's death, he is transformed, by means of the diary, into a witness to his own agony. Through this device, Pablo splits himself in two: a body that suffers and a writing that testifies to this suffering; an experience of the dissolution of the "I" and an experience antagonistic to an "I" that expresses itself. By taking this experience of the "I" to the limit, renouncing love to confront desire, Pablo breaches a dark core that unites pain and pleasure, self-destruction and salvation, agony and orgasm. As Georges Bataille affirms in *Historia del erotismo,* "the desire of the senses is the desire, if not to be destroyed, then at least to burn and lose itself without reservations." Reliving the death of the man who had been his partner, Pablo carries on the ceremonies of suffering and pleasure that launch him into the truth of his desire.

After Transgression

The few films in the history of Argentine cinema that have openly treated the theme of homosexuality find their focus in the issues of transgression and civil rights. This was the tone that prevailed, in particular, during the 1980s, in Enrique Dawi's *Adiós Roberto* (1985) and Américo Ortiz de Zarate's *Otra historia de amor* (1986). The former film, made when AIDS had not yet become part of the social fabric, shows the difficulties of a young kid (Carlos Calvo) in recognizing, in the face of his group of friends, his homosexuality (once again, the fourth, ridiculed *berretín,* "fecal dialectics"). The second movie, *Otra historia de amor,* narrates in a melodramatic vein, but with a greater political consciousness of minority politics, the story of a couple (Arturo Bonín and Mario Pasik) who meet at work and are forced to confront various forms of discrimination. The plea for tolerance and the demand for legal equality of both movies control the entire development of the plot, particularly in *Otra historia de amor.* Recognizing their own desires, making them visible, achieving recognition and understanding, being happy—essentially, this is the gay calvary that the two early films narrate.

The greatest difference that *Un año sin amor* marks from Ortíz de Zarate's and Dawi's works is that in Berneri's film homosexuality is not exhibited as something heroic. Undoubtedly, the idea of the 1980s movies was to accompany the opening up of Argentine society after the last dictatorship. In contrast, in Berneri's film, the social gaze, normative and accusatory, has no place. Not even the cruel vicissitudes that people with AIDS suffer from form part of its story. Pablo does not need to hide the results of his test or conceal from his family that he is HIV-positive. (Nor is there any indication that he has had to do this before the film begins.[89]) There is no condemnation of the difficulty in obtaining the drug AZT, and, in the public hospital, the doctor is an understanding character who does not take advantage of Pablo's illness to unleash a thinly veiled rhetoric of accusation and reproach.

In this sense, we could say that *Un año sin amor* is a movie without a closet, which brackets the relationship between the gay community and the gaze of outsiders to move into its interior, *among* its relationships and *within* its codes. The outside is weakened because what matter are not the difficulties of sexual choice (when one's choice is nonnormative) and the subsequent request for recognition but affect and acts. The history does not ask us to accept homosexual desires; rather, it asks what to do with them.

Pablo is indifferent to social recognition, except when it relates to money, linked to the figure of his father and to the student to whom he teaches French. We might imagine that the father would represent the normative and accusatory gaze, pursuing and hounding the homosexual desire of his son; in reality, his father discriminates against him not because of his homosexuality but because he has made this fact public through his book. His father's fury does not acquire a public character (although he does express it); it is contained within the private realm, that of the family, an institution that Pablo questions.

His argument with his father constitutes the only moment in the film when a "we" and "they" appear: "We helped you all that we could." This is the only time the protagonist must confront another person. In this confrontation, however, "being gay" is one element among many, and it is perhaps less important than "being a son" or "being supported economically." Rather than confronting hostility, Pablo discovers, with the publication of his book, that being gay is interesting, that it causes fascination. He takes advantage of this situation and does not question it, just as earlier he does not respond to his aunt's insult of "fag" or replies to his father that there is nothing (that is, there is no family) about which to argue. There is no heroism with respect to these forms of rejection or the concealed discrimination unveiled with the acceptance of his manuscript for publication. Pablo's heroism, in any case, is in confronting his own desire once he has renounced love and is preparing to die. Yet, in contrast to the philosophers of ancient Greece, he prepares to die not with the weapons of reflexive knowledge but through making use of and offering up his own body. And his diary is the testimony of this offering.

As Gabriel Giorgi brilliantly shows in his *Sueños de exterminio (Homosexualidad y representación en la literatura argentina)* ("Dreams of Extermination: Homosexuality and Representation in Argentine Literature"), the "languages of social hygiene and internal war" dominate in the relationship of normative society to the gay community (2005, 10). In confronting extermination (the "dream of extermination," per Giorgi) as a permanent threat in a society that is terrified of homosexuals (and that fantasizes about terrorizing them when it does not in fact do so), *Un año sin amor* is not emphatic. It does not deny the reality of this situation; it simply focuses on another aspect. This fact does not make *Un año sin amor* a less political film or one less connected to minorities. Rather, by not placing the emphasis on transgression, it diagnoses a paradigm shift that has taken place in recent years.

This change is characterized by the weakening of the force of the obscene: in a regime of visibility in which the sexually explicit is common, accessible, and socially accepted (think of the boom in Internet pornography or the pornographic section in video stores), a movie can no longer find its effectiveness in showing that which, despite having the prestige of the prohibited, has already been seen and accepted (even if in secret). Nor can it exploit the rejection of the gay choice, because although this is still socially controversial, it has acquired a considerable degree of acceptance within certain groups and an assured place, even if by means of stereotypes, in media representations. In this case, AIDS itself establishes a regime of visibility in which what was forbidden to be seen is no longer the law that regulates values and desires. AIDS thus becomes a symbolic illness: "monstrously porno," as the protagonist defines it in his diary, it also resembles a society in which the obscene no longer has a place. Thus, the question is no longer about staging a transgression (what cannot enter on to the stage) but about creating a scene in order to "resexualize Thanatos" and "desexualize Eros," according to Deleuze in his formulation on masochism.[90] In the film, by getting rid of love (of sincerity, commitment, or passion for another person), the protagonist can investigate the links between pleasure and pain; he does so from a homosexual and, as we shall see, *plurisexual,* perspective.

The Paths of Pleasure and Pain

In his experience outside of love, Pablo walks the streets in search of sex, places advertisements in newspapers, frequents gay clubs.[91] He visits two places most often: the sadomasochistic (S/M) sessions and the gay movie theater. In the latter, a pornographic movie is projected while spectators have sexual contact in which *the adoration of the cock* predominates.[92] In a glorification of sex between men, Pablo either hurls himself onto the seat of one of the employees or is penetrated against one of the bathroom walls. The pleasure sought is sexual, and what matters is not the personality of the bodies but how they are physically endowed. In contrast, in the sadomasochistic sessions, pleasure is not obtained solely by means of sexual relations.

In comparison with the coarseness of this world of hook-ups at gay movie theaters (where initial banter is scarcely necessary), the world of S/M is refined and educated. In Pablo's first encounter with Officer Báez, who organizes the sessions, and with another participant who will later become his friend (Juan la Hiena), the three speak of clubs in Paris and San Francisco, of travels, drinks. Despite the fact that pleasure is not obtained solely through sex, the S/M club shares one characteristic with the pornographic movie theater: the dissolution of personality. Pablo seeks relationships in which this experience of dissolution takes place. For this reason, his relationship with his friend Nicolás, who is the only person with whom he shares memories and affect (for example, he is the only one to visit Pablo in the hospital), becomes less interesting than all the casual relationships that arise, whether in the disco, the movie theater, or the sessions organized by the Officer. This is why Nicolás' love for Pablo is not requited. Pablo wants to lose himself, give himself over without restrictions to the demands of pleasure, to the dissolution that this provokes. For in self-dissolution pleasure does not find an "I" but an undertow that drags him in no specific direction.

Before analyzing the meaning of the S/M sessions in *Un año sin amor,* I will list some characteristics of these practices, using, when fitting, examples from the movie:

First, sadomasochism is a staging of the relationships of power on the basis of the body's reactions of pleasure and pain. This power is contractual (that is, consensual) and has been interpreted in diverse ways: as a parody of authority; as a cathartic act for its participants; as a "strategic relation," in Foucault's words; or, according to Leo Bersani, as "unforeseen kinds of relationships."[93] The clearest difference from conventional power relations is that in sadomasochism the roles of "master" and "slave" are interchangeable.

Second, because power in our society is sexist, the masculine runs through the world of S/M in various ways. In the clothing and instruments used, in its attraction for muscular and hairy bodies, in the temerity in confronting pain and transforming it into pleasure, in the exaltation of the military, S/M takes to the limit the "ideal of the strong and protective man" that Pablo Pérez speaks of as he plays with his childhood toys: superheroes, Batman, the wrestlers of the program "Titans in the Ring."[94] As Pablo's commemoration suggests, his entry into S/M is a trip into his own imagination, a redramatization of his fascination with dominant men, with him since childhood.

Third, Foucault, who was very interested in the last years of his life in S/M practices, found that these provided him with an answer to the problem that he had put forth in the first volume of *The History of Sexuality.* Beginning with a critique of the hypothesis that states that sexuality was repressed historically, Foucault avers that since the eighteenth century, sex has been constantly evoked in a series of discourses that shape a regime of power–knowledge–pleasure and "polymorphous techniques of power." Against this obsessive search for the "truth" in sex, Foucault believes that sadomasochism is an investigation of the body in its entirety (not necessarily the erogenous zones) and a desexualization of pleasure.[95] In *Un año sin amor*, the most intense—and, as we shall see, central—scene is the one in which the Officer plays with a knife on Pablo's back and nipples. There is an entire production of bliss, pain, and pleasure focalized on Pablo's torso. "A very good little slave," Báez remarks. Here, as in various scenes with Alejandro, pleasure has less to do with the strictly sexual than with the fact that the *entire* body is submitted to a series of trajectories and unconventional experiences.

Fourth, this experimenting with the limits of the body is expressed in materials that help to traverse and abuse it, at times in scenes of torture that cease only at the request of the slave. (Without a contract, there can be no masochism, as Sacher-Masoch's *Venus in Furs* makes clear.) There are four types of such materials: leather, instruments of torture, skin, and orifices; that is, the impenetrable, the hard, the soft, and the penetrable. The tied-up body, suspended or reclining, unable to react or control its excitement, is also fundamental, as a documentary scene of a leather bar session shows.[96]

Fifth, since Freud's "Beyond the Pleasure Principle," we have known that an organism seeks out pleasure and brackets pain. According to Leo Bersani, a critic who has rigorously examined the relationship between desire and masochism, masochists are no exception to Freud's observations: "Far from enjoying pain, masochists have developed techniques to bypass pain" (1995, 93). Bersani's hypothesis is that in masochism there is a self-displacement in which the "I" relinquishes its power over the world; in this case, pain shields the organism from its undoing. Pain and pleasure constitute the immediate information of our existence.

Finally, and although we could evidently add other characteristics, in the world of S/M there is a macabre culture, an aestheticization of death (aestheticization as the distanced treatment of sensation). This is one of S/M's most complex aspects because, according to some critics, it establishes a link to fascist practices (and, in fact, Nazi paraphernalia is at times used).[97] However, this critique does not take into account the fact that sadomasochism is defined as a community in which power is always incidental, interchangeable, and consensual; nor the fictional and mise-en-scène character of all S/M sessions. In contrast, *Un año sin amor* finds one of its most interesting wagers in this aestheticization of death, because Pablo's entry into the Officer's flock has to do precisely with the fact that he intends to make of death his last work of art—hence the fact that S/M is linked not only to a fascination with power but also to an illness that is aestheticized as much by the mise-en-scène (in its numerous detail shots) as by the protagonist himself. In one of the detail shots, Pablo holds an AZT pill in his hand and remarks, "A unicorn welcomes me." Later, he adds that the pills are "a work of art of the nineties." The aesthetic is compensatory: through writing, it is therapeutic, and through sex, self-destructive. The two extremes (healing and self-destruction) are part of the same process, and, like pleasure and pain, they are enmeshed and mutually implicated. Pablo knows that he is going to die, and he wants to do it in style.

The movie positions itself at once very close to and very far from sadomasochism, that is, in the position of a participant (through Pablo) and through a documentary register. According to Emilio Bernini, the movie "does a formidable job with free indirect discourse. It is the camera's gaze—that is, that of the narrator—but it is at the same time the gaze of Pablo Peréz, the character in the movie. Two gazes coexist in the same act of looking" (see Berneri, García, and Pérez 2007). The gaze, as the story itself, is organized around the documentary impulse. Pablo's excursions resemble at times those of a hidden camera, and the shots of the sadomasochistic sessions shift to a prudent distance, without interfering but also without moving away out of modesty.

The tension in the points of view is translated into the theme of the movie itself: if documentary is the furious drive to take hold of the indices of the real, sadomasochism, in contrast, offers us a mise-en-scène of sexual relations. In the diary, an intimacy appears through the presence of the voice-over. In contrast, in the S/M sessions, the style is lacking in intimacy, documentary, and objective (in that it is impossible to tell whether these scenes are real or acted out). The tension between documentary and staging is also clear within the protagonist himself: the actor Juan Minujín plays the writer Pablo Pérez, and Pablo's book is shown in the film.[98] Pablo commits himself, his own body, twice: as an experience to be observed and as an adventure to be lived—an invitation to self-dissolution and a distanced observation of the loss that this entails.

The film's strategy consists of turning the nightmare of the real around through the theatricalization of desire—a double theatricalization: that of the "I" who writes and that of the "I" who comes undone through the limits of pleasure and pain; that of the screen (the computer screen, the movie screen) and that of bodies. In this last theatricalization Pablo fails, because in wanting to take to the limit the rules of the S/M game, he forges a relationship with Alejandro without the Officer's permission. Yet the punishment—with the consent of Alejandro himself—is not long in coming, and the fantasies of theatricalization are quickly frustrated. The Officer, in the end, is too sadistic. He lacks the masochistic component, the capability of being a slave; in a world in which the reversibility of relationships should predominate, he establishes a tyranny in which he tries to remain an exception.[99]

Ultimately, Pablo cannot make his final journey, that of death. However, the theatricalization of his diary functions perfectly to erase borders, fulfill fantasies, create a world (even if it is one without love). And this is seen in the brutal self-reference to the book from which the film was adapted. For beyond the failures narrated in *Un año sin amor,* Pérez and Berneri find a vanishing point (*punto de fuga*[100]) because they play with theatricalizations at their extreme. In a world that has decided to show everything, they discover, through the mise-en-scène, how pleasure can be established within the folds of this display: whether on screen, in writing, or on the body.

Voyeuristic Film

Un año sin amor is a film almost devoid of women. Pablo's aunt Nefertiti is the only woman who forms part of the plot, and her presence tends to frustrate any idea of identifying women's bodies with visual pleasure. Against the frequent construction in film of the female body as object of desire, the very idea of desirability is here taken to a ludicrous extreme, as Nefertiti constantly appears with a thick layer of face cream that make her ridiculous, promising a beauty that at no point becomes real. Rather, as her frequent telephone conversations indicate, and in contrast to what happens to Pablo, no one desires Nefertiti, and her efforts to render herself desirable are bound to fail.

The other woman who is present in the film is never made visible. I refer to the director, Anahí Berneri, who has decided to make a movie about the world of male homosexuality—that is, a story in which her own identification with the characters and with the events is complex, a story that she observes with a distanced gaze.[101] We could say that the distance of this gaze is precisely one of the successes of *Un año sin amor:* as much in its remote gaze (as when Pablo wanders the streets in search of sex) as in its ethnographic methods (recording scenes as though in a documentary), Berneri chose to portray a world in which she is not directly implicated. The free indirect style, however, calls this distance into question, at times blurring the borders between camera and character, creating an instability in terms of genre. That is, *Un año sin amor* is not a film made from within the gay male community, for a gay audience.

In this shift, what is at play is the multiplication of sex: Pablo's, the director's, and a third sex that forms in this encounter. In this body that is traversed in the S/M sessions, the feminine gaze of the director means that genital difference does not predominate. In this way, the entire story is located under the sign of desire. Hence, the image that defines the film (on posters advertising it) is a photograph of Pablo's back during one of the movie's most intense scenes. We all have a back, and it is here that the pleasure and pain that are at the core of Pablo's adventures are revealed. A pleasure that is not necessarily genital, in which this back is presented to us as though it were a movie screen: scratched, traversed, written on, the back returns *our* gaze.

Like other productions of the new Argentine cinema, *Un año sin amor* sets out not to preach to the audience but to investigate the regime of visibility. In addition, it investigates the regime of sexuality (or of pleasure). The fact that this examination is carried out by a woman alters Pablo Pérez's diary significantly. Whereas the text locates itself within the homosexual saga, the film places its confessions in a plurisexual instance, beyond genitality.

Perhaps it is this combination of gazes of different genders, in addition to the movie's awareness of its place in a "monstrously porno" society—one in which what Zygmunt Bauman calls "liquid love" predominates—which leads *Un año sin amor* to eschew gay stereotypes, not even as negativity.[102] For the movie's theme is not homosexuality but desire, a transversal force that offers resistance to the visual regime in which we live. Given that visuality imposes the distance, domination, and even peace of mind of those who do not feel themselves to be implicated, doesn't Berneri's gaze, implicated in the film's free indirect style, make present the desire of its protagonist? What is more, don't we find ourselves facing the aestheticization of death that attempts to endow the image with *aesthesis* (sensibility)? Isn't this what the protagonist's back, interpolating us from the movie poster, tells us? Within the movie, in an extreme scene for a commercial film, this back causes our gaze to be, per Baudelaire, the knife *and* the wound. Anahí Berneri and Pablo Pérez's *Un año sin amor* responds affirmatively to these questions, entering a terrain that Argentine cinema, both old and new, has rarely entered: that of the extreme experiences elicited by desire and pleasure.[103]

Appendix I

The World of Cinema in Argentina

A revelation on January 17, 2002. I am headed to the Citibank on Cabildo Street, where I have a savings account. I try to enter the bank but cannot because of the number of people waiting. So I give up on my errand. I cross the street to return home, and from the sidewalk facing the bank I see, for the first time, the building in which it is housed. The familiar is made strange; shortly after, it becomes familiar again, but in a slightly disturbing way. I recognize the building's arches and moldings, its fanciful rococo façade. I recognize the Cabildo movie theater, in which I saw so many movies as an adolescent. Although I have been coming to this bank for years, I have never before made this connection. I know movie theaters that have been transformed into video arcades, into evangelical churches,[1] into parking garages, even into bookstores. Yet I knew of none that had become a bank. All my savings were housed in a space that had been shadows, lights, images, sounds, seats, a screen, film.

I remember that around the age of sixteen, I saw Robert Redford's *Ordinary People* (1980) on the same day as Alain Resnais' *Last Year at Marienbad* (1961) in the Hebraica theater. Two or three movies a day (video didn't exist then) in which almost everything was film, film, and only film. These are the adolescent years in which cinephilia is born: a messy love, passionate, without much judgment. I remember once I dragged some friends to see a piece of Italian garbage at the Hebraica, just "because it was *Italian*" and I loved movies from Italy. Film, and we should remember this, was still something linked to the forbidden: Stanley Kubrick's *Barry Lyndon* (1975) had been rated inappropriate for people under the age of fourteen and to see it, one had to perform a juggling act. (In such cases, is bribery an act of corruption?) Luckily, there were some theaters (such as the Boedo on

San Juan Avenue) in which the forbidden could be touched with the eyes, even if only in the mediocre movies of erotic stars Isabel Sarli or María José Cantudo. Film was something as immense, enormous, and dark as the theaters themselves.

Then video came and the theaters grew empty. The process of reviving them was slow, but video also allowed for a reconnection with earlier film that had been unthinkable. We no longer had to wait for an Orson Welles or Billy Wilder retrospective to see their movies; professors could use fragments of films in their classes; a cinephile could set up a film library. Yet because the industry of the spectacle continued to be one of the most lucrative, it was not long before the exhibition of new movies reorganized—in recent years, on a global scale. During the 1990s movie theaters also suffered the effects of the magic word of that period: *conversion.*

The great theaters began to disappear, the pedestrian walkway on Lavalle Street became a ghost town (at least for those of us who loved film), and we saw the arrival of the large chains that constructed their Buenos Aires theaters according to the same designs as theaters in Cincinnati or Bangkok. A shot from Rejtman's *Silvia Prieto* that out-lines the neon lights of the theaters on Lavalle, as though they were an organism living on beyond people, is particularly moving for those of us who lived the absurd spell that this street cast.[2] There was (there still is) the Atlas, which Alberto Prebisch designed in 1966, and which was the theater to see premieres. All of those theaters that had been ours (so to speak) began to disappear or to be split up into smaller theaters. Even the Los Ángeles theater, "the first theater in the world dedicated exclusively to Disney," as its sign proclaims, was divided up, subjected to strange alterations.

The first movie theaters were pockets of fantasy in the city, buildings whose façades resembled exotic palaces, or whose interiors, as in the case of the Ópera theater, simulated a starry sky. The Los Ángeles looked like a castle, and it did not matter that it was painted cardboard. There were also neighborhood theaters where you could see classic films, pseudo-pornography, or unusual movies (in the Moreno theater, in the Caballito neighborhood, Beatles films; in the Boedo, the premiere of Leonardo Favio's *Juan Moreira* [1973] and Fernando Ayala and Héctor Olivera's *Argentinísima* [1972, "Extremely Argentine"]). The appearance of video led many to believe that film as a spectacle was on its way out, but in the 1990s the North American chains arrived. Although these chains were devoted to commercial films and housed in malls, they were also protagonists of the Festival de Cine Independiente (Independent Film Festival). Cinema's forms were changing, and the public (who had grown up with television, MTV, and video) had other habits.

The closing of the great theaters began around 1987, and the rate of closure increased sharply with the economic crisis of the late 1980s. Of the 900 theaters in Argentina in 1984, by the end of the decade less than one half remained (427 in 1990). The lowest point came in 1992, with only 280 working theaters, and the recovery came in the late 1990s, with the multiplex and theaters in the malls. In 1997, there were 589 working theaters, 830 in 1998, 920 in 1999, and in recent years more than 1000 in the entire country—that is, more than at the beginning of the 1980s (Seivach and Perelman 2004, 139). All of this indicates that film's social function has changed, along with its role in the production of images.

In this appendix I am interested in referencing five specific phenomena of the 1990s that have had an impact on film as an institution and on its aesthetics: first, the huge increase in the amount of money needed to finance a film and the infinite production possibilities, from homemade movies to mega productions (which often end up competing in the same space); second, the profound transformations in the cultural function of the administrators of the image[3] and in the institutions where they are trained; third, the appearance of a new exhibition network for films, which found in the festival scene a specific public, critics, and reception; fourth, the foundation of a number of cinema schools, which changed the trade by opening up a new way to enter the world of making movies; finally, the growth of film criticism as an event that is not external to the phenomenon of the new Argentine cinema but forms a part of it, actively fostering it.

Strange Forms of Independence: Film and Production

The category "independent" is exceedingly loose and relates more to production than to aesthetics, as it refers to the financial means with which a movie is made. However, it is difficult to make a clear-cut distinction between production and aesthetics in a medium such as film, in which decisions must constantly negotiate artistic and economic components. The issue becomes even more complex if we keep in mind that the term "independent" has an international sweep but that "production" varies according to the national context. In a globalized cinema, U.S. "indie" productions share space in a festival such as Sundance with independent movies that, in their country of origin, might not strictly be independent (and, if they are, might have little in common with respect to production with their North American counterparts). BAFICI, which carries the label "independent" in its title, in reality showcases productions that can be considered independent only in comparison to costly Hollywood movies. The category "independent," then, has a global character, but its features vary according to the national origin of products, and it ends up being more strategic than objective.

In the United States, the label "independent," or "indie," has been very successful since the late 1980s and has undeniable aesthetic consequences, given that its economic difference from industry films is astronomical (and this difference influences scriptwriting, casting, filming, and postproduction).[4] The label, at any rate, references only one phase of production, as movies are filmed independently but their makers aspire to have them distributed by an important company, as this is the only way to survive in a broad, competitive network. (In the network of global cinema, distributors have an increasingly important role in the film industry.) On the other hand, some major studios have discovered the profitability of creating a special subcategory for indie movies. Major studios see independent film not as an aesthetic antagonist but as a form of production from which they also can benefit. Thus, Richard Linklater's *Before Sunset* (2003) opens with a title for "Warner Independent." Thus, the two types of production (independent and studio) aspire to be part of the same circuit.

The case of Miramax is exemplary, as it began by distributing movies made outside of the major studios. It could even be said that Miramax created the independent label in the late 1980s when it bought and distributed Steven Soderbergh's *Sex, Lies, and Videotape* (1989). From that moment, the Weinstein brothers' company (named after their parents, Miriam and Max) has not stopped growing, and with Quentin Tarantino's *Reservoir Dogs* (1992), it became one of the major companies of the 1990s, until it was absorbed by Disney in an association that ended abruptly when Mickey's company refused to distribute Michael Moore's documentary *Fahrenheit 9/11* (2004).[5]

There is, of course, a genuinely independent tradition in the United States, comprising filmmakers as diverse as John Casavettes,

John Waters, Kenneth Anger, Andy Warhol, Jonas Mekas, and Robert Frank—although here it perhaps more correct to use the term "underground film" (more precise and less confusing) for all but the case of Casavettes.[6]

Another novelty U.S. independent film introduced was that with low costs and good distribution it became possible for an independent film to yield a high return, in many cases greater than that of a commercial film. In 2002, Joel Zwick's *My Big Fat Greek Wedding* became one of the most successful movies in history, not so much for the number of spectators (which was large) but for the difference between the low investment and the profits. To this example can be added Daniel Myrick and Eduardo Sánchez's *Blair Witch Project* (1999) or Robert Rodríguez's *El Mariachi* (1992). Once they leave their country of origin, these unexpected successes enjoy the distribution prerogatives of any Tom Cruise or Angelina Jolie picture.

In any case, the additional fact that U.S. movies are made with private capital means that the difference is due to the quantity of money invested and not the character of the investment. In contrast, in Argentina what is decisive is whether the INCAA supports a film with subsidies and credits, approximating in this way the European model of subsidies and state promotion.[7] The existence of "independent film" in Argentina in the 1990s related not to the amount of money invested but to the fact that many producers and filmmakers sought ways to finance their movies that avoided the INCAA, or turned to it only in postproduction.

Three such strategies were crucial for the establishment of a new generation of filmmakers. First, the making of a film was so fragmented that investment could appear during any of its phases. (Earlier, in contrast, it was customary to film once one had obtained the go-ahead from the INCAA).[8] Second, filmmakers turned to foreign sources of funding (Fond Sud Cinèma, the Hubert Bals Fund, Sundance).[9] Here, too, there was a difference from 1980s film; whereas earlier filmmakers sought artistic co-productions, which often required adaptations or artistic concessions (changes to the screenplay, locations, and casting), these foreign foundations offered the possibility of a financial co-production that did not demand changes to the original project. Third, as these movies sought to insert themselves into and modify existing structures, it is not coincidental that many of those who later made up the new Argentine cinema had actively participated in the enactment of the *ley de cine* and in the protests in front of the Congress for the enactment of this law. Thus, during a time when state protectionism was a bad term, film was subsidized and promoted by the state.

This corporate consciousness achieved the application of the law and its regulation, principally to prevent abuses or partial applications, as in the case of pressure from the Ministry of the Economy, especially during the tenure as minister of Domingo Cavallo (the 1990s). In 1996, the *ley de Emergencia Económica* had the Treasury retain funds that belonged to the INCAA. In 2002, the INCAA stopped being an "autarkic entity" and became a "nonstate public entity" with financial autarky, juridical personnel, and its own patrimony. In 2004, after the exemplary cases of Juan José Campanella's *Luna de Avellaneda,* Martín Rejtman's *Los guantes mágicos,* and Lucrecia Martel's *La niña santa,* the "continuity average" regulation, which protected national movies, was added to the "screen quota" (the obligation to show one national movie per trimester).[10] On one extreme, then, we have the fragmentation of production; on the other, the unionized struggle to impose the idea of a cinema subsidized in its production and distribution.

Outside of official support, however, so many movies are made that the INCAA has a specific policy to help independent films enter the system. Despite the law's benefits, there are those who, for artistic or political reasons, opt to make films outside of the INCAA. This is the case of Mariano Llinás and his productions such as *Balnearios* or *El amor (primera parte),* which he presented in the Museo de Arte Latinoamericano de Buenos Aires (MALBA) with the goal of creating an alternative space for the exhibition of films.[11] It is also the case for a series of movies that, for their own aesthetic or cultural impulse, had no desire to become part of the commercial circuit and preferred to maintain a marginal position or one linked to a specific public. These are the lowest-cost local film productions of the 1990s, among them B-movies, the Saladillo experience, and Raúl Perrone's films.

B-movies have a cult following that expresses its tastes and ideas through the Internet, in journals (the most important and prestigious is *La cosa*), and in books. (Diego Curubeto, with his *Cine bizarro,* among other titles, has been one of the principal cheerleaders of this phenomenon.) There are also film clubs, such as Noctura ("Nocturnal"), led by Cristian Aguirre and Roberto Faggiani, and La Cripta ("The Crypt"), created by Peter Punk and Boris Caligari. In the field of cinematographic production, Pablo Pares, Paulo Soria, and Hernán Sáez's *Nunca asistas a este tipo de fiestas* (2000, "Never Go to These Types of Parties"), *Plaga Zombie* (1997, "Zombie Plague"), and *Plaga Zombie: zona mutante* (2001, released in the United States as *Mutant Zombie*) stand out, having been filmed in a few days and in super VHS or directly in VHS. Ernesto Aguilar's *El planeta de los hippies* (1997, "Planet of the Hippies") and *Mi suegra es un zombie* (2001, "My Mother-in-Law Is a Zombie") were filmed in 16 millimeter. With films based on cheap special effects, tons of makeup, references to cult films, and a love for the monstrous and the poorly made, the B-movie genre has been a phenomenon of cult film in recent years.

Saladillo, a town in the province of Buenos Aires, produced one of the most peculiar filmic experiences of the 1990s. Everything began when one of its residents, Julio Midú, bought a video camera and began to film movies with his neighbors during the summer. During the winter, the results were shown in a local movie theater, and thus began a tradition that continues to this day. A truly amateur filmmaker, Midú, along with Fabio Junco, has not ceased making movies: *Vueltas de la vida* ("Life's Changes"), *Prisioneros* ("Prisoners"), *Dame aire* ("Give Me Air"), *Dulce compañía* ("Sweet Company"), *Gema* ("Gem") (all made in 2001), and *Lo bueno de los otros* (2004, "What Is Good in Others").[12] At the Seventh BAFICI Alberto Yaccelini's *Los de Saladillo,* which investigates the experience developed by Midú and Junca, was screened.

Among low-budget productions, the most notable have been those of Raúl Perrone, who closed the 2003 BAFICI with his movie *La mecha* ("The Fuse"), founded a film school, and directed a program devoted to independent film on cable television. Of all the directors to emerge during the 1990s, Perrone has been the most assiduous in his independent position, attacks upon commercial film, and the construction of his own poetics, which we could call "brutal *costumbrismo.*"[13]

All filmed in his neighborhood (Ituzaingó, in Buenos Aires province), with nonprofessional actors and based on improvisation, his movies tell stories of the daily lives of ordinary people. In Perrone's prolific career we can observe the director's progressive training and his increasing knowledge of cinematographic language. (In *La mecha,* for example, the sound is acceptable and the editing is not careless.) Perrone believes—and this is what has allowed him to make several movies—that film is the necessity of expressing oneself. He is perhaps the only Argentine director who associates "realism" with transparency and spontaneity, with showing things as they are, and with stories as slices of life. In addition to *La mecha,* Perrone has also created the trilogy *Labios de churrasco* (1995, "Barbeque Lips"),

Graciadió (1997, "Thank God"), and *5 pal peso* (1998), in addition to *La felicidad: un día de campo* (1999, "Happiness: A Day in the Countryside"), *Zapada/una comedia beat* (1999, "Zapada/A Beat Comedy"), *Late un corazón* (2002, "A Heart Is Beating"), and *Peluca y Marisita* (2002). As he has fared well with film critics (receiving comparisons to Wim Wenders and Jim Jarmusch), Perrone has become an important reference point of independent film.

We could add numerous works and directors, particularly in the documentary genre, to these examples. Some directors, after achieving a commercial success (such as Gustavo Postiglione with *El asadito* [2000, "The Little Barbecue"]), face the dilemma of how to continue to be independent when the INCAA expresses an interest in sponsoring their movies. A native of Rosario, where he continues to work, Postiglione made *El asadito* in a single day and in 16 millimeter while he was simultaneously filming *El cumple* (2001, "The Birthday") in digital. Among his most striking experiments is the making of a movie during the Sixth BAFICI at the request of the director Quintín and sponsored by the same festival. Shot in video, *Miami* was shown on the last day of the festival. At the 2005 Mar del Plata International Film Festival, Postiglione presented a new version of the film entitled *Miami RMX, ensayo fílmico electrónico,* along with his book *Cine instantáneo,* in which he critiques the depoliticization of the new Argentine cinema. Finally, another interesting example of a film made outside of institutional canons was *Safo, historia de una pasión (una remake),* perhaps the first queer film of the new Argentine cinema, featuring transvestites, gays, and participants in other nonnormative practices. The movie, a remake of Carlos Hugo Christensen's *Safo, historia de una pasión* (1943), was made by Goyo Anchou and the Yago Blass League.[14] In Anchou's version, Safo is played by various transvestites and cross-dressers. The movie was shown in the Centro Cultural Rojas, a very apt space for films made outside of institutional circuits of production, which has a program of movies (coordinated by Sergio Wolf) that rarely make it to the commercial network.

In light of the difficulties of self-management, a large group of filmmakers (in reality, the true protagonists of the new Argentine cinema) consider the enactment of the law and its application extremely important in stabilizing the industry and financing more ambitious projects to compete in commercial networks and in festivals.[15] Within this context, one of the most interesting phenomena in recent years (and one of the least recognized) has been the emergence of a group of young producers, an entire generation, who know cinema well and from the inside, and who have attempted to insert themselves into institutional organs and decision-making processes.

Hernán Musaluppi of Rizoma Films worked with Martín Rejtman and produced *Los guantes mágicos, No sos vos, soy yo,* and *Whisky;* he was also executive producer of *Todo juntos, Silvia Prieto,* and *No quiero volver a casa* ("I Don't Want to Go Home"), in addition to participating in the production of *Mundo grúa* and *Mala época.* In 1997 Daniel Burman and Diego Dubcovsky founded BD Cine, one of the most diversified production companies to emerge in recent years, with the capacity to implement various strategies according to the requirements of each film (co-production with other countries, foundations, grants, credits from the state, and so on). BD Cine produced all of Burman's films and co-produced Walter Salles' *Diarios de motocicleta* ("Motorcycle Diaries") and the films *Garage Olimpo, Nadar solo,* and *Un año sin amor.* Hugo Castro Fau and Pablo Trapero founded Matanza Cine in 2002, which produced, among other films, *Ciudad de María, La mecha,* and *Géminis* ("Gemeni"), in addition to Trapero's films. Alongside the unique space occupied by Lita Stantic, these production companies (principally BD Cine, Matanza, and Rizoma) are characterized by their central role in shaping the new cinema and also by their stable and active structures. They are obliged to finance—in order to stay afloat—two movies a year that can compete with the output of the major studios. It seems clear that the INCAA should be supporting more production companies that are not closely linked to the market and should be financing emergent ones rather than the major studios that design their productions around ticket sales.

In addition to these production companies, which have achieved a high level of continuity and have become reference points in the new cinema, others have managed to achieve stability (although not always in such a clear form) or have been formed by filmmakers trained through different experiences with the objective of operating a production company while doing freelance work. Although Rolo Azpeitía (Azpeitía Cine) lacks an impressive filmography, he is an important reference point for independent producers, having produced Fernando Spiner's *Animalada* and *Herencia.* Verónica Cura (Acqua Films), who worked as production director on Agresti's last films, was executive producer for *Vida en Falcon,* Jorge Gaggero's *Cama adentro,* and Enrique Piñeyro's *Whisky Romeo Zulú* (2004), and was a member of the production crew of Daniel Rosenfeld's *La quimera de los héroes* (2003, "The Chimera of Heroes") and his

Saluzzi, ensayo para bandoneón y tres hermanos (2001, "Saluzzi, for an Accordion and Three Brothers"). Nathalie Cabirón (Tres Planos Cine) produced Juan Villegas' *Sábado* and *Los suicidas,* Ana Katz's *El juego de la silla,* and Diego Fried's *Sangrita.* El "Chino" Fernández (Villavicio Producciones) was responsible for Luis Ortega's movies. Carolina Konstantinovsky was responsible for Alejandro Chomski's *Hoy y mañana* (2003, "Today and Tomorrow") and Celina Murga's *Ana y los otros.* In the documentary genre, in addition to the tremendous media coverage and production of Carmen Guarini and Marcelo Céspedes of Cine Ojo, there is Magoya Films, which produced Nicolás Battle and Rubén Delgado's *Matanza* (2002, "Slaughter") and *Rerum Novarum.* Finally, many director-producers prefer to deal with the executive production themselves, including Lisandro Alonso, Ana Poliak, and Verónica Chen.

This list is undoubtedly incomplete and groups together different operations (production is not the same as executive production). What is fundamental is that in recent years a new generation of producers, with a different profile than traditional producers, has been trained. They began with risky projects and only gradually came to be incorporated into the film market and into the decision-making institutions. (Films such as *Mundo grúa, Caja negra,* and *Sábado,* to name only a few, were made under very precarious conditions.) In 2004, this new generation reached the executive commission of the APIMA (Asociación de Productores Independientes de Medios Audiovisuales [Association of Independent Producers of Audiovisual Media]), one of the five associations of Argentine production companies and one of the most important, with an illustrious legacy. (It had previously been headed up by Pablo Rovito, the producer of Burman and Caetano's *18-J,* Alberto Lecchi's *El juego de Arcibel* [2003, "Arcibel's Game"], and Juán José Jusid's *Bajo bandera* [1997, "Under a Flag"], among others.[16]) This achievement is important because, as one of its members has stated, "through these associations the politics of promotion are discussed with the INCAA."[17]

In contrast to the producers of earlier generations, the new generation has been trained in film schools, understands how to negotiate with international foundations, links the prestige of the producer with the aesthetic qualities of the film, and knows in detail the operation of festivals. From the earlier generations, only Lita Stantic and Alejandro Agresti (with his idea of turning to foreign foundations) shared these characteristics and were able to function as reference points for younger producers.[18] The challenges these producers are currently taking up include demanding transparency in the INCAA's selection process, searching for ways to promote and support new generations of screenwriters and filmmakers, taking advantage of the law to continue to make risky and innovative works, and achieving a stability that allows directors to make a second or third movie.[19]

As Paulina Seivach and Pablo Perelman point out,

> More than a year after the INCAA recovered autarky, a debate about the situation of Argentine cinema and the efficacy of the current mechanisms of promotion was desirable and necessary. Clear and lasting rules are required, so that the private sector assumes the great risks of these undertakings. In addition, a transparent handling of funds and an equal treatment for all projects are necessary.... There remains an underlying doubt about the degree of discretion that the Institute holds to support certain films. (2004, 131–2)

In addition to the benefits of the law, to consolidate a film industry it is crucial to reinforce the operation of institutions and transform them into transparent, democratic, and efficient organizations.

Despite the 2001 economic crisis, the continuity of film production has exceeded expectations; already many young directors are on their second or third movie. During 2005, these included Lisandro Alonso's *Liverpool* (2008), Rodrigo Moreno's *El custodio* (2006, released in the United States as *El Custodio/The Minder,* and the winner of a competition at Sundance), and Juan Villegas' *Los suicidas* (2005, "The Suicides"), his second feature-length film, based on an Antonio di Benedetto novel. At the Seventh BAFICI (2005), a number of directors premiered their second films: Ezequiel Acuña's *Como un avión estrellado* ("Like a Crashed Plane"), Luis Ortega's *Monobloc,* and Ernesto Baca's *Samoa.* Albertina Carri closed the festival with her third feature-length film, *Géminis,* which was produced by Pablo Trapero. In addition, during the recent past a number of new directors have emerged, testifying to the sustained growth of cinematographic production in Argentina. For their *operas primas* not to end up overlooked and moribund in the INCAA's movie theater, it is necessary for producers to create a successful system of distribution that does not cram the theaters with premieres and that allows for the negotiation of favorable conditions with movie theaters, and for those who make up the film world to participate actively in the INCAA's politics to improve selection criteria when it awards prizes and subsidizes new movies.

The Birth of a Nation:
The Culture Industry

The process in which film participates is global and has undergone major transformations in an era characterized more and more by the image. The vast growth of the market in daily life is explained by recent economic and urban changes, and by changes in the visual field. The image has become key in politics, economics, culture, and social relations: in a word, in power. Thus, it is no coincidence that in recent years jobs linked to the design, production, and distribution of images have been increasing in number. Undoubtedly, this is a wide and heterogeneous field, in which administrators of the image occupy different positions, work with different materials, and have different objectives. Inside of this broad field, film is made. As Serge Daney affirms, "[T]here is a narrower mechanism that is film, one that is very condensed and powerful; and there is a broader mechanism, which is the image in general" (2004, 283).

It would be a mistake to believe that the field of film is merely an aesthetic environment and that its identity, materials, and objectives are aesthetic in nature. And this mistake in assessment would be compounded if it were applied to a decade in which cinema, in Argentina, entered into the realm of the culture industries in such an emphatic way. The benefits of the law, the role of patronage that foreign foundations fulfill, and the possibility to make movies with festivals in mind (that is, for a specialized public) can be causes for enthusiasm, but they cannot hide the dangers of an advance toward a fully administered cinema. Such a fate, similar to what has already occurred in the field of visual art, in which material and symbolic value often function independently of contact with the societies into which they are supposedly interpolated, could lead to the creation of a new division between commercial and artistic cinema that would betray film's flexible and ubiquitous character. This is why the creators of images, by means of different strategies, should maintain in tension their relationship with the politics of financial support and promotion.

Theodor Adorno created the term "culture industry" to describe how mercantilization and automatization had reached the more spiritual and creative terrain of arts and of culture more generally. The expression was the result of Adorno's pessimism and the negative impact of his encounter with U.S. culture while he was in exile during the Second World War. In this period, Adorno wrote with

Max Horkheimer what critics deemed "the black book," *Dialectic of Enlightenment* (1944).

At the end of the 1990s, and without any loyalty to those who had coined the term, the municipality of the city of Buenos Aires decided to create the Subsecretaría de Gestión e Industrias Culturales (Subsecretary of Administration and Culture Industries) with the goal of fostering and promoting artistic events.[20] What in the 1940s was cause for unease and dismay—that culture would transform into another area subject to capitalist gain—became, during the 1990s, a reason for rejoicing: culture was an industry and should be among the top priorities in political projects.

As George Yúdice argues, culture is one of the basic resources in economic terms. Through culture, tourism is promoted, consumption encouraged, unemployment mitigated, and money obtained from foundations; that is, cultural and social conflicts are resolved. Festivals such as Buenos Aires No Duerme (Buenos Aires Doesn't Sleep), the Festival Internacional de Danza y Teatro (International Festival of Dance and Theater), and the Festival de Cine Independiente (Festival of Independent Film) are among the events in which large investments underpin the image of Buenos Aires in Argentina and in the world. Although in film these effects have been minimal in comparison with other cultural fields, it became evident that the BAFICI had created a kind of fictitious microclimate: some movies that were successful in the festival were later not exhibited in any commercial theater. One example is Celina Murga's *Ana y los otros,* which was released in France with solid results. The most striking case is Ana Poliak's *Parapalos,* which was the winner of the international competition in the Sixth BAFICI and was never released commercially.

Paolo Virno offers a lucid explication of the metamorphosis of the concept of the culture industry from the Adornian version to our contemporary situation. In his *Gramática de la multitud (Para un análisis de las formas de vidas contemporáneas)* ("A Grammar of the Multitude: For an Analysis of Contemporary Forms of Life"), Virno affirms that contrary to what we might think, the culture industry in its entirety is the paradigm of post-Fordist production (2003, 54). For Adorno and Horkheimer, capitalism had managed to introduce Fordist serialism into artistic creation and in this way subordinate it to something greater: the production of generic commodities. For Virno, in our contemporary era post-Fordism has transformed the preindustrial capacities of the realm of art (the unexpected, informal, unprogrammed) into a norm for the entire realm of labor. We are entering an era in which art no longer resists but generates criteria for conduct, becoming a terrain in which politics and finance intervene to shape it. While this prospect is not very encouraging, the most lucid reaction would appear to be not to succumb to nostalgia for a more or less heroic past (even though we might recover and construct the alternatives that this past contains). During the 1990s, a good many administrators of the image adapted themselves to the politics of power in a society that asked for more and more images to sustain and foment consumption, among which audiovisual media occupied an increasing role. For filmmakers, it was important to penetrate this machine of images, thereby marking, with their own work, a difference in our relations with images.

The City and the Festival

The anecdote of the movie-theater-turned-bank with which I began this appendix is a sign of changes not only in the modes of production and financing of films but also in its modes of circulation and consumption. The arrival of video and cable television; the death of the old, monumental movie theaters and their replacement by multiplexes; the proliferation of film festivals; the new directions that film distribution took; the changes in the advertising of film—all these elements also have aesthetic consequences.

Perhaps the most important phenomenon is the globalization of a thematic repertoire that, although it did not drastically alter a medium that has always been open to all sorts of influences, found in the 1990s a new inflection with the omnipresence of certain stories and with the circulation of cinematographies up until then unknown in Argentina, principally those of Asia (Taiwan, Hong Kong, Korea) and Iran.[21] Film is the first truly global art, as is shown in the multinational expression of film festivals, which reached Argentina in the 1990s, in the broad interests of its public (any well-informed spectator knows something about films made in Iran and in the United States, in Hong Kong and in Denmark), and in the themes of the movies themselves.

Lawrence Kasdan's *The Accidental Tourist* (1988) could not have been made in an era in which globalization was already a fact. In a world full of McDonald's, what sense is there in the story of a writer of guidebooks for U.S. businessmen to feel at home when they travel? Complementarily, Tsai Ming-liang's *Ni neibian jidian* (2001, *What Time Is It Over There?*), a love story that takes place in parallel in Paris and Taipei, could not have been narrated without the simultaneity and equivalences of recent years. In fact, the protagonist, Hsiao-kang (Kang Sheng-li), is a street vendor, one of the most global trades. (Who has not seen, in any bus or subway station in any city in the world, someone selling cheap watches made in China?) Globalization has also generated its own favorite narratives: the portraits of disoriented youth, the stories of characters outside of the social, and, principally, the stories of food and marriage.

The themes of disoriented youth and characters outside of the social emerge in various ways in Argentine film, to such an extent that we can speak, in Ana Amado's terms, of a common place of "disenchanted middle-class youth, youth as a group marginalized by the harshness of a consumer society, and the city as a frame of its aimless trajectories" (2002, 93). The global characters with the greatest longevity in national film have been those outside of the social, apathetic and a little zombie-like, as anticipated in some films from the 1980s: Travis in Wim Wenders *Paris, Texas* (1984), the narcoleptic Mike Waters in Gus Van Sant's *My Own Private Idaho* (1991), Mona the drifter in Agnès Varda's *Vagabond* (1985), the couple in Wong Kar Wai's *Happy Together* (1997). All of these movies show a predilection for nomadic characters who go nowhere, burdened by a spiritual illness that escapes their grasp. Several movies from the 1990s (those of Alonso, Trapero, and Rejtman) can be read as local Argentine variations on this global nomadic theme.

In contrast, tales of food and marriage have barely made an appearance in the new Argentine cinema, and this is because the theme of immigration, as we have seen in the discussion of Caetano's *Bolivia,* has continually been rendered invisible. Other cinematographies, however, have produced numerous versions of the wedding scene that consecrates the amorous union between characters of different racial, national, or religious origins. This scene shows that families must cast off traditional beliefs, and its narrative of the clash of cultures finds its reflection in the terrain of food as a metaphor of daily life and of the originality of mixture. Mira Nair's *Monsoon Wedding* (2001), Joel Zwick's *My Big Fat Greek Wedding* (2002), Ang Lee's *The Wedding Banquet* (1993), and Wayne Wang's *The Joy Luck Club* (1993) are movies in which this story unfolds.

Although Argentine cinema does not seem to have much use for this storyline, the story of food and marriage can be found in Gabriel Lichtmann's *Judíos en el espacio,* which hinges on a Passover Seder. Daniel Burman, the filmmaker most sensitive to these multicultural processes, adds his own particular inflection to them, as in *Esperando al mesías,* where marriage—in contrast to the examples given above—represents not a transgression of the family but an enclosure within its interior.

In her essay "Acá lejos" ("Here Far"), Inés Katzenstein (2003) points out the paradox that despite the cosmopolitanism of the 1990s, local visual arts were not able to move beyond their isolation. In contrast to what we might expect to be a period when the international scene and travel abroad were more accessible,[22] the local artistic scene is marked by anachronism. Similar anachronisms can be found in literature, not so much because of the disarticulation of a scene that lacks the homogeneity of the visual arts but because of literature's own slow pace of translation and diffusion. Globalization did not affect the development of local literature to a great extent, although it did modify the world of publishing. (Paradoxically, the Latin American literary market was never as fragmented as during the 1990s.)

None of this applies to film. Whether because prestigious festivals guaranteed that some movies managed to premiere in commercial movie theaters or because festivals allowed us to keep watch on the state of global cinema, it is clear that film and globalization are part of the same phenomenon. The reopening of the Mar del Plata International Film Festival (www.mdpfilmfestival.com.ar) in 1996 made it clear that exhibition was crucial for the development of the film industry. And although the festivals that took place in Mar del Plata never found a stable, coherent cultural policy, the sections programmed by Nicolás Sarquís ("Detrás de cámara" ["Behind the Camera"] and "Otros horizontes" ["Other Horizons"]) screened for the first and only time consecrated directors who were not shown in commercial theaters and the *operas primas* of directors who were pursuing new trends. However, in addition to eventual problems (as in the personalist direction of the Menemist Julio Mahárbiz, who wanted to make the festival a superficial parade of stars for the press), the festival has two structural problems that it has never been able to overcome. First, its dependence on the national government subjects it to repeated changes and a lack of long-term planning: the festival is too dependent upon power and too oriented to presenting itself as a success of the negotiations of municipal, state, and national governments. Second, the fact that it is an "A," or competitive, festival means that only international premieres can be shown in the official section.[23] Competing only with great difficulty with other festivals of greater continuity and prestige (Cannes, Berlin, San Sebastián), the competitions can never recover the brilliance of the past (when François Truffaut, Joaquim Pedro de Andrade, and Ingmar Bergman, among others, participated).

In contrast, these two drawbacks have been successfully resolved in the BAFICI, created in 1999. First, the festival is an event that is exclusively part of the city of Buenos Aires and thus does not need to deal with officious national and state structures. (The festival was initially directed by Ricardo Manetti, who was then part of the city government, and who is also a recognized university professor and historian of Argentine film.) Second, its regulations, devised by its artistic director, the filmmaker Andrés Di Tella, are fairly simple: the first or second movies of a filmmaker are allowed into the official competition. In contrast to the Mar del Plata festival, this has allowed movies that have premiered at other festivals to be shown; it has also allowed directors who made a very good first film to return with their second work to confirm or disconfirm that initial promise.

Festivals, then, were not only a space for students, spectators, and film people to keep up with the global film scene; they also propelled the new cinema. In 1997, Caetano and Stagnaro's *Pizza, birra, faso* obtained the Jury's Special Prize in the Thirteenth Mar del Plata festival, and in 1999 *Mundo grúa* received various prizes (best director, best actor) in the first BAFICI. Whereas the BAFICI has been more radical in its rejection of standardized products of Argentine cinema, the Mar del Plata festival has had to abide by the INCAA's policies, which promoted the inclusion of television actors (in Mahárbiz's era) and resulted in the inclusion of more conventional productions in the competition. (This by no means prevented the new cinema's presence; in addition to *Pizza, birra, faso,* Luis Ortega's *Caja negra* participated in the competition.[24]) With the creation of the section "Vitrina Argentina" ("Argentine Showcase") in 2005, the Mar del Plata festival managed to incorporate a whole series of independent and experimental products.

With regard to structure, the BAFICI's possibilities were also greater, because they fit in much better with the new international panorama. Buenos Aires has a profile that suits it to competition with other cities in the era of globalization. In his article "Global Cities and the International Film Festival Economy," Julian Stringer writes, "[O]ne might say that all the major festivals established in the immediate postwar period (Berlin, Cannes, Edinburgh, Moscow, London, Venice) were closely aligned with the activities and aims of particular national governments" (2002, 135). Yet, at the end of the twentieth century, the relationship between nation-state and city had been transformed, and the latter had acquired a greater autonomy in the "map of transcultural film exhibition and consumption" (134). Rotterdam, New York, Hong Kong, Berlin, and other cities use their festivals as part of an urban politics that is coordinated with tourism, the production of resources, the promotion of the city as a cultural center, and its location on the new global map.[25]

In addition to traditional festivals made possible by governmental institutions, recent years have seen the appearance of many festivals dedicated to more specific themes. Among these are the Festival Internacional de Cine y Video de Derechos Humanos (International Human Rights Festival of Film and Video; www.derhumalc.org.ar), which takes place in different cities. In 2003, Luis Gutmann founded the Festival de Cine Judío en la Argentina (Festival of Jewish Film in Argentina; www.ficja.com.ar), which has taken place three times. Horror, fantastic, and bizarre film also has its own festival, the Buenos Aires Rojo Sangre (Buenos Aires Red Blood; http://rojosangre. quintadimension.com), as do gay and lesbian film (Diversa—Festival de Cine y Video Gay/Lésbico [Diverse: Festival of Gay/Lesbian Film and Video]; www.diversafilms.com.ar), documentary film (in the presentations driven by Tercer Ojo [Third Eye; www.tercer-ojo.com] and the movement of documentary filmmakers; www.documentalistas. org.ar), working-class film (www.felco.ojoobrero.org), and the shorts of students at the Escuelas de cine (www.ucine.edu.ar/festival).

As Héctor Tizón once said, in Argentina someone has to do something so that someone else can immediately do the opposite: since the BAFICI already existed, in 2005 the BaFREEci—1er Festival Free de Cine y Cultura Independiente, Libre y Gratuita (First Free Festival of Independent and Free Cinema and Video; www.bafreeci.tk/) began, on the same dates as the other festival. We could say that festivals have been able to occupy a parallel and permanent place in the exhibition of films that would have otherwise reached spectators only with great difficulty.

Schools: Training

In addition to changes in production and distribution, a strategic politics of the culture industry, and the culture of festivals, the other major phenomenon in the 1990s was the proliferation of film schools as a nearly obligatory rite of passage for cinematographic creation. Supplanting the old tradition of the *plateau* as a place of apprenticeship, film schools institutionalized the stages of acquisition of technical and artistic knowledge. In addition, some film schools had a strong bearing on production, as many films could be assembled and edited in their studios. The best-equipped schools could lend film equipment and help orient newcomers to the twists and turns of production. The festival culture also became broader through these schools, which organized their own festivals of shorts and presented their projects and curricula at the most important festivals.

In 1991, Manuel Antín established the Fundación Universidad del Cine (Foundation Film University, or FUC). Several factors contributed to making this the most important national school in the promotion of new directors. Its objectives were both technical and strongly oriented toward humanistic education (with professors from the public university); fully equipped studios were created that allowed the university to be transformed into a center of production; and emphasis was placed specifically on film, in contrast to other institutions dedicated to the image in general or to advertising.[26] However, the university's high tuition fees limit access to the wealthier sectors of the population, a condition that is exacerbated during periods of economic crisis.

The best-prepared technicians, having learned their trade through a combination of technical, practical, and humanistic knowledge (and no longer on the set), emerged from the Fundación Universidad del Cine. In fact, many FUC students who specialize in a given area also were able to move into directing films of a high level of narrative and technical quality. A group of assistant directors (Ana Katz, Gabriel Medina), photographers (Guillermo Nieto, Paola Rizzi, Lucio Bonelli), editors (Alejandro Brodersohn, Martín Mainoli, Nicolás Goldbart), and sound editors and designers (Catriel Vildosola, Federico Esquerro, Enrique Bellande, Jesica Suárez, Lisandro Alonso, Carlos López Victorel) were able to work efficiently under the most adverse conditions. The FUC also produced several filmmakers, among them Pablo Trapero, Juan Taratuto, Albertina Carri, Lisandro Alonso, Juan Villegas, Gabriel Lichtmann, Bruno Stagnaro, Rodrigo Moreno, Ulises Rossell, Diego Fried, Alejo Taube, Celina Murga, Damián Szifrón, Andrés Schaer, and Mariano Llinás.

Another important school, with a longer history, is the Escuela Nacional de Experimentación y Realización Cinematográfica (National School of Filmic Experimentation and Execution, or the ENERC), which is dependent on the INCAA and boasts several famous graduates, including Lucrecia Martel and Julia Solomonoff. Ezequiel Acuña (*Nadar solo* and *Como un avión estrellado*) and

Ernesto Baca (*Cabeza de palo* and *Samoa*) graduated from the Centro de Investigación y Experimentación en Video y Cine (Center of Investigation and Experimentation in Video and Film, or the CIEVYC), the school directed by Aldo Paparella.

Recent years have seen the growth of the program in Image and Sound Design at the Universidad de Buenos Aires (UBA), founded in 1988 and dedicated to the audiovisual field more generally. However, the lack of equipment and the gargantuan nature of an institution like the UBA mean that the university is not in a position to offer its students the same technical possibilities that a private university or the ENERC can. In addition, the fact that it operates under the Department of Architecture, Design, and Urbanism speaks to a functional, rather than artistic, emphasis.

The Centro de Investigación Cinematográfica (Center of Cinematographic Investigation, or the CIC), geared toward cinema and theater, has encouraged film critics, including the directors of the journal *Haciendo cine* ("Making Film"). Although it is impossible to provide an exhaustive account of all the institutions that train professionals in film, we should also mention the Carrera de Realización Integral de Cine y Televisión (Degree in the Comprehensive Execution of Film and Television) in trade schools and the Taller de Cine Contemporáneo (Workshop on Contemporary Film), which is dependent on the municipality of Vicente López and from which Leonardo Di Cesare (*Buena Vida Delivery*) graduated.

Outside of Buenos Aires, we find the Taller de Cine de la Universidad Nacional del Litoral (Film Workshop of the National University of the Litoral), founded in 1985 by Raúl Beceyro; the Escuela Provincial de Cine y Televisión de Rosario (State School of Film and Television in Rosario), also dependent upon the state government; and the Escuela de Cine de la Universidad Nacional de Córdoba (Film School of the Córdoba National University). In addition to Antín's creation of the FUC, other directors have founded film schools, among which we can include the Fundación Imaginario (Imaginary Foundation), established by Fernando "Pino" Solanas, and the Escuela de Cine Profesional (School of Professional Film), founded by Eliseo Subiela in 1994. (Oriented toward digital cinema, in 1998 the Escuela de Cine Profesional produced the first all-digital movie made in Argentina: Subiela's *Las aventuras de Dios* [2000, "The Adventures of God"].)

There were other reference points outside of film schools that created study groups and influenced new generations. These include the study groups formed by José Martínez Suárez, and by Edgardo Chibán in the province of Salta.[27] We should highlight also El Amante/Escuela (The Lover/School), founded by the journal of the same name, the first educational institution devoted exclusively to film criticism.

Evidently, it is difficult to provide a full account of film training, given that a single film involves twenty or thirty people (the numbers vary according to the size of the project). Moreover, although the schools mentioned here were fundamental to shaping and producing the new Argentine cinema, it should come as no surprise that in an industry as permeable as cinema many filmmakers or assistant directors have had nontraditional training, as is the case of those who studied in foreign schools (including Paula Grandío and Fernando Alcalde, photographer and assistant director, respectively, of Martel's *La ciénaga*), those who are autodidacts, and those who trained in private workshops.

Criticism and Film Journals

During the 1990s, film criticism diversified and grew stronger in fields where it had been practically nonexistent. In the late 1950s, the previous boom period, film criticism found a home in movie clubs, magazines, and journals, as well as the Mar del Plata festival, created by critics in 1959.[28] Criticism thought of itself as an alternative field that needed to confront the hostility of the more conservative mass media. (In an important case during the 1970s, Tomás Eloy Martínez and Ramiro Casasbellas had to leave the newspaper *La Nación* because they refused to praise William Wyler's *Ben-Hur* [1959], a film backed by a great deal of publicity.) Although they were precarious and marginal, specialized journals provided a means of expression. Yet notable critics, including José Agustín Mahieu and Simón Feldman, were unable to convince the broader public of the early 1960s that a new generation had emerged.

During the 1990s, the situation was entirely different. Movie clubs no longer had this character of critical production,[29] and newspapers were no longer so impenetrable for young critics. These young critics could now help, through their reviews and interviews, to instill the idea that a change had occurred, a generational shift that needed to be heeded. Diego Lerer and Marcelo Panozzo in the newspaper *Clarín,* Diego Battle in *La Nación,* and Luciano Monteagudo and Horacio Bernardes in *Página/12*, through interviews, assessments, and criticism, circulated the idea that a new generation had emerged. (For example, young first-time directors, including Celina Murga and

Pablo Trapero, managed to appear on the cover of the entertainment supplement *Clarín espectáculos*.)

University and critical academic studies constitute another important realm that had been entirely absent from criticism during the 1970s. The growth of the film criticism track in the Arts department of the Philosophy and Letters wing of the Universidad de Buenos Aires meant a renovation in historical studies, an updating of the critical and theoretical arsenal, and the production of theses and books that marked out a possible path for criticism. Generally linked more to the historical study of film, this university criticism has produced the monumental history *Cine argentino* ("Argentine Cinema"), edited by Claudio España, which constitutes a landmark from the point of view of its analyses and the archival images it has recovered.

The FUC and other film schools have given space to criticism, now considered part of cinema itself and no longer something extraneous and sterile. Within the Universidad de Buenos Aires, the Centro Cultural Ricardo Rojas is an important center of the production and dissemination of film criticism; here, several program directors have played an important role, among them Fernando Peña, Andrés de Negri, and Sergio Wolf. The latter edited the book *Cine argentino, la otra historia* (1993, "Argentine Film, the Other Story"), which published articles by critics who would play a role in different media throughout the decade.

Finally, we should consider the proliferation of film journals such as *El amante cine* and *Haciendo cine*, which have managed an unusual continuity for specialized publications. Young critics have achieved continuity in their places of work (magazines and journals) and also participated actively in festivals, especially in the BAFICI, of which Quintín, one of the founders of the journal *El amante cine*, was director for four years, succeeding the first artistic director, Andrés Di Tella. In the festival's seventh year, Quintín was replaced by another film critic, also a historian and collector, Fernando Martín Peña. In 1993, Peña founded the journal *Film*, with Sergio Wolf and Paula Félix-Didier (which ceased publication in 1998). He is also in charge of the film programming for the Museo de Arte Latinoamericano de Buenos Aires (MALBA), where several Argentine films have premiered (the majority of them never having a commercial release) and lost or poorly conserved works have been rescued or restored.

The Internet has a great number of sites devoted to film that follow recent Argentine production very closely. In addition to the sites of print journals (*Hacinedo cine, El amante cine*), there are sites especially created for digital media: *citynema* (founded by Leandro Arteaga, Alejandro Hugolini, and Fernando Varea), *otrocampo* (managed by Victoria Ciaffone and edited by Fernando La Valle), *cineismo* (managed by Guillermo Ravaschino), and *leedor* (co-founded by Alejandra Portela and Guillermo Caneto). With critics from the most diverse backgrounds (many of them students or university graduates), these sites produce a considerable number of reviews, essays, and editorials, in addition to debates, discussion groups, and links.

Of all these phenomena of film criticism, the most pronounced break occurred in the field of language and in a different attitude toward Argentine movies. In this sense, the texts of *El amante cine* were fundamental because, for the first time, criticism did not patronize Argentine productions in the interests of recognizing investment or of defending national projects. Although the journal might not have had a clear program when it began—the fourth issue placed Eliseo Subiela's *El lado oscuro del corazón* (1992, released in the United States as *The Dark Side of the Heart*) on the cover and praised it, only to attack it in later issues—Quintín, Gustavo Noriega, Flavia de la Fuente (all founding members), Gustavo Castagna, Eduardo Russo, Alejandro Ricagno, Jorge García, Rodrigo Tarruela, and other editors established a different tone characterized by its irreverence, nonconformity, humor, subjective opinions, the ignoring of silent pacts, and even direct attacks. In addition, all of these critics had a solid cinephilic background and could sustain these battles with an exhaustive knowledge of film history and the use (which would strengthen as the journal grew) of critical and theoretical sources.

What saved the journal from becoming a committee of blasé and conceited critics, however, was primarily the gradual construction and defense of a canon of universal film that included a few Argentines. (There was an issue devoted to Leonardo Favio in 1993 and cover stories on Aristarain and Agresti.) Also of great importance were the defense of the renovation of national film at the end of the 1990s (with cover stories on Trapero, Villegas, Alonso, Martel, Bielinsky) and the active creation of a repertoire of high-quality international and Argentine works through the editors' extensive participation in the BAFICI from 2001 to 2004. Thus, demolition work (particularly with respect to Argentine film) was accompanied by a proposal for an alternative canon.

The differences between Quintín's increasingly modernist pose (and his full-time devotion to organizing the festival, resulting in an essentially nominal leadership at the journal) and the more narrative conception of film that Noriega, Jorge García, and newer collaborators such as Santiago García and Javier Porta Fouz share became increasingly clear, to the point that Quintín could not return to a journal with which he no longer identified. Currently, the journal is edited by Gustavo Noriega, with Javier Porta Fouz as editor-in-chief. Among the permanent collaborators are Gustavo Castagna, Santiago García, Eduardo Russo, Jorge García, Marcela Gamberini, Leonardo M. D'Esposito, Diego Trerotola, Juan Villegas, Marcelo Panozzo, and several other critics who have been brought in during the most recent phase of the journal.

In contrast to *Film* and even to *El amante cine, Haciendo cine* placed its bets early on the formation of a new Argentine cinema. The cover of the first issue (September 1995) featured an image from Raúl Perrone's *Labios de churrasco,* and was followed by cover stories on Stagnaro, Alejandro Agresti, Gustavo Mosquera, Martín Rejtman, and the Mar del Plata festival. The journal was founded and edited by Hernán Guerschuny and Pablo Udenio; the first issues came out irregularly, but from 2002 the journal achieved a bimonthly continuity and, in 2005, became a monthly publication. More informative in its writing than *El amante cine,* Guerschuny and Udenio's journal has had a strong influence on national production with its participation in festivals (principally in the "Work in Progress" section at the BAFICI) and with its exhibition of national premieres in the Alianza Francesa. Cynthia Sabat edits the journal, and her staff ("the *HC* team") includes the following critics: Nicolás Artusi, Ximena Battista, Eleonora Biaiñ, José María Brindisi, Santiago Calori, Augusto Constanzo, Martín Crespo, Sebastián De Caro, Florencia Eliçabe, Javier Firpo, Julián Gorodischer, Guido Herzovich, Micaela Krolovetzky, Nicolás Maidana, Silvina Marino, Paulo Pécora, Miguel Peirotti, Sebastián Rotstein, Martín Wain, and Nadia Zimerman.

The impact that the new cinema has had on some journals of cultural criticism, such as *Punto de vista, El ojo mucho,* and *Confines,* is another interesting aspect of recent film criticism. These journals began to publish essays on contemporary Argentine cinema using generally more sophisticated language and paying closer attention to cultural debates than those journals devoted exclusively to film. Of all of these journals, *Punto de vista* (with articles by Rafael Filippelli, David Oubiña, Hernán Hevia, Santiago Palavecino, and Raúl Beceyro, among others) has dealt most consistently with the seventh art.

In terms of academic interest in influencing cultural debates through film, we should highlight the role of *Kilómetro 111,* a specialized film journal written by university-trained critics. With lengthy articles, a greater obsession with conceptual precision, and the use of specialized bibliographies, the journal possesses the format of a book and tries to give the box office less prominence. Edited by Emilio Bernini, with Domin Choi, the journal has a staff that includes Mariano Dupont, Daniela Goggi, and Silvina Rival, with the participation of temporary collaborators (although Mauricio Alonso, Jerónimo Ledesma, Daniele Dottorini, Silvia Schwarzböck, Eduardo Russo, and Leonel Livchits have participated in several issues). *Kilómetro 111* has published seven issues, and since the second it has shown an increasing interest in the new Argentine cinema, through roundtables, articles, and film reviews.

In conclusion, film criticism has achieved, in recent years, two objectives shared by all intellectual activities that aspire to intervene in the social sphere: active participation in political decisions in the cultural field and intervention in contemporary debates. This does not mean I am averring that film criticism has reached a high level of debate or a high level of quality in its texts. Even today, it continues to be anchored in the need to produce quickly; the privileged genre of film criticism was, and continues to be, movie reviews. (In fact, in the face of the growth of magazines and Web sites devoted to film, the publication of books on Argentine cinema has been extremely rare.) This *immediacy* (in every sense of the word) of writing is accentuated by one of the deities most sacred to Argentine criticism: taste—as though taste, without rigorous reflection, were not virtually the same as mere habit. Established to a great extent by cinephiles, the cinephilia of criticism has the virtue, in the words of Jacques Rancière, of "rejecting the authority of specialists" and of "intersecting different experiences and knowledge" (2004b). However, it still needs to overcome certain challenges: to be more conceptually risky and to articulate in more extensive writings its stance on film.

Appendix 2

The Policy of Actors

With a heterogeneity that goes beyond a simple attachment to Italian neo-realism, the new Argentine cinema has pursued, in its choice of actors, a politics of the face, the body, and the name. As Raúl Antelo says in discussing the work of Deleuze and Agamben, the face is a political space of enunciation (2004, 121). In faces, bodies, and names, these movies investigate their own links to the real, and they do this in a specifically cinematographic way. For film is, in one of Serge Daney's lovely definitions, "that strange art made with real bodies and real events" (2004, 288). Through their casting policies, the movies of the new cinema broaden the field of perception of a cinema that had generally used a limited number of actors, and they enter into the world of nonprofessional actors.

In the face, there is a search for a blank page—the amateur actor has no repertoire of previously rehearsed gestures—upon which actions and affect can be inscribed. The character follows the screenplay but also embarks upon a trajectory toward himself or herself, his or her past, what happened to him or her at some time and the emotions elicited by that experience. With the body, filmmakers pursue a possible narration. In a society that organizes the visibility of bodies on the basis of a narrow model of beauty, the new cinema shows the body as accumulation, as history, as story. Through names, these films destabilize a fiction closed in upon itself, reflecting upon the materials that make this fiction possible. The names of actors and characters coincide despite the fact that the stories are invented. Experience, story, construction of a fiction: these three elements can be tracked through the original casting of the new Argentine cinema.

The Face

Esteban Sapir's *Picado fino* ("Fine Powder"), filmed between 1993 and 1995 and premiered in 1998, has not left a long legacy in terms of narrative aesthetics, but its casting has had an impact: its faces, clean or virginal in the eyes of the camera, are central to the story's narration. Facundo Luengo (Tomás) and Belén Blanco (Ana), along with other actors, are transformed into bodies that acquire experience as the story progresses.[1] Through its obsession with close-ups, Sapir's movie shows the possibilities of working with the features of a face unknown to the public. In *Picado fino,* the face is seen for the first time before revealing its expressions as the movie progresses. This notion of the cleansing of faces, working on them as though they were virgin territory, can be applied to almost all of the movies of the new Argentine cinema. Rejtman does this in *Los guantes mágicos* with Vicentico when he erases the rock star's face; Martel, too, in *La ciénaga* with the faces of the adolescent actresses, but also with the icon Graciela Borges. This practice extends to the casting of professional actors who are less known on screen or who tend to play secondary roles (Daniel Valenzuela, Roly Serrano, Beatriz Thibaudin, Marcelo Videla, Susana Pampin). Daniel Rosenfeld's *La quimera de los héroes* (2004), for example, lingers on the faces of the Toba Indians who form part of the rugby team in Formosa province that is the subject of the film. Perhaps one of the weakest aspects of this strange and interesting film is precisely its politics of the face, as these Indians never manage to become characters and to have their say in a film that has them as its protagonists. Ultimately, it is their trainer (Eduardo Rossi) who captures the camera's attention.

The face, then, is constructed during the film. This is the first time we have seen this face, and with it we encounter a person rather than an actor. Trapero's *Mundo grúa* ends with a close-up of el Rulo (Luis Margani) that accelerates, for the first time, the film's temporal flow. We first see his face at night, illuminated by the headlights of a car, his cigarette lit in the darkness; then in sunlight and, finally, in darkness once again. What is in this face, or why is it this face that the film offers up to us when it ends? Margani carries on his face the traces of labor—that is, as we have analyzed, the promise of a narrative.

In both *Picado fino* and *Mundo grúa,* although with different goals, this use of faces establishes a documentary connection with the real. To seek out the connections between this face and the real (reducing actorly feigning) appears to be another principle of the new cinema's casting.

In gestures we find perhaps the most political part: the fact that the actors act. Yet a gesture of pain, suffering, or happiness is not a representation or the result of a sedimented technique learned in theater school; it is a recovery of something that happened to this person before. The link with the real flares up here in all its intensity: el Rulo is not playing at suffering but repeating an earlier experience of suffering. The camera accompanies Misael Saavedra in *La libertad,* but Lisandro Alonso manages to create an atmosphere that allows him to go about his daily life (even an act as private as defecating) as though the camera did not exist. In Carri's *Los rubios,* we never know for sure whether gestures are meticulously measured or whether they are spontaneous; this doubt grows because those who give testimony encounter a fictional Albertina Carri, whom they supposedly know, and greet her as though she were the real one. In Alonso's *Los muertos,* the actor Argentino Vargas has the same name as the character in the film: does this mean he also spent time in jail? Does this mean this is the second time he is taking this trip? The movie's vision provides us with no answer. Might it be that, like Carri but with different goals in mind, Alonso is reflecting on the potential of fiction and its materials? For Carri, fiction is one of the privileged terrains in which memory itself (or the memory of children) is investigated. For Alonso, fiction is the adventure to which two bodies are committed: the actor's and the director's.[2] These are two very different ideas about fiction, but they are elaborated from the same point: the virginal face upon which a story is inscribed.

Bodies

Luis Ortega's *Caja negra* is perhaps the best demonstration of work with the bodies of actors. Ortega makes bodies the substance with which he constructs his extreme close-ups. The faces and bodies of the three characters are subject to a series of dissections and contrasting shots. Thus, the movie begins (after an enigmatic scene involving monkeys) with a contrast between the skin of a grandmother (Eugenia Bassi) and that of her granddaughter, Dorotea (Dolores Fonzi). The anguished and strange body of Dorotea's father, Eduardo Couget (curiously, he keeps the same name in the fiction), will sustain the entire narration, which eschews narrative sequence for a composition of states of the body: the grandmother whose body possesses marks of an ending, the adolescent who is losing the best years of her life, the father who moves around the city and appears to be a marionette. Fernando La Valle wrote,

> [W]e could say that the film ends, in its own way, on the formal level, considered as an exercise in the showing of bodies. In this sense the film opens up to a series of variations, centered around the three bodies carefully distinguished from one another, something like the extremes of human visibility: the father's slimness, the grandmother's old age, and Dolores Fonzi's delicious shape. Through a restless framing and editing, these three emblematic bodies undergo a rigorous, striking fragmentation. (www.otrocampo.com)

The body is the story, and not just any body, but extreme bodies, accumulating life and an unbearable burden.

We could also speak of the body in *Mundo grúa*, where el Rulo's physical problems are addressed throughout the film.[3] The choice of el Rulo has consequences in the terrain of bodies and names. El Rulo's body is that of an unemployed worker who tries to enter the workforce in any way possible. This body is juxtaposed with that of another non-professional actor, Federico Esquerro (a sound editor by profession and one of the most outstanding students of the Universidad del Cine). With great judgment, Trapero chooses a body, rather than an actor, because the traces of years of work and unexpected firings cannot be imitated. The same phenomenon occurs with el Rulo's son, the body of a young man who has never worked and who spends his time in a rock band. It is not a question of an aesthetic doctrine, as in the original Italian neorealism; Trapero understands well the difficulties of using nonprofessional actors. Thus, he surrounds them with talented professionals (Adriana Aizenberg, Daniel Valenzuela, and Roly Serrano), who accompany these bodies into the world of acting.

Names

In *Mundo grúa*, Trapero's casting of el Rulo is fitting—something made evident in the prize that Margani received in the First BAFICI and the fact that the character has become an icon of the film. From the movie poster, el Rulo appropriates the movie's story; the boundary between fiction and reality becomes permeable. His name and nickname are the same in real life and in the film, a phenomenon repeated in other films: Misael Saavedra and Argentino Vargas in Alonso's *La libertad* and *Los muertos,* the characters in Caetano's

Bolivia, Eduardo Couget in *Caja negra,* Nicéforo Galván in Raúl Perrone's *La mecha,* and Gastón Pauls in Villegas' *Sábado.* (In fact, *Sábado* was going to be called *Gastón Pauls.*[4]) In *Silvia Prieto* this conceit is realized in a strange way (particularly in a film that is about names). Gabriel Fernández Capello is called "Gabriel" in the movie. As this actor is usually known by his artistic name, Vicentico, it is possible that Rejtman intended to restore his common name, separate from his identity as a rock idol. It is not Vicentico acting but Gabriel. In the film's final scene, the real Silvia Prietos meet up in a gathering in which one of the film's Silvia Prietos (Mirta Busnelli) also participates. In this use of names, the movies establish another link to the real: real people and the fictitious story influence one another by osmosis. The borders between daily life and the adventure of film blur.

Radical in their efforts, all of these movies find meaning (and also politics) not necessarily in the stories that they tell, nor in the call to action, nor in the postulation of a national identity. At times they turn to the meaning of sounds; at other times, to the expressiveness of framing. Here, we see how the choice of actors marks a possible path to reflect on the relationships between film and society and how film and society approach names, faces, and bodies.

Appendix 3

Argentine Films That Premiered between 1997 and Mid-2005

1997 (Twenty-Seven Films)

24 horas (Algo está por explotar) (1997), Luis Barone
Bajo bandera (1997), Juan José Jusid
Buenos Aires viceversa (1996), Alejandro Agresti
Canción desesperada (1996), Jorge Coscia
Cenizas del paraíso (1997), Marcelo Piñeyro
*Comodines (1997), Jorge Nisco
*Dibu, la película (1997), Carlos Olivieri and Alejandro Stoessel
*Dile a Laura que la quiero (1995), José Miguel Juárez
El Che (1997), Aníbal Di Salvo
*El impostor (1997), Alejandro Maci
*El sekuestro (1997), Eduardo Montes Bradley
El sueño de los héroes (1997), Sergio Renán
*Fantasmas en la Patagonia (1996), Claudio Remedi
Graciadió (1997), Raúl Perrone
Hasta la victoria siempre (1997), Juan Carlos Desanzo
Historias clandestinas en La Habana (1996), Diego Musiak
La furia (1997), Juan Bautista Stagnaro
La lección de tango (1997), Sally Potter
*La vida según Muriel (1997), Eduardo Milewicz
Martín (Hache) (1997), Adolfo Aristarain
*Noche de ronda (1997), Marcos Carnevale
Pequeños milagros (1997), Eliseo Subiela
Prohibido (1996), Andrés Di Tella
*Queréme así (Piantao) (1997), Eliseo Alvarez

Sapucay, mi pueblo (1997), Fernando Siro
*Territorio comanche (1997), Gerardo Herrero
Un asunto privado (1995), Imanol Arias

1998 (Thirty-Seven Films)

5 pal peso (1998), Raúl Perrone
Afrodita, el jardín de los perfumes (1998), Pablo César
Aller simple (Tres historias del Río de la Plata) (1994), Noël Burch,
    Nadine Fischer, and Nelson Scartaccini
Asesinato a distancia (1997), Santiago Carlos Oves
Buenos Aires me mata (1998), Beda Docampo Feijóo
Che...Ernesto (1997), Miguel Pereira
*Cohen vs. Rosi (1998), Daniel Barone
*Cómplices (1998), Néstor Montalbano
Corazón iluminado (1998), Héctor Babenco
Crónica de un extraño (1997), Miguel Mirra
*Dársena Sur (1997), Pablo Reyero
*Diario para un cuento (1997), Jana Bokova
Dibu 2, la venganza de Nasty (1998), Carlos Galettini
Doña Bárbara (1998), Betty Kaplan
El desvío (1998), Horacio Maldonado
El faro (1998), Eduardo Mignogna
El juguete rabioso (1998), Javier Torre
*Escrito en el agua (1997), Marcos Loayza
*Fuga de cerebros (1997), Fernando Musa
La cruz (1997), Alejandro Agresti
La herencia del tío Pepe (1997), Hugo Sofovich
La nube (1998), Fernando Ezequiel Solanas
*La sonámbula, recuerdos del futuro (1998), Fernando Spiner
*Los ratones (1965), Francisco Vasallo
*Mala época (1998), Nicolás Saad, Mariano De Rosa, Salvador
    Roselli, and Rodrigo Moreno
Mar de amores (1998), Víctor Dínenzon
Momentos robados (1997), Oscar Barney Finn
*Picado fino (1994), Esteban Sapir
*Pizza, birra, faso (1997), Bruno Stagnaro and Israel Adrián
    Caetano
*Plaza de almas (1997), Fernando Díaz
Secretos compartidos (1998), Alberto Lecchi

Sobre la tierra (1998), Nicolás Sarquís
Sus ojos se cerraron (1998), Jaime Chávarri
Tango (1998), Carlos Saura
Tinta roja (1998), Carmen Guarini y Marcelo Céspedes
Un argentino en Nueva York (1998), Juan José Jusid
Un crisantemo estalla en cinco esquinas (1997), Daniel Burman

1999 (Thirty-Four Films)

Alma mía (1999), Daniel Barone
América mía (1998), Gerardo Herrero
Caminos del Chaco (1998), Alejandro Fernández Mouján
Che, un hombre de este mundo (1998), Marcelo Schapces
Comisario Ferro (1998), Juan Rad
Diablo, familia y propiedad (1999), Fernando Krichmar
El amateur (1998), Juan Bautista Stagnaro
El evangelio de las maravillas (1998), Arturo Ripstein
El mismo amor, la misma lluvia (1999), Juan José Campanella
El secreto de los Andes (1998), Alejandro Azzano
El siglo del viento (1999), Fernando Birri
El viento se llevó lo que (1998), Alejandro Agresti
El visitante (1999), Javier Olivera
Esa maldita costilla (1999), Juan José Jusid
Garage Olimpo (1999), Marco Bechis
H. G. O. (1998), Víctor Bailo and Daniel Stefanello
Héroes y demonios (1999), Horacio Maldonado
Invierno, mala vida (1997), Gregorio Cramer
La cara del angel (1998), Pablo Torre
La edad del sol (1999), Ariel Piluso
La noche del coyote (1998), Iván Entel
La venganza (1999), Juan Carlos Desanzo
Lisboa (1999), Antonio Hernández
Manuelita (1999), Manuel García Ferré
Mundo grúa (1999), Pablo Trapero
Música de Laura (1994), Juan Carlos Arch
Ni el tiro del final (1997), Juan José Campanella
Padre Mujica (1999), Gustavo E. Gordillo
Pozo de zorro (1998), Miguel Mirra
Río escondido (1999), Mercedes García Guevara
Silvia Prieto (1998), Martín Rejtman

Soriano (1998), Eduardo Montes Bradley
Tres veranos (1999), Raúl Tosso
Yepeto (1999), Eduardo Calcagno

2000 (Forty-Three Films)

76 89 03 (1999), Cristian Bernard and Flavio Nardini
**Acrobacias del corazón* (1999), Teresa Costantini
Almejas y mejillones (2000), Marcos Carnevale
Ángel, la diva y yo (1999), Pablo Nisenson
Apariencias (2000), Alberto Lecchi
Botín de guerra (2000), David Blaustein
Buenos Aires plateada (2000), Luis Barone
**Casanegra* (2000), Carlos Lozano Dana
**Cerca de la frontera* (1999), Rodolfo Durán
Chicos ricos (2000), Mariano Galperín
**Cien años de perdón* (1999), José Glusman
**Cóndor Crux* (1999), Juan Pablo Buscarini, Swan Glecer, and
    Pablo Holcer
Corazón, las alegrías de Pantriste (2000), Manuel García Ferré
**El asadito* (1999), Gustavo Postiglione
El astillero (1999), David Lipszyc
El camino (2000), Javier Olivera
**El mar de Lucas* (1999), Víctor Laplace
**El nadador inmóvil* (1998), Fernán Rudnik
Esperando al mesías (2000), Daniel Burman
**Felicidades* (2000), Lucho Bender
**Fuckland* (2000), José Luis Marqués
Harto The Borges (2000), Eduardo Montes Bradley
Invocación (2000), Héctor Faver
**Las huellas borradas* (1999), Enrique Gabriel-Lipschutz
Los días de la vida (2000), Francisco D'Intino
Los libros y la noche (1999), Tristán Bauer
**Los Pintín al rescate* (2000), Franco Bíttolo
Nueces para el amor (2000), Alberto Lecchi
**Nueve reinas* (2000), Fabián Bielinsky
Nunca asistas a este tipo de fiestas (2000), Pablo Parés, Hernán
    Sáez, and Paulo Soria
Ojos que no ven (1999), Beda Docampo Feijóo
Operación Fangio (1999), Alberto Lecchi
Operación Walsh (1999), Gustavo E. Gordillo

Papá es un ídolo (2000), Juan José Jusid
Plata quemada (2000), Marcelo Piñeyro
*Qué absurdo es haber crecido (2000), Roly Santos
Sin querer (1996), Ciro Cappellari
*Sin reserva (1997), Eduardo Spagnolo
Sólo gente (1999), Roberto Maiocco
Solo y conmigo (2000), Carlos Lozano Dana
*Tesoro mío (1999), Sergio Bellotti
Un amor de Borges (2000), Javier Torre
Una noche con Sabrina Love (2000), Alejandro Agresti

2001 (Forty-Seven Films)

*Agua de fuego (2001), Candela Galantini, Sandra Godoy, and
    Claudio Remedi
*Animalada (2000), Sergio Bizzio
Antigua vida mía (2001), Héctor Olivera
Arregui, la noticia del día (2001), María Victoria Menis
*+bien (2001), Eduardo Capilla
*Cabecita rubia (2000), Luis Sampieri
*Cabeza de tigre (2001), Claudio Etcheberry
Campo de sangre (1999), Gabriel Arbós
*Chiquititas, rincónde luz (2001), José Luis Massa
*Cicatrices (1999), Patricio Coll
Ciudad sin luz (1999), Juan Carlos Arch
Contraluz (2001), Bebe Kamín
Dejala correr (2001), Alberto Lecchi
El amor y el espanto (2000), Juan Carlos Desanzo
*El armario (1999), Gustavo Corrado
*El despertar de L (1999), Poli Nardi
El hijo de la novia (2001), Juan José Campanella
El lado oscuro del corazón II (2001), Eliseo Subiela
Gallito ciego (2000), Santiago Carlos Oves
*(h) historias cotidianas (2000), Andrés Habegger
Historias , Argentina en Vivo (2001), Israel Adrián Caetano,
    Bruno Stagnaro, Marcelo Piñeyro, Andrés Di Tella,
    Cristian Bernard, Flavio Nardini, Miguel Pereira,
    Gustavo Postiglione, Albertina Carri, Fernando Spiner,
    Gregorio Cramer, Jorge Polaco, *Vicentico Fernández Capello,
    and Eduardo Capilla
*La ciénaga (2000), Lucrecia Martel

La fuga (2001), Eduardo Mignogna
*La libertad (2001), Lisandro Alonso
*La mujer que todo hombre quiere (2001), Gabriela Tagliavini
Los cuentos del timonel (2001), Eduardo Montes Bradley
*Los pasos perdidos (2001), Manane Rodríguez
*Luna de octubre (1997), Henrique de Freitas Lima
*Maldita cocaína (2000), Pablo Rodríguez
Mil intentos y un invento (1972), Manuel García Ferré
*Nada por perder (2001), Enrique Aguilar
*No quiero volver a casa (2000), Albertina Carri
*¿Quién está matando a los gorriones? (2000), Patricia Martín
   García
*Rerum Novarum (2001), Fernando Molnar,
   Nicolás Batlle, and Sebastián Schindel
*Rodrigo, la película (2001), Juan Pablo Laplace
*Rosarigasinos (2001), Rodrigo Gran
*Saluzzi, ensayo para bandoneón y tres hermanos (2000),
   Daniel Rosenfeld
*Sólo por hoy (2000), Ariel Rotter
*Taxi, un encuentro (2000), Gabriela David
Te besaré mañana (2001), Diego Musiak
*Testigos ocultos (2001), Néstor Sánchez Sotelo
Tobi y el libro mágico (2001), Jorge Zuhair Jury
*Tocá para mí (2001), Rodrigo Fürth
Un amor en Moisés Ville (2000), Antonio Ottone
*Van Van, empezó la fiesta (2000), Liliana Mazure and
   Aaron Vega
Viaje por el cuerpo (2000), Jorge Polaco
*Yo, Sor Alice (1999), Alberto Marquardt

2002 (Forty-Six Films)

Apasionados (2002), Juan José Jusid
*Bahía mágica (2002), Marina Valentini
Bolivia (2001), Israel Adrián Caetano
Cacería (2001), Ezio Massa
*Caja negra (2001), Luis Ortega
*Casi ángeles (2000), Vanessa Erfurth, Carolina Suárez,
   Mario Borgna, Manuel Tello, and Leonel Compagnet
Chúmbale (2001), Aníbal Di Salvo
*Corazón de fuego (2002), Diego Arsuaga

Cortázar: apuntes para un documental (2002),
    Eduardo Montes Bradley
Dibu 3 (2002), Raúl Rodríguez Peila
El bonaerense (2002), Pablo Trapero
El cumple (2002), Gustavo Postiglione
El descanso (2001), *Ulises Rosell, Rodrigo Moreno, and
    *Andrés Tambornino
Estrella del sur (2002), Luis Nieto (II)
Herencia (2001), Paula Hernández
Historias mínimas (2002), Carlos Sorín
I Love You…Torito (2001), Edmund Valladares
Kamchatka (2002), Marcelo Piñeyro
La entrega (2001), Inés de Oliveira Cézar
La fe del volcán (2001), Ana Poliak
Las aventuras de Dios (2000), Eliseo Subiela
Las Palmas, Chaco (2002), Alejandro Fernández Mouján
Los malditos caminos (2002), Luis Barone
Luca Vive (2002), Jorge Coscia
Lugares comunes (2002), Adolfo Aristarain
Marechal, o la batalla de los ángeles (2001), Gustavo Fontán
Matanza (2001), Nicolás Batlle, *Rubén Delgado,
    *Sebastián Menéndez, and *Emiliano Penelas
Mataperros (2001), Gabriel Arregui
Mercano, el marciano (2002), Juan Antín
Micaela, una película mágica (2001), Rosanna Manfredi
Ni vivo, ni muerto (2001), Víctor Jorge Ruiz
No dejaré que no me quieras (2002), José Luis Acosta
Noche en la terraza (2001), Jorge Zima
NS/NC (2001), Fernando Musa
Peluca y Marisita (2001), Raúl Perrone
Sábado (2001), Juan Villegas
¿Sabés nadar? (1997), Diego Kaplan
Samy y yo (2001), Eduardo Milewicz
Temporal (2001), Carlos Orgambi
Todas las azafatas van al cielo (2001), Daniel Burman
Tres pájaros (2001), Carlos Jaureguialzo
Un día de suerte (2002), Sandra Gugliotta
Un oso rojo (2002), Israel Adrián Caetano
Vagón fumador (2000), Verónica Chen
Vidas privadas (2001), Fito Páez
¿Y dón, está el bebé? (2002), Pedro Stocki

2003 (Fifty-Four Films)

Abrazos, tango en Buenos Aires (2003), Daniel Rivas
Assassination Tango (2002), Robert Duvall
Balnearios (2002), Mariano Llinás
Bar "El Chino" (2003), Daniel Burak
Barbie también puede estar triste (2001), Albertina Carri
Bonanza (En vías de extinción) (2001), Ulises Rosell
Bonifacio (2003), Rodrigo Magallanes
Che vo cachai (2002), Laura Bondarevsky
Ciudad de María (2003), Enrique Bellan
Ciudad del sol (2001), Carlos Galettini
Cleopatra (2003), Eduardo Mignogna
Click! (2001), Ricardo Berretta
Código postal (2001), Roberto Echegoyenberri
Don, cae el sol (2002), Gustavo Fontán
El agua en la boca (2003), Federico Augusto Arzeno
El alquimista impaciente (2002), Patricia Ferreira
El día que me amen (2003), Daniel Barone
El fondo del mar (2003), Damián Szifrón
El juego de Arcibel (2003), Alberto Lecchi
El juego de la silla (2002), Ana Katz
El polaquito (2003), Juan Carlos Desanzo
El regreso (2001), Hugo Lescano
El séptimo arcángel (2003), Juan Bautista Stagnaro
En la ciudad sin límites (2001), Antonio Hernán
Gerente en dos ciudades (2001), Diego Soffici
Ilusión de movimiento (2001), Héctor Molina
India Pravile (2003), Mario Sabato
La mecha (2003), Raúl Perrone
La noche de las cámaras despiertas (2002),
    Hernán Andra and Víctor Cruz
La televisión y yo (notas en una libreta) (2002), Andrés Di Tella
Los rubios (2003), Albertina Carri
Marc, la sucia rata (2003), Leonardo Fabio Calderón
Murgas y murgueros (2003), Pedro Fernández Mouján
Nadar solo (2003), Ezequiel Acuña
Nicotina (2003), Hugo Rodríguez
No debes estar aquí (2002), Jacobo Rispa
Nowhere (2002), Luis Sepúlveda (II)
Oscar Alemán, vida con swing (2001), Hernán Gaffet

Por la vuelta (2002), Cristian Pauls
Potestad (2001), Luis César D'Angiolillo
Raúl Barboza, el sentimiento de abrazar (2003), Silvia Di Florio
Sangre (2003), Pablo César
Sé quien eres (2001), Patricia Ferreira
Sol de noche (2002), Pablo Milstein and *Norberto Ludin
Soy tu aventura (2003), Néstor Montalbano
Sudeste (2002), Sergio Bellotti
Tan de repente (2002), Diego Lerman
Todo juntos (2002), Federico León
Un día en el paraíso (2003), Juan Bautista Stagnaro
Un hijo genial (2003), José Luis Massa
Valentín (2002), Alejandro Agresti
Vivir intentando (2003), Tomás Yankelevich
Vladimir en Buenos Aires (2002), Diego Gachassin
Yo no sé qué me han hecho tus ojos (2003),
    Sergio Wolf and Lorena Muñoz

2004 (Sixty-Nine Films)

18-J (2004), Adrián Caetano, Carlos Sorín, Daniel Burman,
    Alberto Lecchi, Alejandro Doria, Lucía Cedrón,
    Juan Bautista Stagnaro, Mauricio Wainrot, Marcelo Schapces,
    and Adrián Suar
Atrapados en el fin del mundo (2003), Eduardo L. Sánchez
Ay, Juancito (2004), Héctor Olivera
Buena Vida Delivery (2003), Leonardo Di Cesare
Cabeza de palo (2002), Ernesto Baca
Casafuerte (2004), Tomás Gotlip and Nicolás Grandi
Chiche bombón (2004), Fernando Musa
Contr@site (2003), Daniele Incalcaterra and Fausta Quattrini
Conversaciones con mamá (2004), Santiago Carlos Oves
Cruz de sal (2003), Jaime L. Lozano
Deuda (2004), Jorge Lanata and Andrés Schaer
Diarios de motocicleta (2004), Walter Salles
Dolores de casada (2004), Juan Manuel Jiménez
Dos ilusiones (2004), Martín Lobo
El 48 (2004), Alejandra Marino
El abrazo partido (2003), Daniel Burman
El cielito (2003), María Victoria Menis
El delantal, Lili (2003), Mariano Galperín

El favor (2003), Pablo Sofovich
El lugar don, estuvo el paraíso (2001), Gerardo Herrero
*El Nüremberg argentino (2004), Miguel Rodríguez Arias
El perro (2004), Carlos Sorín
*El resquicio (2003), Amin Alfredo Yoma
*El tren blanco (2003), Nahuel García, Sheila Pérez Giménez, and
    Ramiro García
*Erreway: 4 caminos (2004), Ezequiel Crupnicoff
*Extraño (2003), Santiago Loza
Familia rodante (2004), Pablo Trapero
*Historias breves IV (2004), Gabriel Dodero, Paula Venditti,
    Jonathan Hoffman, Daniel Bustamante, Lautaro Núñezde Arco,
    Martín Mujica, Pablo Pérez (II), Cecilia Ulrich, Pablo Pupato,
    Fernando Tranquillini, and Camilo José Gómez
*Hotel, hotel (2002), Ofelia Escasany
*Hoteles (2003), Aldo Paparella
*Hoy y mañana (2003), Alejandro Chomski
La cruz del sur (2002), Pablo Reyero
La mayor estafa al pueblo argentino (2002), Diego Musiak
La mina (2003), Víctor Laplace
La niña santa (2004), Lucrecia Martel
La puta y la ballena (2003), Luis Puenzo
La quimera de los héroes (2003), Daniel Rosenfeld
La soledad era esto (2001), Sergio Renán
*La vaca verde (2003), Javier Díaz (II)
*Legado (2001), Vivian Imar and Marcelo Trotta
*Lesbianas de Buenos Aires (2002), Santiago García
Lisboa (2003), Néstor Lescovich
Los esclavos felices (2003), Gabriel Arbós
*Los fusiladitos (2003), Cecilia Miljiker
Los guantes mágicos (2003), Martín Rejtman
Los muertos (2004), Lisandro Alonso
*Los perros (2004), Adrián Jaime
Luna de Avellaneda (2004), Juan José Campanella
Memoria del saqueo (2003), Pino Solanas
*Nietos (Identidad y memoria) (2004), Benjamín Ávila
*No sos vos, soy yo (2004), Juan Taratuto
*NOA, un viaje en subdesarrollo (2004), Diego Olmos and
    Pablo Pintor
*Operación Algeciras (2003), Jesús Mora
*Oscar (2004), Sergio Morkin

Palermo Hollywood (2004), Eduardo Pinto
Patoruzito (2004), José Luis Massa
Peligrosa obsesión (2004), Raúl Rodríguez Peila
Próxima salida (2004), Nicolás Tuozzo
Que lo pague la noche (2003), Néstor Mazzini
Raymundo (2002), Ernesto Ardito and Virna Molina
Rebelión (2004), Federico Urioste
Roma (2004), Adolfo Aristarain
Siglo bohemio (2004), Aníbal Garisto, Mónica Nizzardo, and
  Javier Orradre
Tacholas, un actor galaico porteño (2003), José Santiso
Teo, cazador intergaláctico (2004), Sergio Bayo
Trelew (2003), Mariana Arruti
Tus ojos brillaban (2003), Silvio Fischbein
Un mundo menos peor (2004), Alejandro Agresti
Una de dos (2004), Alejo Taube

2005 (Twenty-Seven Films)

1420, la aventura de educar (2004), Raúl Tosso
…al fin, el mar (2003), Jorge Dyszel
Adiós querida Luna (2003), Fernando Spiner
Buenos Aires 100 kilómetros (2004), Pablo José Meza
Buscando a Reynols (2004), Néstor Frenkel
Cama adentro (2004), Jorge Gaggero
Cielo azul, cielo negro (2003), Paula de Luque and Sabrina Farji
Cuando los santos vienen marchando (2004), Andrés Habegger
El jardín de las hespérides (2003), Patricia Martín García
Géminis (2005), Albertina Carri
Hermanas (2004), Julia Solomonoff
Kasbah (2001), Mariano Barroso
La esperanza (2003), Francisco D'Intino
La vida por Perón (2004), Sergio Bellotti
Manekenk (2003), Juan Schröder
Oro nazi en Argentina (2004), Rolo Pereyra
Otra vuelta (2004), Santiago Palavecino
Papá se volvió loco (2005), Rodolfo Ledo
PyME (Sitiados) (2003), Alejandro Malowicki
Ronda nocturna (2004), Edgardo Cozarinsky
Seres queridos (2004), Teresa de Pelegrí and Dominic Harari
Sólo un ángel (2001), Horacio Maldonado

Un año sin amor (2004), Anahí Berneri
Un buda (2005), Diego Rafecas
Vereda tropical (2004), Javier Torre
Whisky (2003), Juan Pablo Rebella and Pablo Stoll
Whisky Romeo Zulú (2003), Enrique Piñeyro

Epilogue to the 2011 Edition[1]

I finished writing the Spanish-language edition of *Other Worlds* in May of 2005. Since then, much has been written about contemporary Argentine film: three books have been published (Ana Amado's *La imagen justa. Cine argentino y política 1980–2007* [The Right Image: Argentine and Political Film, 1980–2006], Agustín Campero's *Nuevo cine argentino: de Rapado a Historias extraordinarias* [New Argentine Cinema: From *Rapado* to *Historias extraordinarias*], Joanna Page's *Crisis and Capitalism in Contemporary Argentine Cinema*)[2]; the publishing house Picnic began its collection on new Argentine film (Nuevo Cine Argentino), directed by Daniela Fiorini, Aldo Paparella, and Paula Socolovsky; master's theses and doctoral dissertations have been defended; and several research projects are currently underway.[3] In the academic field, of which this book forms a part, the increase has been unprecedented, which makes putting together an "updated" or "revised" version a challenge.[4] Besides all of this we also need to consider the journalistic pieces and blogs that, beyond the insults and banalities that come with this territory, have been the staging ground for many impassioned debates.

While this challenge is great on the level of critical production, it is no less so with respect to the corpus itself. The frustrating story of the sixties generation filmmakers has not repeated itself: many of the directors who emerged at the beginning of the twenty-first century are currently filming on a regular basis, having already made three or more films.[5] In addition, there are new filmmakers with at least two films completed who are only briefly mentioned in the first edition of *Other Worlds*, simply because their *operas primas* had been released only very recently.[6] Today, many film crews are starting up new projects. I mean, specifically, *are starting up*: it is impossible to write this story in any other tense but in the present, an open present, dynamic and decisive.

Many of the principles that governed filmmaking between 2000 and 2004 have changed radically, and what used to be isolated cases now constitute a tendency whose paths are very difficult to predict. What has changed the most are networks of exhibition, and for this reason lists of official releases can be misleading: they constitute only a part of what is being produced and, stranger still, of what is seen.[7] Filmmaking possibilities have also changed and digital is increasingly offering filmmakers other avenues. Production has increased, aesthetic quality has been maintained, and exhibition has diversified. Of course, problems and unusual situations persist: for example, newspapers have not made the same effort as they have in the realm of theater to review releases that debuted in spaces outside those recognized by the INCAA (Instituto Nacional de Cine y Artes Audiovisuales.) Some noteworthy ventures—like the movie theater opened by Daniel Burman, Pablo Rovito and Diego Dubcovsky in the Constitución neighborhood of Buenos Aires—were not commercially viable and had to be rescued by the INCAA, revealing the pressing nature of the problem of exhibition. Another problem is that the auspicious climate of the new Argentine cinema has favored the reception of certain works that would not be as compelling in a different context—although, in reality, this is less a specifically cinematic phenomena than one related to art consumption more broadly. Lastly, the pendulum of politics tests the powers of filmmaking in Argentina, even if the 1994 law, discussed in this book, provides a shield—thus one is faced with an uneven panorama with multiple facets that are difficult to describe and analyze in a few pages. For this reason, this epilogue is more a tentative reflection than a closed account.

Shifts in Production Companies and Anomalous Film

The two most important events in recent Argentine film were the shifts undergone in production companies and the consolidation of an anomalous cinema. As they are outside of the scope of this chapter, I will bracket the success of Juan José Campanella's *El secreto de sus ojos* [The Secret in Their Eyes], (2009), winner of the 2010 Oscar for Best Foreign Film, and the heightened level of mainstream Argentine filmmaking through contributions of filmmakers such as Daniel Burman, Fabián Bielinsky, Juan Taratuto, and Damián Szifrón, among others. The very incorporation of directors from the new cinema into the industry (for example, in the case of Pablo Trapero, Adrián Caetano, Diego Lerman, and others previously mentioned) means that the dividing line between the mainstream and "new Argentine cinema" has become less rigid and pronounced. Evidently, this does not signal capitulation but a change in the state of things, with institutionalization as a necessary moment in order for a living, heterogeneous, and variable movement to be consolidated. But just as there is an institutional path, there is also an alternative, which is the one taken by anomalous cinema: a group of marginalized, bastard, stubborn films that seek to establish a different network and a different experience on the edges of the industry. Not coincidentally, this tendency began in the cinemateques of art museums: it can be understood as the perseverance of a kind of film that either has no place in conventional movie theaters and in the INCAA or has not wanted to be placed there.[8]

Shifts in production companies mean the arrival of a new kind of producer with a keen sense of the contemporary moment, a certain eclecticism, and the capacity to support projects that respond to very different networks. Matanza (headed up by Pablo Trapero), BD Cine (by Diego Burman and Diego Dubcovsky), and Rizoma (Hernán Musaluppi) are production companies that started small and have since learned to diversify their production, to work in different territories, and to find a place within the institutional framework. These and a few others have changed the face of cinematic production in Argentina in recent years.

In this context, these same directors have learned to multiply their strategies and to have their films circulate creatively, dispensing with rigid previous models and taking diverse possibilities into account. The relationship between the budget and the more or less alternative nature of a film is less mechanical; what is fundamental is the elasticity of the different aspects of production of a film. On the one hand there are subsidies that are not unique to filmmaking but are part of a general cultural operation.[9] In a globalized economy, those who make films need to know how to handle different options, in addition to the national laws that protect them. On the other hand, it is necessary to construct a relatively autonomous mechanism to support an industry that requires more funds than other cultural areas. At this crossroads, the new production companies have already proved competitive. In the case of Matanza Cine, three projects are already underway for 2011, among them the second films of both Santiago Palavecino and Gabriel Medina. In addition, both in Matanza Cine and in BD or

Rizoma, those who are heading up these projects do not come from the world of finance (not even the entertainment business) but are people—Pablo Trapero, Daniel Burman, or Hernán Musaluppi (graduate of the Fundación Universidad del Cine, or FUC)—who had their beginnings in independent film and who have had rich experiences working in cinema.

The other event is what I call anomalous film. According to the path sketched out in the subtitle of Agustín Campero's book (From *Rapado* to *Historias extraordinarias*), the trajectory of the new Argentine cinema was, then, from one independent film to another—or, better stated, from one independent film in a hostile environment to another independent film as a strategy and as a fortification of a way of thinking about cinema. Both are political gestures but the contexts are clearly different: while *Rapado* constituted a discovery and learning process in the face of scarce options, *Historias extraordinarias* is a choice, esthetic, political, and vital position. For Llinás, the adventure of cinema is equal to the adventure that he imagines for the characters in his film.

Anomalous film is not a cinema that necessarily confronts an order but one that is, simply, made at the margins of an order. The anomalous does not place itself in opposition to a norm, as Deleuze and Guattari have explained, but is that which differs, the multiple: "*anormal,* a Latin adjective lacking a noun in French, refers to that which is outside rules or goes against the rules, whereas *an-omolie,* a Greek noun that has lost its adjective, designates the unequal, the course, the rough, the cutting edge of deterritorialization."[10] It is, therefore, logical that in anomalous film we are unable to find similar works, or those that opt for a similar esthetic, but instead there are films that differ greatly from one another, by directors such as Gustavo Fontán and Matías Piñeiro, Santiago Loza and Inés de Oliveira Cezar. What is it that unites them? The principle of thinking a cinema outside of itself, a cinema that creates new networks as it is shown: in a museum, at a cultural center, in a movie theater, at a festival. The tentacle-ties of anomalous cinema expand "outside" of the field of cinema, an outside that is, in reality, an organism's respiratory cells: ducts and sites of exchange for air and blood, at once internal and external. In addition to being a filmmaker, Gonzalo Castro is also a novelist and the codirector of the publishing house Entropía. Alejo Moguillansky works in theater and his film cannot be understood outside of the innovations that have been occurring in dance and drama in Buenos Aires in recent years. Federico León is a writer with an even greater "dual citizenship"; he began as a director of theater. Gastón Solnicki, who has been trained in both film and music, could make *süden (El breve regreso de Kagel a la Argentina)* [*süden*: The Brief Return of Kagel to Argentina], based on the visit of the experimental musician to Argentina in 2006. In contrast to the films made at the beginning of the decade 2000–2010, these more recent films set up a dialogue with young writers, as in the case of the directors Juan Villegas and Alejandro Lingenti in *Ocio* (based on the novel by Fabián Casas) and the five directors (Marco Berger, Cecilia del Valle, Francisco Forbes, Andrew Sala and Cinthia Varela) whose first cinematic work was the feature film *Cinco*, based on erotic short stories by Marina Mariasch, Pedro Mairal, Natu Moret, Oliverio Coelho, and Maximiliano Tomas. This turn toward literature can also be observed in the works of Gonzalo Castro (with the Mexican-Peruvian novelist Mario Bellatín) and Santiago Loza (with the Argentine poet Néstor Perlongher). Finally, Mariano Llinás, in the commentary he included in the book edition of *Historias extraordinarias*, displays the double narrative system (both cinematographic and literary) through which we can read the adventures of his characters.[11] A distanced and ironic vision of this phenomenon is offered by Mariano Cohn and Gastón Duprat's *El artista* [The Artist], an acidic portrait of the art world with "actors" who come from different cultural realms (Rodolfo Fogwill, León Ferrari, Horacio González, and Alberto Laiseca). In broad strokes and keeping in mind the necessary simplification of any affirmation, it is clear that whereas the first batch of the new Argentine cinema was preoccupied with settling in and strengthening the specifically cinematographic field (as a language and as an institution), the newer arrivals are more concerned with relocating film within the art world and with establishing connections and lines of flight.

Pablo Fendrik—a filmmaker of violence and entropy, according to Horacio Bernades—made one film with the INCAA (*La sangre brota* [Blood Flows]) and another in anomalous fashion (*El asaltante* [The Mugger]); what is central, however, is that the same drive and the same tendency toward the easy impact run through both: while the first conquers a territory, the second traces a line of flight. The two models are distinct, but they are interwoven and remain active simultaneously.

An extreme case of anomalous film is Mauro Andrizzi's *Iraqi Short Films*, made up of fragments of the war in Iraq uploaded onto YouTube that the director was able to compile before they were taken offline for political reasons. A sort of anti-CNN film made up of e-found footage, *Iraqi Short Films* shoots down various contemporary myths (such as the idea of freedom for Internet users). This is a war film without money, a documentary in which the very soldiers in the film are the witnesses and filmmakers, executing a choral work organized around Andrizzi's editing. *Iraqi Short Films* gives a good sense of anomalous film: the act of making, of putting something out into the world, is prior to the possibilities of its execution. The question *How do I do it?*, which has left so many filmmakers in limbo, is marginalized or rendered less important. A bit like Osvaldo Lamborghini's formula—"publish first, then write"—but transplanted into the realm of movies: release first, then film.

Llinás' *Historias extrodinarias* was the film that inaugurated a new modulation of the image that broke the mold of conventional production. The film debuted at the 2008 BAFICI and was screened later at the MALBA, in one of the series organized by the Cinemateque's director, Fernando Martín Peña, and it did so in an unexpected way, for it did not withdraw into the hermetic language of independent film, although it takes advantage of its successes. In light of presumably narrative and entertaining mainstream movies, Llinás made a *hyper-narrative* and hallucinatory film, much more entertaining than any of the products designed to have an impact on the spectator. Under the influence of Robert Louis Stevenson, Jack London, and Jules Verne in its frenzied imagination, and of Jorge Luis Borges and Adolfo Bioy Casares in its precise, speculative language, it has something of the experience of a group of friends sitting around a campfire telling each other stories in which memories and fabrications are interspersed.[12]

Undoubtedly, other films had already been shown at the MALBA, including Llinás' own *Balnearios*; Alejandro Fadel, Martín Mauregui, Santiago Mitre, and Juan Schnitman's *Amor (primera parte)* [Love (Part I)], Sergio Morkin's *Oscar*, Gustavo Fontán's *El paisaje invisible* [The Invisible Landscape], Mariano Donoso's *Opus*, and Ulises de la Orden's *Río arriba* [Up River], but *Historias extraordinarias* is a film that functions on its own terms and that surprises us in its strangeness. It is monumental—like the works of the architect Franco Salomone, the historical figure recreated in the film—and, also like Salomone's works, it perplexes us. It was in the movie theater of the MALBA, in spite of being an alternative space that does not enjoy the privileges of cinematic legislation, where a large percentage of the anomalous films of recent years debuted, in order to continue later on in their unexpected paths: the films of Inés Oliveira Cézar, Andrizzi's *Iraqi Short Films*, Matías Piñeiro's *Todos mienten* [Everybody Lies], Alejo Moguillansky's *Castro*, Santiago Loza's *Rosa patria* [Pink Fatherland], Ezequiel Acuña's *Excursiones* [Excursions], and so many other films.

The same law that fostered the stabilization of the new Argentine cinema should be rethought to establish new rules for anomalous films that, given the lack of prior financing, need institutional recognition linked both to exhibition and to the financing of future projects. (Regardless of the law, however, anomalous film will continue to be made.)

Shifts in production companies and the anomaly: two possible paths, equally legitimate, both opened up by the new generation of filmmakers, connected to one another, at times contiguous and taking turns. Two ways of producing that have had an impact, and which we can perceive in the stories these films tell.

Beyond Identity

Many narrative drives mark contemporary Argentine culture, but two tendencies are of particular interest to me because they have been very influential in national film and have run through it in different ways. Although articulated differently, these tendencies focus on the question of identity. One tendency consists of those stories that reflect upon identities as though they were already formed realities that must be discovered and strengthened. In contrast to this more essentialist vision, the other tendency sees identity not as something that is fixed, but as a series of processes subject to abrupt changes, not existing prior to narrative but constructed, always precariously, within it.

This distinction does not necessarily imply either positive or negative positions: the essentialist idea of identity can be found in both reactionary movements and in progressive sectors, and the same can be said of the concept of fluid identities. In what I call "a World without Narration," this question is fundamental because the narrative tendency of contemporary art is defined in different ways according to how these narratives are anchored in identities. In light of a world without narrative, do we turn to identities that at their time were effective and more or less defined? Or do we insist upon the empty core within the story's ability to be occupied by anything or anyone, or upon its openness to the unexpected and the accidental?

Two examples of anomalous film demonstrate how the question of production is central, but not determinant, when thinking of identities.

With all of its inversions and transgressions, Santiago Loza's *Rosa Patria* [Pink Fatherland], as its title indicates, nevertheless locates the queer Argentine poet Néstor Perlongher within a national constellation. The fact that the movie ends precisely before Perlongher's bus trip to Brazil (where he would settle and later die of AIDS) is symptomatic, for this is the trajectory that will lead to the writing of the long poem *Cadáveres* [Corpses] and the best of his work (and, judging by the testimonies left, the best of his life). Although the fatherland may be pink , Loza proposes to territorialize Perlongher and return his identity to him as a sense of national belonging. Rather than the neo-baroque poet of permanent deterritorialization, the movie offers us a Perlongher closer to the codes of gay identity that have emerged in recent years than those that we find in the poet's own works.

References to national history also appear in Matías Piñeiro *Todos mienten* [Everybody Lies]; here, however, they do not work to codify identities or to corroborate identities that have already crystallized, but to link them to lies, games, pretending, fighting, and wit. Domingo F. Sarmiento's question—"¿Hai realmente un tipo nacional arjentino?" [Is there really an Argentine national type?][13]—is answered with laughter, with a comic sketch. The referents are seemingly more conventional and monumental than in Loza's film, but from the beginning it is clear that Sarmiento, Juan Manuel Rosas, and even the texts cited in the film (from Sarmiento's *Travels*) are not the object of sacralization but profaned in a game whose rules are never entirely clear and whose meaning constantly escapes us. The characters' lineages are not national but international and reach the very limits of the West and of nations themselves: Helena (a fascinating Romina Paula) has Argentine, Italian, French, and English ancestors, in addition to a German one who ended up living among Indians. The movie's own kinship is no less nomadic than that of its characters. It is hermetic only if we read it as a search for truth, but references to Jean Renoir (one of the chapters is called "Helena and the Men," a play off the title of the 1956 film released in English as *Paris Does Strange Things*) and to Orson Welles (another chapter is titled "F is for True") provide us with a clue to understanding its playful tone.[14] In Renoir's *The Rules of the Game,* a comedy whose successful mise-en-scène is based on the arrival and exit of characters from the frame, Jurieux (Roland Toutain) dies for respecting the rules of his passions: his tireless search for the truth leads him to death. In Welles, the gesture is more decisive because, as Deleuze explains, there is a critique here of the true man. "The 'true world' does not exist and, if it did, would be inaccessible, impossible to describe, and, if it could be described, would be useless, superfluous."[15] Like the paintings of JMR, one of the film's characters, the fakes in *Todos mienten* are also authentic— there is more than one original—and identities are contingent, fragile, and ephemeral. Piñeiro's film opts for difference and mystery, which stand in contrast to the complicity with the spectator and the meaning in Loza's film.

With a very different esthetic proposal and with more excess than reserve, Llinás' *Historias extraordinarias* takes this epic of naming, of an identity that is never fixed nor defined but in permanent narration and process, to an extreme. There are no prior identities here; instead these are formed within a story that bifurcates indefinitely and that, ultimately, is revealed to be full of holes, ambiguities, and surprises. The unstable character of identity appears not only in the proliferation of names but also in the images of identikits, sketched faces that could either be someone in particular or anyone at all.

Historias extraordinarias tells the story of three people whom the omnipresent narrator, an off-screen voice that does not flag at all in the film's entire four hours, calls X, Z, and H. The three stories are independent from one another and are not told in succession but are instead interwoven without ever intersecting. X (Mariano Llinás himself) tells the story of a man who, in the plains of Buenos Aires province (where all of the stories take place), is witness to a crime whose mystery will pursue him until the end. The second story is that of Z, a man who arrives in the town of Federación to replace another man in an office job; his predecessor is named Cuevas and will soon become an obsession for Z, who follows his tracks to Africa. Lastly, we have the story of H, a man who, on a bet, is charged with discovering the surveying monoliths along the Salado River installed by the Fluival Company of the River Plate (Compañía Fluvial del Plata) in order to make an alternative corridor.[16] H must find and photograph these; on his way, he comes across the eccentric César, who was contracted to destroy them. Thus begins a beautiful friendship that ends with the story of the Jolly Goodfellows, a group of intrepid English soldiers who risk everything to defeat the Germans. In between infinite incidents occur and the pleasure of the movie lies not in how each ends, but in following their bifurcations, detours, surprises, and suspensions. Rather than the characters' psychology, what matters are the roles they fulfill, which are nothing more than imaginative modes: X, Z, H; observation, substitution, displacement; the Witness, the Substitute, the Traveler. Yet, in all of its proliferations, in all of its excesses, what is the story being told in Llinás' movie about? *Historias extraordinarias* is a reflection upon the charms of stories and the pleasure of those to whom they are narrated. In a footnote to the book version of the film, Llinás warns the reader-spectator that what the articles in the newspaper *El Telégrafo* [The Telegraph] mention can barely be recognized in the movie, though they are actually written in their entirety; explaining this obsession he says, "this excessiveness lies…in a kind of superstitious and childlike obsession: that fiction should exceed the scene, it should overflow It."[17] This centrifugal element is complemented by another, of a centripetal nature, which is that of the adventure. One scene demonstrates this marvelously: in his search for Cuevas, Z finally reaches Africa. His time there consists of a shot of Z walking through the streets of Maputo, Mozambique. This shot is a fragment of an adventure (the film crew's trip to Africa) that exceeds the film and of which there are only these brief remains, the tip of the iceberg. What is left in the film is the overflow of the adventure of filming the movie itself. (*Historias extraordinarias* was made on a very low budget). In this double movement of exceeding limits (of fiction toward the real, of the adventure toward the story), *Historias extraordinarias* moves toward that childlike world in which the borders between fiction, adventure, and life are erased. It is a child's translation of Jules Verne's *Five Weeks in a Balloon*, Hergé's *Tintín*, or of Stevenson's tales.

This, however, tells us very little about what moves the story; there is nothing in the film that, in the manner of cartoons, infantilizes the audience. Instead, the spectator observes how fiction is constructed throughout the film, its mechanisms. The first sentences that the narrator uses to describe X are fundamental in this sense: "It goes like this: a man, let's call him X, arrives at midnight to any small town in the Buenos Aires province. We know nothing about X…We know he's travelling for his job. We know that this job is gray and bureaucratic, that it's *any old* job." X is an everyman. The epic in this story is similar to how Borges and Bioy Casares understood it: not of the heroism of a people or of elevated characters but of the courage of common men.[18] X, Z, and H are unremarkable characters in a space without qualities (the plains) who are submitted to extraordinary things by a narrator, a kind of magician or conjurer. From this perspective, *Historias extraordinarias* is a story about the emptying out of identity, about the capacity of words to metamorphize and of images to bewitch.

This "anywhere" appears to be located in Buenos Aires province, a space customarily ignored by cinema, except in the guise of rural films about gauchos and horses. (In *Historias extraordinarias*, a lion rather than a horse is the animal of the pampas). Llinás discovers here a wellspring of possible stories, in an enormous variety of registers (detective fiction, the fantastic, realism, the adventure story, among others). According to a footnote in his book, the film's genesis lies in one of the director's fantasies: "to spend a weekend outside of Buenos Aires, holed up, like a John Le Carré character, in an invisible hotel in the provinces." This hotel turns out to be the Gran Hotel Azul, a city in which Llinás discovered the architectural work of Salamone. The city, which at first had seemed insipid to him, becomes "supernatural and uncanny," as in Bioy Casares' *La trama celeste* (*The Celestial Plot,* 1948). "Of this abrupt contrast between the calm monotony of the plains, of the lateral paths and hotels like the Gran Hotel Azul, and the eruption of adventure and the marvelous [of Salomone's work], the idea of this film was born."[19]

The meeting of the ordinary (any character in any space) and the extraordinary (a marvelous character such as Cuevas, César or Salomone, who also renders the space marvelous) characterizes the film's narrative unfolding, its expenditure, while the mise-en-scène is marked by another expenditure: the excess of the off-screen voice, its omnipresence, its level of detail, its *plus* with respect to the image. If modernist film—from Bresson to Godard—has worked with the disassociation between the visual and the aural and if, as seems to be the case, we do not find in Llinás a return to a kind of naive equivalent, then why the repeated use of an extreme version of the off-screen voice to describe what occurs on screen?[20]

Although the word follows the image closely, the latter also exceeds it. And although the image might illustrate the narration, there is always something in words that the image cannot express. But this generalized mechanism that functions in many films acquires in *Historias extraordinarias* a particular inflection: voice and image try to approximate each other as much as possible. "What's going to happen now is the following," we hear. The image concretizes what the voice promises but it does not necessarily make it true. X's conjectures on the case of "Lola Gallo" and the Armas brothers are shown in a series of images in spite of the narrator saying, "However, it's not like that. X is mistaken in every detail, from the very beginning. He will never know it, but everything, every single aspect, of his theory is false." The narrator refutes the character, although this does not prevent him from presenting the entire "theory" in images. Yet the effect is not precisely that of unreliability: rather, after locating this incredulity at the center of modern film, *Historias extraodinarias* opts, through its narrative power, for the enchantment of appearances, conjectures, and imaginations. After nihilism, after incredulity, we must become reenchanted by the image, by the word. They are divided, except in their power to shape, to create adventure, even if this is only an adventure of appearances. And could we not affirm that, in a world that has lost the belief in truth, we must learn to read and observe appearances?[21] The definitive question is not truth but, as in the story that Cuevas tells to Derek, the appearance that we choose.

Choreographies

It would be mistaken to think of anomalous film as continuing a modernist line that resists, from its aesthetic retreat, the ravages of contemporary life. It would be an even greater mistake to see it through the morbid perspective of the death of cinema, an assertion that means little in light of the death of television and, soon, the death of the Internet (deaths that always imply powerful modes of survival). As the playwright Rafael Spregelburd wrote of *Historias extraordinarias*, "good news: the future isn't modern!"

This is why I prefer, rather than to insert these films into a prestigious tradition, to understand them as pulverizing that tradition from the perspective of the present, rereading it through a new lens. I am particularly intrigued by the thrust of certain anomalous films that allows us to consider speculative stories in a world without narration. Thus, rather than modernist nostalgia, I would emphasize these works' search for new configurations that no longer respond to the concepts we use, as though these images and audiovisual expressions were *telling* us things that we were still unable to define with prior categories. As though the ill-fit between words and the flux of life was greater every day and, as a result, these works were asking us to move forward a bit, leading us to rethink our conceptual arsenal and to invent new tools to do so.

These new narratives push us to shake off the tyranny of national narratives and compensatory identities, to create new concepts, and, above all, to work—not only through these concepts but also with affect, ideas, and sensibilities—toward the invention of possible communities. Many recent films have responded to social disintegration and crisis with *choreographic compositions,* images in which what is central is the relationship among bodies, space, and shots. How can other communities be constructed from the community of cinema? Or, how can film be fueled by the communities that it approximates and depicts? How do bodies appear, how do they relate and connect to one another?

These choreographies are a mise-en-scène of the body, an exhibition of the *theatricality* of life and of the force of film to offer us more powerful performances. They are not utopic or revolutionary choreographies (their horizon is never that of the generalized choreographies that we find in Eisenstein's *October* or in Solanas' *The Hour of the Furnaces* or Cuban director Tomás Gutiérrez Alea's *Memoirs of Underdevelopment,* which exhibit the people [*el pueblo*]. Instead, they seek out contingent, local harmonies that form communities. They attempt to reach, as Caetano Veloso's song states, "diverse, possible harmonies, without final judgment."[22]

The theatricality of life or the capacity for performance is increasingly central in our lives because our fate depends upon it. In the context of post-Fordist work, knowing how to communicate is necessary because in the society of the spectacle communication is one of the most valued commodities.[23] Learning to act means learning to live and to survive, and work increasingly requires us to know how to speak, move our bodies, and seduce. "Good appearance required," the want ads state. These are forms of knowledge that go beyond technical ability in a given skill. The same question that we ask ourselves in our free time is replicated in the realm of labor: "Am I interesting?"[24] This space of performance is taken up by various contemporary films but is marked by the idea of subtraction: these are not choreographies of the real but tentative configurations, orchestrated movements, figures in tension with the social, that is, alternative choreographies that abandon the ethnographic gaze of Trapero's *Mundo grúa* or Alonso's *La libertad* and instead invest in conjectural orders closer to the 1990s works of Martín Rejtman.

Let's begin with an example that investigates popular choreographies. Rejtman's *Copacabana* (2006) is a documentary depicting the Bolivian community in Buenos Aires. Beyond the links the film establishes with contemporary documentary films (which are present but are usually noted to legitimize the film and to lend it an unnecessary note of distinction), *Copacabana* resembles the works of Busby Berkeley or Jacques Demy in order to go even further. The choreographies of the Bolivian community shine in their own right; the director's strength lies in observing their operation, rather than setting them up. In spite of what some critics have stated, we do not find here the gaze of a modernist director and a formless community: the Bolivians in *Copacabana,* living in poor conditions in a country that treats them with hostility, debate their problems in assemblies, together confront the problem of immigration and diaspora, and prepare parties with beautiful choreographic numbers that sustain the film's narrative. There is nothing formless here, except to a very removed or prejudicial viewpoint. Nor is this a celebration of a situation that is, in social terms, unfortunate. Instead, the film observes what is under construction, a community that sustains itself through codes and memories, and also through its external enemies. There has always been something rhythmic and danceable in Rejtman's films, but in *Copacabana* the dance is made by others and the director knows how to maintain distance (not as a modernist but due to his interest in the lives of Bolivian immigrants).[25]

Shifting gears, we find another choreographic film in Federico León and Marcos Martínez's *Estrellas* [Stars] (2007), and it is no coincidence that Rejtman and León have together made *Entrenamiento para actores* [Actors' Training] (2009), a film in which they investigate the theatricality with which we operate, not just on stage but in life itself. *Estrellas* is a documentary about Julio Arrieta, a resident of a shanty town, or *villa*, [Villa 21] in the city of Buenos Aires, who makes a living offering actors for publicity, television, and movie castings. In a society marked by theatricality on many levels, the protagonist of *Estrellas* takes advantage of this paradox: those who can best perform as marginalized characters or petty thugs [*chorros*] are those who "in real life" are marginalized individuals or petty thugs. "The place that they do not have in society," Alan Pauls notes, "is the one they find in the spectacle."[26] These actors take advantage of the reality effect that the media pursues: they must pretend that they are not pretending. Arrieta uses all the prejudices and fears of the outsider's gaze, becoming a great manipulator. We are far from the naiveté of "the people" represented in earlier cinema: when *La guerra gaucha* [The Gaucho War] (1942) was made in the early 1940s, "one of the *authentic* gauchos, when he found out we were about to film his movements, shaved off his lovely beard, changed his clothes and...we couldn't use him!"[27] What these "authentic" gauchos did not know how to do was to move within mass media, the "natural" habitat (a second nature) of the residents of the villa. Like all other sectors of society, these are marked by the language of the society of the spectacle and their survival depends upon their ability to take advantage of this medium. Arrieta would leave his beard untouched and would not change his clothes or wear perfume, because he is aware that directors are looking for something "authentic." Regardless of one's social class, surviving requires knowing how to move within the society of the spectacle.

Yet what is this "authentic" that has so often been linked to sincerity, to the national, to tradition? Gastón Solnicki's *süden,* another choreographic film, opens with a declaration of cosmopolitan faith by its protagonist, Mauricio Kagel, the late Argentine musician who had settled in Germany: "I feel good where I can work well: that is my homeland."[28] The statement echoes Cicero's *Tusculanae disputationes*: "Patria est ubicumque bene est" [The homeland is where one is well] (V, 37). While the documentary details the difficulties within Argentina that led to Kagel's exile, it traces the portrait of someone whose homeland, in the end, is music itself. While he affirms this extraterritoriality in German at the beginning of the film, at its end Kagel defines his "ideal interpreter" as one who appropriates the work: "this work is mine." The statement is as much Kagel's as it is of those musicians who accompany him and upon whom he has left his mark, like Solnicki, who performs in many ways the work of a musician.

As the film's title, "The Brief Return of Kagel to Argentina," indicates, brevity and transience are the film's keys: in one of its more intense moments, Kagel conquers the city with *Eine Brise. Acción fugitiva para 111 ciclistas,* which consists of the movement of bicyclists sounding their bicycle horns, singing and using other instruments. It would appear to be superfluous to invoke the avant-garde ancestry of the bicycle—the protagonist of Marcel Duchamp's first readymade. More important are Kagel's own words in the film when he affirms that, in Buenos Aires, "music is essential for life. In some way, music substitutes for what doesn't work in politics, in social life, etc." The fleeting breeze of the cyclists, their choreographic energy, locates Solnicki's film at the intersection between music and the real, between Kagel's journey and the political.

By way of conclusion, let us look at the most choreographic film of them all: Alejo Moguillansky's *Castro.* In this film not only do the characters move through the city as though they were part of a huge dance (with buses accompanying the party), the shots are also formed by a geometric progression, like a melodic phrase with its harmonies, counterpoints, and *ritornellos.* (The director edited more than a dozen films, *Historias extraordinarias,* Carri's *La rabia* [Rage], and Piñeiro's *El hombre robado* [The Stolen Man] among them).[29] In a mise-en-scène that cannot help but evoke Hugo Santiago's *Invasión* [Invasion], the theatrical, the musical, the choreographic, the pictorial, and the cinematographic collide in a cinema in which, like in the short film that Samuel Beckett made with Buster Keaton, slapstick meets metaphysics, in this case a metaphysical search for a certain Castro who, in Lacanian fashion, functions as the *objet petit a.* The name Castro undoubtedly allows for other psychoanalytic interpretations, but what is central is the lack of the real in the midst of daily life. Something similar happens in *Historias extraordinarias* with its proliferation of McGuffins that set the story into motion and, with their strangeness, render it extraordinary on the flat landscape of the pampas. But *Castro* is actually closer to Piñeiro's *Todos mienten* than to *Historias extraordinarias,* for it also has a choreographic mise-en-scène, above all in the arrival and exit of the characters in the shots ("a relay race," as described in Moguillansky's film). Followed by tracking shots that take an a priori route, the movement of the bodies is executed with a spontaneity that means that *Todos mienten* expresses itself like the choreography of an encounter: between rigorous shots and the composition of the actors. In contrast to Llinás' excess, *Castro* and *Todos mienten* refer to what is stated about JMR by one of the characters in Piñeiro's film, that his paintings possess "a geometry of forms that recovers an order in things." (The sentence is deliberately ironic, because the "order" is imposed by cinema, and not by things.) But although they are linked by this central aspect—and this is why the directors presented them at the BAFICI as "sister" films—they diverge with respect to the world they construct.[30]

Castro's story is structured around the lack of work. When his lover Celia (Julia Martínez Rubio) threatens him, saying "either find a job or I'm leaving," Castro (Edgardo Castro) asks himself what is it that he possesses that will help him find work. In contrast to Godard's Pierrot (although his ending is similar), he lacks audacity and the madness of the artist or the bohemian, and when he tries to figure out what he has, he tells himself, "My name is Castro, I'm 38 years old, I need to make money"; "I have you, my body, my head"; or, in more synthetic fashion, "Celia, my body, my head." This verification is dramatic, besides the fact that Castro also forgets that he has feet, in a film in which, above all, one must run, dance, walk, and pursue. Like the man who lives in the room above Castro's, of whom we only hear footsteps. The day that we no longer here them, he has died. Walking is living.

Threatened by his wife and hounded by his ex-wife, Rebeca Thompson (Carla Crespo), the jealous Samuel (Alberto Suárez)—Celia's old flame—the useless Acuña (Esteban Lamothe), and the mercenary Willie/Mugica (Gerardo Naumann), Castro reaches the city with the sole goal of escaping his pursuers, surviving, and getting a job. But this prospect terrifies him: "making a living—he tells himself over and over—is the same as wasting it." The film's choreography invests everything in this economy, of work and savings in the face of waste and *jouissance*. Spending is not justified by social utility but by the pure *jouissance* of the geometric game that takes place within the narrative, in the mise-en-scène, in the city, and, above all, in the bodies with their vicissitudes that resemble silent film slapstick. And as in all intellectual slapstick, the goal is to measure with each stumble the struggle between the order of fantasy and the disorder of the real, between the thrust of desire and the organization of labor. In this pendulum, in this confrontation, the protagonist, oppressed by his indecision (or by the lack of a real solution), decides to take his own life.

Filled with cinephile references, like *Todos mienten* (from Jacques Demy's *The Umbrellas of Cherburg* to Jean-Pierre Melville and Hal Hartley's films), the film shows how persecution acquires a meaning within itself, how an object that would confer it with a broader meaning never appears.

Castro and *Todos mienten* converge again in their purpose: what objective puts these choreographies into motion? In reality, there is no exterior objective or obvious utility: neither labor nor history is sufficiently powerful to confer a reason for living upon these characters. Each choreography must seek out its own economy, its own way of spending and regulating through the movement of bodies, the development of the plot, and precise editing. Its energy also stems from film and literature, evoked through citations both cryptic and explicit. Both films indicate the opening of cinema to other arts (as have Gonzalo Castro's films) and, also paradoxically, a concentration of cinematic language that moves them away from that opening toward the real of the filmmakers from the beginning of the decade. Paraphrasing Mauricio Kagel in *süden*, these movies—like music—function as a substitute that leads us to reflect upon the connections between reality and desire or, better stated, upon the reality of desire.

Consolidation of the Pioneers

Making a high-quality *opera prima* isn't easy, and it's even harder to make second or third films that confirm the expectations generated by the first. Lisandro Alonso, Lucrecia Martel, Pablo Trapero, Albertina Carri, Martín Rejtman, and Adrián Caetano exceeded the expectations placed upon them and made new movies that deserve an analysis beyond what I can accomplish in this epilogue. All of these filmmakers have also had an international impact, have participated in the most important film festivals, and have had their work recognized by top film critics. (In some cases, such as that of Trapero, both public and critics have agreed). Some, such as Lucrecia Martel and Lisandro Alonso, were recognized by international critics in the monumental survey published in *Film Comment* in February 2010.[31]

After the rupture that *Los rubios* inaugurated in cultural life, it seemed unlikely that Albertina Carri would be able to create a work of such density. *Los rubios* was a kind of cinematic release, an exorcism, and a liberation, and the question that it forced viewers to grapple with seemed to be directed at the filmmaker herself: and now what? Paradoxically, having made *Los rubios* to free herself from something that oppressed her, Carri now had to make another movie to free herself from *Los rubios*. After the failure of *Geminis*, *La rabia* (2008) relocated and artistically resolved, in the realm of fiction, the tensions of *Los rubios*. Several motifs link the two films: the past as a kind of set piece recalls the countryside [*el campito*] of *Los rubios,* just as the cartoons recall the playmobiles and Nati's screams recall Analía Couceyro's invectives in the earlier film. (Even in its title, "rabia" appears to erase and rewrite "rubios.") Parricide has been mentioned as a way of reading *Los rubios*; *La rabia* ends in parricide.[32] The intensity of a scream that makes the significant arise from the insignificant is the core of Carri's work: that is, the unexpressable knot formed by violence and memory.[33] But there is a fundamental difference between the two films, and it lies in an archaic substratum that evokes the work of Pier Paolo Pasolini and Bruno Dumont's *Flandres*. If *Los rubios* was Carri's history, her childhood, *La rabia* shows that, in another realm, this childhood was also like any other, that is, subjected to a culture based on fear and slaughter, on the fantasies of masculine power, on women and children's fantasies of escape, on the gaze that is witness to something that exceeds it or terrorizes it, or to something that it cannot see—a true war of the pig, as in Bioy Casares' novel (*Diary of the War of the Pig,* 1969).

With *La rabia*, Carri once more searches for the link between what is said and what is omitted. "You have to make pretty things: little animals, flowers," the mother (Analía Couceyro) says to her daughter, Nati (Nazarena Duarte), but the girl, although mute, knows how to capture all the frequencies and modulations that surround her, and to pour them into her fantasies. With her drawings, Nati is able to express partially what overwhelms her, and this is something that her parents, who would prefer her to make "little flowers," cannot understand. This lack of receptivity to the *jouissance* of others (and this archaic succumbing to her own *jouissance*) is what unleashes the tragedy in the film. In all the spaces of living creatures (and animals have a central role in the film), harm and destruction are generalized but not indiscriminate: as Iván Pinto points out, the patriarchal macho directs these against women and children. The last link of the biological chain is found in Nati who, to defend herself, withdraws into her own animality and tries to free herself through the fantasy of her drawings. Pleasure and pain are indiscernible for her, an inability that makes her an indecipherable character, one who is out of control: the drawings protect her from anguish and her shrieks are her way of being in the world.[34]

After the perturbing *Fantasma* [Ghost], in which Lisandro Alonso experimented with the relationship between cinephilia (within the emblematic space of the Lugones, the Buenos Aires art-house movie theater) and characters outside of the world of cinema, in *Liverpool* he once again takes up the tension between the director's gaze and inaccessible characters, installed in their silence and nomadism, without our being aware of what it is they are searching for, or what they feel or think as they search. In *Liverpool*, Alonso's poetics remain faithful to his earlier movies. As in *La libertad* or in *Los muertos,* the protagonist's exteriority is represented by the containers from the quantifiable world of merchandise through which Alonso's characters must inevitably emerge: the wood that Misael must sell in *La libertad,* or the shirt that Vargas, the protagonist of *Los muertos*, must sell, or his encounter with a prostitute, "the apotheosis of empathy with merchandise," in the words of Walter Benjamin. Yet this exteriority, this world of quantities, of "three and two: five," as the salesman says in *Los muertos*, is something that Alonso's characters traverse or abandon in order to penetrate other types of incommensurable relationships, a force field that cannot be measured or controlled.

Although taking up the threads of Alonso's earlier films, *Liverpool* simultaneously opens up new paths. When Farrell (Juan Fernández) leaves the boat behind, Alonso's poetics inaugurates a shift that anticipates future mutations. Once he reaches Usuhaia, Farrell goes to see his mother and Analía (Giselle Irrazabal), the mentally disabled daughter that he has presumably abandoned. Farrell returns to his town to find out whether his mother is "alive," but when he finds her he is unable to establish any contact with her. In the face of a hopeless situation of remorse or reproach (this aspect is never clarified in the film), Farrell decides to leave, but the camera prefers to stay. In an act that oscillates between the fictional and the real, the protagonist abandons the story after leaving Analía with a key ring with the word "Liverpool"—the name of the port city that marks the character's errancy—that she will later squeeze between her hands. Both women, weakened by their different illnesses, are almost-people, pure life that cannot say "I." "A difficult inheritance," as one of the characters puts it. When it stays back in the town as the protagonist is leaving, the story chooses Analía, as though there were something in this life, reduced to the biological, that the protagonist refused to understand. A purely tactile life, maternal and feminine, emerges in all its intensity in one of the film's most emotional moments, when the daughter rests her head on a tree, as though seeking out the rest that others have not given her. Between the vegetative and mercantile states, Analía touches what is most real: the heart that she draws on a sheet of paper (and that Farrell is unable to appreciate), the tree that she lies up against, the key ring that she squeezes between her hands—a pure world of affect, visible in earlier Alonso films, but here taking on all the emotional, filmic, and revulsive weight, in the skin of these women who, for the first time in Alonso's oeuvre, are anchored in a fixed territory.

In *La mujer sin cabeza* [The Headless Woman] Lucrecia Martel has reasserted her place as the master of blind and deaf zones. With *Leonera* [Lion's Den] (2008) and *Carancho* [Vulture], Trapero has not only consolidated his narrative gifts but also deepened the combination of investigation and realism, of action film and tragic reflection. In *Crónica de una fuga* [Chronicle of an Escape] (2006), Adrián Caetano continues to rewrite genre film through extreme and realistic situations, depicting life in a concentration camp during the last military dictatorship in Argentina.[35] They were pioneers, and today they have an oeuvre.

A Cinema of the Political

The difficulty in gaining access to the realm of politics—or the direct closing off of this possibility—has led cinema to a reflection on the political. Rather than being linked to action or to the imagery of the people (as in Pino Solanas' documentaries to this day), the films of the new Argentine cinema have reflected upon conditions linked to the possibility of politics and, for this reason, have shied away from commonplace notions and moved their attention to the emergent modalities of the political, often silenced or deemed less important. Whenever it has approached themes that are central to public debates—like the theme of the disappeared—this new cinema has renewed our perception of the issues concerned, as Carri's *Los rubios* did and as Nicolás Prividera *M* would do later. The general principal is to move away from politics as traditionally understood in order to rethink the political and address, against common sense, *what is important*. The playwright and theatrical director Rafael Spregelburd, in his polemic with the playwright Griselda Gambaro, affirmed his position with respect to theater, a position that is, however, equally valid for cinema: "when we refer to *what is important,* the basic question is who determines what is important and, accordingly, what is the role of the artist within a situation dominated politically by what is important as a communitarian agreement, when this is defined by common sense, a sense that I believe actually destroys the senses."[36] In the case of film, the "heavy inheritance" of political cinema—with all the aesthetic decisions that this implies—has been placed to one side in order to focus more freely on where precisely domination and subjection occur.

In this way, contemporary Argentine film shifts the political question toward immigration, the work of memory, lifestyles, sexualities and the redefinition of gender, the operations of repressive societies—and even car crashes, as in Trapero's *Carancho*, where these are symptoms of a perverse and deficient social mechanism.

Affect and gender were present, as never before, in various films: Anahí Berneri's *A Year without Love*, Lucía Puenzo *XXY*, Santiago Otheguy's *La león* [The Lion], Delfina Castagnino's *Lo que más quiero* [What I Most Want]. Far from the stereotypical and repressive stereotypes of Juán José Campanella's *El hijo de la novia* [Son of the Bride] (2001), but from the non-normative demands of the first films exclusively about gays made in Argentina (I am thinking, for example, of Ortiz de Zarate's *Otra historia de amor* [Another History of Love]), these stories have also touched upon an anomalous notion of gender relations. While in *Otra historia de amor* the relationship between Raúl and Jorge is scandalous, in Lerman's *Tan de repente* Mao and Lenin's choice is one among many: "We aren't lesbians," they say. And something similar happens in the other films I have mentioned here.

Although more fable than case study, Lucía Puenzo's *XXY* has led viewers to question their ideas about the body, sex, and gender.[37] In addressing the possibility of a breakdown of binary sexuality, the film left viewers without a language and even without an image—in this respect, the differing opinions over whether we see the genitals of Alex (Inés Efrón), the film's hermaphrodite protagonist, are interesting. In Flavia and Quintín's blog, "La lectora provisoria," where a large part of this debate took place, we see a clash between those who argued for a specifically cinematographic reading of *XXY* and those who insisted upon the political question of gender (especially Mauro Cabral, a transgender activist who was earlier known by the pseudonym Burdégano). Those who defended the language of cinema maintained a position that consisted in subordinating all these issues to a reading of the film's shots. This position draws inspiration from Godard's dictum that "a tracking shot is a moral issue." And although in agreement with this statement, I do not believe that all moral questions can be resolved with a tracking shot. Cabral wanted to address—and the resistance to his position made this clear—a discussion about how our imagination functions with respect to sex and the body, and how we are trapped in conventional and often ignorant versions.[38] I do not believe that cinema can or should give answers to these questions solely through its formal operations.

In spite of Argentina being a country shaped indelibly by immigration, immigrants have been rendered invisible, when not directly vilified. In *Habitación disponible* [Room Available], Diego Gachassin addressed the relationship between immigration, a people, and discrimination through an intense scene in which the protagonists, a Ukrainian family, arrive at the Plaza de Mayo in the midst of a protest following the 2001 economic crisis in Argentina. Instead of joining the groups in the plaza, the mother and her children realize that they are not part of "the people" and leave the plaza (literally, backing out of the scene). Rejtman's *Copacabana* also focused on Bolivian immigrants but with a very different gaze than Caetano's, years earlier, *Bolivia*. Once again, the category of the people reveals itself to be insufficient or exclusionary.

Many films have addressed closed-off societies, especially the concentration camp–like the universe of gated communities (including Ariel Winograd's *Cara de queso* [Cheese Face] and Marcelo Piñeyro's *Las viudas de los jueves* [The Thursday Widows]), for the purpose of protesting the social relations in these environments. In contrast, Celina Murga's *Una semana solos* [*A Week Alone*] (2007) does not attempt to wage a protest but to see how a way of life and a system of power operate—in this sense, it is closer to Trapero's *El bonaerense*, also the story of a closed-off society, than to other films about gated communities. If in these films there is a ruthless gaze that nevertheless contains a certain emotiveness (as in *Cara de queso*), Murga's film features a distanced, ethnographic gaze, with a radical reflection upon the mise-en-scène, upon how to render the scene of this way of life.

Una semana solos is full of details: the gated community with its domesticated landscape and implacable beauty; the children who don't need their parents because a whole security system cares for them; the necessity of killing time because boredom is the corollary of the peacefulness that reigns during the afternoon; the young woman Esther (Natalia Gómez Alarcón) who takes care of the children and who doesn't suffer, although she misses her daughter who does not live in the gated community; and an overwhelming emptiness. It remains so until the day Juan (Ignacio Giménez), the boy with the bowl cut and Esther's brother, appears. Juan's presence sets off in the children of this environment an entire system of differences and resistance that become clear when they visit the pool. Juan is neither a servant nor a member of the group of owners and for this reason his extraterritorial and erratic position reveals the position and idiosyncrasy of the other characters. (His status is so problematic that it demands an exception to the regulations.)

Una semana solos is a film about propriety and laws or, better stated, about how propriety and the law are inseparable. The law appears in the film under the guise of regulations—that is, as norms established by the gated community in order to live together and to assure the safety of their neighbors. The fact that these rules are subject to constant modification (and without the need for a bureaucratic process), instead of requiring a certain fulfillment, shows how transgression in the film is always minor, allowing for modifications and indulgence. If it had dealt with the law, *Una semana solos* would have led to tragedy: the boy with the bowl cut would have been an extreme victim of the oppressive cordon that separates the gated community from its outside. In contrast, the regulation imposes banality: the offensive seriousness of their actions, their dark and sinister density, never comes to the surface and is not submitted to a process of recognition and, as a result, of catharsis. The modalities of domination and reproduction are subtle and for this reason more effective: there is no consolation for the spectator as in *Las viudas de los jueves,* an absence that would demonstrate that this happy life is a mask that hides a world of corruption and violence. Murga chooses another path: that of showing a prank that does not turn into tragedy, in order to exhibit a deficient and perverse citizenship. The film achieves all of this through the gaps in the story and the mise-en-scène. Instead of protesting, Murga prefers to use visual elisions and silences to make us see.

Murga's film allows us to generalize more broadly about the contemporary: our links to tradition and to the past are in such a state of crisis that, rather than judge them, it is preferable to observe their operations. In this relationship, the indexical image of film brings us a fragment of the past-present and a document that demands that we rethink—always a bit melancholically, due to the loss—these links. This is what many recent documentaries have done, whether with a personal inflection (as in Andrés di Tella's work), or about collective memory (as in Carri and Prividera), or about the historical past (as in investigative documentaries such as Lorena Muñoz's *Los próximos pasados* [The Next Pasts] or Herman Szwarcbart's *Un pogrom en Buenos Aires* [A Pogrom in Buenos Aires]). In these last two examples, exercising cinematographic memory shows the cracks in the preservation of historical patrimony, through the rigorous research of cultural historians.

In the case of documentaries about memory, some filmmakers understood that if they turned to the genre's conventional language this would lead to a stagnant understanding of memory. The use of protagonists' testimony as an indisputable source, the recourse to talking heads, the videograph, and the inserting of found footage marked the path for a self-satisfied memory and a very flat understanding of how time works. (These strategies are exhibited as remains in films such as Carri's *Los rubios* and María Inés Roqué's *Papá Iván*). It was Andrés di Tella, with his *Montoneros, una historia* [Montoneros: A History], who first addressed the necessity of articulating a reflection upon memory that was simultaneously also a reflection about genre. *Los rubios* inaugurated a rupture—as I analyze here in the chapter "*Los rubios*: Mourning, Frivolity, and Melancholy"—followed by Nicolás Prividera's *M,* which demonstrated the existence of a corpus (which can be traced back to Carlos Echeverría's *Juan como si nada hubiera sucedido* [Juan as if Nothing had Happened], 1987). Evidently, this corpus is neither monolithic nor homogenous, but what these films have in common is their overcoming of the false dichotomy (which still reigns in some documentaries and in spheres of politics) between a glorious past and an impoverished present that futilely tries to imitate it.

In the Prologue to *Other Worlds* I indicated the increasing importance of documentary and the difficulty of including it at that point in a book that did not purport to be exhaustive, or to be a history of recent Argentine film. At any rate, rather than treat documentary as a genre, I still prefer to speak of *the documentary* [lo documental] as a *feature* that runs through both fiction and documentary films, in different ways but with similar intensity. While the genre is defined by the testimonial use of indexical images, the documentary as a feature emerges simultaneously with the index itself—that is, it is inherent to the cinematographic image. The importance of visible traces in contemporary Argentine film is accompanied by the privilege likewise accorded to the linguistic index, which we can see in the narrator's use of demonstrative pronouns ("here," "this one") and, above all, in the use of the first person ("I"). This leads to a split, because the image is the not-person (at most it could be compared to the third person), while language contains the first person as though it were inscribed in the image. Therefore, in what is known as first-person documentary what we find is, in fact, a struggle between the first and third persons. And in certain cases, above all in documentaries about the disappeared, rather than a first-person documentary we should speak of documentaries about the difficulty of enunciating, whether in first, second, or third person. On the basis of their own experience, these filmmakers (many of them children of the disappeared) are well aware of the difficulties that arise before being able to say *I,* because since childhood their identities or the identities of those around them were suspended or questioned.

But this tension is also visible in documentaries that opt for a first-person poetics in which the "I" is exhibited with such intensity that the spectator cannot avoid asking about its limits, gaps, and manipulations. With *La televisión y yo* and *Fotografías* Andrés di Tella visits both his paternal line, of a pioneering industrialist, and his maternal line, paradoxically exotic. (Which is more exotic, Argentines in India, Indians who come to Argentina, or the London in which these Argentines have run aground?) In these travels, the materials never cease to divert him toward the moment in the story that exceeds the personal. The documentary as genre and as feature is never first person but a struggle between the first and third persons, between the animate and the inanimate, between construction and capturing, between life that grows and the image that detains it. Perhaps the power of the indexical image in recent years lies in this: the struggle of the real to leave its trace, the force of life.

To speak of the documentary as a feature, or to speak of narrative as an adjective, is to point to the most pressing phenomenon of recent cultural artifacts, which in some way can be synthesized as the return of the real. In its approach to the new Argentine cinema, *Other Worlds* participated in this idea. In a world increasingly trapped in spectacle and in the administration of daily life, film brings its indexes and its narratives to investigate how these might construct communities in a world that, although at times inhospitable, can also lead to *jouissance*.

Buenos Aires, September 2010

Notes

Introduction

1. According to Richard Sennett, "In the creation of the American Republic, the political analyst Judith Shklar argues, the value of hard work defined the ethos of the self-respecting citizen" (Sennett 2003, 57).
2. "The Cunning Tricks of the Aesthetic: Cinematographic Form and the Experience of the Present" was the title of the graduate seminar that I taught in the Master's Program in Culture in the Department of Social Sciences and in the Master's Program in Discursive Analysis in the Department of Philosophy and Literature, both at the University of Buenos Aires. Seminar discussions with students, along with the work they presented, were important in the development of this book. In the chapters that follow, I cite unpublished monographs by author name and seminar title.
3. In the years since the Spanish edition of this book was published, many of the directors whose work is analyzed here have gone on to make more films or have achieved international recognition. See the Bibliography for some recently published analyses.
4. Documentaries have become so important in recent years that in the seventh year of the Buenos Aires Internacional Festival de Cine Independiente (Buenos Aires International Festival of Independent Film) a documentary that entered the official competition was selected as the best film (Mercedes Álvarez's *El cielo gira*, "The Sky Turns"). Critical interest in the genre also grew. Among the texts produced on Argentine film, see Andrés Di Tella's "El documental y yo" (2002) and the fifth issue of the journal *Kilómetro 111 (Ensayos sobre cine)* (2004), which includes Emilio Bernini's "Un estado (contemporáneo) del documental. Sobre algunos films argentinos recientes" ("A [Contemporary] State of the Documentary: On Some Recent Argentine Films") and Mauricio Alonso's review of Sergio Wolf and Lorena Muñoz's *Yo no sé qué me han hecho tus ojos* (2003, released in the United States as *I Don't Know What Your Eyes Have Done to Me*). *Imágenes de lo real: la representacion de lo politico en el documental argentino* ("Images of the Real: The Representation of the Political in Argentine Documentary"), a volume edited by Josefina Sartora and Silvina Rival with contributions by prestigious film critics, including Mariano Mestman, Eduardo Russo, Ricardo Parodi, Gustavo Castagna, Raúl Becero, Jorge Ruffinelli, and Emilio Bernini, was published in 2007.

1   On the Existence of the New Argentine Cinema

1. The critic Horacio Bernardes, in his writings on the "new Argentine cinema" for the Argentine newspaper *Pagina/12*, has proposed the acronym NCA, showing how the denomination functions as a useful mark of identification.

2. On the culmination of the new Argentine cinema's trajectory through film festivals around the world, see "Floating Below Politics" by Larry Rohter, published in the *New York Times* on May 1, 2005. The article begins with the following resounding affirmation: "Iran had its moment, Finland and Korea, too. But at film festivals around the world these days, much of the talk is focused on Argentina and the emerging crop of young directors who have been winning prizes and praise from Berlin and Rotterdam to Toronto and Miami." Although Rohter's corpus is superficial (he mentions as examples *Nueve reinas, La niña santa,* and *El abrazo partido* [2003, "The Lost Embrace"]), he goes on to conclude: "They do not share an aesthetic, the way the French New Wave or Brazilian Cinema Novo did, and some of them did not even know one another until they met at film festivals in Europe or North America. 'To call us a movement or something like that would be excessive, because it isn't that yet and I don't know if it will ever be,' Ms. Martel, 38, said during a recent interview at a bookstore and café near her home in the suburbs here. 'We've been nurtured by the same crisis, but that's about it,' she added, referring to the recurring political and economic turmoil that has characterized Argentine life for decades."

3. This was clearly demonstrated when students who would go on to be directors, regardless of their interest in political protests more generally, participated en masse in the protest that demanded the passing of the *ley de cine* and its enforcement in the early 1990s (see note 7).

4. The film consists of eight shorts with scripts that had received prizes and were produced by the state-sponsored source of funding for film, the Instituto Nacional de Cine y Artes Audiovisuales (INCAA). The shorts are as follows: Pablo Ramos' "La ausencia" ("Absence"), Daniel Burman's "Niños envueltos" ("Stuffed Grape Leaves"), Jorge Gaggero and Matías Oks' "Ojos de fuego" ("Eyes of Fire"), Bruno Stagnaro's "Guarisove, los olvidados" ("Guarisove, the forgotten ones"), Andrés Tambornino and Ulises Rosell's "Dónde y cómo Olivera perdió a Achala" ("Where and How Olivera Lost Achala"), Sandra Gugliotta's "Noches áticas" ("Attic Nights"), Lucrecia Martel's "Rey muerto" ("Dead King"), and Adrián Caetano's "Cuesta abajo" ("Downhill"). Later, new editions of *Historias breves* were released; the second part (1997) is divided into two, given the quantity of shorts, as in the third edition (1999, "Ojo izquierdo" ["Left Eye"] and "Ojo derecho" ["Right Eye"]). *Historias breves IV* was released in 2004.

5. In her interview with Trapero for the film magazine *El amante cine* (1999), Claudia Acuña writes: "*Mundo grúa* consumed forty thousand dollars, 14 months of filming, and 27 years of Pablo, paid in full, the cash of each scene."

6. We should also keep in mind the technological transformations that, for example, allow filmmakers to make a movie on video and then hope for funding from a festival to convert it to film. This was what happened with Santiago Loza's *Extraño* (2003, distributed internationally as *Strange*) and Ana Katz's *El juego de la silla* (2002, distributed internationally as *Musical Chairs*).

7. The *ley de Fomento y Regulación de la Actividad Cinematográfica* ("Law to Foster and Regulate Cinematographic Activity") was passed in 1994, although it took a few years for it to come into full effect. It regulates professional activity in the field of cinema and guarantees state funding and support for national cinema.

8. In 2005, the Mar del Plata International Film Festival screened more than sixty Argentine films, similar to the number screened at the BAFICI during the same year, indicating an increase in production and the variety of formats.

9. See Appendix 1 for details of some of these efforts.

10. The "screen quota" regulates the obligation to exhibit one Argentine movie every trimester in movie theaters.

11. On the place of Agresti and his film in his generation, see Christian Gunderman's essay "Filmar como la gente: la *imagen-afección* y el resurgimiento del pasado en *Buenos Aires viceversa* (1996) de Alejandro Agresti" ("Film Like the People: Image-Complaint and the Resurgence of the Past in Alejandro Agresti's *Buenos Aires viceversa*"), in Amado (2004, 83–109).

12. A movie theater that specializes in art-house films, located in the state-sponsored Teatro General San Martín (Buenos Aires). [Translator's note.]

13. Subsidies given for project development go from $15,000 to a maximum of $50,000. Iberomedia grants loans, but not subsidies, to more advanced projects; these can reach up to $200,000.

14. See Claudio España's essay, as well as my own, "La generación del 60" ("The Generation of 1960"), both in España (2005b).

15. In contrast to those directors who approached artistic co-productions as a means to pay production expenses, and who thus found themselves obliged to alter screenplays to insert characters of other nationalities or to film in foreign locations, the filmmakers of the new cinema, following the pioneering examples of Alejandro Agresti and Martín Rejtman, had access to foundations that did not impose conditions once a screenplay was realized and worked with a cosmopolitan idea of cinematographic execution.

16. Bazin wrote, "Le décor naturel est au décor construit ce que l'acteur amateur est au professionnel" (2000, 315). Although it is difficult to generalize about the use of natural sets in the new cinema (especially in a country where studios are very precarious), it is important to note that they differ substantially from those presented in earlier cinema: from bizarre natural sets that nevertheless are not exotic (Mariano Llinás' *Balnearios* [2002, "Beach Towns"], Ulises Rosell's *Bonanza (En vías de extinción)* [2001, "Bonanza: Endangered Species"], Rosell and Rodrigo Moreno's *El descanso* [2002, "The Break"]), to the capacity to broaden the map of daily life. On the innovation that the representation of urban space meant for one of the movies of the new cinema, see Adrián Gorelik (1999) on *Mala época*.

17. *Costumbrismo* is the literary genre in Spanish-language theater, novels, and chronicles whose purpose and major emphasis is the demonstration of local habits, customs, and speech. [Translator's note.]

18. Paradoxically, Adolfo Aristarain, a director who in the early 1980s opted for a narrative cinema in which the political imperative was reformulated in an original way, has in recent years made several movies responding to the imperative of identity: *Martín (Hache)* [1997, "Martin (H)"], *Lugares comunes* [2002, distributed in the United States as *Common Ground*], and *Roma* [2004, "Rome"]).

19. Jameson maintains this position in different articles (1986a, 1995) and extends it to the whole of Latin American, Asian, and African production (that is, the Third World). In *The Time Image*, Deleuze analyzes the productions of the Brazilian filmmaker Glauber Rocha and other filmmakers of political cinema, stressing, "Kafka suggested that 'major' literatures always maintained a border between the political and the private, however mobile, whilst, in minor literature, the private affair was immediately political and 'entailed a verdict of life or death'"; "the private affair merges with the social—or political—immediate" (1986, 218).

20. In this sense, Andrés Di Tella's third documentary, *La televisión y yo (notas en una libreta)* (2002, "Television and I: Sketches in a Notebook"), is exemplary: it was exhibited in different partial versions (in the Museo Nacional de Bellas Artes, in the fourth year of the BAFICI) before arriving at the definitive version.

21. The characterization in this chapter is more an instrument to understand the tendencies of the new cinema than a classification that decides what does and what does not constitute the new Argentine cinema. As such, there are productions that share some of these features but not others, and if they are mentioned here it is to allow us to think in terms of contrast and difference. Enrique Piñeyro's *Whisky Romeo Zulú* (2004) links aerial accidents, the movie's theme, to television images that appear as another reality at the film's end. The principle of exteriority, in contrast, is included in the main character (Piñeyro himself), who ends up offering us the correct moral and political point of view on the facts narrated.

22. In terms of their impact, it is enough to consider the size of their public, unthinkable for the directors of the new cinema. Puenzo's *La historia oficial*, for example, was watched by more than 1.5 million spectators, and Bemberg's *Camila* by more than 2 million, without counting those who watched the films on television. These figures speak to a quantitative efficacy that should not be overlooked when we reflect upon the changes produced in film in recent years.

23. In some genres, such as detective fiction, the coincidental is absolutely excluded. (For a narrative reflection on this exclusion, see Jorge Luis Borges' "Death and the Compass"). In other narratives, there are accidents, but these are often motivated (an illness is a moral stain, a worker's accident is a denouncement of an exploitative system, etc.). At any rate, we should mention the great number of narrators who introduce chance and unmotivated accidents as part of their poetics, especially the surrealists, and André Gide and his concept of the "gratuitous act."

24. In *Silvia Prieto* the accident that befalls one of the women who delivers soap samples, which is not shown, is the reason that Silvia must change jobs. That is, this accident twists the course of the story. Diego Trerotola made this observation of the offscreen accident to me.

25. During the 1980s, and earlier still, Argentine cinema was obsessed with the question of how to represent characters who exercised some kind of institutional power: businesspeople, politicians, police chiefs, members of the military. These were the terminals of a societal mechanism that made the course of history change. It is interesting to note the utter absence of these kinds of characters in the new Argentine cinema, even in those films that would be most inclined to represent them. (I am thinking, for example, of *Los rubios* or *El bonaerense*). This is because these films are less interested in showing the representatives of power than in displaying the functioning of social machinery and its less obvious components.

26. Los Kjarkas, a Bolivian group created in 1965 by the Hermosa brothers, has had a number of international hits, including "Florcita azul" ("Little Blue Flower") and "Lambada, llorando se fue" ("Lambada Went Away Crying"). In Quechua, Kjarkas means "force," or "fortress." See Jaime Reyes, http://loskjarkas.com/biografia.html.

27. Given the position of the characters, we could even say that the television set creates the spatiality and the position of the customers in the bar.

28. On the televisual characteristic of the zoom, Serge Daney writes, "In its daily (secular) use, the zoom-in has become less a desire to signify or a figure of style than a sort of automatic reflex, empty of meaning, on the part of the cameraman, indicating only that 'we are on television.' But at the same time, the zoom-in, with its insinuating side, like a beast of prey, continues to 'mean something': precisely, a violation" (2004, 197).

29. This also has political consequences, given that, as Oscar Landi has shown, "television constitutes the field of vision as the great strategic issue of political power; the electronic struggle to order and educate people's perceptions thus becomes one of the central aspects of our era" (1992, 90).

30. Beyond this opposition between the real and the mental, however, Deleuze and Bazin agree that neo-realism must be valorized for its mise-en-scène. We should reflect upon the fact that the film theorist who has put forth the fiercest defense of realism is also the one who has imposed most forcefully the idea of the mise-en-scène.

31. There is a difference between the documentary and the indexical that is proper to cinema and the documentary as a genre. Considering the filmic image as an index, I understand that all films (except animation) have a documentary basis and, thus, that the opposition that should guide reflection on the "documentary" genre is the one produced between fiction and testimony, and not the one between fiction and documentary. The documentary genre would, in broad outline, be the testimonial use of the documentary features of the cinematographic register.

32. See Schwarzböck (2001) and the roundtable organized by the journal *Kilómetro 111*, in Acuña, Lerman, and Villegas (2004).

2   Film, the Narration of a World

1. Ironically, the advertisement for the Ford Falcon from the 1970s that opens and closes Gaggero's film shows, to extol the car's size, how a large family can comfortably fit into it.

2. One exception that shapes the family is the stories of Jewish families in which a reencounter appears to be possible and is filled with meaning. I refer to the films of Daniel Burman (in particular, *El abrazo partido*) and to Gabriel Lichtmann's *opera prima, Judíos en el espacio (¿o por qué es diferente esta noche a las demás noches?)* (2005, "Jews in Space [or Why Is This Night Different From Any Other?]").

3. Here and throughout, the term "popular" refers to "the people" (*el pueblo*), a category that is not clearly defined except in opposition to foreign, elite, or other "nonorganic" forms of culture and social life. It should not be confused with the English term "popular culture" (*cultura de masas*), which refers to mass culture. [Translator's note.]

4. In *Monobloc* ("Notepad"), Ortega's second feature-length film, the components of sedentary disintegration reach their limit in the history of an adolescent (Carolina Fal) who states, "Perla [her mother, played by Graciela Borges] and my godmother [Rita Cortese] are my only world." In this film, Ortega abandons the austerity of his *opera prima* and develops in excess what was in his earlier work more mannered and sentimental: the score that extends, in this later film, to the acting, photography, and narration.

5. Nor can the gaze endure the accident; as I have indicated, it always occurs offscreen.

6. The case of Enrique Bellande's *Ciudad de María,* analyzed below, which tells of the transformation of San Nicolás from a "city of steel" to a city of pilgrimage, is an interesting one. The construction of a large cupola is among the visual leitmotifs of the film. Jean Cocteau's phrase is fitting here: "Nothing so resembles a house in ruins as a house being constructed."

7. Of the YPF service stations of the 1930s, Anahí Ballent and Adrián Gorelik write that these constructions are "frankly modernist, almost didactic commands of the avant-garde, with the explicit vocation of generating a progressive, urban imagination" in Argentina (2001, 191).

8. The inclusion of one filmic citation in *La niña santa* must have surprised several of these critics; it referred not to Torre Nilsson but to Raúl de la Torre's *Heroína* (1972, "Heroine"), the movie that Mercedes Morán's character watches on television. Is this an homage to one of the few Argentine directors besides Nilsson and others from the generation of the 1960s who placed an emphasis on the feminine gaze and experience? Or is it more a dedication to Graciela Borges, who plays a translator at a medical conference in that film?

9. For Deleuze on naturalism, see also his analysis of Zola, included in *Logic of Sense.*

10. At one point, Pablo says to el Cordobés: "You're going to have a kid, didn't you know?" To which he replies: "Not me, Sandra." Sandra is, moreover, the only character for whom the father's authority plays a central role and who has a stable home. (In fact, various scenes are shot in her room.)

11. In *Rapado* the character escapes on his motorcycle, but when it breaks down he must return to Buenos Aires. In contrast, in the story that is the source for the movie, Lucio goes to Mar del Plata, where the text ends. The only film in which there is an escape from the police is *Pizza, birra, faso*, and in that film Uruguay is the analog for Mexico in U.S. film noir or crime fiction. The story ends on the border, just before the protagonist can board the ferry. In addition, Lerman's *Tan de repente* and Pablo Reyero's *La cruz del sur* (2003, "The Southern Cross") take place on the Atlantic coast.

12. The script was published as a book (León 2005).

13. Filippelli (2002) analyzes *Todo juntos* using the category of the shot.

14. In his review of the film, Salas speaks of "three ghosts" that hound the couple: the video of the slaughtering of the pig, his supposed infidelity, and, finally, the taxi driver (2004, 175). Diego Trerotola's review of the film in *El amante* (2003) is also very good.

15. I would like to thank Diego Trerotola, who suggested this reading of the movie's ending to me.

16. Estrella roja ("Red star") refers to an LSD tab of the same name. Cf. the song "Mil horas" ("A Thousand Hours") on the album *Vasos y besos* (1983, "Cups and Kisses") by Los Abuelos de la Nada ("The Grandparents of Nothingness"): "In the circus you're a star/A red star that imagines it all." Rosario Bléfari and Gonzalo Córdoba are part of the rock band Suárez.

17. The movie is a catalog of the motorcycles (from the Zanella to the most famous ones) that traverse the story at various levels: from the video games that Dreizik's character plays to the real motorcycles that populate the film.

18. The term "dysfunctional" has been subject to various critiques because it is based on a normative idea of the family. This is why I am avoiding this term, preferring to speak instead of the disintegration of the model of the patriarchal family, without implying decadence, abnormality, or irreparable loss. Rather, what interests me is the intersection between normative models that continue to function and those costumes, habits, or familial ties that have transformed the social panorama but are still presented as novel and not yet conceptualized.

19. In his *Tratado de semiótico* (*A Theory of Semiotics*), Umberto Eco explains Peirce's system of signs. According to Eco, one of the great virtues of Peirce's conception of the sign lies in the fact that it supposes neither *intentionality* nor *artificiality* (1995, 32).

20. In fact, Bazin uses a similar example to Peirce's: that of a fingerprint (2000, 16).

21. See note 3.

22. See chapter 1, note 17.

23. An earlier version of the film included a final shot in which Misael was looking into the camera and smiling. This shot was later eliminated from the definitive version, although in reality it suggested more a sense of complicity and artificiality than one of interference.

24. This characteristic also applies to the whole boom of commercial film produced during the 1990s under the auspices of television. In these films (Jorge Nisco and Daniel Barone's *Comodines* [1997; released in the United States as *Cops*], Eduardo Mignogna's *La fuga* [2001, "The Escape"], Juan José Jusid's *Un argentino en Nueva York* [1998, "An Argentinian in New York"]),

the commodity narrates without any mediation whatsoever. These are the prolongations, we could say, of the sociopolitical story of the 1990s that Beatriz Sarlo has defined as *"the bourgeois novel of the marketocratic ratio-nalization,* a truly impoverished material to replace the political identity that Menemism set out to dissolve" (1990, 4; italics in original). Although these films do not hold up to a cinematographic analysis, they are interesting from a cultural point of view. Is there a more pathetic "first world" than that repre-sented by the encounter between the protagonist played by Franchella and the doubles of Woody Allen and Whoopi Goldberg, the latter transformed into a waitress at a fast-food joint? Just as Juan José Jusid's *Made in Argentina* (1986) was not a great film but served as a *direct* testimony of the Alfonsín years (and also began in New York), Jusid's *Un argentino en Nueva York* inadvertently illustrates the social imagination during the Menem years.

25. This characteristic, according to Marx, is typical of the commodity: "The form of wood, for instance, is altered, by making a table out of it. Yet, for all that, the table continues to be that common, every-day thing, wood. But, so soon as it steps forth as a commodity, it is changed into something transcendent. It not only stands with its feet on the ground, but, in relation to all other com-modities, it stands on its head, and evolves out of its wooden brain grotesque ideas, far more wonderful than 'table-turning' ever was" (translation from www.marxists.org/archive/marx/works/1867-c1/ch01.htm).

26. The other important economic transaction is the sale of the peppers that the family produces. The theme comes up in the lunch scene and is linked to the family's decadence, for they must sell to Mercedes (Silvia Baylé), José's current partner and the former lover of Gregorio (Martín Adjemián), Mecha's husband.

27. Toward the end of his argument, Agamben prefers to speak—in an anti-avant-garde turn typical of the 1970s—of the "unexperiencable," referring to shock and novelty: "To experience something means divesting it of novelty, neutralizing its shock potential." And, "new is what cannot be experienced, because it lies 'in the depths of the unknown'" (1993, 41).

28. Benjamin had divided experience into *Erfahrung* (the integration of events into collective memory) and *Erlebnis* (the separation of events from these meaningful contexts and the linking of them to the flux of life). For an exposition of this difference, see Jay (1988, 67).

29. To give only one example of an intensive use of this concept of experience, we can think of Georges Bataille and what he deems "interior experience," related to the extreme (the heterogeneous) and the nondiscursive, which finds its most radical practice in eroticism and mysticism.

30. "I'm looking for my daughter, Olga," Argentino Vargas says. And the grandson replies: "Yes, she's my mom." In this way, the direct familial link between them (grandfather–grandson) is blocked.

31. In the same book, Benjamin avers, "Prostitution, in which the woman represents merchant and merchandise in one, acquires a particular significance" (1999, 896).

32. This asymmetry between Vargas' forced situation and the director's choice is highlighted throughout the story by means of the negation of any identifi-cation between character and director. The sequence shots and the music of

Flormaleva achieve this. This is not the place to analyze how Alonso himself knew how to take advantage of new situations in the global circulation of films in festivals that provide these movies with prestige. The festival circuit is a realm with which Alonso is quite familiar: his training, along with his short stay in film school, emerged from his participation in the "Primer plano" section that Nicolás Sarquís curated in the Mar del Plata festival, which is characterized by showing alternative and independent cinema or national cinematographies unfamiliar in Argentina. (It was in this series that the films of the new Iranian cinema were first shown.)

33. His grandson is also shown climbing a tree and picking a fruit that he will eat. This idea of survival is repeated, in a very different vein, in the case of the director himself, who worked out an entire strategy of exhibition to avoid a foreseeable failure at the box office. (The movie was shown in the Sala Leopoldo Lugones of the Teatro Municipal General San Martín and was framed by important publicity.) One could say that the film itself was almost able to do without the traditional cinema market.

34. It is clear that a shirt is not necessarily a commodity, but it is presented in *Los muertos* as an object of transaction and valorized according to its price.

35. On the themes of perception, interest, and the human condition, see the developments of Bergson and Deleuze in Marrati (2003, 42–4). The "first material moment of subjectivity" consists, according to Deleuze, in a subtraction of the perception from that which interests us (1986a, 63). The action-image ("the virtual action of things on us") and the affection-image ("living matter") form the second and third moment of subjectivity (65).

36. The doll has an Argentine jersey, which would seem to encourage a reading in terms of national allegory, but no other indication in the film would allow us to develop such a reading.

37. Once again, a confrontation between two types of experience: the *naturalness* of Vargas' world and the *artificiality* of cinema.

38. Life in the city as something stripped of all genuine experience is an anti-avante-garde cliché that also appears in Agamben's book, cited above: "Today, however, we know that the destruction of experience no longer necessitates a catastrophe, and that humdrum daily life in any city will suffice" (1993, 13).

39. Alonso's asceticism makes every object acquire a certain abstraction and become part of a series: knives, razors, machetes, children, the objects of survival (fruit, a honeycomb, a goat). Whereas the adults can more or less do without commodities, the children in the film are almost all imprisoned in a world that is already commodified: the prostitute's daughters (unable to defend themselves against their mother's negligence), the boys who buy candy, the baby carriage (the only node of modernity in the ranch that Vargas visits to deliver the letter), his grandson's little football player.

40. In only two moments does this incommunicability appear to shatter: in jail (but in the context of a world of people excluded from public life) and when Vargas leaves one of the sugar bowls he had made in prison as a gift for María, the girl to whom he needed to deliver the letter. A true gift that Vargas leaves when he departs the next morning, it is nevertheless given stealthily, and almost as a payment for the night he spent at the ranch.

41. This camera on the truck marks one of the caesuras that divide the film into three parts: his life in prison until the police truck leaves him on the road, his stay in the town (the camera abandons him once again when he enters the river with his canoe), and his journey down the river. The initial and final sequences form a sort of epilogue and prologue, related to one another through the use of Flormaleva music on the soundtrack.

42. In traditional documentaries in which a traveler or explorer penetrates nature, the camera tends to follow behind, giving the spectator the sense that he or she is discovering the surroundings with the traveler and that potential surprises are in store. (Some fiction films, such as Francis Ford Coppola's *Apocalypse Now*, take great advantage of this effect). In contrast, in *Los muertos* the camera tends to wait for the protagonist as if the space to be traversed lacks any possible shock.

43. The initial sequence of *Los muertos* corresponds in a sense to the "dream" scene in *La libertad*. Since Alfred Hitchcock's *Vertigo*, green has connoted death and recollection. As innumerable scholars of colors have demonstrated, the meaning that we attribute to a particular color is arbitrary and depends upon cultural context. The importance of Hitchcock's works allows us to suppose that in the realm of the cinematographic image, green can be reutilized with these connotations (as in François Truffaut's *The Green Room* (1978, in French *La chambre verte*), based on a Henry James story).

44. In addition, the sequence has inspired admiration for Alonso's manual skill, leading one critic to wonder whether he used a steady-cam (Mauricio Teste, "Los olvidados" ["The Forgotten Ones"], at www.otrocampo.com). At any rate, it is the skill of a body transformed by technology (without or without a steady-cam) and not that of a "naturally" skilled body such as that of the film's protagonist.

45. In the worlds of the exchange of objects in Rejtman's other films, counting is also present. In *Rapado*, the owner of the video arcade says of the chips: "One for five, ten for forty-five, 100 for 420." And in a later scene (subject to inflation): "One for ten, ten for ninety, 100 for 800." In *Los guantes mágicos*, Alejandro does the math during a taxi-cab ride: from a total of twenty-three pesos, Alejandro ends up with four; six go to Luis, who bought the car, ten for the taxi call station, and three for Susana, who booked the trip.

46. The man whom Silvia meets in Mar del Plata is named Armani, in reference to the brand of his jacket. A secondary character appears wearing a shirt from the Disco supermarket chain, where he works.

47. Nowhere is this more clearly demonstrated than in the Russian porn actors of *Los guantes mágicos*, who live in Canada, travel to Argentina to film a movie, and use their bodies as commodities.

48. This circulation is based on a potentially ridiculous substitution, but one that is not without a certain logic, constituting Rejtman's particular, curious sense of humor. An extreme case of this is the young woman who hands out samples of Brite soap, who is run over by a bus, and who is substituted by Silvia, who goes to work in the deceased woman's clothing.

49. In *Silvia Prieto*, each object enters into seriality: the little doll; the former husband's money, in dollars; sliced chicken breasts; cups of coffee in the café; clothing (the film begins with a misunderstanding at a laundromat); couples;

characters' names (Armani, Brite, Silvia Prieto). Everything is duplicated, as it is during a happy hour, one of the motifs of *Los guantes mágicos*.

50. Something similar occurs with the Renault 12 that challenges a drag race in *Los guantes mágicos*: It has stickers that distinguish it from all the other Renault 12s.

51. In the short story "Quince cigarillos" ("Fifteen Cigarettes") in *Velcro y yo* (1996, "Velcro and I"): "What a shame that I haven't run into any of Mariano's old high school friends. I've just gotten here and I want to get back in touch. A casual encounter around a circumstance like this one [Mariano is in jail], which brings people together, is always better than any old phone call" (Rejtman 1996, 95). The melancholy of such encounters is never entirely dark; it is nuanced by the ironic distance of the absurd: in *Los guantes mágicos* it is the brother of a grade-school classmate (they run into each other in the end, but they do not recognize one another); in *Silvia Prieto*, Garbuglia mixes up the names of his former classmates.

52. *Madame de…* tells the story of the title character, who sells a pair of earrings in the shape of a heart that her husband (Charles Boyer) had given her. The husband later discovers this fact and recovers the earrings to give them as a gift to his lover. The lover visits Constantinople and parts with the earrings, which find themselves in a jewelry store where an Italian diplomat (Vittorio de Sica) buys them. The diplomat travels to Paris and falls in love with Madame de…, to whom he ends up giving the earrings. Her husband discovers the betrayal and challenges the diplomat to a duel, eventually killing him. In his text "Postproducción," Rejtman mentions *Madame de…*, *La ronde*, and Ophuls' *Le plasir* (1999, 144, 152). He also refers several times to Guy de Maupassant, the writer on whose work the episodes in *La plasir* are based.

53. In her astute review of *Silvia Prieto*, Silvia Schwarzböck speaks of "residues" of the classics (1999). She begins her article by affirming that "while movies can be similar to other films or to extra-cinematographic reality,…*Silvia Prieto* eschews both possibilities."

54. I am, of course, using these comparisons in a different way than is customary when film criticism speaks of Bresson and the rigor of the mise-en-scène—what David Bordwell, borrowing from Noel Burch, deemed "parametric narration," a type of narration that differs from plot-based films (1996, 275). In this sense, Ophuls tends to orchestrate his mise-en-scenès around spiral forms, in a constant search for the superposition of shots through frames, glass, rails, and other objects. In this sense, Rejtman is closer to Bresson's asceticism. See Beatriz Sarlo's comparisons in Birgin and Trímboli (2003).

55. Cavell analyzes the following films: Preston Sturges' *The Lady Eve* (1941), Frank Capra's *It Happened One Night* (1934), Howard Hawks' *Bringing Up Baby* (1938) and *His Girl Friday* (1940), and George Cukor's *The Philadelphia Story* (1940) and *Adam's Rib* (1949).

56. In the screwball comedy the wedding is always special, unique, impetuous. The lovers get married after an hour and have to wake up the priest, or they arrive late to the ceremony, etc. In contrast, in *Silvia Prieto* the wedding is like any other.

57. Evidently, a name can accumulate certain signifiers in a given context. The name "Juan Domingo" (Perón's first names) would be loaded with

connotations in Argentina but not in other countries. There are also names such as Soledad ("Solitude"), Violeta ("Violet"), Amparo ("Refuge"), and Libertad ("Liberty"), as well as those given to remember a relative or an event. Yet, rather than the meaning, what characterizes the proper name is the absolutely contingent character of what it designates.

58. The original Spanish text here uses two different terms: *regalo* ("present") and *don* ("gift"). The latter, which has a more powerful sense than the former, alludes to anthropological literature. [Translator's note.]

59. Exchange in Rejtman has the outrageous dynamic of comedy, in which the voices of exchange are unpredictable and move from the affective to the economic and back. It would be a mistake to think that this value of arbitrary exchange is set against a more genuine use value. To speak of use value with respect to Rejtman's films is to restore a notion of depth and hidden truth to be revealed that is totally foreign to his aesthetics.

60. When Silvia Prieto goes to buy a present for her double (whom she has not yet met), she has to choose among different brands of shampoo ("Revlon, Helena Rubinstein, Sedal, Wellapon, Plusbelle, Springtime…"), among different types ("normal, dry"), and also among different bottle sizes. She introduces herself into the series of commodities and appropriates something to give it to someone whom she does not know and who has just made her enter into the world of dispossession.

61. The purity of this act is heightened by the fact that Silvia takes the money out of circulation and buries it in one of the flowerpots on her balcony.

62. The *lack of relief,* which is one of the personal marks of Rejtman's films, leads spectators and critics to appropriate a moment of the film and read it as key, in a gesture that always ends up violent. Beatriz Sarlo, for example, in an excellent reading of the film, affirms that "Silvia's only profoundly personal act" is to send her canary to her mother in Mendoza, which ends up being more a projection of the critic herself than a reading derived from the film. One of the participants of the seminar "Centro de Pedagogiás de Anticipación," in a comment on Sarlo's review, proposed a well-argued interpretation of the film as "feminist…because all in all it is women who make men circulate. I think it is interesting because here we find a social imagination in which women fight over men and pass them among themselves, as men used to do with women. It's a more fair circulation, isn't it?" (both in Birgin and Trímboli 2003, 137, 148). Alejandro Portela, in her review "Corazónes geométricos" ("Geometric Hearts"), published at www.leedor.com, affirms that "the country Silvia Prieto" is a "cinematographic metaphor of identity" in Argentina. *Silvia Prieto's* neutrality, then, presents spectators with a challenge: what part of the surface will we appropriate to create a reading? What clues should we follow if all clues are false? (*Pistas falsas,* or "False Clues," is the title of a book of Gabriel's poems in the film.) What is *Silvia Prieto* about, for us?

63. A legendary center of avant-garde production in the field of visual arts in Buenos Aires during the 1960s and 1970s. [Translator's note.]

64. Once again, technological advances highlight the artificiality of artistic languages, as in the case of dubbing. In recent years, improvement in theater acoustics, the generalized use of the Dolby system ("optical stereophonic sound on film," created in 1975), and the possibility of manipulating sound

with computers (to splice together different parts, to temporalize sound, to reformat it, etc.) have all made the elaboration of sound as extensive an act as work on the image. Francis Ford Coppola, for example, has spent as long developing sound as on filming (Stam 2001, 212–13). In contrast, at times technical limitations pose true challenges for filmmakers, as happened in Adrián Caetano's *Bolivia*. According to Carolina Duek, in a paper presented in the seminar on "The Cunning Tricks of the Cinematographic Form," "The role of music in editing is well known. As they did not have money to film with two sound tracks, they had to do it with a single one. This meant that the ambient sound could not be 'superimposed' upon the music. For this reason, the dialogues in the movie would seem to form a part not only of the plot but also of the ambient sound, which in other cases is occupied by soundtracks."

65. Some films that include indigenous languages, such as Lautaro Murúa's *Shunko* (1960), subtitle these parts to facilitate comprehension.

66. In addition to the possibility of mere coincidence, the final scene of *Los guantes mágicos*, which takes place in the northeastern province of Salta, might be an homage to Lucrecia Martel, a native of the province, and to all the recent cinematographic production from Salta, in which the critic Edgardo Chibán played an important role. Rodrigo Moscoso, the director of *Modelo 73* (2001, "73 Model") and Rejtman's editor Martín Mainoli are also from Salta.

67. The original Spanish text here uses the term *representatión* throughout the discussion of this scene, which means both theatrical performance and the English term "representation." [Translator's note.]

68. The thereminvox is an instrument invented by a Russian musician, a pioneer in the field of sound and electronics. It has the additional peculiarity of forcefully incorporating a visual dimension, for the musician's hands touch not the metal rod but the electromagnetic waves emitted (one hand regulates the volume and the other the pitch); thus the musician appears to be performing magic. To interpret the role of the musician, Martel chose one of the most renowned thereminvox players in Argentina, Manuel Schaller, who transmits with his body a strange sensation of solemnity and mystery.

69. I thank Jimena Rodríguez for calling my attention to this passage. According to Lerer, the rhyme was sung by children in Spain, inspired by the good Dr. Gannon of the television program *Centro Médico;* it was not in the original script but was invented by one of the girls during the movie's casting call.

70. The first vision that Jano has of Helena is through a mirror, as though it is not her body he sees but its reflection. In addition, it is the reflection of her back, as in Amalia's back, when he presses up against her. The camera insistently shows us the nape of Jano's neck. *La niña santa* thus finds one of its themes: what bodies do beyond what we can see, as symbolized by the parts of our own bodies that we cannot observe.

71. The movie poster represents precisely this moment, when she turns her head to confront Jano, her pursuer, who flees.

72. This polarity is also present in the stories of vocation narrated in the catechism classes. In one, "a mother" warns a truck driver that there has been an accident on the highway; when he arrives at the scene of the accident, he discovers the same mother lying dead, next to her son, whose life has been saved because of this warning. The other story is of a "worldly woman" who

sees her friends die in an accident and decides to dedicate her life to caring for forlorn people. Paradoxically, the first mother dies (although she saves her son), whereas the second is saved. Whether obedient or transgressive, both women are punished by these stories and, as the litany sung in the catechism classes goes, these figures are always "lost."

73. For her part, Helena receives phone calls from the new wife of her ex-husband, reminding her of her role as mother and wife, but she does not answer them.

74. According to Adriana Cavarero, this represents "the nature of women as a specific, passionate nature, considered disordered, dangerous, and incapable of regulating itself from *within*. Therefore, it is seen to need discipline from *without*, which is generally the role of men" (1998, 303).

75. At night, Helena suffers the same discomfort as the character in the movie she is watching on television, Graciela Borges in Raúl de la Torre's *Heroína*. Instead of invoking Torre Nilsson (the director to whom she had been compared after her first film), Martel turns to Raúl de la Torre, the first Argentine director with an exclusively feminine thematic. In addition to *Heroína*, see *Juan Lamgalia y Sra.* (1970, "Mr. and Mrs. Juan Lamgalia"), *Crónica de una señora* (1971, "Chronicle of a Lady"), and *Sola* (1976, "Alone"), all of which feature Graciela Borges.

76. Helena recites to her daughter some of the verses of the *romancero* ("The gentlemen goes off to hunt/to hunt like he tended to do/he brings the tired dogs with him/the lost falcon was there") so that she will stop reciting her litanies ("Mother of divine grace/Purest mother/Most chase mother/Virginal Mother/Immaculate Mother…Health for the sick/Refuge for sinners/Console to the afflicted/Help to the Christians/Queen of the Angels…Queen of the Virgins/Queen of all Saints/Queen conceived without original sin"). The poem that Helena recites is from the "Romance of the Infanta," a cruel but beautiful story in which a knight leaves a young girl in love and promises to return once he has received her mother's permission to marry her. When he returns, the girl is no longer there, and he punishes himself by cutting off his own hands and feet. As often happens in Martel's films, the mother comes between desire and its object.

77. The fundamental position of the woman in relationship to desire lies in the fact that, in the words of Pierre Bourdieu, "she is condemned to be seen through the dominant, that is, masculine, categories" (1998, 89).

78. "Did Mary conceive through the ear, as Augustine and Adobard assert?" asks Beckett in *Molloy*. According to Lucas Margarit, an Argentine specialist on Beckett, there is nothing recorded on the identity of Adobard. (There was an Agobardo of Lyon, who lived in the eighth century, but most likely this is an invention of Beckett's.) The reference to Saint Augustine is to the reelaborations in his sermons of the phrase "the Word made flesh" (sermons 72/A, 7; 215–4 and 293 B, 4). In the Bible we also find some references to conception through the ear, including Romans I, 5:17: "Mary conceived the Word."

79. Roland Barthes writes of Ignacio of Loyala: "At the beginning of the modern era, in Ignatius' century, one fact seems to begin to modify the exercise of the imagination: a reordering of the hierarchy of the five senses. In the Middle Ages, historians tell us, the most refined sense, the perceptive sense *par excellence*, the one that established the richest contact with the world, was hearing: sight came in only third place, after touch. Then we have the reversal: the eye becomes

the prime organ of perception (Baroque, art of the thing seen, attests to it). This change is of great religious importance. The primacy of hearing, still very prevalent in the sixteenth century, was theologically guaranteed: the Chuch bases its authority on the word, faith is hearing: *auditum verbi Dei, id este fidem;* the ear, the ear alone Luther said, is the Christian organ. Thus a risk of a contradiction arises between the new perception, led by sight, and the ancient faith based on hearing. Ignatius sets out, as a matter of fact, to resolve it: he attempts to situate the image (or interior 'sight') in orthodoxy, as a new unit of the language he is constructing" (1976, 65).

80. Classifications of sound in film have always been problematic and are almost always described as a function of the visual. For the sound whose origin is not perceivable in the image, two terms are used: "nondiegetic" and "diegetic." As can be seen from previous examples, in *La niña santa*, sound is presented in offscreen space, later to reveal itself in the scene. On this theme, see Michel Chion's indispensible books (1999, among others), and the succinct but exhaustive treatment of the term "Sound" in Russo (1998).

81. The literature on the relationship between the privileging of the visual (ocularcentrism), masculine control (phalocentrism), and the preeminence of reason (logocentrism) in the West, particularly in the realm of French post-structuralism and feminism, is extensive. A lucid analysis of these positions with respect to cinematographic criticism can be found in Martin Jay (1993). In her essay "La tecnología del género," Teresa de Lauretis proposes, per Foucault, that the body of the woman saturated with sexuality is "perceived as an attribute or a property of the male" (1987, 14) and that "in the phallic order of patriarchal culture and in its theory, woman is unrepresentable except as representation" (20). That is, the order of representation, to which the cinematographic apparatus belongs, is constituted by the masculine gaze.

82. Ricardo Vallarino, in a note published at www.bazaramericano.com, interprets the ending differently and suggests a strong value judgment of the movie: "The problem with the film lies in the fact that, with a narration that tends toward a climax, it does not satisfy. In fact, it is opportune: Jano is trapped and goes on stage, everything is set for the moving denouement, and Martel nevertheless denies us this. Why? Why does Martel omit this imminent ending? My hypothesis is that, turning to a potent identification, Martel wants to deprive us of catharsis without turning to a Brechtian distance. This discomfort is evident in all that relates to sex: sex scenes are interrupted; no orgasm, no ecstasy, is ever shown. The sense of dissatisfaction, of frustration, is the goal. In the severity of her story, the director determines her creatures (her world) by dark, unconscious forces and, for good or for bad, decides to maintain the character of 'openness,' leaving us with a shot (once again) of the pool. Everything is absolutely closed, and at the same time open; everything is absolutely determined and, at the same time, everything is possible." Vallarino seems to overlook both Amalia's masturbation scene and the long kiss on the mouth that she gives Josefina.

83. See note 67.

84. This is a photocopy of a text written, according to Josefina, by "M.V.D." in the seventeenth century. Perhaps a full reading of the text lets us see better its strange logic: "I was dressed one day in Divine Charity, and then I saw the Lord who had an enemy of mine dead in his arms, for whom I had prayed.

He said to me: 'Here is our son, whom do you love more? Me or my son?' I responded that I loved our son more, that is, that I preferred to suffer more in our world for the salvation of a soul than to be in glory with Our Lord.''

85. There are, of course, exceptions, but they are few; generally, the source of the sound is, as it were, at arm's length. Almost invariably, these are sounds that technological apparatuses of reproduction emit: the car radio, the keys of a cell phone, the televisions where a pornographic film is playing, the noise of a car alarm, music from a CD.

86. This difference in the composition of the shot could be extended to elisions, so important for both directors. In Martel, the ellipsis always has to do with what is hidden, with a lack, with what is silenced or what cannot be said or shown. In contrast, in Rejtman, the ellipsis is a leap, a segmentation, the movement from one thing to another.

87. In both *Silvia Prieto* and *Los guantes mágicos,* it is unusual for one character to appear behind another. An interesting example is the shot in *Los guantes mágicos* in which Alejandro appears driving a bus behind his copilot. A cut follows and, in the following scene, Alejandro appears in the place of the copilot and this character is now driving.

88. New Order is the name that the group Joy Division took after the death of their lead singer, Ian Curtis. They are an emblematic band for the late 1980s, one that marks the persistence of youth in a man who is no longer young.

89. In fact, there exists a subculture of the Renault 12, and it can be found at www.renault12club.com.ar.

90. Something similar occurs with the brands of shampoo that Silvia Prieto must choose from.

91. A music entirely different from Piranha's (which almost functions as a kind of torture).

92. According to Rejtman, "I included El otro yo in *Silvia Prieto* because, in reality, the name of the group interested me. I chose it because, quite literally, the movie is talking about that, 'the other I.' When I wrote the scene—and I don't know how this happened, because I hadn't yet heard them—I wrote about a girl who sings in a hardcore band with guttural noises and they had a song like that, basically. It was serendipitous. It's not that I liked that music in particular....In *Silvia Prieto* the theme of *language* is more important than that of *identity.* Silvia Prieto's problem is not that there are other people like her, but rather that there are others with the same name. The name is what matters" (in Fontana 2002, my emphasis).

93. I prefer the phrase "typical places" because it is more descriptive than the evaluative "common places." It seems to me that the first phrase better expresses the neutrality of Rejtman's gaze.

94. This tendency to fulfill the conventions of a genre continued in many movies of the 1990s, including Alberto Lecchi's *Perdido por perdido* (1993, "Since It's Already Failed"), Desanzo's *Al filo de la ley* (1992, "At the Edge of the Law"), and Mario Levin's *Sotto voce* (1996), which do not belong to the "new cinema." There were also important contributions to a rereading of the genre in Marcelo Piñeyro's *Cenizas del paraíso* (1997, released in the United States as *Ashes from Paradise*) and Fabián Bielinsky's *Nueve reinas,*

which had very solid screenplays (the first by Aída Bortnik, the second by the film's director). Among the younger filmmakers, it was Damián Szifron—the most coherent filmmaker dedicated to well-constructed commercial movies—who revisited the genre with *El fondo del mar* (2003, released in the United States as *The Bottom of the Sea*). For an overview of detective/crime film of the 1980s, see the article by Elena Goyti and David Oubiña in España (1994).

95. For a reading of the use of genre in *Un oso rojo* that contrasts the film with Godard's use of genres and the supposed superiority of classic film ("Classic film was always right. If it was beautiful it is because it was right"), see Oubiña (2003).

96. This first part stems from a short by Lerman based on César Aira's *La prueba* ("The Test"). Aira's novel, as the director has stated more than once, was only a starting point. In fact, *Tan de repente* takes only the two first parts of the novel: Marcia's encounter with Mao and Lenin and the dialogue in the Pumper Nic (in the movie, in a McDonald's). In the novel, the "test of love" consists of Mao and Lenin's crazed robbery of a supermarket, replete with fires, burnt bodies, severed heads, and other violence. In Lerman's movie, it is the entrance into the sea. The anticommodity violence is substituted for a romantic cliché. In both cases, Marcia joins her new friends. In addition to the anecdotes and various dialogues, the play of speeds is also present in Aira's novel: "Outside of her story [Marcia] felt herself slipping too quickly, like a body in ether with no resistance….She did not feel it, shouldn't feel it, because she was part of the system, but all those kids were wasting their time. It was the way that they had of being happy. That's what it was about, and Marcia was capturing it perfectly, even though she wasn't able to participate in it. Or she thought she couldn't" (1992, 8–9). Both novel and film show how Marcia ends up participating in the quicker and more intense world of Mao and Lenin. For a reading of the encounter between the new Argentine cinema and the new literary generation, focusing on the figure of Lerman, see Speranza (2002).

97. The "serendipitous encounter" evidently has poetic connotations and recalls Lautréamont's phrase that the surrealists later adopted as their motto: "the chance encounter of an umbrella and a sewing machine on a dissecting table." The parachutist's song is sung in an invented language that phonetically resembles Russian or Finnish.

98. The song was written specially for the movie by Juan Ignacio Bouscayrol.

99. Villegas had already made a lovely short entitled *Rutas y veredas* (1995, "Routes and Sidewalks"), in which a mysterious urban sadness gives the film its tone.

100. I recall an anecdote about a five-year-old girl who was taken backstage after seeing a play. Her mother told her: "Now you're going to meet Gastón Pauls" (it could have been a different actor; I don't remember). To which the girl responded: "No, mommy, *he* is going to meet *me*. I already know him from TV."

101. The comment that Natalia makes to Martín when he comes home is very funny: "Have you been crashing again?"

102. Various examples could be included in a fairly heterogeneous series of films of education or formation—from literary adaptations of classic examples of the *Bildungsroman*, such as Wim Wenders' version of *Wilhelm Meister* and Peter Handke's *Falsche Bewegung* (1975), to the properly cinematographic inflection

typical of U.S. film, where an older (and wiser) character initiates another into a discipline: from John Avildesen's *The Karate Kid* (1984) to Martin Scorsese's *The Color of Money* (1986). The initiation of a novice into the institution of the police constitutes a subgenre and has many examples: Dennis Hopper's *Colors* (1988), with Robert Duvall and Sean Penn; John Herzfield's *15 Minutes* (2001), with Robert DeNiro and Edward Burns; and many others.

103. The title of the film is the name of the police force of the Buenos Aires metropolitan area, which the protagonist joins. [Translator's note.]

104. This taking on of the point of view is corroborated by the cameo by Trapero himself, as one of the agents who receives the diploma with Zapa's promotion.

105. Although the story starts before Zapa's entry into the police, the black background of the opening credits and the large fade-out make this first part of the narration a kind of prologue. We could say that Zapa did not commit the crime and instead was an accomplice because he was tricked, but from the juridical point of view he is a participant and therefore guilty. Ultimately, the judge (a stage that is not reached) should determine whether his participation was intentional or unintentional, two options that imply an enormous variation in the character of the punishment. I wish to thank Juan Balerdi for specifying the juridical situation of this "case."

106. This double identity is constituted by the sharp division between the institution and what lies outside of it; whereas *inside* strong, almost familial, ties are created, the *outside* is perceived as a place of risk under enemy control. One of the police officers in his substation understands perfectly this double identity when he explains to Mendoza that someone who kills a cop is, for the police, a "black" but, for others, "a hero."

107. This idea of dispossession linked to subject formation was presented by Shyla Wilker in the seminar on cinema that I taught at the UBA.

108. In the shots in the shoot-out scene, the nature of Trapero's realism can also be perceived. In almost all movies spectator and characters rely on images of both sides, moving within a space with a relatively clear idea of the movements of the opponent, but in *El bonaerense* only Zapa's position can be perceived, and the space as a whole is chaotic, confusing, and disorienting.

109. There are also elements of Trapero's film that have little to do with the workings of the Buenos Aires police, despite the fact that the mise-en-scène reinforces the reality effect of the images. One of these is the jacket with the label "La bonaerense" ("The Buenos Aires police force"), invented by the film's costume designers, worn by the police officers who visit Zapa at his home. (I owe this observation to Mariana Galvani, from the seminar on "The Cunning Tricks of the Cinematographic Form.")

110. Corruption is not opposed to good intentions; its efficacy lies in its tendency to be inseparable from these. Without the prioritizing of friendships, rewards, affections, preferences, or "good turns" (*gauchadas*) in the interpersonal workings of an institution, there would be no corruption, or it would exist to a lesser extent.

111. For many aspects of what I examine in this chapter, I have consulted Richard Sennett's intelligent study on the relationships between personality and institution, especially *Respect in a World of Inequality* (2003).

3   A World without Narration

1. As domestic or private life is also of public interest, it is difficult to restrict ourselves to a classical definition of politics as human activity in the realm of the *polis* or public life. However, we think that in the tradition of Argentine political film—in which *La hora de los hornos* (1969) is the most important milestone—politics is associated with power, action, and the transformation of the public space and private life through relationships of control linked to the state. In recent years (think only of the feminist slogan "The personal is political"), the very idea of politics has been transformed.

2. The idea of national culture is affirmed despite all that has happened in recent years. Solanas spends time on the Rolling Stones' visit to the presidential palace in Olivos and omits, or chooses not to include, all the visits of Argentine musicians and artists (folklorists, tango players, rock musicians) to the presidential estate. Everything continues as it was before. For a vision of the militant cinema of the 1970s, Mariano Mestman's work (2001) is indispensable.

3. A very different case—and perhaps the only one that continues, though in a very different vein, the legacy of the Liberation Film Group—is that of films about *piqueteros*, those involved in the social movement of civil disobedience for the rights of the unemployed that began in the mid-1990s. This cinema took the baton from the political film of the 1980s, with the difference that new technologies and a lack of censorship allowed these *piqueteros* to participate more collectively and actively in the making of their works. In *El rostro de la dignidad* (1999, "The Face of Dignity"), the activists of Solano's Movimento de Trabajadores Desocupados (MTD, Movement of Unemployed Workers) assemble to decide how to end the movie. Completely indifferent to the institution of film (which *La hora de los hornos* tried to combat), these movies had their own film festival in the Cosmos movie theater in Buenos Aires in December 2001. (I take this information from Christian Dodaro's paper "Memories of light and repulsive aesthetics" from the seminar on film at the UBA. See also Dodaro and Salerno (2003) and the Alavío group's Web site, which states: "Making technologies and skills accessible and available to exploited sectors by democratizing audiovisual production and language is a priority of Grupo Alavío's work. For over 10 years, Alavío has been participating in working class struggles, supporting with audiovisual materials. As activists struggling for social revolution, the debate of whether the reach of the camera is enough is an inevitable discussion. 'We are working to construct an identity and thinking that reflects the working class' and exploited sectors' specific interests and necessities. The camera is a tool, another weapon' "; www.revolutionvideo.org/alavio/englishhome.html.)

4. Here and throughout, the term "popular" refers to "the people" (*el pueblo*), a category that is not clearly defined except in opposition to foreign, elite, or other "nonorganic" forms of culture and social life. It should not be confused with the English term "popular culture" (*cultura de masas*), which refers to mass culture. Note that "popular" has a more political sense in Spanish than in English; it carries a sense of poor, lower-class people or workers. The same is true of *el pueblo*. [Translator's note.]

5. According to Cecilia Flaschland, in the Social Science Department of the UBA (where there is a group named after Roberto Carri, Albertina's father), *Los rubios* elicited the following reaction: "If the director had not had the last name Carri, we would have done an *escrache*." [The term *escrache* refers to the public exposure by leftist groups of people who participated with impunity in the last military dictatorship, often by marking on their door their link to the violent regime. Translator's note.]

6. The text comes from the work of Juan Díaz del Moral and acts as an epigraph for Alberto Carri's work. In a reading of the "writing of the father" in *Los rubios*, Hugo Salas (in a text included in his blog "elconsensoreverenciado") debates Kohan's (2004a) reading of this passage.

7. In these cases there is a key difference from Alejandro Agresti's *Buenos Aires viceversa* (1996), which films a protest by children of the disappeared during the last dictatorship and has the protagonist join the protest to find out about her past. As Ana Amado pointed out to me in conversation, it is from the inclusion of the protest in the narrative diegesis that the films analyzed here are distancing themselves.

8. This is what happened to Héctor Anglada, one of the characteristic faces of the new cinema, who tragically died in a motorcycle accident in 2002. Anglada trained with Adrián Caetano and participated in his first shorts, filmed in Córdoba; his first television part was in Channel 13's *Gasoleros* ("Thrifty People"), playing a trash collector.

9. The *cacique* is someone who is powerful at the local level but whose function is not always clear to an outsider. (The *cacique* can be a mayor, but also a baker, a doctor, or, as in this case, a trash picker.) The *cacique* is a conventional figure in Latin American cultural politics. A good example is García Márquez's dentist who also holds power in the town ("Un día de estos") in *Los funerales de la Mamá Grande* (translated into English as *Big Mama's Funeral.*)

10. On the figure of the plebeian in Argentine culture, see Christian Ferrer's interesting essay in Birgin and Trímboli (2003). Ferrer analyzes the plebeian imagination as an alliance between popular culture and political power.

11. Manu Chao is the musician who perhaps best represents the hopes of anti-globalization groups. Kevin Johansen is an Argentine–U.S. musician who treats the imagination of globalization with intelligence, especially in his "Mc Donald" and *Sur o no sur* ("South or No South").

12. This populist-lumpen line has been returning in recent festivals, and Jorge Gaggero, in his *Cama adentro* (2003, released in the United States as *Live-In Maid*) and *Vida en Falcón*, is one of the filmmakers who affirms it. The first film opened the festival and the second won the audience choice award.

13. In film, Olmedo was a "wasted talent." He made several movies, but all of them (except perhaps Enrique Cahen Salaberry's *Mi novia él...* [1975, "My Fiancée the..."]) were mediocre, and his televisual talents (improvisation, rapid exits, changes in tone, games with the space of the set) were not apparent. According to Martín Johan (in a conversation we had), this "waste" is what makes Olmedo so attractive, because it stages one of the strongest ideas of our cultural imagination: the idea that Argentines would be much better, brilliant even, given other circumstances.

14. I am not claiming that Ulises Rosell read Landi's book but that both participate in a rehabilitation of Olmedo that ran throughout the 1990s. For a reading of Landi's book when it was first published, see Beatriz Sarlo's review (1992), in which she objects to the contemporary or "Realpolitik" stance towards the televisual image that ultimately eliminates thought from all critical operations.

15. From the perspective from which we are analyzing this film, the total absence of references to Peronism and to Eva Perón is also striking. The only political party mentioned is the Unión Cívica Radical, which, according to one of the women interviewed, is "homophobic." Once again, everything indicates that *Lesbianas de Buenos Aires* works with displacements and inversions of traditions.

16. This invisibility is evident in the history of Argentine film, which has virtually ignored lesbians, except when they are linked to criminal activity, as in Emilio Vieyra's *Sucedió en el internado* (1985, "It Happened in the Institution") and *Correccional de mujeres* (1986, distributed in the United States as *Women's Reformatory*) and Aníbal de Salvo's *Atrapatadas* (1984, released in the United States as *Condemned to Hell*), all of which take place in jails or other disciplinary institutions. (Barney Finn's chapter, included in *De la misteriosa Buenos Aires* [1981, "Of the Mysterious Buenos Aires"], constitutes an exception.) The most interesting precursor of this link between lesbianism and criminality comes in Daniel Tinayre's *Deshonra* (1952, "Dishonor"). Among Argentine directors, Tinayre is one of the most inclined to show sexual conflicts. Despite the film's Peronist propaganda and melodrama, prison life in *Deshonra* suggests sexual relationships between some of the inmates. Male homosexuality has had better luck, although it has often been represented satirically. After efforts such as Enrique Dawi's *Adiós Roberto…* (1985, "Goodbye, Roberto…") and Américo Ortiz de Zárate's *Otra historia de amor* (1986, "Another Love Story"), we have to wait until Verónica Chen's *Vagón fumador* (2001, "Smokers Only") and, in particular, Anahí Berneri's *Un año sin amor*, based on the story of Pablo Pérez, to see intelligent and nonprejudicial representations.

17. I am aware that this reading develops a somewhat indirect aspect of the film, so I reproduce here part of Moira Soto's review, which does justice to the movie's central theme: "Neither *lesbian chic* nor paternalistic, thuggish condescension. Neither hypocritical voyeurism nor spying disguised as pedagogical or sociological dissemination. In these close encounters with the young women of the film's title, Santiago García, with a fine-tuned, empathetic attitude, deserves the trust that his brave lesbians offer to him in revealing themselves, from the personal—so linked to social rejection that denies them a visible, egalitarian place in the world—with moving sincerity" (2004).

18. Deleuze classifies frames as physical, geometric, or dynamic. In geometric framing, "there are many different frames in the frame…it is by this dovetailing of frames that the parts of the set or of the closed system are separated, but also converge and are reunited." The physical conception of the frame, in contrast, "produces imprecise sets" (1986a, 14).

19. *Rey muerto*, Martel's short film in *Historias breves*, already included "the people" through television and in the comments the parishioners make with respect to the famous incident when the journalist Silvia Fernández Barrio was doing a story on the attack on the Israeli embassy and a passer-by touched her bottom. The sarcastic comments of the parishioners (later the protagonists of a *machista* patriarchal drama) make clear the place of the popular in Martel's cinema and how the people, together with the media, have an impact on the construction of the feminine. It bears mentioning that in an unconventional way, this vulgar molestation of Fernández Barrio reappears in Jano's touching of Amalia in *La niña santa*.

20. This gaze can also be found in Martel's documentary on the Argentine writer Silvina Ocampo, based on a script by Adriana Mancini and Graciela Speranza, which constructs a story of her life around the figure of her maid.

21. Just so the reader does not think that the blind man riding a motorcycle is a religious miracle: he rides a two-seater, with his cousin at the front, pedaling.

22. The film's beginning is direct: a journalist from Channel 13 faces the camera and explains to viewers the nature of the report: "*According to tradition, the Virgin appeared to Gladys Motta on September 25, 1983.*" But just what is this tradition that is only fifteen years old and can call itself "tradition"? With the end of traditions, will we be condemned to live with paradoxically brief traditions projected into the future by television?

23. A similar opposition can be found in Sebastián Schindel, Fernando Molnar, and Nicolás Battle's *Rerum Novarum* (2001), which juxtaposes Villa Flandria films from the 1950s and 1960s with contemporary images of a textile factory in ruins. (The town was built around the Flandria textile factory, founded by the Belgian immigrant Julio Steverlinck, the model of a modern boss and progressive Catholic, who was inspired by the encyclical *Rerum Novarum*.) In the film we also see how the factory brought hospitals, schools, clubs, and a movie theater to the town. The story centers on a musical group (organized among the factory workers by Steverlinck in 1937) that continued to function after the factory's closure in 1996. The biographical sketches are more personal and affectionate and leave the sociological and political aside. Of course, the opposition between film and video can be a consequence of the era, but in both Bellande's film and *Rerum Novarum* the appearance of celluloid as materiality is underlined.

24. Strangely enough, Bellande's second movie is an institutional documentary for Techint on the construction of a gas pipeline 731 kilometers in length. In the words of Gustavo Noriega, "the fantastic project of the gas pipeline has such characteristics, and this is the focus that Bellande privileges: to show a unique combination of a group physical effort and engineering genius," a "fascinating exaltation of human effort and its half-truths" (2005, 27).

25. Even a Disney-Pixar film for children has detected this change: in *Monsters, Inc.* the monsters work on a Fordist assembly line, but their raw material is children's fear, from which they extract energy for their city.

26. Séptimo Regimiento actually existed, and el Rulo was the group's bassist.

27. The evocation of the past is exclusively oral. At the barbeque that el Rulo throws with Adriana, his friends get together to look at photographs (never

shown), sing Manal songs, and recall Séptimo Regimiento. This despite the fact that Trapero could have incorporated the hit song, which appears in Fernando Ayala's *El professor patagónico* (1970, "The Patagonian Professor.") El Rulo finally returns to Patagonia (to Comodoro Rivadavia), not as a musician but as a worker.

28. Central de Trabajadores de la Argentina, one of the most progressive unions that opposed the Menem government during the 1990s.

29. Politics no longer pursues the goal of changing the status of labor; rather it aims to conserve or recover it. This nostalgia for the monuments of labor (the admiration that large, empty factories inspire) is a theme not only of narrative documentaries such as *Rerum Novarum* but also of works of political activism, such as Carlos Mamud, Patricia Digilio, and Nora Gilges' *Laburantes (Crónicas del trabajo recuperado)* (2003) ("Workers [Tales of Recovered Work]"), which speaks of the cooperatives that unemployed workers form in their places of work.

30. Detail shots of machines and of people trying to fix them are a hallmark of Trapero's films: Zapa making a key, the protagonist of *Familia rodante* fixing the engine of his mobile home. They show his love for machines and for the capacity of human labor to make them operate.

31. According to Eduardo Russo, video and light equipment rendered the great cranes of classic film obsolete. Russo also says that "this eccentric support would become one of the most archetypical elements of studio filming"; he writes of "totemic figures" and "coveted fetishes of Hollywood's Golden Age" (1998, 122).

32. This scene was undoubtedly filmed at the Maxi movie theater in Buenos Aires on 9 de Julio Avenue, where one can see the projector and the projectionist through a huge window.

33. Both Rafael Filipelli (1999) and Domin Choi (n.d.) point out the organic nature of *Mala época* and the procedures and intersections that transform it from a collection of shorts into a feature film.

34. Earlier, Omar had written in his notebook, "Today it seems that...." The subsequent shot does not allow us to find out how the sentence ends.

35. Adrián Gorelik (1999; also in Birgin and Trímboli 2003) has written two excellent analyses of politics in this movie based on its representations of urban space: "It is this definitive failure of politics as an instrument of change and of society as its actor that I think should be seen as the basis of these new representations of the city" (1999, 31).

36. In addition to the work of Sander Gilman, Jesús Martín-Barbero's studies and Alejandro Grimson's various works on the Bolivian community in Buenos Aires (2000) are of great interest. In collaboration with Sergio Wolf, Grimson made a documentary on the Bolivian community in this city. On the problem of stereotypes in film, especially peripheral film, see Ella Shohat and Robert Stam's panorama: "1. Revealing oppressive patterns of prejudice in what might at first glance have seemed random and inchoate phenomena; 2. Highlighting the psychic devastation inflicted by systematically negative portrayals on those groups assaulted by them, whether through the internalization of the stereotypes themselves or through the negative effects of

their dissemination; and 3. Signaling the social functionality of stereotypes, demonstrating that they are not an error of perception but rather a form of social control, intended as what Alice Walker calls 'prisons of image' " (1994, 198).

37. These power relations are not necessarily ones of domination. Subaltern groups can also use these stereotypes, as in George Grosz's illustrations of obese German fat cats wearing frock coats and top hats.

38. Few films have continued the theme of immigrants in Argentina inaugurated by Caetano. One of the exceptions is Diego Gachassin's *Vladimir en Buenos Aires* (2002), which tells the story of a Russian immigrant. Gachassin has continued with this theme in his second feature-length film, *Habitación disponible* (2005, "Room Available"), co-directed with Eva Poncet and Marcelo Burd.

39. There is one character who never appears and who has been successful: "el Turco" ("the Turk," the Argentine term for people of Middle Eastern descent). Is the character of the *turco* a stereotyped figure, or does he correspond in some way to a social observation? In *Bolivia*, the *turco* is the one who escaped his class and who is doing well, because the principal talent of *turcos* is that they know how to do business, and their basic attribute in the social imaginary is a lack of morals. This combination is very useful in times of crisis. Thus, in Rodolfo Enrique Fogwill's novel *Los pichiciegos* (translated in 2007 as *Malvinas Requiem: Visions of an Underground War*), the *turco* organizes the subsistence economy of the troops. Similarly, the author Jorge Asís has projected this figure onto himself and onto his literature. All of this indicates that the strength of stereotypes does not lie in their truth, although they can simplify and condense little pieces of reality that encourage false categories in the social imagination. One *turco* may be a wise guy, but this says nothing about the nature of *turcos* (a racial or national category that is, in addition, quite vague).

40. The title of this section, "The Failure to Adjust," is a translation of *Señal de desajuste*. It is a play on the term *señal de ajuste*, the bars that appear on the screen in order to adjust the colors of a television set. [Translator's note.]

41. The elided subject of "they're terrible" refers to another stereotype: *yanquis*, or people from the United States.

42. On this relationship between stereotype and experience, see Jesús Martín-Barbero's analysis (1993, 128ff), based on Richard Hoggart's arguments in *The Uses of Literacy*.

43. This is why I think it was a good decision to include Caetano's film in Claudia Torre and Álvaro Fernández Bravo's introductory book on college writing (2003).

44. At any rate, the fact that a Bolivian was sleeping in a bar would not make the statement that Bolivians are good-for-nothing true. The stereotype sees the particular as being based on a general category (nation, race, sex, class) that supposedly explains it.

45. These gazes sanction an entire logic of bodies based on the small territories that each character occupies in the bar: Freddy at the grill, the taxi drivers in the space of the customers, Enrique behind the cash register. Each time

Freddy leaves the territory of the grill (where, without papers, he finds the precarious protection of a job), the gazes mark that he has just crossed a border. The city is also a hostile space, and Freddy finds relief only in the spaces of entertainment of the Bolivian community, where people fight, but not over racial or national issues. Freddy dies at the limit between the bar that provided him with a job and the city that wants to expel him.

46. In addition to its potential physical effect, the insult, in acts of discrimination, strips the target of his or her rights.

47. This is seen also in his final speech, where el Oso defends Héctor (to whom the boss denies work because he is gay) despite the fact that his homosexuality was the source of discrimination in other scenes. On top of this sexual discrimination, another form is traced: the scorn directed at those Argentines who are not from Buenos Aires, like Héctor, who is from the province of Córdoba.

48. Christian Gundermann (2005), in his work on desire in recent Argentine film, says of *Bolivia:* "One of the last 'postcards' is the sign 'Grill Cook Wanted,' a shot that obviously explains retrospectively the dialogue between the men's voices, but that also takes on a special significance at the end of the film when the bar's owner again hangs up the same sign in the door after Freddy's death (murdered by a xenophobe whom the bar owner had told him to kick out because of his drunkenness). This shot of the sign symbolizes all the structural brutality of an environment in which not only is the immigrant worker replaceable, but his death (which occurred while he was following an order) is a non-event, one that cannot be elaborated."

49. As cited in Sigfried Kracauer's *Orpheus in Paris (Offenbach and the Paris of His Time)* (1938).

50. See my article "Maravillosa melancholia (sobre *Cazadores de utopías* de David Blaustein)" ("Marvelous Melancholy [On David Blaustein's *Cazadores de utopias*]"), in Sartora and Rival (2007).

51. The *montoneros* were a left-wing armed militant group of Peronist origins that operated in the 1970s. They were persecuted by the military dictatorship that came to power in 1978. [Translator's note.]

52. Almost all of the testimonies in Andrés Habegger's *(h) historias cotidianas* (2001, "Stories of Daily Life") make reference to the explanations given to children about the fate of their parents. In Albertina Carri's case, as she states in her movie, when she was told at the age of twelve what had happened, "she didn't understand anything."

53. Of these three movies, only *(h) historias cotidianas* is explicitly linked to an institution, HIJOS (Hijos por la Igualdad y la Justicia contra el Olvido y el Silencio; "Children for Equality and Justice against Forgetting and Silence"), a group that since 1996 has used political and artistic acts to activate memory and condemn the impunity of those involved in the last dictatorship. Albertina Carri was never part of this group, and María Inés Roqué has continued to live in Mexico, where her mother and brother were also exiled. It was there that Roqué made her film, with support from the CONACULTA (Centro de Capacitación Cinematográfica; "Center for Cinematographic Funding"), part of the Fondo Nacional Para la Cultura y las Artes de México. Blaustein made his film in Argentina, with his own production company.

54. I am citing Oscar Espinosa's reading, presented in the seminar on cinematic form at the UBA.

55. Aumont speaks of "visual touch" and shows how the haptic returns periodically in the very optical medium of cinema (1997, 111–13). For an insightful review, see Antonia Lant's "Haptical cinema" (1995), a critique of Alois Riegl and Noël Burch.

56. In the case of *Los rubios*, we should also speak of a failure of oral–auditory representation, since the movie proposes that we not listen to *what those who are giving testimony want to say* (or what they think they are saying) but rather practice listening to the gaps, lapses, spontaneities. This explains Carri's critique in the film for the ex-activists' testimonies having "everything neatly set up" (*todo armadito*).

57. This is why it is not a coincidence that Carri's subsequent project has nothing to do with the theme of *Los rubios*.

58. By "heroism" I refer both to the individual bravery of these activists and to the epic context that makes these heroic acts possible. Of course, it is unnecessary to deny the heroic stature of these men and women from the past to recover the present; what I object to is this recovery as a denigration of the present.

59. Almost all political documentaries fall into this trap of naturalization, but few in such a systematic and monotonous way as Blaustein's *Cazadores de utopias*. For an analysis of the testimony of the mother through the lens of gender, see Amado (2004, 64–5).

60. They are Cristian Czainik (the son of Antonio Czainik, disappeared in August 1977), Ursula Méndez (the daughter of Silvia Gallina, disappeared in November 1976), Florencia Gemetro (the daughter of José María Gemetro, disappeared in February 1977), Claudio Novoa (the son of Gastón Gonçalvez, murdered in 1976), Martín Mórtola Oesterheld (the son of Raúl Mórtola and Estela Oesterheld, murdered in December 1977, and grandson of the cartoonist Héctor Oesterheld), and Victoria Ginzberg (daughter of Mario Ginzberg and Irene Bruchstein, disappeared in March 1977).

61. María Laura Guembe offers a different interpretation in a paper that she wrote for the seminar on cinematic form at the UBA: "He does not elude the first person but rather cedes to it and multiplies it in order to respond to those questions that mobilize his own search," adding about the director's research process: "Norberto Habegger was kidnapped in Brazil while returning from one of his trips. Andrés and his mother confirmed the news a week after it occurred. More than twenty years later, Andrés began a detailed investigation into his father's story, moved—as we read in the Historias Orales de la Asociación Civil Memoria Abierta ["Oral Histories of the Civil Association of Open Memory"]—by 'a pressing need to be able to bury him, in the good sense of the word.' He wanted to be linked to his father's history with greater autonomy: 'to detach myself a bit from the version that my mother had always given me of him.... I no longer wanted to know anything about his activism. I wanted to know in reality who he was in order to know who I was.'" Andrés Habegger's history can be read at www.memoriaabierta.com.ar.

62. Although they may appear to be mixing oil and water, these types of combinations have been very fruitful for directors of the new Argentine

Cinema, who have tried to combine in their own way and in the audiovisual context of the 1990s what Serge Daney has called "film's two legs": avant-garde and mainstream film. With respect to *Los guantes mágicos*, for example, Martín Rejtman has spoken of a combination of Robert Bresson's *Balthazar* (1966) and John Carpenter's *Christine* (1983) (Pauls 2004).

63. One of the witnesses refers to Albertina's mother as "Rasputin," a rather strange label for someone whose primary goal in life was to foment the revolution.

64. In fact, Martín Kohan speaks of "total impassiveness [*indolencia*]" with respect to Carri (2004a, 27). Etymologically, *indolencia* is "the absence of pain" (*dolor*) and, by extension, "the lack of mourning." Mourning and pain (*duelo* and *dolor*) have the same root. Emilio Bernini speaks, in contrast, of a "*lack of interest* in accessing the familial and public past" (2004, 46, my emphasis). Now, not even in film do we need to believe everything we see. Are these writers not able to perceive, beyond the visual, the waves of pain that rock the director when she opens her car window or when she witnesses the testimony of the woman who turned her father in? To evaluate its implications, Martín Kohan's essay should be related to his novel *Dos veces junio* (2002, "June, Twice"), one of the most interesting written narratives on the dictatorship years.

65. The term *campito* suggests a child's view of a place of vacation and, simultaneously, the concentration camps (*campos*) where political prisoners were detained during the military dictatorship. This play between *campito* (the diminutive of countryside) and *campo* is lost in English. [Translator's note.]

66. A seminal multimedia artistic project/event, executed in the city of Rosario in 1968, which linked avant-garde practices to leftist protest. [Translator's note.]

67. In relation to the Malvinas/Falkland Islands war, for example, Federico Moura's group composed the song "El banquete" ("The Banquet"), which has the following lyrics: "They've sacrificed young calves/to prepare an official dinner/they've authorized a ton of money/but they're promising a masterly menu/The chefs are famous/they're going to offer us the latest recipes./The stew seems overdone/someone told me it's from the day before yesterday." The Moura brothers, often accused of frivolity, knew very well what repression was, as they had a brother who had been disappeared. In its time, Virus did what Carri does in her film: it opened a window to let in some fresh air.

68. When Carri affirms, with a photograph of a slaughterhouse, "I don't like dead cows; I like beautiful architecture," a complex relationship between politics and aesthetics begins to be sketched out. This image leads her to the sense that the photographer was tortured, which turns out to be the case. In her interview, the photographer compares the camera to the electric prod used by the dictatorship in torture sessions, and Carri says, "It seems like I'm missing a chapter in art history." Politics and art mutually condition each other in a game of associations that goes beyond the will, connecting the sinister to the frivolous, and form with suffering. These two photographs (of the beautiful architecture and of the dead cow) are the two small windows of the aesthetic from which Carri spies on politics.

69. Film, however, has dedicated itself with great intensity to the study of the relationship between childhood and politics, from the famous cases of neorrealism (Vittorio de Sica's *The Bicycle Thief,* Rossellini's *Alemania ano cero* ["Germany Year Zero"] and *The Greatest Love* [1951]) to various postwar films, such as René Clément's *Forbidden Games* (1952). At any rate, children are *inside* of politics as victims (or they testify to something that they cannot endure or understand, or they are used by those in power). In Latin American cinema, the list of films condemning the treatment of children is extensive.

70. One of the strangest examples is a television commercial featuring a boy who wants to take his dog on vacation and who sings an ode to the military. The song, with new lyrics, became a frequent presence at mobilizations against the dictatorship, as well as at soccer matches.

71. In fact, the nonexpiring nature of these crimes has meant that nearly all of the hierarchy of the military dictatorship currently find themselves under house arrest.

72. Among the many books that focus on these subjects, Juan Gelman and Mara La Madrid's *Ni el flaco perdón de Dios* (1997) is indispensable. With respect exclusively to activist organizations, Cristina Zuker's *El tren de la Victoria: una saga familiar* (2003, "Victory Train: A Family Saga") contains chilling cases.

73. The theory of the *foco,* per Ernesto "Che" Guevara, which stated that one little fire is enough to make the whole country burn. [Translator's note.]

74. This is not the case with all forms of urban guerrilla organization. In Brazil, for example, entering into an organization meant cutting family ties. At any rate, in the case of Argentina we need to keep in mind the Peronist victory of 1973 and the fact that many activists in armed organizations were publicly known. There is a fair consensus that the *montoneros'* shift to secrecy in 1975 was a mistake, as it exposed many activists to a precarious situation.

75. This danger is not comparable, of course, to the repression that would come with the dictatorship, when the military attacked those who were at risk and those who were not and, under no circumstances, applied the law. One of the great difficulties involved in reflecting on the period before the military coup of March 1976 is this *hiatus,* which makes it impossible to hypothesize relationships of cause and effect.

76. Several films of the 1990s deal with the relationship between childhood and dictatorship. Some were institutional documentaries of denunciation, such as David Blaustein's *Botín de guerra* (2000, "Spoils of War"), on the work of the Abuelas de la Plaza de Mayo (Grandmothers of the Plaza de Mayo) to recover children born in captivity during the dictatorship. Others deal with the perceptions that a child could have of state terrorism after his or her family has been torn apart. Marcelo Piñeyro's fictional film *Kamchatka* (2003) turns, like *Los rubios,* to the projection that a child makes onto his games (in this case, a game of military strategy) owing to situations that overwhelm him that he cannot explain.

77. On the other hand, we must not forget that the majority of children whose parents were disappeared learned of their fate in a fragmentary

way. *(h) historias cotidianas*, for example, tells how one daughter of the disappeared discovered her situation in a chance conversation with the woman who took care of her. At any rate, I would see the testimony collected by Gelman and La Madrid as an aberrant effect of state terrorism rather than as a political act.

78. Santiago Girald, the assistant director of *Los rubios*, and an actor in the film, told me that parental authorization is required to include a child; thus, in this case, Carri had no choice. I am interested in highlighting the way she incorporates this refusal to include her nephew's testimony into the film.

79. "The country is the space of fantasy or where my memory begins," the voice-over of the director states.

80. Interestingly enough, one of the first scenes, of cars on the street, is shot from above in such a way that they seem miniature.

81. Based on a comic, this movie became one of the most important cult films of the twentieth century, paving the way for all sorts of citations and adaptations, from mass film culture (Jim Sharman's *The Rocky Horror Picture Show*, Tim Burton's *Mars Attacks!*), to rock (the album cover of Ringo Starr's *Goodnight Vienna*, the world of David Bowie), and others. *Los rubios* adds itself to this long line of memorabilia. In the chapter that she compiles for *Historias de Argentina en Vivo* (2001, "Stories of Argentina, Live"), Carri refers to these science fiction films from the 1950s in her discussion of the musical invasion of "alternative" rockers (Leo García, María Gabriela Epumer, Rosario Bléfari, Richard Coleman, Francisco Bochatón).

82. I do not believe *Los rubios* shows that the past cannot necessarily be constructed, but rather something more interesting: that if we refuse the commonplaces constructed about this era, its reconstruction becomes more difficult.

83. This speech is accompanied by playmobiles that take on different outfits granted to them by the gaze of others. One of *Los rubios*' themes is precisely this: Why do they always see me as a daughter?

84. This reading is freely inspired by Femenías (2003, 170ff).

85. Even very personal movies such as *Papá Iván* end up being secondary to chronology, as though the time of memory were linear.

86. *Los tres berretines* was made by Lumiton studios, and Enrique T. Susini is listed as its director, although various testimonies suggest that the direction was in fact shared by members of the film crew.

87. The essay was originally published in the journal *Sur* (Number 4, 1931) and was included in the first edition of Borges' collection of essays *Discusión* (1932). Borges eliminated the essay from later editions (*Borges en Sur* 1999, 119). An incisive reading of the text can be found in Daniel Balderston's "La dialéctica fecal: el pánico homosexual y el origen de la escritura en Borges" ("Fecal Dialectics: Homosexual Panic and the Origin of Writing in Borges"), in his *El deseo, enorme cicatriz luminosa (Ensayos sobre homosexualidades latinoamericanas)* ("Desire, enormous, luminous scar [Essays on Latin American Homosexualities]," 2004).

88. The term *autofiction*, coined by Serge Doubrovsky, refers to the literary genre that links two types of narrative that are a priori contradictory: a

story, such as autobiography, based in the identity between author, narrator, and character, and the use of fiction, originating in the genre of the novel, which renders any autobiographical pact impossible. Pablo Peréz's novel was published by Perfil in 1998 with the title *Un año sin amor (Diario del Sida)* ("A Year without Love [An AIDS Diary]"). An excellent reading of the book can be found on Daniel Link's blog, "Enfermedad y cultura: política del monstruo" ("Illness and Culture: Politics of the Monster"), http://linkillo. blogspot.com.

89. On this characteristic, specific to the process of illness, see Susan Sontag's *Illness As Metaphor: and, AIDS and Its Metaphors* (1990).

90. See *Sacher-Masoch y Sade* (1969, 107), translated into English as *Sacher-Masoch: An Interpretation*. I am using Deleuze's analyses only partially, as he refers to Sacher-Masoch's novels and to the clinical diagnosis of masochism in a situation that applies only partially to sadomasochistic practices. (In fact, one of his goals is to deconstruct Freud's linking of Sade and Sacher-Masoch, who for him represent different, and even opposing, symptoms.)

91. The lack of love is the condition necessary for the diary to continue: "Should I fall in love, I would not be able to write this diary anymore."

92. The term is used intentionally: Pablo Peréz's book *El mendigo chupapijas* ("The Beggar Who Sucks Cock"), in fact, takes place in these movie theaters. Here, oral sex is presented as the beggar's only activity and source of income. Originally self-published, the book was edited and released by Mansalva in 2006.

93. For a playful and meticulous appraisal of the role that S/M practices played in Foucault's work, see James Miller's *The Passion of Michel Foucault*, where he employ the expression "strategic relation" (1993, 263).

94. Certain characters in "Titans in the Ring," such as Mr. Moto or Mercenario Joe, would not be out of place in a leather bar.

95. Foucault's opinions were expressed in interviews that he gave to gay magazines after his stay in San Francisco as visiting professor at the University of California–Berkeley in 1975. These texts were included in *Dits et ecrits* (Gallimard; partially excerpted in English in *The Essential Works of Michel Foucault, 1954–1984*). "Desexualization" does not mean that there is no sex but that the discourse of sex articulated around genitality is subverted. As Foucault says in an interview cited by Miller, one should aim, in the new feminist and gay social movements, not at "liberation" of "sex-desire" but "at a general economy of pleasure not based on sexual norms" (1993, 273).

96. In effect, this scene consists of a meeting of sadomasochists that the cameras record without intervening or being seen by the participants. On the filming of this scene, see Emilio Bernini, Silvia Schwarzböck, and Daniel Goggi's interview with Anahí Berneri, Santiago García, and Pablo Pérez in the journal *Kilómetro 111* (2007).

97. See Michele Marzano (2006, 235), and the bibliography therein; see also the bibliography in Linden et al. (1982).

98. The casting call: Are they gay? Do they practice S/M? The answer is irrelevant.

99. In an interview he gave in the 1970s, Foucault distances himself from Sade—to whom he had referred on numerous occasions—calling him a "sergeant of sex."

100. The author plays here with the perspectival term from the visual arts and the idea of *fuga*, of escape (as in *línea de fuga*, "line of flight"). [Translator's note.]

101. In the interview in *Kilómetro 111*, Berneri says: "I came to the gay world with an exterior gaze....I happened to find a gaze that was exterior to a world that I don't belong to, where I'm never going to belong. In a sense, sexual orientation allowed me, in clubs or in certain places, to look at a distant world, where I'm invisible." Santiago García makes a similar remark in the same interview, with respect to his film *Lesbianas de Buenos Aires:* "In my case, I'm not part of the lesbian community, clearly. What's more, I can't be a part of that community, notwithstanding the fact that a militant Mexican activist (a woman) once characterized me as *lesbiano* [that is, as a male lesbian], authorizing that name for me." See Berneri, García, and Pérez (2007).

102. One scene involving a gay man who responds to Pablo's announcement could be considered a reference to a stereotyped character. However, this scene was cut from the film and is available only as an "extra" on the DVD version.

103. We cannot say that the film has predecessors in Argentine cinema. If I were forced to give examples of movies that it might resemble, I would name Hugo del Carril's *La Quintrala* (1955) and Leopoldo Torre Nilsson's *La casa del ángel* (1976, "The House of the Angel"). In both of these films there is a relationship between pleasure and self-dissolution.

Appendix 1: The World of Cinema in Argentina

1. The prize for most creative adaptation undoubtedly goes to the evangelical church set up on Rivadavia Avenue in the old General Roca movie theater. As the parishioners wanted to recycle the marquee and to save on signage (which is very expensive), they used the neon from the former theater and transformed it for its new function. Now, you can read "Jesuscristo es la Roca" ("Jesus Christ Is the Rock").

2. For many years, Lavalle was "the street of the movies," and it even had a certain touristy charm. There were more than three theaters per block along the stretch that extended from 9 de Julio Avenue to Florida Street. Certain theaters became mythic for different generations: the best theater in Argentina, the theater where cult films were shown that then became a site of pornographic films and gay adventures, the theaters in which various movies could be seen one right after the other, the theater in which you could experience 3D film, and so on.

3. By "administrators of the image" I mean all of those workers linked to the creation of audiovisual products, whether for television, film, advertisement, computers, or the like.

4. Because in the United States actors have become the most important investment, given that their presence guarantees a film's success, it is common for independent filmmakers to take scripts to their agents to tempt them, ensure their participation, and, as a consequence, guarantee the financing of their films.

5. In the words of Quentin Tarantino, the 1990s were "the beginning of the big independent American film wave," in which Miramax played an important role.

6. All of these directors, with the exception of Warhol and Waters, have had retrospectives in recent years: Anger at Mar del Plata, and Casavettes, Mekas, and Frank at the BAFICI.

7. Before the 1994 reform, the INCAA was called the Institution Nacional de Cinematografía (National Institute of Cinematography). The same law establishes a division between movies recognized by the institute ("national movies," according to the law) and those made in Argentina but outside of the institute's aegis ("Argentine movies"). The latter, for example, do not receive the benefits of the screen quota or of subsidies. For a detailed commentary on Law 17741, see Raffo 2003.

8. Some examples: Caetano's *Bolivia* began as an independent film (Caetano used some rolls that he had gotten ahold of); it later obtained Lita Stantic's support and, ultimately, was sponsored by the INCAA, a source of funding that was not yet established when Caetano began filming. Lerman's *Tan de repente* has a first section that formed part of a short the director made at film school. Later, it was produced by Lita Stantic and supported by the INCAA. Luis Ortega started filming *Caja negra* once it had been accepted into the official competition of the Mar del Plata Film Festival.

9. See the following anecdote that Rejtman recounts in an interview with Pablo Udenio and Hernán Guerschuny (1996):

—How did you get Alejandro Agresti interested in the movie?
—I sent him the script. And he was a big help in making the movie.
Regardless of the state of our relationship today, a large part of the movie was possible because Alejandro promised to put in a lot of things that he put in. In this sense I am completely grateful; it's one of the factors that made the movie possible. Not the only one, but one of them. Plus, I went to Europe with the intention of getting money for the film. I sent Agresti the screenplay from Paris. At the same time, I ran into [filmmaker and author] Edgardo Cozarinsky, who told me, "Go to see Marcos Müller in the Netherlands; he's the director of the Rotterdam festival. There's the Hubert Bals Fund there, they might have some cash for you." Then he read it and confirmed it. Within a week he gave me fifteen thousand dollars. It was really strange. Certain things just happen.

10. The "continuity average" is the number of spectators required for a movie to remain in theaters. To regulate this, "different percentages were established for the size of the theater, time of year, and number of copies of the film" (Seivach and Perelman 2004, 52). This regulation could protect films, such as *Los guantes mágicos* or *La niña santa*, that had an acceptable audience but were displaced by the productions of large distributors with greater market impact.

11. Mariano Llinás' belligerent attitude toward the INCAA and other aspects of the film world can be followed in the articles that he has written for the

film magazine *El amante cine:* "In general terms, [the INCAA] defends the strongest, those directors and producers who should have left the shelter of the state decades ago to prove that their abilities were at the level of their airs; and ignores or obstructs the path of the weakest, the youngest, the most daring, the best" (2004, 48).

12. See their website, www.fatam.com.ar. The Muestra Nacional de Cine con Vecinos (National Exhibition of Film with Neighbors) debuted in 2004, with a second version in Saladillo in October 2005.

13. See Chapter 1, note 17.

14. Yago Blass was a successful radio and theater actor who never obtained a similar level of recognition in movies, where he embarked upon independent and experimental productions that linked him more to Ed Wood than to the avant-garde. Gregorio Anchou describes one of Blass' experiments thus: "[I]n spite of the negligent impact of his return to the big screen, he tried yet again with one of the worst movies in the history of Argentine film, *Una mujer diferente* (1956, *A Different Woman*), a Molgar production (a company whose components are unknown to us), in which he tried to put into practice, with hilarious results, the 'sequence shot per act' that Alfred Hitchcock had realized in *Rope*" ("Veinticinco años de producción independiente: las fronteras ignoradas" ["Twenty-Five Years of Independent Production: Unknown Frontiers"] in España 2000).

15. I should point out that the law not only determines benefits but also indicates responsibilities, above all with respect to labor. Independent Argentine film has tended to get around, to the extent that it is possible, labor obligations imposed by the law, because their fulfillment would not allow movies to get made. It would be necessary to study in detail whether, with the benefits that the law establishes, this tendency has been reversed in recent years.

16. In addition to the APIMA, the following are recognized associations of producers: Asociación General de Productores (General Association of Producers, AGP), Asociación de Productores y Realizadores Independientes (Association of Independent Producers and Filmmakers, APRI), Asociación Productores de Cine y Medios Audiovisuales (Association of Film and Audiovisual Media Producers, APROCINEMA), and Asociación de Realizadores y Productores de Artes Audiovisuales (Association of Filmmakers and Producers of Audiovisual Arts, APROAT).

17. The following figures show the composition of the INCAA's Fondo de Fomento Cinematográfico (Fund for Cinematographic Promotion) from 1999 to 2002:

Year	Tickets sold	Commercial videos	Television
1999	$15,169,978	$4,711,435	$31,024,827
2000	$16,495,345	$3,617,863	$29,294,353
2001	$13,291,360	$4,254,010	$28,210,354
2002	$11,624,933	$3,743,000	$25,659,305

As can be observed immediately, television has been the principal source of the institute's revenue. (*Source:* CEDEM 2004, Secretaria de Desarrollo Económico, GCBA, in the INCAA's database.)

18. Alejandro Agresti also produced *Rapado* and was a reference point for the new generations until 1998, when he came out in defense, in his typically spectacular fashion, of the management of Julio Mahárbiz at a point when the *ley de cine* was being blocked. Gustavo Noriega wrote in a note for the film magazine *El amante cine:* "This foul-mouthed and haughty guy is no longer the mythic figure in exile who filled the cafés of Buenos Aires with reproaches and reprimands, while placing his bets on the out-dated and irrelevant Mahárbiz and Cavallo (Minister of Economics under Menem). He will continue to be the director of *Boda secreta* and *El acto en cuestión*, so this misstep can be resolved in his favor as long as he goes back to filming with that earlier rigor and magic" (2001).

19. One of the most perverse facts in the history of Argentine cinema is that some directors have made several movies without critical or commercial success while others have achieved continuity only with great difficulty. This is manifest in the undeserved failure of almost all of the generation of the 1960s (Rodolfo Kuhn, David José Kohon, Lautaro Murúa) and of various filmmakers in recent decades.

20. In the words of Jorge Telerman, vice-chief of the government of the city of Buenos Aires, "[I]n order to attend to the economic dimension of culture, the Subsecretary of Administration and Culture Industries was created, forging an important alliance with the Secretariat of Economic Development, in order to incorporate culture industries into the records and indicators of the City's economic activity" (www.campus-oei.org/pensariberoamerica).

21. In the 1950s, film expanded its repertoire, as manifested in the recognition by metropolitan centers (basically European) of other cinematographies. These are the years of the consecration of Bergman, Mizoguchi, Kurosawa, and Savajit Ray.

22. The one-to-one dollar/peso exchange rate during the 1990s allowed a broad swath of the Argentine middle class to travel abroad. [Translator's note.]

23. There are only seven "A" festivals in the world; the most important are Cannes, Berlin, and San Sebastián. The Mar del Plata festival does not have the continuity, history, or prestige of its competitors that would tempt directors to premiere their movies there. In addition, the festival occurs at a difficult time of year, between Berlin and Cannes.

24. At the Sixteenth Mar del Plata festival, directed by Claudio España and with Miguel Onaindia at the head of the INCAA, the artistic quality improved considerably, but maintaining that quality was impossible owing to the political events that led to the fall of de la Rúa's government in 2001. After the crisis that directly affected the seventeenth festival, its direction fell to filmmaker Miguel Pereira, the organizer of the most recent festivals, who managed to establish a group of program organizers (many of whom had already collaborated with Claudio España) who made the 2005 festival one of the best in recent times. Despite these changes and debacles, we should point out the continuity of the cycle "La mujer y el cine" ("Women and Film"), directed by Marta Bianchi, created when the festival started up again.

25. Recent facts (the lack of governmental financing of recent BAFICIs and the expulsion of Quintín as director) lead us to think, however, that government employees are unaware of the function of festivals. We encounter once again the squandering of resources and the lack of a coherent policy with respect to culture.
26. According to the university's own figures, in 1991 there were fewer than 1,000 students and in 2003 there were almost 12,000.
27. Martín Mainoli presented a documentary film, *La filia*, on Edgardo Chibán, who passed away in 2000, at the 2006 BAFICI. Chibán's influence was fundamental in *La ciénaga*, as Lucrecia Martel has pointed out several times.
28. There is a debate over when the first Mar del Plata festival took place. When Julio Marhábiz started the festival up again in 1996, he deemed the 1954 screening the first. However, 1954's was not a competitive festival, despite the presence of important figures—Errol Flynn, who spent all of his money at the casino; Gina Lollobrigida, who, according to the anti-Peronists, walked around naked with Perón at the presidential palace; Jeanne Moreau; and Trevor Howard. Edward G. Robinson withdrew from the event when he realized that it was a political move on Perón's part in the face of the production problems that Argentine cinema was facing. The first Mar del Plata International Film Festival took place in 1959 and was supported by the Asociación de Cronistas Cinematográficos (Association of Cinematographic Journalists); it would not have seen itself as a continuation of the screening during Perón's second presidency.
29. It is necessary to note the important role that movie clubs played during the last dictatorship, especially the Cine-Club Núcleo (Nucleus Movie Club) led by Salvador Samaritano, where cinephiles could see movies that did not reach commercial movie theaters. Movie clubs and film festivals were also important because of the possibility they offered of seeing historic or otherwise inaccessible movies, as at the seminal Sala Lugones del Teatro General San Martín, directed by the film critic for the newspaper *Página/12*, Luciano Monteagudo. During the 1980s, the end of censorship and the arrival of video diminished the importance of these clubs.

Appendix 2: The Policy of Actors

1. The movie is dedicated to Facundo Luengo, an actor with an astonishing and mysterious face, who died in an accident after filming; he was only a little over twenty years old.
2. In fact, Alonso's most recent project takes this idea of adventure to its extreme: *Liverpool* takes place in Antarctica.
3. Luis Margani's body acquires operations that are narrative (he is not allowed to work because the "ART [Aseguradora de Riegos de Trabajo; work-related insurance] doesn't protect" him), temporal (he is no longer like he used to be; he's "sixty pounds over weight"), and aesthetic (he is not attractive in conventional terms, yet he is the star of the film).
4. Albertina Carri presents a curious case in her choice of an actress to represent the reconstruction of her past. In this film, acting is precisely the social

role that provides people with identity through the gaze of others. Carri places this intense burden of the identitarian demand upon the actress and appears herself as a nonactor in the film, refusing to play this role—this part—assigned to her.

Appendix 3: Argentine Films That Premiered between 1997 and Mid-2005

This appendix covers the period from 1997 (the year in which *Pizza, birra, faso* premiered at the Mar del Plata Film Festival) to mid-2005, when I finished writing the text. It could not have been produced without the valuable statistics compiled by various film scholars: Raúl Manrupe and Alejandra Portela's (2004) *Un diccionario del films argentinos II (1996–2002)*, Diego Trerotola's personal database, and the database at cinenacional.com, directed and founded by Diego Papic and Pablo Wittner. (I should point out that despite the usefulness of cinenacional.com, its lists are compiled not according to film titles but through the suggestions of members of the cast/crew.) I indicate *operas primas* with an asterisk (*). In the case of works executed as collaborations, an asterisk is present if this is the first film of all of the filmmakers; otherwise, an asterisk is placed next to the name of those filmmakers for whom this is their first film.

Epilogue to the 2011 Edition

1. I would particularly like to thank Agustín Campero who gave me access to many of the films discussed in this epilogue. I would also like to thank Sergio Wolf, who offered guidance for my research on the cultural panorama of the past few years and offered me some tips for analysis, such as shift in production companies.

2. Joanna Page: *Crisis and Capitalism in Contemporary Argentine Cinema* (Durham and London, Duke University Press, 2009); Ana Amado: *La imagen justa. Cine argentino y política 1980–2007* (Buenos Aires, Colihue, 2009); Agustín Campero: *Nuevo cine argentino: de Rapado a Historias extraordinarias* (General Sarmiento, IDH-UNGS—Biblioteca Nacional, 2009). In the 2009 Buenos Aires Book Fair (Feria del Libro), I had the opportunity to present Ana Amado's book; my review of Joanna Page's book can be found in the journal *A Contracorriente* (http://www.ncsu.edu/project/acontracorriente/).

3. In light of the fact that the first thesis specifically devoted to film at the University of Buenos Aires was only defended in 2005, the number defended recently is relatively high. I helped or was in dialogue with the following writers of film theses, among others: Hernán Sassi, Esteban Dipaola, Enrique Oyhandi, Malena Verardi.

4. I have tried not to repeat here what appears in my previously published essays, including the following: *Estudio crítico sobre* El bonaerense [Critical Study of *El bonaerense*] (colección Nuevo Cine Argentino, Buenos Aires,

Picnic, 2008); "Con el cuerpo en el laberinto: sobre *M* de Nicolás Prividera" [With the Body in the Labyrinth: on Nicolás Privadera's *M*], in Josefina Sartora and Silvina Rival (eds.): *Imágenes de lo real (La representación de lo político en el documental argentino* [Images of the Real: The Representation of the Political in Argentine Documentary]), Buenos Aires, Libraria, 2007; "Maravillosa melancolía. *Cazadores de utopías*: una lectura desde el presente" [Marvelous Melancholy: *Cazadores de utopiás:* A Reading from the Present], in María José Moore and Paula Wolkowicz (eds.): *Cines al margen (Nuevos modos de representación en el cine argentino contemporáneo* [Cinemas at the Margins: New Modes of Representation in Contemporary Argentine Film]), Buenos Aires, Libraria, 2007; *Oriente grau zero:* Happy together *de Wong Kar Wai* (Río de Janeiro, Fórum de Ciência e Cultura/ UFRJ, 2009) [The East Degree Zero: Wong Kar Wai's *Happy Together*]; the Prologue to Ignacio Amatriain's *Una década de nuevo cine argentino (1995–2005). Industria, crítica, formación, estéticas de* [A Decade of New Argentine Film, 1995–2005: Industry, Criticism, Training, Aesthetics], *Buenos Aires, Ediciones Ciccus*, 2010; "Nuevos cines argentinos: el retorno de lo diferente" [New Argentine Cinemas: The Return of the Different] in the exhibition catalog, *Do novo ao novo Cinema Argentino: birra, crise e poesia* [From the New to the New Argentine Cinema: Beer, Crisis, and Poetry], São Paulo—Rio de Janeiro—Brasil, Centro Cultural Banco do Brasil, agosto de 2009; "Monobloc de Luis Ortega" in Marcelo Panozzo (coord.): *Bafici 10 años—Cine Argentino 99–08*, Buenos Aires, Bafici—Gobierno de la Ciudad de Buenos Aires, 2008; "Testimonio de una disolución. Sobre *Un año sin amor* de Anahí Berneri" [Testimony of a Dissolution: on Anahí Berneri's *A Year without Love*], in Adrián Melo (comp.): *Otras historias de amor (Gays, lesbianas y travestis en el cine argentino* [Other Love Stories: Gays, Lesbians, and Transvestites in Argentine Film]), Buenos Aires, ediciones Lea, 2008 (included in the first English edition of this book) and "New Argentine Cinema" en *ReVista (Harvard Review of Latin America)*, Volume VIII, number 3, fall 2009 / winter 2010 (with a translation by June Erlick).

5. These are: Pablo Trapero, Martín Rejtman, Juan Villegas, Lisandro Alonso, Lucrecia Martel, Albertina Carri, Federico León, and Adrián Caetano

6. These include Santiago Loza, Alejo Moguillansky, Mariano Llinás, Matías Piñeiro, Gonzalo Castro and Cecilia Murga.

7. See Atilio Roque González's essay, "Buen cine en Buenos Aires. Exhibición alternativa de cine en la Capital Federal" [Good Film in Buenos Aires: Alternative Film Exhibition] available on-line at *estadistica.buenosaires. gov.ar.*

8. The term "bastard" should not be understood in a pejorative sense. I take inspiration from Jorge Luis Borges's comment that "film is a bastard art"— referring to film's capacity to work with different languages at different levels and entering into a more fluid relationship to the present than to tradition. See the book that I co-authored with Emiliano Jelicié, *Borges va al cine* [Borges Goes to the Movies], Buenos Aires, Libraria, 2010.

9. George Yúdice develops the idea of culture as a resource in his *El recurso de la cultura: usos de la cultura en la era global*, Barcelona: Gedisa, 2002.

10. Gilles Deleuze and Félix Guattari, *A Thousand Plateaus: capitalism and schizophrenia*. Minneapolis: University of Minnesota Press, 1987, p. 269.

11. The script was later published in book form with Llinás' own footnotes as *Historias extraordinarias*, Buenos Aires, Mondadori, 2009.

12. Although the Borgesean influence is clear, the presence of Bioy Casares is much stronger in the characters' sentimental and amorous tangents, recounted in a tone that recalls some of his novels.

13. The question is found in *Viajes por Europa, África y América 1845–1847 y diario de gastos* [Travels in Europe, Africa, and America 1846–1847 and Travel Expenditures], Nanterre, FCE / Archivos, 1993, p. 387. In this quote I have left Sarmiento's particular spelling intact. Piñeiro's film tells of the games that eight characters (four men and four women, some the descendants of Rosas and of Sarmiento) play with Sarmiento's book in a country estate called *El Chajá*. The name implicates the scenario of enclosure and escape that defines the game: "The most common name for this bird, *chajá*, comes from Guaraní and in this language means 'Let's go!' or 'Escape!,' a presumably deformation of the onomatopoeia of the shriek of these birds upon being surprised, in this way warning others of their species in their proximity so that they can flee from the potential predator." (Source: Wikipedia.)

14. Other references abound: the chapter "Un tiro en la tarde" [A Shot in the Afternoon] recalls John Ford's *The Man Who Shot Liberty Valance* (titled in Spanish *Un tiro en la noche*), a film with which it also establishes a kinship. "La historia de los ocho" [The Story of the Eight] duplicates Jacques Rivette's *La bande des quatre* (*The Gang of Four*, 1989), undoubtedly the director whom Piñeiro most closely resembles. "Todo está bien si termina bien" might be both a translation of Shakespeare's *All's Well That Ends Well*, with an echo of Godard's *Tout va bien*, although this seems less likely. (At any rate, there is a very clear reference to Godard's *Pierrot le fou* when the characters paint their faces red while perched in a tree, a scene which simultaneously alludes to Alejo Moguillansky's *Castro*). Helen's last sentence ("Ahora me toca a mí" [Now It's My Turn] makes a reference to the last sentence in Hugo Santiago's *Invasión*: "Ahora nos toca a nosotros" [Now It's Our Turn]). I note these references not to read Piñeiro as trapped in the inheritance of the masters but as part of the hermeneutic and burlesque game that the film sets up.

15. This is a paraphrase of Nietzsche's found in *Cinema 2: the time-image*. Minneapolis: University of Minnesota Press, 1989, p. 13, in a discussion of an Orson Welles' film.

16. As in Enrique Bellande's *Ciudad de María* and Schindel, Molnar and Battle's *Rerum Novarum*, the use of the filmic in the Institucional de Compañía Fluvial del Plata invokes the discourses of modernity and progress observed by the more fluid and multitemporal character of video.

17. All quotations from the script and comments by Llinás are from the book *Historias extraordinarias*, op.cit.

18. Emiliano Jelicié and I analyze this theme in *Borges va al cine* (Buenos Aires, Libraria, 2010).

19. *Historias extraordinarias*, op. cit., p. 48. On the parallels between the film and Salamone's work, see Patricio Fontana's essay, "*Historias extraordinarias*: una extensión que no aqueja," in *Otra parte*, 15, Spring 2008.

20. In his "Ficciones," published in *El amante cine*, Santiago Palavecino, observes that the narrator plays "a very subtle dialogical game, forging relationships of emphasis, anticipation, syncopation, and supplement with the image. One that is always extremely assertive. (Number 192, 2008, available at: http://www.elamante.com/).

21. I agree with Santiago Palavecino (op. cit.) on this point, who observes that, "*Appearance* is the key word here: the very substance of the cinematographic image, it is also the land that Llinás has chosen to excavate, to find the riches hidden there.")

22. The line is from the song "Fora da orden," included on the CD *Circuladô de fulô*.

23. See Paolo Virno, *Gramática de la multitud*, op. cit.

24. This is the question that the characters in Mariano Pensotti's anomalous theatrical work, *El pasado es un animal grotesco* [The Past Is a Grotesque Animal], ask. This work has numerous connections to the new Argentine cinema. (In fact, one of the characters in the play wants to be a film director; another studies marketing: "Mario always liked movies, but feels that his own life is not worthy of playing anywhere.") (*El pasado es un animal grotesco*, Buenos Aires, Gayo, 2010, p. 14).

25. In stark contrast to the lack of protest in Argentina when the exploitive labor conditions of many members of this community was revealed. (In fact, the only protests were launched by Bolivians themselves, as though this were an issue that only concerned the immediate victims of the situation).

26. See "Los actores sociales" [Social Actors] in the "Radar" section of *Página/12*, Sunday, December 9, 2007.

27. This anecdote is cited in César Maranghello, *Artistas Argentinos Asociados: La epopeya trunca* de Buenos Aires, del Jilguero, 2002, p. 52.

28. The title *süden* is taken from the piece *Die Stücke der Winderose* (*The Rose of the Winds*), which consists of five cardinal points: *Osten, Süden, Nordosten, Nordwesten, Südosten*. (A version directed by Reinbert de Leeuw and played by the Schönberg Ensemble was edited by the Naïve label). I take the title from the copy of the film I worked with (although I did not find it in official records of the film).

29. In fact, despite not being a musical, the film features a choreographic director, Luciana Acuña, member of the Krapp dance company.

30. At any rate, the three films are also connected by their insistence upon *writing*, posters, chapters, etc.

31. *La mujer sin cabeza (The Headless Woman)* was voted the second best film of 2009; Lucrecia Martel and Lisandro Alonso appear in second and third place, respectively, as the best new directors of the decade.

32. See Cecilia Flaschland's *Pasado argentino reciente* [The Recent Argentine Past], written with Pablo Luzuriaga, Violeta Rosemberg, Julia Rosemberg, and Javier Trímboli, a multimedia text used for teacher training and edited by the Argentine Ministry of Education.

33. In Carri's films, memory is not linked only to the past but also to the marks that life leaves on the body, the affect, the gaze, language…In this sense memory is linked more to the slip than to conscious or already formulated language. See Iván Pinto's excellent interview with Carri on the website *La fuga* (http://lafuga.cl/entevista-a-albertina-carri/5).

34. I am drawing from Georges Didi-Huberman, *La invención de la histeria (Charcot y la iconografía de la Salpêtriere)*, Madrid, Cátedra, 2007, pp. 343 and ss.

35. See Silvia Schwrazböck's *Estudio crítico sobre Crónica de una fuga* [Critical Study on *Chronicle of an Escape*], Buenos Aires, Picnic Editorial, 2007.

36. See Spregelburd's response to Gambaro, Ñ, May 12, 2007.

37. As Mauro Cabral has effectively pointed out in his posts on the internet.

38. A more critical reading of Puenzo's film can be found in Diego Trerotola, "La diferencia entre el cine y la literatura" [The Difference between Film and Literature], in Adrián Melo (comp.): *Otras historias de amor (Gays, lesbianas y travestis en el cine argentino)* [Other Love Stories: Gays, Lesbians, and Transvestites in Argentine Cinema], Buenos Aires, ediciones Lea, 2008.

Bibliography

Abbagnano, Nicola. 1961. *Diccionario de filosofía*. México DF: Fondo de Cultura Económica.

Acuña, Claudia. 1999. "El neorrealista bonaerense (Entrevista a Pablo Trapero)." In *El amante cine*, number 88.

Acuña, Ezequiel, Diego Lerman, and Juan Villegas. 2004. "Los no realistas (conversación)." In *Kilómetro 111 (Ensayos sobre cine)*, number 5.

Agamben, Giorgio. 1993. *Infancy and History: Essays on the Destruction of Experience*. London; New York: Verso.

Aguilar, Gonzalo. 2001a. "Los precarios órdenes del azar." In *Milpalabras (Letras y artes en revista)*, number 1.

Aguilar, Gonzalo. 2001b. "Renuncia y libertad (sobre una película de Lisandro Alonso)." In *Milpalabras (Letras y artes en revista)*, number 2.

Aira, César. 1992. *La prueba*. Buenos Aires: Grupo Editor Latinoamericano.

Alabarces, Pablo. 2004. "Cultura(s) [de las clases] popular(es), una vez más: la leyenda continúa. Nueve proposiciones en torno a lo popular." In *Potlatch (Cuaderno de antropología y semiótica)*, number 1 (Spring).

Alonso, Mauricio. 2004. "Distancias (*Yo no sé qué me han hecho tus ojos* de S. Wolf y L. Muñoz)." In *Kilómetro 111 (Ensayos sobre cine)*, number 6.

Altamirano, Carlos. 1996. "Montoneros." In *Punto de vista*, number 55.

———. (ed.). 2002. *Términos críticos. Diccionario de sociología de la cultura*. Buenos Aires: Paidós.

Amado, Ana. 2002. "Cine argentino. Cuando todo es margen." In Pensamiento de los confines, number 11.

———. 2003a. "Herencias, generaciones y duelo en las políticas de la memoria." In *Revista iberoamericana*, number 202 (January–March).

———. 2003b. "Imágenes del país del pueblo." In *Pensamiento de los confines*, number 12.

———. 2004. "Ordenes de la memoria y desórdenes de la ficción." In Ana Amado and Nora Dominguez (eds.), *Lazos de familia. Herencias, cuerpos, ficciones*. Buenos Aires: Paidós.

Antelo, Raúl. 2004. *Potências da imagem*. Argos: Chapecô.

Arendt, Hannah. 1993. *La condición humana*. Barcelona: Paidós.

Augé, Marc. 1995. *Non-places: Introduction to an Anthropology of Supermodernity*. Trans. John Howe. London; New York: Verso.

Aumont, Jacques. 1997. *El ojo interminable*. Buenos Aires: Paidós.

Balderston, Daniel. 2004. *El deseo, enorme cicatriz luminosa (Ensayos sobre homosexualidades latinoamericanas)*. Rosario: Beatriz Viterbo.

Ballent, Anahí and Adrián Gorelik. 2001. "País urbano o país rural: la modernización territorial y su crisis." In Alejandro Cattaruzza (ed.), *Nueva historia Argentina (Crisis económica, avance del Estado e incertidumbre política, 1930–1943)*. Buenos Aires: Sudamericana.

Barthes, Roland. 1976. *Sade/Fournier/Loyola*. Trans. Richard Miller. New York: Hill and Wang.

———. 1986. *The Rustle of Language*. Trans. Richard Howard. New York: Hill and Wang.

———. 2005. *The Neutral*. Trans. Rosalind E. Krauss and Denis Hollier. New York: Columbia University Press.

Bataille, Georges. 1976. *Breve historia del erotismo*. Buenos Aires: Editorial Calden.

Bauman, Zygmunt. 1999. *In Search of Politics*. Stanford: Stanford University Press.

———. 2000. *Liquid Modernity*. Cambridge, UK: Polity Press; Malden, MA: Blackwell.

Bazin, André. 2000. *Qu'est-ce que le cinéma?* Pari s: Du Cerf.

Beceyro, Raúl. 1997. "Fantasmas del pasado." In *Cine y política*. Santa Fe: Universidad Nacional del Litoral.

———. 1998. "Adiós al cine 2." In *Punto de vista*, number 60.

Beceyro, Raúl, Rafael Filippelli, David Oubiña, and Alan Pauls. 2000. "Estética del cine, nuevos realismos, representación (Debate sobre el nuevo cine argentino)." In *Punto de vista*, number 67.

Benjamin, Walter. 1986. *Sobre el programa de la filosofía futura y otros ensayos*. Barcelona: Planeta-Agostini.

———. 1989. *Discursos interrumpidos I*. Buenos Aires: Aguilar.

———. 1999. *The Arcades Project*. Cambridge, MA: Belknap Press.

Bentivegna, Diego. 2003. "Realismo, naturalismo, verdad (sobre *El bonaerense* de Pablo Trapero)." Retrieved from: www.otrocampo.com (site no longer available).

Bergson, Henri. 2002. *La risa (Ensayo sobre el significado de lo cómico)*. Buenos Aires: Losada.

Bernades, Horacio, Diego Lerer, and Sergio Wolf (eds.). 2002. *New Argentine Cinema: Themes, Auteurs and Trends of Innovations/Nuevo cine argentino: temas, autores y estilos de una renovación*. Buenos Aires: Ediciones Tatanka.

Berneri, Anahí, Santiago García, and Pablo Pérez. 2007. "Minorías (entrevista)." In *Kilómetro 111 (Ensayos sobre cine)*, number 7.

Bernini, Emilio. 2003. "Un proyecto inconcluso (Aspectos del cine argentino contemporáneo)." In *Kilómetro 111 (Ensayos sobre cine)*, number 4.

———. 2004. "Un estado (contemporáneo) del documental. Sobre algunos films argentinos recientes." In *Kilómetro 111 (Ensayos sobre cine)*, number 5.

Bersani, Leo. 1995. *Homos*. London: Harvard University Press.

Birgin, Alejandra and Javier Trímboli (eds.). 2003. *Imágenes de los noventa*. Buenos Aires: Libros del Zorzal.

Bobbio, Norberto. 1993. *Igualdad y libertad*. Barcelona: Paidós.

Bordwell, David. 1996. *La narración en cine de ficción*. Barcelona: Paidós.

Bordwell, David and Noël Carroll. 1996. *Post-Theory: Reconstructing Film Studies*. Madison: University of Wisconsin Press.

Borges, Jorge Luis. 1999. *Borges en Sur*. Buenos Aires: Emecé.

Bourdieu, Pierre. 1998. *La dominación masculina*. Barcelona: Anagrama.

———. 1999. *Meditaciones pascalianas*. Barcelona: Anagrama.

Butler, Judith. 1997. *Excitable Speech (A Politics of the Performative)*. New York: Routledge.

Caetano, Israel Adrián. 1995. "Agustín Tosco Propaganda (manifiesto)." *El amante cine*, number 41.

Caparrós, Martín and Eduardo Anguita. 1998. *La voluntad: una historia de la militancia revolucionaria en la Argentina*, 3 vols. Buenos Aires: Norma.

Cavarero, Adriana. 1998. "La pasión de la diferencia." In Silvia Vegetti Finzi (ed.), *Historia de las pasiones*. Buenos Aires: Losada.

Cavell, Stanley. 1981. *Pursuits of Happiness: The Hollywood Comedy of Remarriage*. Cambridge, MA; London: Harvard University Press.

CEDEM. 2004. "Informes cuatrimestrales coyuntura económica de la Ciudad de Buenos Aires: IX. industrias culturales." Available at: www.cedem.gov.ar.

El cine argentino. 1997. CD-Rom de la Fundación Cinemateca Argentina.

Cháneton, July. 2004. "Los padres según los hijos, en *(h) historias cotidianas* de Andrés Habegger," mimeo.

Chion, Michel. 1999. *El sonido (Música, cine, literatura…)*. Barcelona: Paidós.

Choi, Domin. n.d. "La ciudad de la melancolía." Retrieved from: www.otrocampo. com (site no longer available).

Coma, Javier and José Maria Latorre. 1981. *Luces y sombras del cine negro*. Barcelona: Fabregat.

Correas, Carlos. 1998. "Tres filmes argentinos." In *El ojo mocho*, number 12/13.

Cozarinsky, Edgardo. 2003. "Notas sobre un filme argentino (*Tan de repente* de Diego Lerman)." In *Kilómetro 111 (Ensayos sobre cine)*, number 4.

Culler, Jonathan. 1975. *Structuralist Poetics, Structuralism, Linguistics, and the Study of Literature*. Ithaca, NY: Cornell University Press.

Daney, Serge. 1998. *Perseverancia*. Buenos Aires: El Amante/Tatanka.

———. 2004. *Cine, arte del presente*. Buenos Aires: Santiago Arcos.

de Lauretis, Teresa. 1987. *Technologies of Gender*. Bloomington: Indiana University Press.

Deleuze, Gilles. 1969. *Sacher-Masoch y Sade*. Córdoba: Editorial Universitaria.

———. 1986a. *Cinema 1: The Movement-Image*. Trans. Hugh Tomlinson and Barbara Habberjam. Minneapolis: University of Minnesota Press.

———. 1986b. *Cinema 2: The Time-Image*. Trans. Hugh Tomlinson and Robert Galeta. Minneapolis: University of Minnesota Press.

———. 1990. *The Logic of Sense*. New York: Columbia University Press.

———. 1995. "Optimismo, pesimismo y viaje (Carta a Serge Daney)." In *Conversaciones*. Valencia: Pretextos.

D'Epósito, Leonardo. 2005. "'El perro' en 'El año de transición.'" In *El amante cine*, number 153.

Di Tella, Andrés. 2002. "El documental y yo." In *Milpalabras (Letras y artes en revista)*, number 4.

Dodaro, Christian and Daniel Salerno. 2003. "Cine militante: repolitización, nuevas condiciones de visibilidad y marcos de lo decible." *Segundas jornadas de jóvenes investigadores*, Instituto de Investigación Gino Germani, Universidad de Buenos Aires.

Dupont, Mariano. 2003. "*El bonaerense* (Pablo Trapero)." In *Kilómetro 111 (Ensayos sobre cine)*, number 4.

Eco, Umberto. 1990. "T.V.: la transparencia perdida." In *La estrategia de la ilusión*. Barcelona: Lumen-De la Flor.

———. 1995. *Tratado de semiótica*. Barcelona: Lumen.

Edgard, Andrew and Peter Sedgwick. 1999. *Key Concepts in Cultural Theory*. London; New York: Routledge.

España, Claudio (ed.). 1994. *Cine argentino en democracia, 1983–1993*. Buenos Aires: Fondo Nacional de las Artes.

———. 2000. *Cine argentino 1933–1956: industria y clasicismo*. Buenos Aires: Fondo Nacional de las Artes.

———. 2005a. *Cine argentino 1957–1983: modernidad y vanguardias I*. Buenos Aires: Fondo Nacional de las Artes.

———. 2005b. *Cine argentino 1957–1983: modernidad y vanguardias II*. Buenos Aires: Fondo Nacional de las Artes.

Femenías, María Luisa. 2003. *Judith Butler: introducción a su lectura*. Buenos Aires: Catálogos.

Filippelli, Rafael. 1996. "Adiós (al cine) a la voluntad de forma." In *Punto de vista*, number 56.

———. 1998. "Adiós al cine 1." In *Punto de vista*, number 60.

———. 1999. "Ellos miran: la perspectiva de *Mala época*." In *Punto de vista*, number 64.

———. 2001. "El último representante de la Nouvelle Vague." In *El amante cine*, number 115.

———. 2002. "Una cierta mirada radical." In *Punto de vista*, number 73.

———. 2004. "*Goodbye Dragon Inn*: el espacio y sus fantasmas." In *Punto de vista*, number 79.

Flores D'Arcais, Paolo. 1996. *Hannah Arendt: existencia y libertad*. Madrid: Tecnos.

Fontana, Patricio. 2002. "Martín Rejtman. Una mirada sin nostalgias." In *Milpalabras (Letras y artes en revista)*, number 4.

Frisby, David. 1986. *Fragments of Modernity*. Cambridge, MA: MIT Press.

García Canclini, Néstor. 1999. *La globalización imaginada*. Buenos Aires: Paidós.

———. 2002. *Latinoamericanos buscando lugar en este siglo*. Buenos Aires: Paidós.

Getino, Octavio and Susana Vellegia. 2002. *El cine de las historias de la revolución (Aproximaciones a las teorías y prácticas del cine político en América Latina, 1967–1977)*. Buenos Aires: Altamira.

Gilman, Sander. 1985. *Difference and Pathology: Stereotypes of Sexuality, Race and Madness*. Ithaca, NY: Cornell University Press.

Giorgi, Gabriel. 2005. *Sueños de exterminio (Homosexualidad y representación en la literatura argentina)*. Buenos Aires: Beatriz Viterbo.

Godard, Jean-Luc. 1989. *Godard par Godard: les annèes cahiers*. París: Flammarion.

González, Horacio. 2003. "Sobre *El bonaerense* y el nuevo cine argentino." In *El ojo mocho*, number 17.

González, Horacio and Eduardo Rinesi. 1993. *Decorados*. Buenos Aires: Manuel Suárez editor.

Gorelik, Adrián. 1999. "*Mala época* y la representación de Buenos Aires." In *Punto de vista*, number 64.

Grignon, Claude and Jean-Claude Passeron. 1992. *Lo culto y lo popular. Miserabilismo y populismo en sociología y literatura*. Madrid: Ediciones La Piqueta.

Grimson, Alejandro. 2000. *Interculturalidad y comunicación*. Buenos Aires: Norma.

Gundermann, Christian. 2005. "La obturación de los flujos. Deseo y objetividad en el Nuevo cine argentino," mimeo.

Hernández Arregui, Juan José. 1969. *Nacionalismo y liberación*. Buenos Aires: Hachea.

Jameson, Fredric. 1986. "Third World Literature in the Era of Multinational Capitalism." In *Social Text*, number 15 (Fall).

———. 1995. *Marcas do visível*. Trans. Ana Lúcia Gazzola et al. Rio de Janeiro: Graal.

———. 2003. "The End of Temporality." In *Critical Inquiry*, volume 29, number 4 (Summer).

Jay, Martin. 1988. *Adorno*. México: Siglo XXI.

———. 1993. *Downcast Eyes: The Denigration of Vision in Twentieth-Century French Thought*. Berkeley: University of California Press.

———. 2003. *Campos de fuerza (Entre la historia intelectual y la crítica cultural)*. Buenos Aires: Paidós.

Julien, Isaac and Kobena Mercer. 1996. "De Margin and De Centre." In David Morley and Kuan-Hsing Chen (eds.), *Stuart Hall (Critical Dialogues in Cultural Studies)*. London: Routledge.

Katzenstein, Inés. 2003. "Acá lejos." In *Ramona (revista de artes visuales)*, number 37.

King, John, Ana López, and Manuel Alvarado (eds.). 1993. *Mediating Two Worlds*. London: British Film Institute.

Kohan, Martín. 2004a. "La apariencia celebrada." In *Punto de vista*, number 78.

———. 2004b. "Una crítica en general y una película en particular." In *Punto de vista*, number 80.

Kracauer, Siegfried. 1989. *Teoría del cine*. Paidós: Barcelona.

———. 1938. *Orpheus in Paris (Offenbach and the Paris of His Time)*. New York: Alfred Knopf.

Landi, Oscar. 1992. *Devórame otra vez (Qué hizo la televisión con la gente, qué hace la gente con la televisión)*. Buenos Aires: Planeta.

Lant, Antonia. 1995. "Haptical cinema." In *October,* number 74.

León, Federico. 2005. "Todo juntos." In *Registros (Teatro reunido y otros textos).* Buenos Aires: Adriana Hidalgo.

Lerer, Diego. 2003. "Lobo suelto, cordero atado." In *Clarín,* July 17.

Linden, Robin Ruth, Darlene R. Pagano, Diana E.H. Russell and Susan Leigh Star (eds). 1982. *Against Sadomasochism: A Radical Feminist Analysis.* East Palo Alto, CA: Frog in the Well.

Link, Daniel. 2005. "Enfermedad y cultura: política del monstruo." Available at: http://linkillo.blogspot.com.

Llinás, Mariano. 2004. "El Imperio contraataca." In *El amante cine,* number 153.

Macón, Cecilia. 2004. "*Los rubios* o del trauma como presencia." In *Punto de vista,* number 80.

Man, Paul de. 1990. *La resistencia a la teoría.* Madrid: Visor.

Manrupe, Raúl and Alejandra Portela. 2004. *Un diccionario de films argentinos II (1996–2002).* Buenos Aires: Corregidor.

Marrati, Paola. 2003. *Gilles Deleuze: cine y filosofía.* Buenos Aires: Nueva Visión.

Martín-Barbero, Jesús. 1993. *Communication, Culture and Hegemony: From the Media to Mediations.* London; Newbury Park, CA: Sage.

M.B. 2003. "Vidas privadas en espacios públicos (El cineasta y director de teatro Federico León define a su película *Todo juntos* como 'la mirada subjetiva de una relación')." In *Página/12,* August 10.

Mestman, Mariano. 2001. "Postales del cine militante argentino en el mundo." In *Kilómetro 111 (Ensayos sobre cine),* number 2.

Miller, James. 1993. *The Passion of Michel Foucault.* New York: Simon & Schuster.

Mongin, Olivier. 1997. *Violencia y cine contemporáneo.* Buenos Aires: Paidós.

Noriega, Gustavo. 2000. "El rey de la chatarra (Ulises Rosell y *Bonanza*)." In *El amante cine,* number 104.

———. 2001. "Historia de una búsqueda (Los 10 años de *El amante* y el cine argentino)." In *El amante cine,* number 117.

———. 2002. "Freddy toma soda (sobre *Bolivia* de Adrián Caetano)." In *El amante cine,* number 120.

———. 2005. "Un fantasma recorre Perú (sobre *Camisea* de Enrique Bellande)." In *El amante cine,* number 156.

Nun, José. 1995. "Populismo, representación y menemismo." In Various authors, *Peronismo y menemismo (Avatares del populismo en la Argentina).* Buenos Aires: El cielo por asalto.

Orozco, Olga. 1998. *Relámpagos de lo invisible (Antología).* Buenos Aires: Fondo de Cultura Económica.

Ortiz, Renato. 1994. *Mundialização e cultura.* São Paulo: Brasiliense.

Oubiña, David. 2003. "El espectáculo y sus márgenes. Sobre Adrián Caetano y el nuevo cine argentino." In *Punto de vista,* number 76.

Pauls, Alan. 2004. "Vamos de paseo (entrevista a Martín Rejtman)." In *Radar, Página/12,* May 30.

Peirce, Charles. 1885. "One, Two, Three: Fundamental Categories of Thought and of Nature." Manuscript, W 5:245, 1885.

Pérez, Martín. 2004. "Para saber cómo es la libertad (Entrevista a Lisandro Alonso)." *Radar*, September 26.

Pérez, Pablo. 2006. *El mendigo chupapijas*. Buenos Aires: Mansalva.

Quintín. 2000. "Lucrecia Martel antes de la largada. Es de Salta y hace falta." In *El amante cine*, number 100.

———. 2001. "El misterio del leñador solitario (Entrevista a Lisandro Alonso)." In *El amante cine*, number 111.

Raffo, Julio. 2003. *Ley de Fomento y Regulación de la Actividad Cinematográfica, comentada*. Buenos Aires: Lumiere.

Rancière, Jacques. 1991. *Breves viajes al país del pueblo*. Buenos Aires: Nueva Visión.

———. 2001. "D'une image à l'autre? Deleuze et les âges du cinéma." In *Le fable cinématographique*. Paris: du Seuil.

———. 2002. *La división de lo sensible (Estética y política)*. Salamanca: Consorcio Salamanca.

———. 2004a. *Disagreement*. Minneanapolis: University of Minnesota Press.

———. 2004b. "Les écarts du cinéma." In *Trafic*, number 50.

Rejtman, Martín. 1992. *Rapado*. Buenos Aires: Planeta.

———. 1996. *Velcro y yo*. Buenos Aires: Planeta.

———. 1999. *Silvia Prieto*. Buenos Aires: Norma.

Rest, Jaime. 1979. *Conceptos de literatura moderna*. Buenos Aires: Centro Editor de América Latina.

Rival, Silvina and Domin Choi. 2001. "Última tendencia del cine argentino sobre *La libertad* de Lisandro Alonso." In *Kilómetro 111 (Ensayos sobre cine)*, number 2.

Rohmer, Eric. 2000. *El gusto por la belleza*. Barcelona: Paidós.

Rohter, Larry. 2005. "Floating below Politics." In *The New York Times*, May 1.

Russo, Eduardo. 1998. *Diccionario del cine*. Buenos Aires: Paidós.

Said, Edward. 1983. *The Word, the Text and the Critic*. Cambridge, MA: Harvard University Press.

Salas, Hugo. 2004. "Duro ese cuerpo (reseña de *Todo juntos* de Federico León)." In *Kilómetro 111 (Ensayos sobre cine)*, number 5.

Santiago, Silviano. 2004. *O cosmopolitismo do pobre: crítica literária e crítica cultural*. Belo Horizonte: Universidade Federal de Minas Gerais.

Sarlo, Beatriz. 1990. "Menem." In *Punto de vista*, number 39.

———. 1992. "La teoría como chatarra (Tesis de Oscar Landi sobre la televisión)." In *Punto de vista*, number 44.

———. 1998. "La noche de las cámaras despiertas." In *La máquina cultural*. Buenos Aires: Ariel.

Sartora, Josefina and Silvina Rival (eds.). 2007. *Imágenes de lo real: la representacion de lo politico en el documental argentino*. Buenos Aires: Libraria.

Schwarzböck, Silvia. 1999. "El enigma de Silvia Prieto." In *El amante cine*, number 87.

———. 2000. "Último tren a Constitución." In *El amante cine*, number 104.

Schwarzböck, Silvia. 2001. "Los no realistas." In *El amante cine*, number 115.

Seivach, Paulina and Pablo Perelman. 2004. "La industria cinematográfica en la Argentina: entre los límites del mercado y el fomento estatal," mimeo, Observatorio de Industrias Culturales.

Sennett, Richard. 2003. *Respect in a World of Inequality.* New York: W.W. Norton.

Shohat, Ella and Robert Stam. 1994. *Unthinking Eurocentrism: Multiculturalism and the Media.* New York: Routledge.

Simmel, Georg. 1919. "Das Abenteuer." In *Philosophische Kultur: Gesammelte Essays,* 2nd edn. Leipzig: Alfred Kroner.

Sloterdijk, Peter. 2002. *El desprecio de las masas (Ensayo sobre las luchas culturales de la sociedad moderna).* Valencia: Pre-textos.

Solanas, Fernando and Octavio Getino. 1973. *Cine, cultura y descolonización.* Buenos Aires: Siglo XXI.

Sontag, Susan. 2003. *La enfermedad y sus metáforas/El sida y sus metáforas.* Buenos Aires: Taurus.

Soto, Moira. 2004. "Sobre *Lesbianas de Buenos Aires* de Santiago García." Available at: www.malba.org.ar.

Speranza, Graciela. 2002. "Nuevo cine, ¿nueva narrativa?" In *Milpalabras (Letras y artes en revista),* number 4.

Stam, Robert. 2001. *Teorías del cine. Una introducción.* Buenos Aires: Paidós.

Stam, Robert and Toby Miller. 2000. *Film Theory (An Anthology).* Oxford: Blackwell.

Stam, Robert, Robert Burgoyne, and Sandy Flitterman-Lewis. 1999. *Nuevos conceptos de la teoría del cine.* Buenos Aires: Paidós.

Stendhal. 1966. *Del amor.* Madrid: Ferma.

Stewart, Susan. 2001. *On Longing: Narratives of the Miniature, the Gigantic, the Souvenir, the Collection.* Durham, NC; London: Duke University Press.

Stringer, Julian. 2002. "Global Cities and the International Film Festival Economy." In Mark Shiel and Tony Fitzmaurice (eds.), *Cinema and the City (Film and Urban Societies in a Global Context).* Oxford: Blackwell.

Svampa, Maristella. 2000. "Identidades astilladas. De la patria metalúrgica al heavy metal." In *Desde abajo. La transformación de las identidades sociales.* Buenos Aires: Biblos.

Torre, Claudia and Álvaro Fernández Bravo. 2003. "Los marginados modernos." In *Introducción a la escritura universitaria (Ciudades alteradas. Nación e inmigración en la cultura moderna).* Buenos Aires: Granica.

Trerotola, Diego. 2003. "Polvos de una relación (sobre *Todo juntos* de Federico León)." In *El amante cine,* number 138.

Udenio, Pablo and Hernán Guerschuny. 1996. "Cinéfilo es una palabra rara (Entrevista a Martín Retjman)." In *Haciendo cine,* number 5 (October).

Vezzetti, Hugo. 2003. *Pasado y presente. Guerra, dictadura y sociedad en la Argentina.* Buenos Aires: Siglo XXI.

Virno, Paolo. 2003. *Gramática de la multitud (Para un análisis de las formas de vidas contemporáneas).* Buenos Aires: Colihue.

Williams, Raymond. 1983. *Keywords, a Vocabulary of Culture and Society.* Oxford: Oxford University Press.

Index

Breinigsville, PA USA
09 February 2011
255158BV00001B/2/P